DAILY SECRETS OF CHRISTIAN LIVING

OF

CHRISTIAN LIVING

Compiled by Al Bryant
from the writings of

Andrew Murray

Bethany Fellowship INC.
MINNEAPOLIS, MINNESOTA 55438

Published by Bethany Fellowship, Inc.
6820 Auto Club Road, Minneapolis, Minnesota 55438

Printed in the United States of America

Library of Congress Cataloging in Publication Data

Murray, Andrew, 1828-1917.
    Daily secrets of Christian living.

    Includes index.
    1. Devotional calendars.   I.   Bryant, Al,
1926-   II.   Title.
BV4811.M797   1978   242'.2   77-17187
ISBN 0-87123-500-5

CONTENTS

January .... The Secret of Intercession

February .... The Secret of Persevering Prayer

March .... The Secret of the Faith Life

April .... The Secret of Adoration

May .... The Secret of the Abiding Presence

June .... The Secret of United Prayer

July .... The Secret of Fellowship

August .... The Secret of the Cross

September .... The Secret of Brotherly Love

October .... The Secret of Power from on High

November .... The Secret of God's Saving Plan

December .... The Secret of the Throne of Grace

About the Author

ANDREW MURRAY's life spanned nearly a century and his influence for the cause of Christ was crucial during the nineteenth and early twentieth century. That influence lives on in the rich heritage of devotional writings which he left to later generations. Most of the meditations in this book first appeared in his "Pocket Companion" series, but this is the first time they are available within the covers of one book.

Born at Graaff Reinet, South Africa, in 1828, Murray attended schools in Scotland and Holland. Ordained in 1848, he pastored churches throughout South Africa from 1850 to 1906. Taking a forthright conservative theological stance, he led the opposition to liberalism within the ranks of the Dutch Reformed Church during the 1860s. He became known both for his preaching ability and his comsummate skill as a devotional writer, making a worldwide reputation for himself. His most famous book was *Abide in Christ*, reflecting the "deeper life" emphasis in his writings and spoken ministry.

May this collection capture the hearts and lives of a new generation of Christians striving for the deeper life!

Al Bryant

About the Compiler

After a two-year stint in the army during and after World War II, Mr. Bryant attended Grand Rapids Junior College, Wheaton College, and the University of Michigan. He received a B.A. degree in journalism from the University of Michigan.

He just completed his sixth year on the board of directors for the Christian Counseling Center, an interdenominational psychological agency in Grand Rapids.

He is the author/compiler of more than forty books. There are more than two and one-half million of his books in print.

He was for more than 25 years associated with Zondervan Publishing House in various capacities, and is now Senior Editor of Word Books, of Waco, Texas.

January

The Secret of Intercession

January 1

Intercession

Pray one for another.—James 5:10

What a mystery of glory there is in prayer! On the one hand, we see God in His holiness and love and power waiting, longing to bless man; and on the other, sinful man, on the other end of the scale, bringing down from God by prayer the very life and love of heaven to dwell in his heart.

But how much greater the glory of intercession when a man makes bold to say to God what he desires for others, and seeks to bring down on one soul, or hundreds and thousands, the power of the eternal life with all its blessings.

Intercession! Would one not say that this is the holiest exercise of our boldness as God's children, the highest privilege and enjoyment connected with our communion with God—the power of being used by God as instruments for His great work of making men His habitation and showing forth His glory?

Would one not think that the church would count this one of the chief means of grace, and seek above everything to cultivate in God's children the power of an unceasing prayerfulness on behalf of the perishing world?

Would one not expect that believers, who have to some extent been brought into the secret, would feel what strength there is in unity, and what assurance there is that God will certainly avenge His own elect who cry day and night to Him? It is when Christians cease from looking for help in external union, and aim at all being bound together to the throne of God, by an unceasing devotion to Jesus Christ, and *an unceasing continuance in supplication for the power of God's Spirit,* that the church will put on her beautiful garments, and put on her strength, too, and overcome the world.

January 2

The Opening of the Eyes

And Elisha prayed and said: Lord, open his eyes that he may see.... And Elisha said, Lord, open the eyes of these men, that they may see. —2 Kings 6:17, 20

How wonderfully the prayer of Elisha for his servant was answered! The young man saw the mountain full of chariots of fire and horsemen about Elisha. The heavenly host had been sent by God to protect His servant.

A second time Elisha prayed. The Syrian army had been struck with blindness, and so led into Samaria. There Elisha prayed for the opening of their eyes, and lo, they found themselves hopeless prisoners in the hand of the enemy.

We wish to use these prayers in the spiritual sphere. First of all, to ask that our eyes may see the wonderful provision that God has made for His church, in the baptism with the Holy Spirit and with fire. All the powers of the heavenly world are at our disposal in the service of the heavenly kingdom. How little the children of God live in the faith of that heavenly vision—the power of the Holy Spirit, on them, with them, and in them, for their own spiritual life, and as their strength joyfully to witness for their Lord and His work!

But we will find that we need that second prayer, too, that God may open the eyes of those of His children who do not as yet see the power which the world and sin have upon His people. They are as yet unconscious of the feebleness that marks the church, making it impotent to do the work of winning souls for Christ, and building up believers for a life of holiness and fruitfulness. Let us pray especially that God may open all eyes to see what the great and fundamental need of the church is, in intercession to bring down His blessing, that the power of the Spirit may be known unceasingly in its divine efficacy and blessing.

January 3

Man's Place in God's Plan

The heaven, even the heavens, are the Lord's: but the earth hath
he given to the children of men.—Psalm 115:16

God created heaven as a dwelling for himself—perfect, glorious, and most holy. The earth He gave to man as his dwelling—everything very good, but only as a beginning, with the need of being kept and cultivated. *The work God had done, man was to continue and perfect.* Think of the iron, the oil, and the coal hidden away in the earth, of the steam hidden away in the water. It was left to man to discover and to use all this, as we see in the network of transportation systems that span the world. God had created all to be thus used. He made the discovery and the use dependent on the wisdom and diligence of man. What the earth is today, with its cities and habitations, with its cornfields and orchards, it owes to man. The work God had begun and prepared was to be carried out by man in fulfillment of God's purpose. And so nature teaches us the wonderful partnership to which God calls man for the carrying out of the work of creation to its destined end.

This law holds equally good in the kingdom of grace. In this great redemption God has revealed the power of the heavenly life and the spiritual blessings of which heaven is full. *But He has entrusted to His people the work of making these blessings known, and making men partakers of them.*

What diligence the children of this world show in seeking for the treasures God has hid in the earth for their use! Shall not the children of God be equally faithful in seeking for the treasures hid in heaven, to bring them down in blessing on the world? It is by the unceasing intercession of God's people that His kingdom will come and His will be done on earth as it is in heaven.

January 4

Intercession in the Plan of Redemption

O thou that hearest prayer, unto thee shall all flesh come.—Psalm 65:2

When God gave the world into the power of man, made in His own image, who should rule over it as a viceroy under Him, it was His plan that Adam should do nothing but with God and through God, and God himself would do all His work in the world through Adam. Adam was in very deed to be the owner, master, and ruler of the earth. When sin entered the world, Adam's power was proved to be a terrible reality, for through him the earth, with the whole race of man, was brought under the curse of sin.

When God made the plan of redemption, His object was to restore man to the place from which he had fallen. God chose His servants of old, who, through the power of intercession, could ask what they would and it should be given them. When Christ became man, it was that, as man, both on earth and in heaven, He might intercede for man. And before He left the world, He imparted this right of intercession to His disciples in the sevenfold promise of the farewell discourse (John 15-17), that whatever they should ask He would do for them.

God's intense longing to bless seems in some sense to be graciously limited by His dependence on the intercession that rises from the earth. He seeks to rouse the spirit of intercession that He may be able to bestow His blessing on mankind. God regards intercession as the highest expression of His people's readiness to receive and to yield themselves wholly to the working of His almighty power.

Christians need to realize this as their true nobility and their only power with God—the right to claim and expect that God will hear prayer. It is only as God's children begin to see what intercession means in regard to God's kingdom that they will realize how solemn their responsibility is.

Each individual believer will be led to see that God waits for him to take his part. He will feel in very truth that the highest, the most blessed, the mightiest of all human instrumentalities for the fulfillment of the petition, "as in heaven, so on earth," is the intercession that rises day and night, pleading with God for the power of heaven to be sent down into the hearts of men. Oh, that God might burn into our hearts this one thought: Intercession in its omnipotent power is according to His will and is most certainly effectual!

January 5

God Seeks Intercessors

He saw that there was no man, and wondered that there was no intercessor.—Isaiah 59:16

From of old God had among His people intercessors to whose voice He had listened and given deliverance. Here we read of a time of trouble when He sought for an intercessor, but in vain. And He wondered! Think of what that means —the amazement of God that there should be none who loved the people enough or who had sufficient faith in His power to deliver, to intercede, on their behalf. If there had been an intercessor, He would have given deliverance; without an intercessor His judgments came down (see Isa. 64:7; Ezek. 22:30, 31).

Of what infinite importance is the place the intercessor holds in the kingdom of God! Is it not indeed a matter of wonder that God should give men such power, and yet that there are so few who know what it is to take hold of His strength and pray down His blessing on the world!

Let us try to realize the position. When God had in His Son wrought out the new creation, and Christ had taken His place on the throne, the work of the extension of His kingdom was given into the hands of men. He ever liveth to pray; prayer is the highest exercise of His royal prerogative as Priest-King upon the throne. All that Christ was to do in heaven was to be in fellowship with His people on earth. In His divine condescension God has willed that the working of His Spirit shall follow the prayer of His people. He waits for their intercession, showing the preparation of heart—where and how much of His Spirit they are ready to receive.

God rules the world and His church through the prayers of His people. "That God should have made the extension of His kingdom to such a large extent dependent on the faithfulness of His people in prayer is a stupendous mystery and yet an absolute certainty." God calls for intercessors: in His grace He has made His work dependent on them; He waits for them.

January 6

Christ As Intercessor

He is able to save them to the uttermost that come unto God by him, seeing he ever liveth to make intercession for them.—Hebrews 7:25

When God had said in Isaiah that He wondered that there was no intercessor, there followed the words: "Therefore his arm brought salvation unto him. The Redeemer shall come to Zion" (Isa. 59:16, 20). God himself would provide the true intercessor in Christ His Son, of whom it had already been said: "He bare the sin of many, and made intercession for the transgressors" (Isa. 53:12).

In His life on earth Christ began His work as Intercessor. Think of the high-priestly prayer on behalf of His disciples and of all who should through them believe in His name. Think of His words to Peter, "I have prayed for thee, that thy faith fail not"—a proof of how intensely personal His intercession is. And on the cross He spake as intercessor: "Father, forgive them."

Now that He is seated at God's right hand, He continues as our great High Priest, the work of intercession without ceasing. But with this difference: *He gives His people power to take part in it.* Seven times in His farewell discourse He repeated the assurance that what they asked He would do.

The power of heaven was to be at their disposal. The grace and power of God waited for man's bidding. Through the leading of the Holy Spirit they would know what the will of God was. They would learn in faith to pray in His name. He would present their petition to the Father, and through His and their united intercession the church would be clothed with the power of the Spirit.

January 7

The Intercessors God Seeks

I have set watchmen upon thy walls, O Jerusalem; they shall never hold their peace day nor night: ye that are the Lord's remembrancers, take ye no rest and give him no rest. —Isaiah 62:6, 7

Watchmen are ordinarily placed on the walls of a city to give notice to the rulers of coming danger. God appoints watchmen not only to warn men—often they will not hear—but also to summon Him to come to their aid, whenever need or enemy may be threatening. The great mark of the intercessors is to be that they are not to hold their peace day or night, to take no rest, and to give God no rest, until the deliverance comes. In faith they may count upon the assurance that God will answer their prayer.

It is of this our Lord Jesus said: "Shall not God avenge his own elect, who cry to him day and night?" From every land the voice is heard that the church of Christ, under the influence of the power of the world and the earthly-mindedness it brings, is losing its influence over its members. There is but little proof of God's presence in the conversion of sinners or the holiness of His people. With the great majority of Christians there is an utter neglect of Christ's call to take part in the extension of His kingdom. The power of the Holy Spirit is but little experienced.

Amid all the discussions as to what can be done to interest young and old in the study of God's Word, or to awaken love for the services of His house, one hears but little of the indispensable necessity of the power of the Holy Spirit in the ministry and the membership of the church. One sees but little sign of the conviction and confession that lack of prayer causes the workings of the Spirit to be feeble, and that only by united fervent prayer can a change be brought about. If ever there was a time when God's elect should cry day and night to Him, it is now. Will you not, dear reader, offer yourself to God for this blessed work of intercession, and learn to count it the highest privilege of your life to be a channel through whose prayers God's blessing can be brought down to earth?

January 8

The School of Intercession

Who in the days of his flesh, when he had offered up prayers and supplications with strong crying and tears, . . . and was heard in that he feared.—Hebrews 5:7

Christ, as Head, is Intercessor in heaven; we, as the members of His Body, are partners with Him on earth. Let no one imagine that it cost Christ nothing to become an intercessor. Without this He could not be our example. What do we read of Him? "When thou shalt make *his soul an offering for sin,* he shall see his seed. . . . He shall see of the travail of his soul. . . . I will divide him a portion with the great, because *he hath poured out his soul unto death*" (Isa. 53:10-12). Notice the thrice-repeated expression in regard to the pouring out of His soul.

The pouring out of the soul—that is the divine meaning of intercession. Nothing less than this was needed if His sacrifice and prayer were to have power with God. This giving of himself over to live and die that He might save the perishing was a revelation of the spirit that has power to prevail with God.

If we as helpers and fellow laborers with the Lord Jesus are to share His power of intercession, there will need to be with us, too, *the travail of soul that there was with Him, the giving up of our life and its pleasures for the one supreme work of interceding for our fellowmen.* Intercession must not be a passing interest; it must become an ever-growing object of intense desire, for which above everything we long and live. It is the life of consecration and self-sacrifice that will indeed give power for intercession (Acts 15:26; 20:24; Phil. 2:17; Rev. 12:11).

The longer we study this blessed truth and think of what it means to exercise this power for the glory of God and the salvation of men, the deeper will become our conviction it is worth giving up everything to take part with Christ in His work of intercession.

January 9

The Name of Jesus the Power of Intercession

Hitherto have ye asked nothing in my name. At that day ye shall ask in my name; ask and ye shall receive, that your joy may be full. —John 16:24, 26

During Christ's life upon earth, the disciples had known but little of the power of prayer. In Gethsemane, Peter and the others had utterly failed. They had no conception of what it was to ask in the name of Jesus, and to receive. The Lord promised them that in that day which was coming, they would be able to pray with such a power in His name that they might ask what they would and it should be given to them.

"Hitherto nothing." *"In that day* ye shall ask in my name and shall receive."* These two conditions are still found in the church. With the great majority of Christians there is such a lack of knowledge of their oneness with Christ Jesus, and of the Holy Spirit as the spirit of prayer, that they do not even attempt to claim the wonderful promises Christ here gives. But where God's children know what it is to abide in Christ and in vital union with Him, and to yield to the Holy Spirit's teaching, they begin to learn that their intercession avails much, and that God will give the power of His Spirit in answer to their prayer.

It is faith in the power of Jesus' name, and in our right to use it, that will give us the courage to follow on where God invites us to the holy office of intercessors. When our Lord Jesus, in His farewell discourse, gave His unlimited prayer promise, He sent the disciples out into the world with this consciousness: "He who sits upon the throne, and who lives in my heart, has promised that what I ask in His name I shall receive. *He will do it."*

Oh, if Christians but knew what it is to yield themselves wholly and absolutely to Jesus Christ and His service, how their eyes would be opened to see that intense and unceasing prayerfulness is the essential mark of the healthy spiritual life; and that the power of all-prevailing intercession will indeed be the portion of those who live only in and for their Lord!

January 10

Prayer the Work of the Spirit

God has sent forth the Spirit of his Son into your hearts, crying, "Abba, Father."—Galatians 4:6

We know what "Abba, Father" meant in the mouth of Christ in Gethsemane. It was the entire surrender of himself to the very death that the holy will of God's love in redemption of sinners might be accomplished. In His prayer He was ready for any sacrifice, even to the yielding of His life. In that prayer we have revealed to us the heart of Him whose place is at the right hand of God, with the wonderful power of intercession that He exercises there, and the power to pour down the Holy Spirit.

It is to breathe the very Spirit of His Son into our hearts that the Holy Spirit has been bestowed by the Father. Our Lord would have us yield ourselves as wholly to God as He did; to pray like Him, that God's will of love should be done on earth at any cost. As God's love is revealed in His desire for the salvation of souls, so also the desire of Jesus was made plain when He gave himself for them. And He now asks of His people that the same love should fill them, too, so that they might give themselves wholly to the work of intercession, and, at any cost, pray down God's love upon the perishing.

And lest anyone should think this is too high and beyond our reach, *the Holy Spirit of Jesus is actually given into our hearts* that we may pray in His likeness, in His name, and in His power. It is the man who yields himself wholly to the leading of the Holy Spirit who will feel urged, by the compulsion of a divine love, to the undivided surrender to a life of continual intercession, because he knows that it is God who is working in him.

Now we can understand how Christ could give such unlimited promises of answer to prayer to His disciples; they were first going to be filled with the Holy Spirit. Now we understand how God can give such a high place to intercession in the fulfillment of His purpose of redemption; it is the Holy Spirit who breathes God's own desire into us *and enables* us to intercede for souls.

January 11

Christ Our Example in Intercession

He shall divide the spoil with the strong, because ... He bare the sin of many and made intercession for the transgressors.—Isaiah 53:12

"He made intercession for the transgressors." What did that mean to Him? Think of what it cost Him to pray that prayer effectually. He had to pour out His soul as an offering for sin, and to cry in Gethsemane: "Father, Thy holy will of love be done."

Think of what moved Him thus to sacrifice himself to the very uttermost! It was His love to the Father—that His holiness might be manifest, and love to souls—that they might be partakers of His holiness.

Think of the reward He won! As Conqueror of every enemy, He is seated at the right hand of God, with the power of unlimited and assured intercession. And He would see His seed, a generation of those of the same mind with himself, whom He could train to share in His great work of intercession.

And what does this mean for us when we indeed seek to pray for the transgressors? That we, too, yield ourselves wholly to the glory of the holiness and the love of the Father, that we, too, say: Thy will be done, cost what it may; that we, too, sacrifice ourselves, even to pouring out our soul unto death.

The Lord Jesus has in very deed taken us up into a partnership with himself in carrying out the great work of intercession. He in heaven and we on earth must have one mind, one aim in life—that we should, from love to the Father and to the lost, consecrate our lives to intercession for God's blessing. The burning desire of Father and Son for the salvation of souls must be the burning desire of our hearts, too.

What an honor! What a blessedness! And what a power for us to do the work because He lives, and by His Spirit pours forth His love into our hearts!

January 12

God's Will and Ours

Thy will be done.—Matthew 26:42

It is the high prerogative of God that everything in heaven and earth is to be done according to His will, and as the fulfillment of His desires. When He made man in His image it was, above all, that his desires were to be in perfect accord with the desires of God. This is the high honor of being in the likeness of God—that we are to feel and wish just as God. In human flesh man was to be the embodiment and fulfillment of God's desires.

When God created man with the power of willing and choosing what he should be, He limited himself in the exercise of His will. And when man had fallen and yielded himself to the will of God's enemy, God in His infinite love set about the great work of winning man back to make the desires of God his own. As in God, so in man, desire is the great moving power. And just as man had yielded himself to a life of desire after the things of the earth and the flesh, God had to redeem him and to educate him into a life of harmony with Himself. His one aim was that man's desire should be in perfect accord with His own.

The great step in this direction was when the Son of the Father came into this world, to reproduce the divine desires in His human nature, and in His prayer to yield himself up to the perfect fulfillment of all that God wished and willed. The Son, as Man, said in agony and blood, "Thy will be done," and made the surrender even to being forsaken of God, that the power that had deceived man might be conquered and deliverance procured. In the wonderful and complete harmony between the Father and the Son when the Son said, "Thy will be done," the great redemption was accomplished.

And this is now the great work of appropriating that redemption, that believers have to say, first of all for themselves and then in lives devoted to intercession for others: "Thy will be done in heaven as on earth." As we plead for the church—its ministers and its missionaries, its strong Christians or its young converts—for the unsaved, whether nominally Christian or heathen, we have the privilege of knowing that we are *pleading for what God wills*, and that through our prayers His will is to be done on earth as in heaven.

January 13

The Blessedness of a Life of Intercession

Ye that are the Lord's remembrancers, take ye no rest and give him no rest, till he make Jerusalem a praise in the earth. —Isaiah 62:6, 7

What an unspeakable grace to be allowed to deal with God in intercession for the supply of the need of others!

What a blessing, in close union with Christ, to take part in His great work as Intercessor, and to mingle my prayers with His! What an honor to have power with God in heaven over souls, and to obtain for them what they do not know or think!

What a privilege, as a steward of the grace of God, to bring to Him the state of the church or of individual souls, of the ministers of the Word, or His messengers away in heathendom, and plead on their behalf till He entrusts me with the answer!

What blessedness, in union with other children of God, to strive together in prayer until the victory is gained over difficulties here on earth, or over the powers of darkness in high places!

It is indeed worth living for, to know that God will use me as an intercessor, to receive and dispense here on earth His heavenly blessing, and above all the power of His Holy Spirit.

This is in very deed the life of heaven, the life of the Lord Jesus himself, in His self-denying love, taking possession of me and urging me to yield myself wholly to bear the burden of souls before Him, and to plead that they may live.

Too long have we thought of prayer simply as a means for the supplying of our need in life and service. May God help us to see what a place intercession takes in His divine counsel, and in His work for the kingdom. And may our hearts indeed feel there is no honor or blessedness on earth at all equal to the unspeakable privilege of waiting upon God and bringing power down from heaven, and of opening the way on earth for the blessing He delights to give!

January 14

The Place of Prayer

These all continued with one accord in prayer and supplication.—
Acts 1:14

The last words which Christ spoke before He left the world give us the four great notes of His church: "Wait for the promise of the Father." "Ye shall receive power after that the Holy Ghost is come upon you." "Ye shall be witnesses unto me." "Both in Jerusalem and unto the uttermost part of the earth."

United and unceasing prayer, the power of the Holy Spirit, living witnesses to the living Christ, from Jerusalem to the uttermost part of the earth—such are the marks of the true gospel, of the true ministry, of the true church of the New Testament.

A church of united and unceasing prayerfulness, a ministry filled with the Holy Spirit, the members living witnesses to a living Christ, with a message to every creature on earth—such was the church that Christ founded, and such the church that went out to conquer the world.

When Christ had ascended to heaven the disciples knew at once what their work was to be, continuing with one accord in prayer and supplication. They were to be bound together, by the love and Spirit of Christ, into one Body. It was this that gave them their wonderful power in heaven with God and upon earth with men.

Their one duty was to wait in united and unceasing prayer for the power of the Holy Spirit, as the enduement from on high for their witness to Christ to the ends of the earth. A praying church, a Spirit-filled church, a witnessing church, with all the world as its sphere and aim—such is the church of Jesus Christ.

As long as it maintained this character, it had power to conquer. But alas, as it came under the influence of the world, how much it lost of its heavenly, supernatural beauty and strength! How unfaithful in prayer, how feeble the workings of the Spirit, how formal its witness to Christ, and how unfaithful to its worldwide mission!

January 15

Paul As an Intercessor

I bow my knees unto the Father, that he would grant you to be strengthened with might by his Spirit.—Ephesians 3:14, 16

We think of Paul as the great missionary, the great preacher, the great writer, the great apostle "in labours more abundant." We do not sufficiently think of him as the intercessor who sought and obtained, by his supplication, the power that rested upon all his other activities, and brought down the blessing that rested on the churches that he served.

We see above what he wrote to the Ephesians. Think of what he said to the Thessalonians (1 Thess. 3:10, 13): "Night and day praying exceedingly that we might perfect that which is lacking in your faith, to the end he may stablish your hearts unblameable in holiness." To the Romans (1:9): "Without ceasing I make mention of you always in my prayers." To the Philippians (1:4): "Always in every prayer of mine for you all, making request with joy." And to the Colossians (1:9; 2:1): "We do not cease to pray for you. I would that ye knew what great conflict I have for you."

Day and night he cried to God in his intercession for them, that the light and the power of the Holy Spirit might be in them; and as earnestly as he believed in the power of his intercession for them, did he also believe in the blessing that theirs would bring upon him. "I beseech you, that ye strive together with me in your prayers to God for me" (Rom. 15:30). "God will yet deliver us, ye also helping together by prayer for us" (2 Cor. 1:10, 11). "Praying also for me, that I may open my mouth boldly" (Eph. 6:18, 19; Col. 4:3, 2 Thess. 3:1). "This shall turn to my salvation through your prayer" (Phil. 1:19).

The whole relationship between pastor and people depends on the united continual prayerfulness. Their whole relationship to each other is a heavenly one, spiritual and divine, and can be maintained only by unceasing prayer. It is when ministers and people wake up to the consciousness that the power and blessing of the Holy Spirit is waiting for their united and unceasing prayer, that the church will begin to know something of what Pentecostal Apostolic Christianity is.

January 16

Intercession for Laborers

The harvest truly is plenteous, but the labourers are few; pray ye therefore the Lord of the harvest, that he will send forth labourers into his harvest.—Matthew 9:37, 38

The disciples understood little of what these words meant. Christ gave them as a seed-thought, to be lodged in their hearts for later use. At Pentecost, as they saw how many of the new converts were ready in the power of the Spirit to testify of Christ, they must have felt how the ten days of continuous united prayer had brought this blessing, too, as the fruit of the Spirit's power—laborers in the harvest.

Christ meant to teach us that, however large the field may be, and however few the laborers, prayer is the best, the sure, the only means for supplying the need.

What we need to understand is this: it is not only in time of need that the prayer must be sent up, but the whole work is to be carried on in the spirit of prayer, so that the prayer for laborers will be in perfect harmony with the whole of our life and effort.

In the China Inland Mission, when the number of missionaries had gone up to 200, at a conference held in China they felt so deeply the need of more laborers for districts quite unprovided for that after much prayer they felt at liberty to ask God to give them within a year 100 additional laborers and the funds to meet the expenses. They agreed to continue in prayer day by day throughout the year. At the end of the time the 100 suitable men and women had been found, with the needed support money.

To meet the need of the world, its open fields, and its waiting souls, the churches all complain of the lack of laborers and of funds. Does not Christ's voice call us to the united and unceasing prayer of the first disciples? God is faithful, by the power of His Spirit, to supply every need. Let the church take the posture of united prayer and supplication. God hears prayer.

January 17

Intercession for Individual Souls

Ye shall be gathered one by one, O ye children of Israel.—Isaiah 27:12

In our human body every member has its appointed place. It is so, too, in society and in the church. The work must always aim at the welfare and the highest perfection of the whole, through the cooperation of every individual member.

In the church the thought is found too often that the salvation of men is the work of the minister; whereas he generally only deals with the crowd, but seldom reaches the individual. This is the cause of a twofold evil. The individual believer does not understand that it is necessary for him to testify to those around him—for the nourishment and the strengthening of his own spiritual life, and for the ingathering of souls. Unconverted souls suffer unspeakable loss because Christ is not personally brought to them by each believer they meet. The thought of intercession for those around us is all too seldom found. Its restoration to its rightful place in the Christian life—how much that would mean to the church and its missions!

Oh, when will Christians learn the great truth that "what God in heaven desires to do *needs prayer on earth as its indispensable condition.*" It is as we realize this that we will see that intercession is the chief element in the conversion of souls. All our efforts are vain, without the power of the Holy Spirit given in answer to prayer. It is when ministers and people unite in a covenant of prayer and testimony that the church will flourish, and that every believer will understand the part he has to take.

What can we do to stir up the spirit of intercession? There is a twofold answer. Let every Christian, as he begins to get an insight into the need and the power of intercession, make a beginning in the exercise of it on behalf of single individuals. Pray for your children, for your relatives and friends, for all with whom God brings you into contact. If you feel you have not the power to intercede, let the discovery humble you and drive you to the mercy-seat. *God wants every redeemed child of His to intercede for the perishing.* It is the vital breath of the normal Christian life—the proof that it is born from above.

Then pray intensely and persistently to God to lay the power of His Holy Spirit on you and His children around you, that the power of intercession may have the place that God will honor.

January 18

Intercession for Ministers

A nd for me.—Ephesians 6:19
Praying also for us.—Colossians 4:3
Finally, brethren, pray for us.—2 Thessalonians 3:1

These expressions of Paul suggest the strength of his conviction that the Christians had power with God, and that their prayer would in very deed bring new strength to him in his work. He had such a sense of the actual unity of the Body of Christ, of the interdependence of each member, even the most honorable, on the life that flowed through the whole body that he seeks to rouse Christians, both for their own sakes and for his sake and for the sake of the kingdom of God, with his call: "Continue in prayer, and watch in the same with thanksgiving, withal praying also for us."

The church depends upon the ministry to an extent we little realize. The place of the minister is so high, as the steward of the mysteries of God, as the ambassador for God to beseech men in Christ's name to be reconciled to Him, that unfaithfulness or inefficiency must bring a terrible blight on the church he serves. If Paul, after having preached for twenty years in the power of God, still needed the prayer of the church, how much more does the ministry in our day need it?

The minister needs the prayer of his people. He has a right to it. He is in very truth dependent on it. *It is his task to train Christians for their work of intercession on behalf of the church and the world.* He must begin with training them to pray for himself. He may have to begin still farther back and learn to pray more for himself and for them. Let all intercessors, who are seeking to enter more deeply into their blessed work, give a larger place to the ministry, whether of their own church or of other churches.

Let them plead with God for individual men, and for special circles. Let them continue in prayer and watch therein, that ministers may be men of power, men of prayer, and full of the Holy Spirit. O brethren, pray for the ministry!

January 19

Prayer for All Saints

With all prayer and supplication praying at all seasons in the Spirit, and watching thereunto in all perseverance and supplication for all the saints.—Ephesians 6:18 (R.V.)

Notice how Paul repeats the words in the intensity of his desire to reach the hearts of his readers. "With *all* prayer and supplication praying at *all* seasons in the Spirit, and watching thereunto in *all* perseverance and *all* supplication." It is "all prayer, all seasons, all perseverance, all supplication." The words claim thought if they are to meet with the needed response.

Paul felt so deeply the unity of the Body of Christ, and he was so sure that that unity could be realized only in the exercise of love and prayer that he pleaded with the believers at Ephesus unceasingly and fervently to pray for all saints, not only in their immediate circle, but in all the church of Christ of whom they might hear, "Unity is strength." As we exercise this power of intercession with all perseverance, we will be delivered from self with all its feeble prayers, and lifted up to that enlargement of heart in which the love of Christ can flow freely and fully through us.

Often the great shortcoming in true believers is that in prayer they are occupied with themselves and with what God must do for them. Let us realize that we have here a call to every believer to give himself without ceasing to the exercise of love and prayer. It is as we forget ourselves, in the assurance that God will take charge of us, and yield ourselves to the great and blessed work of calling down the blessing of God on our brethren that the whole church will be fitted to do its work in making Christ known to every creature. This alone is the healthy and the blessed life of a child of God who has yielded himself wholly to Christ Jesus.

Pray for God's children and the church around you. Pray for all the work in which they are engaged, or ought to be. Pray at all seasons in the Spirit for all God's saints. There is no blessedness greater than that of abiding communion with God. And there is no way that leads to the enjoyment of this more surely than the life of intercession for which these words of Paul appeal so pleadingly.

January 20

Missionary Intercession

When they had fasted and prayed, and laid their hands on them, they sent them away.—Acts 13:3

"How to multiply the number of Christians, who will individually and collectively wield this force of intercession for the conversion and transformation of men, *that is the supreme question of foreign missions.* Every other consideration and plan is secondary to that of wielding the forces of prayer."

"That those who love this work, and bear it upon their hearts, will follow the scriptural injunction to pray unceasingly for its triumph, we take for granted. To such, not only the morning watch and the hours of stated devotion, but all times and seasons will witness an attitude of intercession that refuses to let God go until He crowns His workers with victory."

Missions have their root in the love of Christ, as that was proved on the cross and now lives on in our hearts. As men are so earnest in seeking to carry out God's plans for the natural world, so God's children should be at least as wholehearted in seeking to bring Christ's love to all mankind. Intercession is the chief means appointed by God to bring the great redemption within the reach of all.

Pray for the missionaries that the Christ-life may be clear and strong, that they may be men of prayer and filled with love, in whom the power of the spiritual life is made manifest.

Pray for the native Christians that they may know the glory of the mystery among the heathen, Christ in them the hope of glory.

Pray for the baptism classes, and all the pupils in schools, that the teaching of God's Word may be in power. Pray specially for the native pastors and evangelists that the Holy Spirit may fill them to be witnesses for Christ among their fellow countrymen.

Pray, above all, for the church of Christ that it may be lifted out of its indifference, and that every believer may be brought to understand that the one object of his life is to help to make Christ King on the earth.

January 21

The Grace of Intercession

Continue in prayer, and watch in the same with thanksgiving, withal praying also for us. —Colossians 4:2, 3

There is nothing that can bring us nearer to God and lead us deeper into His love than the work of intercession. There is nothing that can give us a higher experience of the likeness of God than the power of pouring out our hearts into the bosom of God in prayer for men around us. There is nothing that can so closely link us to Jesus Christ, the great Intercessor, and give us the experience of His power and Spirit resting on us, as the yielding of our lives to the work of bringing the great redemption into the hearts and lives of our fellowmen. There is nothing in which we will know more of the powerful working of the Holy Spirit than the prayer breathed by Him into our hearts, "Abba, Father," in all the fullness of meaning that it had for Christ in Gethsemane.

There is nothing that can so help us to prove the power and the faithfulness of God to His Word as when we reach out in intercession to the multitudes, either in the church of Christ or in the darkness of heathenism. As we pour out our souls a living sacrifice before God, with the one persistent plea that He will, in answer to our prayer, open the windows of heaven and send down His abundant blessing, God will be glorified, our souls will reach their highest destiny, and God's kingdom will come.

There is nothing that will so help us to understand and to experience the living unity of the Body of Christ, and the irresistible power it can exert, as the daily and continued fellowship with God's children in the persistent plea that God will arise and have mercy upon Zion, and make her a light and a life to those who are sitting in darkness. O fellow Christian, how little we realize what we are losing in not living in fervent intercession! What may we not gain for ourselves and for the world if we allow God's Spirit, as a Spirit of grace and of supplication, to master our whole being!

In heaven Christ lives to pray; His whole communion with His Father is prayer: an asking and receiving of the fullness of the Spirit for His people. God delights in nothing so much as prayer. Shall we not learn to believe that the highest blessings of heaven will be unfolded to us as we pray more?

January 22

United Intercession

There is one body, and one Spirit.—Ephesians 4:4

Our own bodies teach us how essential for their health and strength it is that every member should take its full share in seeking the welfare of the whole. It is even so in the Body of Christ. There are, unfortunately, too many who look upon salvation only in connection with their own happiness. There are those, again, who know they live not unto themselves, and truly seek in prayer and work to bring others to share in their happiness; but they do not yet understand that in addition to their personal circle or church, they have a calling to enlarge their hearts to take the whole Body of Christ Jesus into their love and their intercession.

Yet this is what the Spirit and the love of Christ will enable them to do. It is only when intercession *for the whole church, by the whole church,* ascends to God's throne, that the Spirit of unity and of power can have its full sway. We should be thankful for the desire that has been awakened for closer union between the different branches of the church of Christ. And yet the difficulties are so great and, in the case of different nationalities of the world, so apparently insuperable, that the thought of a united church on earth appears beyond reach.

Let us bless God that there is a unity in Christ Jesus, deeper and stronger than any visible manifestation could make it; and that there is a way in which even now, midst all diversity of administrations, the unity can be practically exemplified and utilized as the means of an unthought-of accession of divine strength and blessing in the work of the kingdom.

It is in the cultivation and increase of the Spirit and in the exercise of intercession that the true unity can be realized. As believers are taught the meaning of their calling as a royal priesthood, they are led to see that God is not confined in His love or promises to their limited spheres of labor, but invites them to enlarge their hearts, and like Christ—we may say like Paul, too—to pray for all who believe, or can yet be brought to believe, that this earth and the church of Christ in it will by intercession be bound to the throne of heaven as it has never yet been.

January 23

Unceasing Intercession

Pray without ceasing.—1 Thessalonians 5:17

How different is the standard of the average Christian, with regard to a life in the service of God, from that which Scripture gives us. In the former the chief thought is personal safety—grace to pardon our sin and to live such a life as may secure our entrance into heaven. How high above this is the Bible standard—a Christian surrendering himself with all his powers, with his time and thought and love wholly yielded to the glorious God who has redeemed him, and whom he now delights in serving, in whose fellowship is heaven begun.

To the former the command "Pray without ceasing" is simply a needless and impossible life of perfection. Who can do it? We can get to heaven without it. To the true believer, on the contrary, it holds out the promise of the highest happiness, of a life crowned by all the blessings that can be brought down on souls around through his intercession. And as he perseveres it becomes increasingly his highest aim upon earth, his highest joy, his highest experience of the wonderful fellowship with the holy God.

"Pray without ceasing." Let us take that word in a large faith, as a promise of what God's Spirit will work in us, of how close and intimate our union to the Lord Jesus can be, and our likeness to Him, in His ever blessed intercession at the right hand of God. Let it become to us one of the chief elements of our heavenly calling, to be consciously the stewards and administrators of God's grace to the world around us.

As we think of how Christ said, "I in them, and thou in me," let us believe that just as the Father worked in Him, so Christ *the interceding High Priest will work and pray in us.* As the faith of our high calling fills our hearts, we will begin literally to feel that there is nothing on earth for one moment to be compared with the privilege of being God's priests, walking without intermission in His holy presence, bringing the burden of the souls around us to the footstool of His throne, and receiving at His hands the power and blessing to dispense to our fellowmen.

This is indeed the fulfillment of the word of old, "Man created in the likeness and the image of God."

January 24

Intercession, the Link Between Heaven and Earth

Thy will be done, as in heaven, so on earth.—Luke 11:2

When God created heaven and earth, He meant heaven to be the divine pattern to which earth was to be conformed; "as in heaven, so on earth" was to be the law of its existence.

The word calls us to think of what constitutes the glory of heaven. God is all in all there. Everything lives in Him and to His glory. Think of what this earth has now become, with all its sin and misery, the great majority of the race without any knowledge of the true God, and the remainder nominally Christians, yet for the greater part utterly indifferent to His claims, and estranged from His holiness and love. What a revolution, what a miracle is needed, if the word is to be fulfilled: "As in heaven, so on earth"!

And how is this ever to come true? *Through the prayers of God's children our Lord teaches us to pray for it. Intercession is to be the great link between heaven and earth.* The intercession of the Son, begun upon earth, continued in heaven, and carried on by His redeemed people upon earth, will bring about the mighty change: "As in heaven, so on earth." As Christ said, "I come to do thy will, O God," until He prayed the great prayer in Gethsemane, "Thy will be done." So His redeemed ones, who yield themselves fully to His mind and Spirit, make His prayer their own, and unceasingly send up the cry, "Thy will be done, as in heaven, so on earth."

Every prayer of a parent for a child, of a believer for the saving of the lost, or for more grace to those who have been saved, is part of the great unceasing cry going up day and night from this earth, "As in heaven, so on earth."

But it is when God's children not only learn to pray for their immediate circles and interests, but enlarge their hearts to take in the whole church and the whole world that their united supplication will have power with God and hasten the day when it shall indeed be, "As in heaven so on earth"—the whole earth filled with the glory of God. Child of God, will you not yield yourself, like Christ, to live with this one prayer: "Father, Thy will be done on earth as in heaven"?

January 25

The Fulfillment of God's Desires

*The Lord hath desired Zion for his habitation. Here will I dwell;
for I have desired it.*—Psalm 132:13, 14

Here you have the one great desire of God that moved
Him in the work of redemption. His heart longed for man
to dwell with him and in him.

To Moses He said: "Let them make me a sanctuary; that
I may dwell among them." And just as Israel had to prepare
the dwelling for God, even so His children are now called
to yield themselves for God to dwell in them, and to win others
to become His habitation. As the desire of God toward us
fills the heart, it will waken within us the desire to gather
others around us to become His dwelling too.

What an honor! What a high calling, to count my worldly
business as entirely secondary, and to find my life and my
delight in winning souls in whom God may find His heart's
delight! "Here will I dwell; for I have desired it."

And this is what I can above all do through intercession.
I can pray for those around me that God will give them His
Holy Spirit. It is God's great plan that man himself shall
build Him a habitation. It is in answer to the unceasing intercession of His children that God will give His power and blessing. As this great desire of God fills us, we shall give ourselves wholly to labor for its fulfillment.

Think of David, when he thought of God's desire to dwell
in Israel, how he said: "I will not give sleep to my eyes,
nor slumber to mine eyelids, until I find out a place for the
Lord, an habitation for the mighty God of Jacob." Shall not
we, to whom it has been revealed what that indwelling of
God may be, give our lives for the fulfillment of His heart's
desire?

Oh, let us begin, as never before, to pray for our children,
for the souls around us, and for all the world. And that not
only because we love them, but specially because God longs
for them, and gives us the honor of being the channels through
whom His blessing is brought down. Children of God, awake
to the realization of what it means that God is seeking to
train you as intercessors, through whom the great desire of
His loving heart may be satisfied!

January 26

The Fulfillment of Man's Desire

Delight thyself in the Lord; and he shall give thee the desires of thine heart.—Psalm 37:4

God is love, an ever-flowing fountain, out of which streams the unceasing desire to make His creatures the partakers of all the holiness and the blessedness there is in Himself. This desire for the salvation of souls is in very deed God's perfect will, His highest glory.

This loving desire of God, to get His place in the heart of men, He imparts to all His children who are willing to yield themselves wholly to Him. It is in this that the likeness and image of God consist—to have a heart in which His love takes complete possession, and leads us to find spontaneously our highest joy in loving as He does.

It is thus that our text finds its fulfillment: "Delight thyself in the Lord" (and in His life of love) "and he will give thee the desires of thine heart." Count upon it that the intercession of love, rising up to heaven, will be met with the fulfillment of the desire of our heart. We may be sure that, as we delight in what God delights in, such prayer is inspired by God and will have its answer. And our prayer becomes unceasingly, "Thy desires, O my Father, are mine. Thy holy will of love is my will too."

In fellowship with Him we get the courage, with our whole will and strength, to bring the persons or the circles in which we are interested, in an ever-growing confidence, that our prayer will be heard. As we reach out in yearning love, we will get the power to take hold of the will of God to bless, and to believe that God will work out His own blessed will in giving us the desire of our hearts, because the fulfillment of His desire has been the delight of our souls.

We then become, in the highest sense of the word, God's fellow laborers. Our prayer becomes part of God's divine work of reaching and saving the lost. And we learn to find our happiness in losing ourselves in the salvation of those around us.

January 27

My Great Desire

One thing have I desired of the Lord, that will I seek after; that I may dwell in the house of the Lord all the days of my life, to behold the beauty of the Lord, and to enquire in his temple.—Psalm 27:4

Here we have man's response to God's desire to dwell in us. When the desire of God toward us begins to rule the life and heart, our desire is fixed on one thing, and that is, to dwell in the house of the Lord all the days of our life, to behold the beauty of the Lord, to worship Him in the beauty of holiness. And then to inquire in His temple and to learn what it means that God has said: "I the Lord have spoken it, and will do it. And I will yet for this be inquired of by the house of Israel to do it for them."

The more we realize the desire of God's love to give His rest in the heart, and the more our desire is thus quickened to dwell every day in His temple and behold His beauty, the more the Spirit of intercession will grow upon us, to claim all that in His New Covenant God has promised. Whether we think of our church and country, of our homes and schools, of our nearer or wider circle; whether we think of the unsaved and all their needs, or the unsaved and their danger, the thought that God is indeed longing to find His home and His rest in the hearts of men, if He be only "inquired of," will rouse our whole being to strive for Zion's sake not to hold our peace. All the thoughts of our feebleness and unworthiness will be swallowed up in the wonderful assurance that He has said of human hearts: "This is my rest for ever; here will I dwell; for I have desired it."

As our faith sees how high our calling is, how indispensable God has made fervent, intense, persistent prayer as the condition of His purpose being fulfilled, we will be drawn to give up our life to a closer walk with God, to an unceasing waiting upon Him, and to a testimony to our brethren of what God will do in them and in us.

Is it not wonderful beyond all thought, this divine partnership, in which God commits the fulfillment of His desires to our keeping? Shame upon us that we have so little realized it!

January 28

Intercession Day and Night

Shall not God avenge his own elect, which cry day and night unto him, though he bear long with them?—Luke 18:7

When Nehemiah heard of the destruction of Jerusalem, he cried to God: "Hear the prayer of thy servant which I pray before thy face day and night." Of the watchmen set on the walls of Jerusalem, God said: "Which shall never hold their peace day nor night." And Paul writes: "Night and day praying exceedingly, to the end he may stablish your hearts unblameable in holiness before our God and Father" (1 Thess. 3:10, 13, R.V.).

Is such prayer night and day really needed and really possible? Most assuredly, when the heart is first so entirely possessed by the desire that it cannot rest until this is fulfilled. The life has so come under the power of the heavenly blessing that nothing can keep it from sacrificing all to obtain it.

Then a child of God begins to get a real vision into the need of the church and of the world, a vision of the divine redemption which God has promised in the outpouring of His love into our hearts. He gets a vision of the power of true intercession to bring down the heavenly blessing, a vision of the honor of being allowed as intercessors to take part in that work. Then it comes as a matter of course that he regards the work as the most heavenly thing upon earth—as intercessor to cry day and night to God for the revelation of His mighty power.

Let us learn from David, who said: "The zeal of thine house hath consumed me"; from Christ our Lord, of whom these words were so intensely true, that there is nothing so much worth living for as this one thought—how to satisfy the heart of God in His longing for human fellowship and affection, and how to win hearts to be His dwelling-place. And shall not we, too, give ourselves no rest until we have found a place for the Mighty One in our hearts, and yielded ourselves to the great work of intercession?

God grant that our hearts may be so brought under the influence of these divine truths that we may in very deed yield ourselves to make our devotion to Christ, and our longing to satisfy the heart of God, the chief object of our life.

January 29

The High Priest and His Intercession

We have such an high priest, who is able to save them to the uttermost that come unto God by him, seeing he ever liveth to make intercession for them.—Hebrews 7:25, 26; 8:1

In Israel, what a difference there was between the high priest and the priests and Levites. The high priest alone had access to the Holiest of All. He bore on his forehead the golden crown, "Holiness to the Lord," and by his intercession on the great Day of Atonement bore the sins of the people. The priests brought the daily sacrifices, and stood before the Lord, and came out to bless the people. The difference between high priest and priest was great. But still greater was the unity; they formed one body with the high priest, sharing with him the power to appear before God to receive and dispense His blessing to His people.

It is even so with our great High Priest. He alone has power with God, in a never-ceasing intercession, to obtain from the Father what His people need. And yet, infinite though the distance be between Him and the royal priesthood that surrounds Him for His service, the unity and the fellowship into which His people have been taken up with Him is no less infinite than the apparent diversity. The blessing that He obtains from His Father for us, He holds for His people to receive from Him through their fervent supplication, to be dispensed to the souls among whom He has placed them as His witnesses and representatives.

As long as Christians simply think of being saved, and of a life which will make that salvation secure, they never can understand the mystery of the power of intercession to which they are called.

But when once they realize that salvation means a vital life union with Jesus Christ, an actual sharing of His life dwelling and working in us, and the consecration of our whole being, to live and labor, to think and will, and find our highest joy in living as a royal priesthood, the church will put on her strength, and prove, in fellowship with God and man, how truly the likeness and the power of Christ dwell in her.

January 30

A Royal Priesthood

Call unto me, and I will answer thee, and show thee great and mighty things which thou knowest not.—Jeremiah 33:3

As you plead for the great mercies of the new covenant to be bestowed, take with you these thoughts:

(1) The infinite willingness of God to bless. His very nature is a pledge of it. He delights in mercy. He waits to be gracious. His promises and the experience of His saints assure us of it.

(2) Why then does the blessing so often delay? In creating man with a free will, and making him a partner in the rule of the earth, God limited himself. He made himself dependent on what man would do. Man by his prayer would hold the measure of what God could do in blessing.

(3) Think of how God is hindered and disappointed when His children do not pray, or pray but little. The low, feeble life of the church, the lack of the power of the Holy Spirit for conversion and holiness, is all due to the lack of prayer. How different would be the state of the church and of heathendom if God's people were to take no rest in calling upon Him!

(4) And yet God has blessed, just up to the measure of the faith and the zeal of His people. It is not for them to be content with this as a sign of His approval; but rather to say, If He has thus blessed our feeble efforts and prayers, what will He do if we yield ourselves wholly to a life of intercession?

(5) What a call to penitence and confession that our lack of consecration has kept back God's blessing from the world! He was ready to save men, but we were not willing to sacrifice our wholehearted devotion to Christ and His service.

Children of God, God counts upon you to take your place before His throne as intercessors. Awake, I pray you, to the consciousness of your holy calling as a royal priesthood. Begin to live a new life in the assurance that intercession, in the likeness and the fellowship with the Lord Jesus in heaven interceding, is the highest privilege a man can desire. In this spirit take up the word with large expectations: "Call unto me, and I will answer thee, and show thee great and mighty things which thou knowest not."

January 31

Intercession, a Divine Reality

And another angel came, ... and there was given unto him much incense, that he should offer it with the prayers of all saints upon the golden altar which was before the throne.—Revelation 8:3

Are the thoughts to which this series has given utterance not a sufficiently grave indictment of the subordinate place given to intercession in the teaching and practice of the church, with its ministers and members? Is it not of supreme importance to make it an essential, altogether indispensable element in the true Christian life? To those who accept God's Word in its full meaning, there can be no doubt about the answer.

Intercession is, by amazing grace, an essential element in God's redeeming purpose—so much so that without it the failure of its accomplishment may lie at our door. Christ's intercession in heaven is essential to His carrying out of the work He began upon earth, but He calls for the intercession of the saints in the attainment of His object. Just think of what we read: "All things are of God, who hath reconciled us to himself by Jesus Christ, and hath given to us the ministry of reconciliation." As the reconciliation was dependent on Christ's doing His part, so is the accomplishment of the work He calls on the church to do her part. We see how Paul regarded intercession day and night as indispensable to the fulfillment of the work that had been entrusted to him. It is but one aspect of that mighty power of God which works in the heart of His believing people.

Intercession is indeed a divine reality. Without it, the church loses the joy and the power of the Spirit life for achieving great things for God. Without it, the command to preach the gospel to every creature can never be carried out. Without it, there is no power for the church to recover from her sickly, feeble life and conquer the world. And in the life of the believer, minister or member, there can be no entrance into the abundant life and joy of daily fellowship with God, except as he takes his place among God's elect—the watchmen and remembrancers of God, who cry to Him day and night.

Church of Christ, awake, awake! Listen to the call, "Pray without ceasing." Take no rest, and give God no rest.

May God help us to know and to fulfill our calling!

The Secret of Persevering Prayer

February 1

Parables on Prayer

I say unto you, Though he will not rise and give him, because he is his friend, yet because of his importunity he will rise and give him as many as he needeth.—Luke 11:8

Our Lord Jesus thought it of such importance that we should know the need of perseverance and importunity in prayer that He spoke two parables concerning this: the parable of the importunate friend (from which our verse for today is quoted) and the story of the unrighteous judge (see Luke 18:1-8). This is proof sufficient that in this aspect of prayer we have at once its greatest difficulty and its highest power. He would have us know that in prayer all will not be easy and smooth.

In the parables our Lord represents the difficulty as existing on the side of the persons to whom the petition was addressed, and the importunity as needed to overcome their reluctance to hear. In our relationship with God the difficulty is not on His side, but on ours. In connection with the first parable He tells us our Father is more willing to give good things to those who ask Him than any earthly father to give His child bread. In the second He assures us that God longs to avenge His elect speedily. The need for urgent prayer cannot be because God must be made willing or disposed to bless; the need lies altogether in ourselves. But because it was not possible to find any earthly illustration of a loving father or a willing friend from whom the needed lesson of importunity could be taught, He takes the unwilling friend and the unjust judge to encourage us in the faith, that perseverance can overcome every obstacle.

The difficulty is not in God's love or power, but in ourselves and our own incapacity to receive the blessing. And yet, because there is this difficulty with us, this lack of spiritual preparedness, there is a difficulty with God too. His wisdom, His righteousness, yes, His love, dare not give us what would do us harm if we received it too soon or too easily. And so in all ages men have prayed, with a sense that there were difficulties in the heavenly world to overcome. As they pleaded with God for the removal of the unknown obstacles, and in that persevering supplication were brought into a state of utter brokenness and helplessness, of entire resignation to Him and His will, and of faith that could take hold of Him, the hindrances in heaven and in themselves were together overcome. As God conquered them, they conquered God. As God prevailed with them, they prevailed with God!

The Elements of True Prayer

I have set watchmen upon thy walls, O Jerusalem. . . . Ye that make mention of the Lord, keep not silence, and give him no rest, till he establish, and till he make Jerusalem a praise. . . .—Isaiah 62:6, 7

Prayer is at once indispensable and irresistible. What unknown and untold power and blessing are stored up for us in heaven? How that power can make us a blessing to men!

How is it to be sought in prayer continually and persistently? How may they who have the heavenly power pray it down upon others? How can it defy all the power of the world, and fit men to conquer that world for Christ? It is the power of the heavenly life, the power of God's own Spirit, that waits for prayer to bring it down.

In all this kind of prayer there is little thought of personal need or happiness. It is the desire to witness for Christ and bring Him and His salvation to others. It is the thought of God's kingdom and glory that must possess His disciples.

If we would be delivered from the sin of restraining prayer, we must enlarge our hearts for the work of intercession. The attempt to pray constantly for ourselves must be a failure; it is in intercession for others that our faith and love and perseverance will be aroused, and the power of the Spirit be found which can fit us for saving men. We are asking how we may become more faithful and successful in prayer. Let us see how the Master teaches us in the parable of the friend at midnight that intercession for the needy calls forth the highest exercise of our power of believing and prevailing prayer. (See Luke 11:5-8.) Intercession is the most perfect form of prayer: it is the prayer Christ ever lives to pray on His throne. Let us learn the elements of true prayer:

(1) Notice *the urgent need:* here intercession has its origin. The friend came at midnight—an untimely hour. He was hungry, and could not buy bread. To pray aright, we must keep eye and heart open to the need around us.

(2) Note *the willing love.* The friend took his weary, hungry friend into his house, and into his heart, too. It is the very nature of love to forget itself for the sake of others.

(3) Note *the sense of impotence.* We often speak of the power of love, yet the strongest love can be utterly impotent. A mother might be willing to give her life for her dying child, and yet not be able to save it. The friend at midnight was most willing to give his friend bread, but he had none, so he went begging. This is what we must do today.

February 3

The Holy Spirit and Prayer

Cornelius, thy prayer is heard, and thine alms are had in remembrance in the sight of God. —Acts 10:31

In the outpouring of the Holy Spirit in the house of Cornelius at Caesarea, we have another testimony to the wondrous interdependence of the action of prayer and the Spirit, and another proof of what will come to a man who has given himself to prayer. Peter went up at midday to pray on the housetop. And what happened? He saw heaven opened, and there came the vision that revealed to him the cleansing of the Gentiles: with that came the message of the three men from Cornelius, a man who "prayed alway," and had heard from an angel, "Thy prayers are come up before God"; and then the voice of the Spirit was heard saying, "Go with them."

It is Peter praying to whom the will of God is revealed, to whom guidance is given as to going to Caesarea, and who is brought into contact with a praying and prepared company of hearers. No wonder that in answer to all this prayer a blessing comes beyond all expectation, and the Holy Spirit is poured out upon the Gentiles. The teaching and the power of the Holy Spirit are alike unalterably linked to prayer.

It is still prayer that is the only secret of true church extension; that is guided from heaven to find and send forth God-called and God-empowered men. To prayer the Holy Spirit will show the men He has selected; to prayer that sets them apart under His guidance He will give the honor of knowing that they are men "sent forth by the Holy Spirit." It is prayer that is the link between the king on the throne and the church at His footstool; the human link that has its divine strength in the power of the Holy Spirit who comes in answer to it.

As one looks back upon the history of the church, how clear the two great truths stand out: where there is much prayer there will be much of the Spirit; where there is much of the Spirit there will be ever-increasing prayer. So clear is the living connection between the two that when the Spirit is given in answer to prayer it ever wakens more prayer to prepare for the fuller revelation and communication of His divine power and grace. If prayer was thus the power by which the early church flourished and triumphed, is it not the one need of the church today?

February 4

Asking for the Holy Spirit

If ye, then, being evil, know how to give good gifts unto your children: how much more shall your heavenly Father give the Holy Spirit to them that ask him?—Luke 11:13

Christ had just said (v. 9), "Ask, and it shall be given you. . . ." God's giving is inseparably connected with our asking. He applies this especially to the Holy Spirit. As surely as a father on earth gives bread to his child, so God gives the Holy Spirit to them that ask Him. The whole ministration of the Spirit is ruled by the one great law: *God must give, we must ask.* When the Holy Spirit was poured out at Pentecost with a flow that never ceases, it was in answer to prayer. The inflow into the believer's heart, and His outflow in the rivers of living water, ever still depend upon the law: Ask, and it shall be given.

The story of the birth of the church in the outpouring of the Holy Spirit, and of the first freshness of its heavenly life in the power of that Spirit, will teach us how *prayer on earth*, whether as cause or effect, *is the true measure of the presence of the Spirit of heaven.* As little as the·power of the Spirit could be given without Christ sitting on the throne, *could it descend without the disciples on the footstool of the throne.* For all the ages the law is laid down here at the birth of the church, that whatever else may be found on earth, the power of the Spirit must be prayed down from heaven. The measure of believing, continued prayer will be the measure of the Spirit's working in the church. Direct, determined, definite prayer is what we need.

At Samaria Philip had preached with great blessing, and many had believed. But the Holy Spirit, as yet, was fallen on none of them. The apostles send down Peter and John to pray for them, that they might receive the Holy Spirit. The power for such prayer was a higher gift than preaching, the work of the men who had been in closest contact with the Lord of glory, the work that was essential to the perfection of the life that preaching and baptism, faith and conversion, had only begun. Surely of all the gifts of the early church for which we should long there is none more needed than the gift of prayer—prayer that brings down the Holy Spirit on believers. This power is given to the men who will say: "We will give ourselves to prayer."

February 5

The Place of Prayer in the Believer's Life

And there is none that calleth upon thy name, that stirreth up himself to take hold of thee.—Isaiah 64:7

Prayer does not have the place it ought to have in our Christian lives. This is a shortcoming all of us are willing to confess. Our difficulties seem to make a true and full prayer life almost impossible. But blessed be God! "The things that are impossible with men are possible with God." "God is able to make all grace abound toward you, that ye, having all sufficiency in all things, may abound to all good work."

Let us believe that God's call to much prayer need not be a burden and cause of continual self-condemnation. He means it to be a joy. He can make it an inspiration, giving us strength for all our work, and bringing down His power to work through us in our fellowman. Let us not fear to admit to the full the sin that shames us, and then to face it in the name of our mighty Redeemer. *The light that shows us our sin and condemns us for it will show us the way out of it, into the life of liberty that is well pleasing to God.* If we allow this one matter, unfaithfulness in prayer, to convict us of the lack in our Christian life which lies at the root of it, God will use the discovery to bring us not only the power to pray that we long for, but the joy of a new and healthy life, of which prayer is the spontaneous expression.

How can our communion with the Father, in continual prayer and intercession, become what it ought to be if we and the world around us are to be blessed? We must begin by going back to God's Word to study what *place God means prayer to have* in the life of His child and His church. A fresh sight of what prayer is according to the will of God, of what our prayers can be through the grace of God, will free us from those feeble, defective views of effective prayer which lie at the root of our failure. As we with our whole heart and soul consent to it and rejoice in it, all thought of task and burden, of self-effort and strain, will pass away in the blessed faith that as simple as breathing is in the healthy natural life so will praying be in the Christian life that is led and filled by the Spirit of God.

February 6

The Intercessor's Prayer

And he saw that there was no man, and wondered that there was no intercessor.—Isaiah 59:16

We must all face the question of whether the call of God for our time and attention is of more importance than that of man. If God is waiting to meet us, and to give us His blessing and power from heaven for His work, it is a short-sighted policy to put other work in the place which God and waiting on Him should have.

I remember a man of God who put it this way: "I rise in the morning and have half an hour in my room before breakfast with God in the Word and in prayer. I go out, and am occupied all day with a multiplicity of engagements. I do not think many minutes elapse without my breathing a prayer for guidance or help. After my day's work, I return in my evening devotions and speak to God of the day's work. But of the intense, definite, importunate prayer of which Scripture speaks one knows little." What, he asked, did I think of such a life?

We all know the difference between a man whose profits are just enough to maintain his family and keep up his business, and another whose income enables him to extend the business and to help others. There may be an earnest Christian life in which there is prayer enough to keep us from going back, and just enough to help us maintain the position to which we have attained, without much growth in spirituality or Christlikeness. The attitude is more defensive, seeking to ward off temptation, than aggressive, reaching out after higher attainment. If there is indeed to be a going after victory, striving from strength to strength, with some large experience of God's power to sanctify ourselves and to bring down rich blessing on others, there must be more definite and persevering prayer. The Scripture teaching about crying day and night, continuing steadfastly in prayer, watching unto prayer, being heard for his opportunity, must in some degree become our experience if we are really to be intercessors.

Praise God for Difficulties

And he spake a parable unto them to this end, that men ought always to pray, and not to faint.—Luke 18:1

God has so constituted us that the clearer our insight is into the reasonableness of a demand, the more hearty will be our surrender to it. One great cause of our laxity in prayer is that there seems to be something arbitrary, or at least something incomprehensible, in the call to such continued prayer. If we could see that this apparent difficulty is a divine necessity, and in the very nature of things the source of unspeakable blessing, we would more readily give ourselves to continue in prayer with gladness of heart. The call to importunity opens to us one of our greatest privileges.

Have you ever noticed what a part difficulties play in our natural lives? They call out man's powers as nothing else can, strengthening and enobling character. We are told that one reason for the greater strength of will and purpose typical of the northern nations, like Holland and Scotland, over the nations of the sunny South, such as Italy and Spain, is that the climate of the latter has been too beautiful, too easy and relaxing. The difficulties of the former have been their greatest boon. Nothing worthwhile is found without labor and effort. What is education but a daily developing and disciplining of the mind by new difficulties presented to the pupil to overcome? The moment a lesson has become easy, the pupil moves on to something higher and more difficult. With race as with the individual, it is in the mastering of difficulties that our highest attainments come.

It is even so in our communion with God. If we needed merely to kneel down and ask, and get up, and go away, what unspeakable loss to our spiritual lives! It is in the difficulty and delay that calls for persevering prayer, that the true blessing and blessedness of the heavenly life will be found. There we are brought to know our own weakness and unworthiness. We discover how earthly and unspiritual we are, how little we have of God's Holy Spirit. We are brought to yield to God's Spirit to pray in us, to take our place in Jesus Christ, and abide in Him as our only pleas with the Father. There our will and strength and goodness are crucified, and we rise in Christ to newness of life, with our whole will dependent upon God and set upon His glory. We must praise God for the need and the difficulty of importunate prayer, as one of His choicest means of grace.

February 8

Importunate Prayer

For every one that asketh receiveth; and he that seeketh findeth; and to him that knocketh it shall be opened.—Matthew 7:8

In importunity there are various elements. The chief of these are perseverance, determination, and intensity. It begins with our refusal at once to accept a denial. It grows to the determination to persevere, to spare no time or trouble, till an answer comes. It rises to the intensity in which the whole being is given to God in supplication, and the boldness comes to lay hold of God's strength. At one time it is quiet and restful; at another, passionate and bold. Now it takes time and is patient; then again it claims at once what it desires. In whatever different shape, it always means: God hears prayer; therefore I must be heard!

Think of the wonderful instances among the Old Testament saints: Abraham, as he pleads for Sodom. Time after time he renews his prayer until the sixth time he has to say: Let not my Lord be angry. He doesn't stop until God consents to His petition, until he has learned how far he can go, has entered into God's mind and rests in God's will. And for his sake, Lot was saved.

Think of Jacob, when he feared to meet Esau. The angel of the Lord met him in the dark and wrestled with him. When the angel saw that he could not prevail, he said, "Let me go." And Jacob said, "I will not let thee go." That boldness forced from the reluctant angel the blessing. It was so pleasing in God's sight that a new name was given Jacob: Israel, he who striveth with God, "for thou hast striven with God and with men, and hast prevailed."

As an intercessor, Moses used importunity with God and prevailed. He proves that the man who truly lives near to God, and with whom God speaks face to face, becomes partaker of that same power of intercession which there is in Him who is at God's right hand and ever lives to pray.

Think of Elijah in his prayer—first for fire, then for rain. In the former you have the importunity that claims and receives an immediate answer. In the latter, bowing himself down to the earth, his face between his knees, his answer to his servant who had gone to look toward the sea and said, "There is nothing," was, "Go again seven times." Here was the importunity of perseverance.

February 9

Prayer As a Servant

If ye abide in me, and my words abide in you, ye shall ask what ye will, and it shall be done unto you. —John 15:7

Here on earth the influence of one who asks a favor for others depends entirely on his character and the relationship he bears to him with whom he is interceding. It is what he is that gives weight to what he asks. It is the same with God. Our power in prayer depends upon our life. Where our life is right, we shall know how to pray so as to please God, and prayer will secure the answer. "If ye abide in *me*," our Lord says, ye shall ask and it shall be done unto you. It is the prayer of *a righteous man*, according to James 5:16, that availeth much. We receive whatever we ask, John says, "because we keep his commandments, and do the things that are pleasing in his sight" (1 John 3:22). All lack of power to pray properly and perseveringly, all lack of power in prayer with God, points to some lack in the Christian life. It is as we learn to live the life that pleases God that God will give us what we ask.

Let us learn from the Lord Jesus, in the parable of the vine, what the healthy, vigorous life is, that may ask and receive what it will. Hear His voice, "If ye abide in me, and my words abide in you, ye shall ask what ye will, and it shall be done unto you." And again at the close of the parable: "Ye did not choose me, but I chose you, and appointed you, that you should go and bear fruit, and that your fruit should abide: that whatsoever ye shall ask the Father in my name, he may give it you."

And what is now, according to the parable, the life that one must live to bear fruit, and then ask and receive? What is it we are to do or be that will enable us to pray as we should, and to receive what we ask? The answer is in one word: it is the branch life that gives power in prayer and for prayer. We are branches of Christ, the living Vine. We must simply live like branches, and abide in Christ, then we shall ask what we will and it shall be done unto us. We all know what a branch is, what is its essential characteristic. It is simply a growth of the vine, produced by it and appointed to bear fruit. It has only one reason for existence: it is there at the bidding of the vine, that through it the vine may bear fruit and ripen it. Its only work is to serve the vine, that through it the vine may do its work. That is the work of the believer, the branch of Christ the heavenly Vine.

February 10

Prayer and God's Presence

Therefore the children of Israel could not stand before their enemies, but turned their backs before their enemies, because they were accursed: neither will I be with you any more, except ye destroy the accursed from among you. —Joshua 7:12

God's presence restored means victory secured. Then, we are responsible for defeat. Then, there must be sin somewhere causing it. Then, we ought at once to find out and put away the sin. We may confidently expect God's presence the moment the sin is put away. Surely each one is under the solemn obligation to search his life to see what part he may have in this evil.

God never speaks of sin to His people except with a view of saving them from it. *The same light that shows the sin will show the way out of it.* The same power that breaks down and condemns will, if humbly yielded to and waited on in confession and faith, give the power to rise up and conquer. It is God who is speaking to His church and to us about this sin: "He wondered that there was no intercessor" (Isa. 59:16). "I wondered that there was none to uphold" (Isa. 63:5). "I sought for a man . . . that should stand in the gap before me . . . and found none" (Ezek. 22:30). The God who speaks thus is He who will work the change for His children who seek His face. He will make the Valley of Achor, of trouble and shame, of sin confessed and cast out, a door of hope. Let us not fear, let us not cling to the excuses and explanations which circumstances suggest, but simply confess: We have sinned; we are sinning; we dare sin no longer.

In this matter of prayer we are sure God does not demand of us impossibilities. He does not weary us with an impractical ideal. He asks us to pray no more for grace to enable us to do so. He will give the grace to do what He asks, and so to pray that our intercessions shall, day by day, be a pleasure to Him and to us, a source of strength to our conscience and our work, and a channel of blessing to those for whom we labor.

God dealt personally with Joshua, Israel, and Achan. Let us each allow Him to deal personally with us concerning this sin, this restraining prayer, and its consequences in our life and work; concerning the deliverance from sin, its certainty and blessedness. Take quiet time and be still before God that He may take this matter in hand. Leave yourself in God's hands.

February 11

The Prayer of a Healthy Man

Is there no balm in Gilead; is there no physician there? why then is not the health of the daughter of my people recovered?—Jeremiah 8:22

It is evident that as long as this defeated spirit prevails, there can be little prospect of improvement. Discouragement must bring defeat. One of the first objectives of a physician is to awaken hope; without this he knows his medicines will often profit little. No teaching from God's Word as to the duty, the urgent need, the blessed privilege of more prayer, effectual prayer, will accomplish much, while the secret whisper is heard: There is no hope.

Our first care must be to find out the hidden cause of the failure and despair, and then to show how divinely sure deliverance is. We must, unless we are to rest content with our state, listen to and join in the question, "Is there no balm in Gilead?" We must listen, and receive into our hearts, the divine promise with the response it met with, "Return, ye backsliding children, and I will heal your backslidings. Behold, we come unto thee, for thou art the Lord our God." We must come with the personal prayer and the faith that there will be a personal answer. Shall we not even now begin to claim it in regard to the lack of prayer, and believe that God will help us? "Heal me, O Lord, and I shall be healed."

It is always important to distinguish between the symptoms of a disease and the disease itself. Feebleness and failure in prayer is a sign of feebleness in the spiritual life. If a patient were to ask a physician to give him something to stimulate his feeble pulse, he would be told that this would do him little good. The pulse is the index of the state of the heart and the whole system: the physician strives to have health restored. What everyone who wants to pray more faithfully and effectually must learn is: his whole life is in a sickly state and needs restoration. It is as he looks not only at his shortcoming in prayer, but at the lack of faith in his life, of which this is a symptom, that he will become fully alive to the serious nature of the disease. He will then see the need for a radical change in his whole life and walk if his prayer life, which is simply the pulse of the spiritual system, is to indicate health and vigor. Prayer is meant to be as simple and natural as breathing or working to a healthy man. The reluctance we feel and the failure we confess are God's own voice calling us to acknowledge our disease, and come to Him for healing.

February 12

Prayer and the Impotent Man

Jesus ... saith unto him, Wilt thou be made whole? The impotent man answered him, Sir, I have no man ... to put me into the pool. ... Jesus saith unto him, Rise ... and walk.—John 5:6-8

This story invites us to notice three things: Christ's question first appeals to the will, and asks for the expression of consent. He then listens to the man's confession of his utter helplessness. Then comes the ready obedience to Christ's command that rises up and walks.

(1) Wilt thou be made whole? About the answer of the impotent man there could be no doubt. Who would not be willing to have his sickness removed? But we need to press the question in the spiritual realm. Some will not admit that they are sick. And some will not believe that Christ can make a man whole. And some will believe it for others but they are not sure it is for them. At the root of all lies the fear of the self-denial and the sacrifice that will be needed. The walk in Christ and like Christ is too hard. They simply do not will to be made whole.

(2) Secondly, Christ wants us to look up to Him as our only Helper. "I have no man to put me in" must be our cry. Here on earth there is no help for me. Exercise builds strength in normal muscles, but sickness needs special measures. Your soul is sick; your inability to walk joyfully in the Christian way is a sign of disease. Don't be afraid to confess it and to admit that there is no hope for restoration unless an act of God's mercy heals you. Come to Christ for healing. He can in one moment make you whole.

(3) The third thing Christ asks is this: the surrender of faith. When He spoke to the impotent man, His word of command had to be obeyed. The man believed there was truth and power in Christ's word; in that faith he rose and walked. By faith he obeyed. And what Christ said to others was for him, too. "Go thy way; thy faith hath made thee whole." Of us, too, Christ asks this faith that His word changes our impotence into strength, and fits us for that walk in newness of life for which we have been quickened in Him. If we do not believe this, if we will not take courage and say, with Paul, "I can do all things in Christ, which strengtheneth me," we cannot obey. If we accept and trust an unseen Christ as our strength, and go on in that strength, we will then know Christ as the strength of our lives. We will know, and tell, and prove that Jesus Christ has made us whole.

February 13

Prayer and Walking with God

For which is easier, to say, Thy sins be forgiven thee; or to say, Arise, and walk!—Matthew 9:5

There are many marks of spiritual health. Our text leads us to one: walking. Jesus said to the sick man, "Arise and walk," and with that restored him to his place among men in full health and vigor, able to take his part in all the work of life. It is a wonderfully suggestive picture of the restoration of spiritual health. To the healthy, walking is a pleasure, to the sick a burden, if not an impossibility. How many Christians there are to whom, like the maimed and the halt and lame and the impotent, movement and progress in God's way is indeed an effort and a weariness. Christ comes to say, and with a word He gives the power, arise and walk.

Just think of the walk to which He restores and empowers us. It is a life like that of Enoch and Noah, who "walked with God." A life like that of Abraham, to whom God said, "Walk before me," and who himself said, "The Lord before whom I walk." A life of which David sings, "They shall walk in the light of thy countenance," and Isaiah prophesies, "They that wait upon the Lord will renew their strength; they shall run and not be weary, they shall walk and not faint." Even as God the Creator faints not, nor is weary, they shall walk with Him, waiting on Him, never exhausted or feeble. It is a life concerning which it could be said of the last of the Old Testament saints, Zacharias and Elizabeth, "They were both righteous before God, walking in all the commandments and ordinances of the Lord blameless." This is the walk Jesus came to make possible and true to His people in greater power than ever before.

Hear what the New Testament says of it: "That like as Christ was raised from the dead by the glory of the Father, so we also should walk in newness of life." It is the Risen One who says to us, "Rise and walk." He gives the power of the resurrection life. It is a walk in Christ. "As ye have received Christ Jesus the Lord, so walk ye also in him." It is a walk like Christ. "He that saith he abideth in him ought so to walk even as he walked." It is a walk of faith, all its power coming simply from God and Christ and the Holy Spirit to the soul turned away from the world. "We walk by faith and not by sight."

Five Marks of True Prayer

What things soever ye desire, when ye pray, believe that ye receive them, and ye shall have them. —Mark 11:24

Here we have a summary of the teaching of our Lord Jesus on prayer. Nothing will so much help to convince of the sin of our laxity in prayer, to discover its causes, and to give us courage to expect entire deliverance, as the careful study and the believing acceptance of that teaching. The more heartily we enter into the mind of our blessed Lord, and set ourselves simply just to think about prayer as He thought, the more surely will His words be as living seeds. They will grow and produce in us their fruit—a life and practice exactly corresponding to the divine truth they contain.

Do let us believe this: Christ, the living Word of God, gives in His words a divine quickening power which brings what they say, which works in us what He asks, which actually fits and enables for all He demands. Learn to look upon His teaching on prayer as a definite promise of what He, by His Holy Spirit dwelling in you, is going to work into your very being and character.

Our Lord gives us five marks, or essential elements, of true prayer: first, the heart's *desire*; then the expression of that desire in *prayer*; with that, the *faith* that carries that prayer to God; in that faith, the *acceptance* of God's answer; then comes the *experience* of the desired blessing.

Do you truly desire that God would enable you so to pray that your life may be free from continual self-condemnation, and that the power of His Spirit may come down in answer to your petition? Come and *ask it of God*. Kneel down and pray for it in a single definite sentence. When you have done so, kneel still in faith, believing in God who answers. Believe that you do now receive what you have prayed; believe that you *have* received. If you find it difficult to do this, kneel still, and say that you do it on the strength of His own word. You have asked and received grace in Christ to prepare you step by step to be faithful in prayer and intercession. The more simply you hold this, and expect the Holy Spirit to work it in you, the more surely and fully will the word be made true to you: Ye shall have it. God himself who gave the answer will work it in you.

February 15

Three Lessons in Prayer

The Spirit also helpeth our infirmity: for we know not how to pray as we ought; but the Spirit himself maketh intercession for us with groanings which cannot be uttered. And he that searcheth the hearts knoweth what is the mind of the Spirit, because he maketh intercession for the saints according to God. —Romans 8:26, 27

The Holy Spirit has been given to every child of God to be his life. He dwells in him, not as a separate being in one part of his nature, but as his very life. He is the divine power or energy by which his life is maintained and strengthened. All that a believer is called to be or to do, the Holy Spirit can and will work in him. If he does not know or yield to the holy Guest, the blessed Spirit cannot work, and his life is a sickly one, full of failure and sin. As he yields, and waits, and obeys the leading of the Spirit, God works in him all that is pleasing in His sight.

This Holy Spirit is, in the first place, a Spirit of prayer. He was promised as a "Spirit of grace and supplication" (Zech. 12:10), the grace for supplication. He was sent forth into our hearts as "the Spirit of adoption, whereby we cry, Abba, Father." He enables us to say in true faith and growing apprehension of its meaning, "Our Father which art in heaven." As we pray in the Spirit, our worship is as God seeks it to be—"in spirit and in truth." Prayer is just the breathing of the Spirit within us; power in prayer comes from the power of the Spirit in us, waited on and trusted in. Failure in prayer comes from feebleness of the Spirit's work in us. If we are to pray aright, the Spirit must be right in us. Our prayer is the index of the Spirit's work in us.

There are three simple lessons that the believer, who would enjoy the blessing of being taught to pray by the Spirit of prayer, must know. The first is: Believe that *the Spirit dwells in you* (Eph. 1:13). As long as we measure our power, for praying aright and perseveringly, by what we feel, or think we can accomplish, we will be discouraged when we hear how much we ought to pray. But when we quietly believe that the Holy Spirit as a Spirit of supplication is dwelling with us, our hearts will be filled with hope. Second, *beware above everything of grieving the Holy Spirit* (Eph. 4:30) by sin, unbelief, selfishness, unfaithfulness to His voice in conscience. Third, *be filled with the Spirit* (Eph. 5:18). Only the healthy spiritual life can pray aright.

February 16

The Yielded Prayer

Praying in the Holy Spirit.—Jude 21

At the time of your conversion you knew little about the Holy Spirit. Later on you heard of His dwelling in you, and His being the power of God in you for all the Father intends you to be, and yet His indwelling and inworking have been something vague and indefinite, and hardly a source of joy or strength. At conversion you did not yet know your need of Him, and still less what you might expect of Him. But your failures have taught it to you. And now you begin to see how you have been grieving Him by not trusting and not following Him, by not allowing Him to work in you all God's pleasure.

All this can be changed. Just as you, after seeking Christ and praying to Him, and trying without success to serve Him, found rest in accepting Him by faith, just so you may even now yield yourself to the full guidance of the Holy Spirit, and claim and accept Him to work in you what God would have. Just accept Him in faith as Christ's gift to be the Spirit of your whole life, of your prayer life too, and you can count on Him to take charge.

"I will pour (out)... the spirit of supplication" (Zech. 2: 10). Do you begin to see that the mystery of prayer is the mystery of the divine indwelling? God in heaven gives His Spirit in our hearts to be there the divine power praying in us, and drawing us upward to our God. God is a Spirit, and nothing but a like life and Spirit within us can hold communion with Him. It was for this that man was created—that God might dwell and work in Him and be the life of his life. It was this divine indwelling that sin lost. It was this that Christ came to exhibit in His life, to win back for us in His death, and then to impart to us by coming again from heaven in the Spirit to live in His disciples. It is this, the indwelling of God through the Spirit, that alone can explain and enable us to appropriate the wonderful promises given to prayer. God gives us the Spirit of supplication, too, to maintain His divine life within us as a life out of which prayer ever rises upward.

February 17

Pray in My Name!

Whatsoever ye shall ask IN MY NAME, that will I do.—John 14:13

"In my name" is repeated six times over in John 14 (vv. 13, 14, 15, 16) and 16 (vv. 23, 24, 26). Our Lord knew how slow our hearts would be to take it in, and He so longed that we should really believe that His name is the power in which every knee should bow, and in which every prayer could be heard, that He did not weary of saying it over and over: *In my name!* Our asking and the Father's giving are to be equally in the name of Christ. Everything in prayer depends upon our understanding and applying this principle—in my name.

Here on earth Christ as man came to reveal what prayer is. To pray in the name of Christ we must pray as He prayed on earth; as He taught us to pray; in union with Him, as He now prays in heaven. We must in love study, and in faith accept, Him as our Example, our Teacher, our Intercessor. Christ's life and work, His suffering and death, it was all prayer, all dependence on God, trust in God, receiving from God, surrender to God. Your redemption, O believer, is a redemption wrought by prayer and intercession; your Christ is a praying Christ. The life He lives in you, the life He lived for you, is a praying life that delights to wait on God and receive all from Him. To pray in His name is to pray as He prayed.

Our Lord taught us to pray in secret, in simplicity, with the eye on God alone, in humility, in the spirit of forgiving love. But the chief truth He reiterated was this: pray in faith. And He defined that faith not only as a trust in God's goodness or power, but as the definite assurance that we have received the very thing we ask. Then, in view of the delay in the answer, He insisted on perseverance and urgency. These purify all that is of the flesh, and tested and strengthened by that spiritual power, we can do all things—even casting the mountains into the sea.

Christ, the Intercessor, is our life; He is our head, and we are His body; His Spirit and life breathe in us. As in heaven, so on earth, intercession is God's chosen, God's only channel of blessing. Let us learn from Christ what glory there is in it; what is the way to exercise this wondrous power; what part we have to take in the work for God. Fear not to plead the name; His promise is a threefold cord that cannot be broken: *Whatsoever ye ask—in My name—shall be done unto you!*

February 18

My God Will Hear Me!

The Lord will hear when I call upon him.—Psalm 4:3

My God will hear me. What a blessed certainty! We have God's word for it in numberless promises. We have thousands of witnesses to the fact that they have found it true. We have experienced it in our own lives. We have had the Son of God come from heaven with the message that if we ask, the Father will give. We have had Jesus praying on earth, and being heard. And we have Him in heaven now, sitting at the right hand of God and making intercession for us. God hears prayer; God delights to answer prayer. We must confess with shame how little we have believed this wondrous truth, in the sense of believing and receiving it into our hearts and allowing it to possess our whole beings. That we accept a truth is not enough; the living God, of whom the truth speaks, must in its light so be revealed that our whole life is spent in His presence, with the consciousness as clear as in a little child toward its earthly parent—I know for certain my father hears me.

My God will hear me. What wondrous grace! Think of God in His infinite majesty, His altogether incomprehensible glory, His unapproachable holiness, sitting on a throne of grace, waiting to be gracious—inviting, encouraging you to pray with His promise: Call unto me, and I will answer thee. Think of yourself, in your nothingness and helplessness as a creature; in your wretchedness and transgressions as a sinner; in your feebleness and unworthiness as a saint; and praise the glory of that grace which allows you to say boldly of your prayer for yourself and others, "My God will hear me" (Micah 7:7).

My God will hear me. What a blessed prospect! I see it—all the failures of my past life have been due to the lack of this faith. My failure, especially in the work of intercession, has had its deepest root in this—I did not live in the blessed assurance, *My God will hear me!* Commonplace and insignificant though I be, filling but a very little place, so that I will scarce be missed when I go—even I have access to this infinite God, with the confidence that He hears me. One with Christ, led by the Holy Spirit, I dare to say: I will pray for others, for I am sure my God will listen to me. What a blessed prospect before me—every earthly and spiritual anxiety exchanged for the peace of God, who cares for all and hears prayer.

February 19

The God Who Hears Prayer

I have called upon thee, for thou wilt hear me, O God.—Psalm 17:6

My God will hear me. What a deep mystery! There are difficulties that can arise to perplex even the most honest heart. There is the question of God's sovereign, all-wise, all-disposing will. How can our wishes, often so selfish, overrule or change the perfect will? Were it not better to leave all to His disposal, who knows what is best and loves to give us the very best? Or how can our prayer change what He has ordained before? Then there is the question as to the need of persevering prayer, and long waiting for the answer. If God is Infinite Love, delighting more to give than we to receive, where is the need for pleading, wrestling, the urgency and the long delay of which Scripture and experience speak? Arising out of this is another question—the multitude of apparently vain and unanswered prayers. How many have pleaded for loved ones seemingly in vain? These questions can be answered, in various ways, but we must remember this: As little as we can comprehend God can we comprehend this, one of His most blessed attributes, He hears prayer! The Holy Spirit can enable us to believe and rejoice in it, even where every question is not yet answered. He will do this, as we lay our questionings before God, trust His faithfulness, and give ourselves humbly to obey His command to pray without ceasing.

My God will hear me. What a solemn responsibility! How often we complain of darkness, feebleness, failure, as if there was no help for it. And God has promised in answer to our prayer to supply our every need, and give us light, and strength, and peace. Would that we realized the responsibility of having such a God, and such promises, with the sin and shame of not availing ourselves of them to the utmost. How confident we should feel that the grace, which we have accepted and trusted to enable us to pray as we should, will be given.

There is more. This access to a prayer-hearing God is specially meant to make us intercessors for our fellowmen. Even as Christ obtained His right of prevailing intercession by giving himself a sacrifice to God for men, and through it receives the blessings He dispenses, so, if we have truly with Christ given ourselves to God for men, we share His right of intercession, and are able to obtain the powers of the heavenly world for them, too. The power of life and death is in our hands (1 John 5:16). My God will hear me: the deeper our entrance into this wonderful truth, the greater our effectiveness as intercessors!

February 20

God Seeks Intercessors

There is none that calleth upon thy name, that stirreth himself to take hold of thee.—Isaiah 64:7

God seeks intercessors. There is a world with its perishing millions, with intercession as its only hope. How much of love and work is comparatively vain, because there is so little intercession. A thousand millions living as if there never had been a Son of God to die for them. Thirty millions every year passing into outer darkness without hope. Fifty millions bearing the Christian name, and the great majority living in utter ignorance or indifference. Millions of feeble, sickly Christians; thousands of wearied workers, who could be blessed by intercession, who could themselves become mighty in intercession. Souls, each one worth more than worlds, are worth nothing less than the price paid for them in Christ's blood, and within reach of the power that can be won by intercession.

God seeks intercessors. There is a God of glory able to meet all these needs. He delights in mercy, He waits to be gracious, He longs to pour out His blessing. The love that gave the Son to death is the measure of the love that each moment hovers over every human being. And yet He does not help. And there they perish, and it is as if God does not move. If He does so love and long to bless, there must be some inscrutable reason for His holding back. What can it be? Scripture says it is because of our unbelief. It is the faithlessness and consequent unfaithfulness of God's people. He has taken them into partnership with himself; He has honored them, and bound himself, by making their prayer one of the standard measures of the working of His power. Lack of intercession is one of the chief causes of lack of blessing.

God seeks intercessors. There is a third magnitude to which our eyes need to be opened: the wondrous privilege and power of intercessors. There is a false humility which makes a great virtue of self-depreciation, because it has never seen its utter nothingness. If it knew that, it would never apologize for its feebleness, but glory in its utter weakness, as the one condition of Christ's power resting on it. Faith sees something of the divine fitness and beauty of this scheme of salvation through intercession, wakens the soul to a consciousness of its wondrous destiny, and girds it with strength for the blessed self-sacrifice to which it calls.

February 21

The Heavenly Vision

Go and inquire for one called Saul of Tarsus; for, behold, he prayeth.
—Acts 9:11

If Paul, as a pattern of prayer, is not as much studied or appealed to as he is in other respects, it is not because he is not in this too as remarkable a proof of what grace can do, or because we do not, in this respect, as much stand in need of the help of his example. A study of Paul as a pattern for prayer will bring a rich reward of instruction and encouragement. The words our Lord used of him at his conversion, "Behold he prayeth," may be taken as life-style.

The heavenly vision which brought Paul to his knees ever ruled after in his life. Christ at the right hand of God, in whom we are blessed with all spiritual blessings, was everything to him. To pray and expect the heavenly power in his work and on his work, from heaven direct by prayer, was the simple outcome of his faith in the glorified One. In this, too, Christ meant him to be a pattern from whom we might learn that, just in the measure in which the heavenliness of Christ and His gifts are known and believed so prayer will become the spontaneous rising of the heart to its life source.

It is of as much importance to know *what* Paul prayed, as how frequently and earnestly he did so. Intercession is a spiritual work. Our confidence in it will depend much on our knowing that we ask according to the will of God. The more distinctly we ask heavenly things, which we feel at once God alone can bestow and which we are sure He will bestow, the more direct and urgent will our appeal be to God alone. The more impossible the things are that we seek, the more we will turn from all human work to prayer and to God alone.

In all His instructions, our Lord Jesus spoke more often to His disciples about their praying than their preaching. In the farewell discourse, He said little about preaching, but much about the Holy Spirit and their asking whatsoever they would in His name. If we are to return to this life of the first apostles and of Paul, we must have the courage to confess past sin and to believe that there is deliverance. To break through old habits, to resist the clamor of pressing duties, to make every other call subordinate to this one, whether others approve or not, will not be easy at first. But the men and women who are faithful will not only have a reward themselves, but will also become benefactors to their brethren.

February 22

The God Who Seeks Intercessors

I chose you, and appointed you, that ye should go and bear fruit, that whatsoever ye shall ask of the Father in my name, he may give it you.—John 15:16

God seeks intercessors. When He called His people out of Egypt, He separated the priestly tribe, to draw nigh to Him and stand before Him and bless the people in His name. From time to time, He sought and found and honored intercessors, for whose sake He spared or blessed His people. When our Lord left the earth He said to the inner circle He had gathered around Him—an inner circle of special devotion to His service, to which access is still free to every disciple—"I chose you, and appointed you, that whatsoever ye shall ask of the Father in my name, he may give it you." And since that time, down through the ages, these men have had their successors, men who have proved how surely God works in answer to prayer.

God seeks intercessors. Though God has His appointed servants in Israel, watchmen set by himself to cry to Him day and night and give Him no rest, He often had to wonder and complain that there was no intercessor, none to stir himself up to take hold of His strength. And He still waits and wonders in our day that there are not more intercessors, that all His children do not give themselves to this highest and holiest work. He wonders to find multitudes of His children who have hardly any conception of what intercession is. He wonders to find multitudes more who have learned that it is their duty, and seek to obey it, but confess that they know but little of taking hold upon God or prevailing with Him.

God seeks intercessors. He longs to dispense larger blessings, to reveal His power and glory as God, His saving love, more abundantly. He seeks intercessors in larger number, in greater power, to prepare the way of the Lord. He seeks them. Where would He seek them but in His church? And how does He expect to find them? He entrusted to His church the task of telling of their Lord's need, the task of encouraging and training and preparing them for His holy service. And He ever comes again, seeking fruit, seeking intercessors. As Christ seeks the lost sheep until He finds it, God seeks intercessors.

Revive Thy Work, O Lord!

O Lord, revive thy work in the midst of the years.—Habakkuk 3:2

Revive Thy work, O Lord! Revival is God's work; He alone can give it; it must come from above. We are frequently in danger of looking to what God has done and is doing, and to count on that as the pledge that He will at once do more. And all the time it may be true that He is blessing us up to the measure of our faith or self-sacrifice and cannot give larger measure until there has been a new discovery and confession of what is hindering Him. Or we may be looking to all the signs of life and good around us, and congratulating ourselves on all the organization and agencies that are being created, while the need of God's mighty and direct interposition is not rightly felt and the entire dependence upon Him not cultivated. Regeneration, the giving of divine life, we all acknowledge to be God's act, a miracle of His power. The restoring or reviving of the divine life, in a soul or in a church, is as much a supernatural work. "Surely the Lord God will do nothing, but he revealeth his secret unto his servants the prophets." It is God who is to give the revival; it is God who reveals His secret; it is the Spirit of absolute dependence upon God, giving Him the honor and the glory, that will prepare for it.

Revive Thy work, O Lord! A second lesson suggested here is: the revival God is to give will be given in answer to prayer. It must be asked and received direct from God himself. Those who know anything of the history of revivals will remember how often this has been proved—both larger and local revivals have been directly traced to special prayer. If there is to be revival—a mighty, divine revival—it will need, on our part, corresponding wholeheartedness in prayer and faith. Let no one believer think himself too weak to help, or imagine he will not be missed. If he first begin, the gift that is in him may be so stirred that, for his circle or neighborhood, he will be God's chosen intercessor. Let us think of the need of souls, of all the sins and failings among God's people, of the little power there is in so much of the preaching, and begin to cry every day, "Wilt thou not revive us again, that thy people may rejoice in thee?" (Ps. 85:6). And let us have the truth engraved deep in our hearts: every revival comes, as Pentecost came, as the fruit of united, continued prayer. Any coming revival must begin with a great prayer revival. It is in the prayer closet, with the door shut, that the sound of abundance of rain will first be heard!

February 24

A Lesson in Revival

I dwell with him that is of a humble and contrite heart, to revive the heart of the contrite ones.—Isaiah 57:15

Revive Thy work, O Lord! Another lesson we need to learn is that it is to the humble and contrite that the revival is promised. We want the revival to come upon the proud and the self-satisfied, to break them down and save them. God will give this, but only on the condition that those who see and feel the sin of others take their burden of confession and bear it, and that all who pray for and claim in faith God's reviving power for His church shall humble themselves with the confession of its sins. The need for revival always points to previous decline; and decline was always caused by sin. Humiliation and contrition have ever been the conditions of revival. In all intercession, confession of man's sin and God's righteous judgment is ever an essential element.

Throughout the history of Israel we continually see this. It comes out in the reformations under the pious kings of Judah. We hear it in the prayer of men like Ezra, Nehemiah, and Daniel. In Isaiah, Jeremiah, and Ezekiel, as well as in the minor prophets, it is the keynote of all the warnings as of all the promises. If there be no humiliation and forsaking of sin, there can be no revival or deliverance: "These men have set up their idols in their hearts. . . . Shall I at all be inquired of them?" (Ezek. 14:3). "To this man will I look, even to him that is poor and of a contrite spirit, and that trembleth at my word" (Isa. 66:2). Amid the most gracious promises of divine visitation, there is ever this note: "Be ashamed and confounded for your ways, O house of Israel" (Ezek. 36:32).

We find the same in the New Testament. The Sermon on the Mount promises the kingdom to the poor and them that mourn. In the epistles to the Corinthians and Galatians the religion of man, or worldly wisdom and confidence in the flesh, is exposed and denounced; without its being confessed and forsaken, all the promises of grace and the Spirit will be vain. In the letters to the seven churches of Revelation, the key word of His message is—not to the unconverted, but to the church—repent! Men want a revival as the outgrowth of their agencies and progress. God's way is opposite: it is out of death, acknowledged as the desert of sin, confessed as utter helplessness, that He revives.

February 25

Stewards of the Love of God

Let a man so account of us, as of the ministers of Christ, and stewards of the mysteries of God. Moreover it is required in stewards, that a man be found faithful.—1 Corinthians 4:1, 2

A steward is the man to whom the king or master entrusts his treasures and goods, to apportion to those who have a right to them. God in heaven needs men on earth to make known the treasures of His love, and to give them to those who have need. The minister of the gospel is a steward of the mystery of God, and above all of the deep mystery of His everlasting love, and all the blessings that flow from it.

It is required in stewards that a man be found faithful; he must devote himself wholly to his life task. He must be faithful at his work, and always at his post in the palace or house where the treasures are stored. So the minister of the gospel must himself be faithful, living each day in the love and fellowship of God. He must be faithful not only to God, but to his fellowmen, caring for the needs of the souls entrusted to him, and ready to recommend God's love and to share it with others. This divine love is a mystery, and can only dwell in a heart set apart for God and satisfied with His love, which flows from Him as a stream of living water.

O child of God, seek to have a deeper insight into what the office of a servant of God means as a steward of the wonderful love of God to sinners. Pray much and often for your ministers that God may hide them in the secret of His tabernacle, so that they may be faithful stewards of the mystery of God, and chiefly of the mystery of divine love.

And you, my beloved brethren, to whom the love of God in heaven, and of Christ on the cross, is entrusted, remember that your congregation, your church, and your people are dependent on your faithfulness in living a heavenly life in fellowship with God. Then you will be able with joy, and in the power of the Holy Ghost, to pass on the love of God to souls who so greatly need it.

February 26

Intercession

If a man see his brother sinning, he shall ask, and God will give him life.—1 John 5:16

In the last night, when the Lord Jesus promised to send the Holy Spirit to His disciples, He said: "In that day ye shall know that I am in the Father and ye in me, and I in you." "Abide in me and I in you"; "He that abideth in me, and I in him, beareth much fruit." The things and the fruit thereof would be attained by prayer. They would pray, and He would grant their desires.

He made a sevenfold promise: "Whatsoever ye shall ask in my name, that will I do" (John 14:13). "If ye shall ask anything in my name, that will I do" (v. 14). "If . . . my words abide in you, ye shall ask what ye will, and it will be done unto you" (15:7).

"I appointed you that whatsoever ye shall ask the Father in my name he may give it you" (15:16). "If ye shall ask anything of the Father, he will give it you in my name" (16:23). "Ask and ye shall receive, that your joy may be full" (16:24). "In that day ye shall ask in my name" (16:26).

Read the above seven texts over and over until you are convinced that the believer who abides in Christ has the right to pray for souls, and that Christ and the Father will answer his prayer.

Remember, too, that you are a branch of the heavenly Vine, not only for your own salvation, but that you may bear much fruit in the conversion of souls. It is as an intercessor that grace is granted you to pray for others, believing assuredly that God will answer you.

Think of the change that would come over a community if every believer in it would take time to pray for those who do not believe. How God would be glorified in our bearing much fruit! Dear child of God, take time to allow God to write these glorious promises upon your heart.

February 27

A Personal Call

*We trust not in ourselves, but in God who delivered us, and will
yet deliver us.*—2 Corinthians 1:9, 10

*Some preach Christ of contention, supposing to add affliction to my
bonds. For I know that this shall turn to my salvation, through your
prayer, and the supply of the Spirit of Jesus Christ.*—Philippians
1:16-19

Texts like these prove that there were still Christians in
the churches under the full power of the Holy Spirit on whom
Paul could count for effectual, much-availing prayer. When
we plead with Christians to pray without ceasing, a large
number quietly decide such a life is not possible for them.
They have not any special gift for prayer; they have not that
intense desire for glorifying Christ in the salvation of souls;
they have not yet learned what it is, under the power of the
constraining love of Christ, to live not unto themselves, but
unto Him who died for them and rose again.

And yet it is to such we bring the call to offer themselves
for a wholehearted surrender to live entirely for Christ. We
ask them whether they are not ashamed of the selfish life,
that simply uses Christ as a convenience to escape from hell
and to secure a place in heaven. We come to them with the
assurance that God can change their lives and fill their hearts
with Christ and His Holy Spirit. We plead with them to believe
that with God all things are possible. He is able and willing,
yes, rather, most anxious to restore them to the Father's house,
to the joy of His presence and service.

One step on the way to the attainment of this will be that
they listen to the call for men and women who will every
day and all the day, in the power of Christ's abiding presence,
live in the spirit of unceasing intercession for all saints, that
they receive the power of the Holy Spirit, and acknowledge
that this is nothing less than a duty, a sacrifice that Christ's
love has a right to claim, and that He by His Spirit will indeed
work in them. The man, however far he may have come short,
who accepts the call as coming from Christ, and draws near
to God in humble prayer for the needed grace, will have taken
the first step in the path that leads to fellowship with God,
to a new faith and life in Christ Jesus, and to the surrender
of his whole being to that intercession of the Spirit that will
help to bring Pentecost again into the hearts of God's people.

February 28

Waiting Upon God

On thee do I wait all the day.—Psalm 25:5

Waiting upon God—in this expression we find one of the deepest truths of God's Word in regard to the attitude of the soul in its conversation with God.

Waiting upon God. Just think—that He may reveal himself in us; that He may teach us all His will; that He may do to us what He has promised; that in all things He may be the Infinite God.

It is the attitude of soul with which each day should begin. On awaking in the morning, in the inner chamber, in quiet meditation, in the expression in prayer of our ardent longings and desires, in the course of our daily work, in all our striving after obedience and holiness, in all our struggles against sin and self-will—in everything there should be a waiting upon God to receive what He will bestow, to see what He will do, to allow Him to be the Almighty God.

Meditate on these things, and they will help you truly to value the precious promises of God's Word.

"They that wait upon the Lord shall renew their strength; they shall mount up with wings as eagles." There we have the secret of heavenly power and joy.

"*Wait on the Lord,* be of good courage, and he shall strengthen thine heart; *wait, I say, on the Lord.*"

"Rest in the Lord, and wait patiently for him."

The deep root of all scriptural theology is this: Absolute dependence on God. As we exercise this spirit, it will become more natural and blessedly possible to say: "On thee do I wait all the day." There we have the secret of true, uninterrupted, silent adoration and worship.

Has this series helped to teach us the true worship of God? If so, the Lord's name be praised.

Or have we only learned how little we know of it? For this, too, let us thank Him.

If we long for a fuller experience of this blessing, let us reread these meditations with a deeper insight as to what is meant, and the absolute need of a life in which the soul each day and all the day waits upon God. May the God of all grace grant this.

March

The Secret of the Faith Life

March 1

The Image of God

And God said, Let us make man in our image, after our likeness.—
Genesis 1:26

Here we have the first thought of man—his origin and his destiny entirely divine. God undertook the stupendous work of making a creature, who is not God, to be a perfect likeness of Him in His divine glory. Man was to live in entire dependence on God, and to receive directly and unceasingly from Him the inflow of all that was holy and blessed in the divine being. God's glory, His holiness and His love, were to dwell in him, and shine out through him.

When sin had done its terrible work and spoiled the image of God, the promise was given in Paradise of the seed of the woman, in whom the divine purpose would be fulfilled. "God's Son, the effulgence of his glory, and the very image of his substance" (Heb. 1:3) was to become a Son of man, in whom God's plan would be carried out, His image revealed in human form. The New Testament takes up the thought of creation, and speaks of those who are "fore-ordained to be conformed to the image of his Son"; of "the new man renewed after the image of him that created him"; and gives the promise: "We know that when he shall be manifested, we shall be like him; for we shall see him as he is."

And, between the eternal purpose and its eternal realization, we have a wonderful promise in regard to the life here upon earth. "We all, beholding the glory of the Lord, are changed into the same image, from glory to glory, as by the Spirit of the Lord" (2 Cor. 3:18).

It was of this that Paul had said just before: "Shall not the ministration of the Spirit be glorious by reason of the glory that excelleth?" Let us take home the promise of the text as the possible and assured experience for daily life to everyone who gives Christ His place as the glorified One. Let us keep the heart set upon the glory of that image of God in Christ, in the assurance that the Spirit will change us into the same image day by day, from glory to glory. O my soul, take time to believe firmly and confidently that this promise will be made true in your Christian life. God Almighty, who created man in His image, seeks now to work out His purpose in changing you into the image of Christ Jesus by the power of the Holy Spirit.

March 2

The Obedience of Faith

The Lord appeared to Abram, and said unto him: I am God Almighty: walk before me, and be thou perfect. And I will multiply thee exceedingly.—Genesis 17:1, 2

In Abraham we see how God not only asks for faith, and rewards faith, but also how He works faith by the gracious training He gives. When God first called him, He at once gave the great promise, "In thee shall all the families of the earth be blessed" (Gen. 12:3). When he reached the land, God met him with the promise that the land should be his (Gen. 12:7). When Abraham returned from the battle against the kings, God again met him to renew the promise (15:5).

Before the birth of Isaac, in the words of our text, He sought to strengthen his faith (Gen. 17). And once more in the plains of Mamre, He spoke: "Is anything too hard for the Lord?" Step by step God led him until his faith was perfected for full obedience in the sacrifice of Isaac. As "by faith Abraham obeyed to go out," so by faith, at the close of forty years, he was able, without any promise, in fact in apparent conflict with all the promises, to obey God's will to the very utmost.

Children of Abraham, children of God, the Father makes great demands on your faith. If you are to follow in Abraham's footsteps, you, too, are to forsake all, to live in the land of spiritual promise, with nothing but His Word to depend upon, separated unto God. For this you will need a deep and clear insight that the God who is working in you is the Almighty who will work all His good pleasure.

Do not think that it is a little thing or easy to live the life of faith. It needs a life that seeks to abide in His presence all day. Bow before God in humble worship until He speaks to you, too: *"I am God Almighty: walk before me, and be thou perfect. And I will multiply thee exceedingly."* When Abraham heard this, he "fell on his face: and God talked with him." There you have the secret birthplace of the power to trust God for everything that He promises.

So only can we go out like Abraham when we are called to a life of true consecration to God, and of the obedience of faith to the very uttermost. Walk in the footsteps of Abraham. Hide deep in your heart the testimony of God's Word: "He was strong in faith, giving glory to God; being fully persuaded, that what he had promised, he was able to perform."

March 3

The Love of God

Thou shalt love the Lord thy God with all thine heart, and with all thy soul, and with all thy might. —Deuteronomy 6:5

God taught Abraham what it was *to believe in God with all his heart;* he was strong in faith, giving glory to God. Moses taught Israel what the first and great commandment was: *to love God with all their heart.* This was the first commandment as the origin and fountain out of which the others naturally proceed. It has its ground in the relationship between God as the loving Creator, and man made in His image as the object of that love. In the very nature of things it could never be otherwise; man finds his life, his destiny, and his happiness in nothing but just this one thing: *loving God with all the heart, and all the strength.* Moses said: "The Lord had a delight in thy fathers, to love them" (Deut. 10:15); such a God was infinitely worthy of being loved. All our religion, all our faith in God and obedience to Him, our whole life, is to be inspired by the one thought: We are to love God with all our heart and all our strength. Every day the child of God has as his first duty to live out this command.

How little Israel was able to obey the command, we all know well. But before Moses died, he was able, after speaking of the judgments God would bring upon His people for their sins, to make known the promise: *"The Lord thy God will circumcise thine heart"*—with a circumcision not made with hands, but the circumcision of Christ on the cross (Col. 2:11)— *"to love the Lord thy God with all thine heart, and with all thy soul"* (Deut. 30:6).

This blessed promise was the first indication of the New Covenant, in which Jeremiah foretold of the law so written in the heart by the Holy Spirit that they should no more depart from God but walk in His ways. But how little have Christians understood this; how easily they rest content with the thought that it is impossible.

Let us learn the double lesson. This perfect heart, loving God with all our might, is what God claims, is what God is infinitely worthy of, is what God—blessed be His name!— *will himself give and work in us.* Let our whole soul go out in faith to meet, to wait for, and to expect the fulfillment of the promise—to love God with the whole heart is what God himself will work in us.

March 4

The Joyful Sound

Blessed is the people that know the joyful sound: they walk, O Lord, in the light of thy countenance. In thy name do they rejoice all the day.—Psalm 89:15, 16

"Glad tidings of great joy" was what the angel calls the gospel message. This is what is here spoken of as "the joyful sound." That blessedness consists in God's people walking in the light of God and rejoicing in His name all the day. Undisturbed fellowship, never-ending joy is their portion. Even in the Old Testament such was at times the experience of the saints. But there was no continuance; the Old Testament could not secure that. Only the New Testament can and does.

In every well-ordered family one finds the father delighting in his children and the children rejoicing in their father's presence. And this mark of a happy home on earth is what the heavenly Father has promised and delights to work in His people; *walking in the light of His countenance, and rejoicing in His name all the day.* It has been promised, it has been made possible in Christ through the Holy Spirit filling the heart with the love of God. It is the heritage of all who are seeking to love God with all their heart and strength.

And yet how many there are of God's children who simply think it impossible and have even given up, with the hope, the desire for a life of rejoicing in God's presence all the day. And yet Christ promised it so definitely: "These things have I spoken unto you, that my joy may be in you, and that your joy may be fulfilled."

Let us think of the Father's longing to have the perfect confidence and love of His children, of the children's need of the Father's presence every moment of the day for their happiness and strength. Let us think of the power of Christ by the Holy Spirit to maintain this life in us; and let us be content with nothing less than the blessedness of them who know the joyful sound: *"They walk in the light of thy countenance, and rejoice in thy name all the day; for thou art the glory of their strength!"*

The deeper we seek to enter into God's will for us, the stronger our faith will be that the Father can be content with nothing less than this, His child walking in the light of His countenance and rejoicing in His name all the day; and the stronger will the assurance come that what the Father has meant for us will be wrought in us through Christ and the Holy Spirit. Let us just hold fast the word—*all the day.*

March 5

The Thoughts of God

As the heavens are higher than the earth, so are my thoughts higher than your thoughts. —Isaiah 55:9

In giving us His promises of what He will work in us, God reminds us that, as high as the heavens are above the earth, so high His thoughts are above ours—altogether beyond our power of spiritual apprehension.

When He tells us that we are made in the image of God, that by grace we are actually renewed again into that image, and as we gaze upon God's glory in Christ, we are changed into the same image as by the Spirit of the Lord: this is indeed a thought higher than the heavens. When He tells Abraham of all the mighty work He was to do in him, and in his seed, and through him in all the nations of the earth, that again is a thought higher than the heavens—man's mind could not take it in. When God calls us to love Him with all our hearts, and promises to renew our hearts so that we shall love Him with all our strength, that again is a thought out of the very heights of heaven. And when the Father calls us to a life here on earth in the light of His face and rejoicing in His name all the day, we have a gift out of the very depths of God's heart of love.

What deep reverence, humility, and patience should be ours in waiting upon God by His Holy Spirit to impart to our hearts the life and the light that can make us feel at home with these thoughts dwelling in us. What need of daily, tender, abiding fellowship with God if we are in very deed to enter into His mind and to have His thoughts make their home in us. And what a faith especially is needed to believe that God will not only reveal the beauty and the glory of these thoughts, but will actually so mightily work in us that their divine reality and blessing shall indeed fill our inmost being.

Just think of what Isaiah says, as quoted by Paul (1 Cor. 2:9): Things which eye saw not, and ear heard not, and which entered not into the heart of man, whatsoever things God prepared for them that love Him. But unto us God revealed them through the Spirit. When Christ promised His disciples that the Holy Spirit from the throne in heaven should dwell with them, He said that the Spirit would glorify Him, would fill us with the light and life of the heavenly world.

March 6

The New Covenant in Jeremiah 31

I will make a new covenant with the house of Israel. I will put my law in their inward parts, and in their hearts will I write it.— Jeremiah 31:31, 33

When God made the first covenant with Israel at Sinai, He said, "If ye will obey my voice indeed, and keep my covenant, then ye shall be a peculiar treasure unto me from among all peoples" (Ex. 19:5). But Israel, alas, had not the power to obey. Their whole nature was carnal and sinful. In the covenant there was no provision for the grace that should make them obedient. The law only served to reveal their sin.

In our text God promises to make a new covenant in which provision would be made to enable men to live a life of obedience. In this new covenant, the law was to be put in their inward parts and written in their heart, "not with ink, but *with the Spirit of the living God,"* so that they could say with David: "I delight to do thy will, O my God; yea, thy law is within my heart." The law, and delight in it, would, through the Holy Spirit, take possession of the inner life with all its powers. Or, as we have it in Jeremiah 32:40, after God had said: "Is there anything too hard for me?": *"I will make an everlasting covenant with them; and I will put my fear in their hearts, that they shall not depart from me."*

In contrast with the Old Testament and its weakness, which made it impossible to continue faithful, this promise ensures a continual, wholehearted obedience as the mark of the believer who takes God at His Word and fully claims what the promise secures.

Learn the lesson that in the new covenant God's mighty power will be shown in the heart of everyone who believes the promise: *"They shall not depart from me." "It shall be even so as it hath been spoken unto me."* Bow in deep stillness before God and believe what He says. The measure of our experience of this power of God keeping us from departing from Him will ever be in harmony with the law: *"According to your faith be it unto you."*

We need to be at great pains to keep the contrast between the Old and the New Testament very clear. The old had a wonderful measure of grace, but not enough for the continual abiding in the faith of obedience. That is the definite promise of the New Testament, the fruit of heart renewal and the power of the Holy Spirit leading the soul and revealing the fullness of grace to keep us "unblameable in holiness."

March 7

The New Covenant in Ezekiel

I will sprinkle clean water upon you, and ye shall be clean; from all your filthiness will I cleanse you. And I will put my Spirit within you, and cause you to walk in my statutes, and ye shall keep my judgments. —Ezekiel 36:25-27

Here we have the same promise as in Jeremiah, the promise of such a heart cleansing from sin, and such a gift of the Spirit in the new heart, as would secure their walking in His statutes and keeping His judgments. Just as in Jeremiah God had said: "I will put my law in their inward parts, and *put my fear in their hearts, that they shall not depart from me,*" so here: "*I will cause you to walk in my statutes, and ye shall keep my judgments.*" In contrast with the old covenant, in which there was no power to enable them to continue in God's law, the great mark of the new covenant would be a divine power enabling them to walk in His statutes and keep His judgments.

"Where sin abounded, grace did much more abound," working wholehearted allegiance and obedience. Why is this so little experienced? The answer is very simple: The promise is not believed, is not preached; its fulfillment is not expected. And yet how clearly we have it in a passage like Romans 8:1-4. There the man who had complained of the power "bringing him into captivity under the law of sin," thanks God that he is "now in Christ Jesus"; and that the law of the Spirit of life in Christ Jesus has made him free from the law of sin and death, so that the requirement of the law is fulfilled in all who walk after the Spirit.

Once again, why are there so few who can give such testimony, and what is to be done to attain to it? Just one thing is needed—the faith in an omnipotent God, who will by His wonderful power do what He has promised: "*I the Lord have spoken it, and will do it.*" Oh, let us begin to believe that the promise will come true: "I will cleanse you from all your filthiness, *and ye shall be clean; and will cause you to walk in my statutes, and ye shall keep them.*" Let us believe all that God here promises, and God will do it. To an extent beyond all power of thought, God has made His great and glorious promises dependent on our faith! and the promises will work that faith as we believe them. "According to your faith, be it unto you." Let us this very day put it to the proof.

March 8

The New Covenant and Prayer

Call unto me, and I will answer thee, and will shew thee great things, and difficult, which thou knowest not. —Jeremiah 33:3

I the Lord have spoken it, and I will do it. For this moreover will I be inquired of by the house of Israel, to do it for them. —Ezekiel 36:36, 37

The fulfillment of the great promises of the new covenant is made dependent on prayer. In answer to the prayer of Jeremiah, God had said: *"I will put my fear in their hearts, that they shall not depart from me."* And to Ezekiel He had spoken: *"I will cause them to walk in my statutes, and ye shall keep my judgments."* To us in our unbelief, and our judging of the meaning of God's Word according to human thought and experience, there is no expectation of these promises being truly fulfilled. We do not believe that God means them to be literally true. We have not the faith in the mighty power of God that is waiting to make His promise true in our experience.

And God has said that without such faith our experience will be only partial and very limited. He has graciously pointed out the way in which such faith can be found. It is in the path of much prayer. *"Call unto me, and I will answer thee, and show thee great things, and difficult which thou knowest not. Moreover, will I be inquired of by the house of Israel, to do it for them."*

It is when individual men and women turn to God with their whole heart to plead these promises that He will fulfill them. It is in the exercise of intense, persevering prayer that faith will be strengthened to take hold of God and surrender itself to His omnipotent working. And then as one and another can testify of what God has done and will do, believers will help each other and take their place as the church of the living God—pleading for and firmly expecting that His promises will be fulfilled in larger measure, as a new enduement for the great work of preaching Christ in the fullness of His redemption to perishing men.

The state of the church, the state of our ministers and members, and our own state call for unceasing prayer. We need to pray intensely and persistently that the need of the power of the Holy Spirit may be deeply felt, and that a strong faith may be roused in the hearts of many to claim and to expect His mighty working. *"I the Lord have spoken it, and I will do it."*

March 9

The New Covenant in Hebrews

For I will be merciful to their iniquities, and their sins will I remember no more.—Hebrews 8:12

Christ is called in this epistle the Mediator of a better covenant, enacted upon better promises (8:6). In Him the two parts of the covenant find their complete fulfillment. First of all, He came to atone for sin, so that its power over man was destroyed and free access to God's presence and favor was secured. And with that came the fuller blessing, the new heart, freed from the power of sin, with God's Holy Spirit breathing into it the delight in God's law, and the power to obey it.

These two parts of the covenant may never be separated. And yet, alas, how many there are who put their trust in Christ for the forgiveness of sin, and yet never think of claiming the fullness of the promise—the new heart cleansed from sin, with the Holy Spirit breathing in it such love and delight in God's law, and such power to obey, that they have access to the full blessing of the new covenant, being God's people and knowing Him as their God.

Jesus Christ is "the mediator of the new covenant," with the forgiveness of sin in the power of His blood, and the law written in the heart in the power of His Spirit. Oh, that we could understand that just as surely as the complete pardon of sin is assured, the complete fulfillment of the promises, "I will put my fear in their hearts, *that they shall not depart from me*"; "I will cause you to walk in my statutes, *and ye shall keep them,*" may be expected, too.

But remember what God said to Abraham: "I am God Almighty . . . is anything too hard for the Lord?" He spoke that word to Jeremiah, too, in regard to the new covenant. It needs strong, wholehearted desire for a life wholly given up to Him. It means to set aside all our preconceived opinions, and in faith to believe in the mighty power of God. It means a surrender to Jesus Christ as the Mediator of the new covenant, a willingness to accept our place with Him, crucified to the world and to sin and to self; it means a readiness to follow Him at any cost.

In one word, it means a simple, wholehearted acceptance of Christ as Lord and Master, heart and life wholly His. God hath said it, and will do it. *"I the Lord have spoken it, and I will perform it."*

March 10

The Trial of Faith

And Naaman's servants came near, and spake unto him, and said: "My father, if the prophet had bid thee do some great thing, wouldst thou not have done it? How much rather then, when he saith to thee, Wash, and be clean?"—2 Kings 5:13

In Naaman we have a striking Old Testament illustration of the place faith takes in God's dealing with man. It gives us a wonderful discovery of what faith really is. Think first of how intense the desire was for healing on Naaman's part. He would do anything, appeal to the king of Syria and the king of Israel; he would undertake a long journey and humble himself before the prophet, who did not even deign to come out and see him. In this intensity of desire for blessing we have the root of a strong faith. And it is just this seeking for God and His blessing which is too much lacking in our religion today.

The second mark of faith is that it has to give up all its preconceived opinion and to bow before the Word of God. This was more than Naaman was willing to do, and he turned away in a rage. It was well for him that a wise and faithful servant gave him better advice. Faith is often held back by the thought how such a simple thing as to accept God's Word can effect such a mighty revolution in the heart.

And then comes the third mark of faith. It submits implicitly to the word of God: "Wash, and be clean." At first all appears vain, but faith proves itself by obedience. It does it not once or twice, but seven times in the assurance that the mighty wonder will be wrought. It takes the simple word, "Wash, and be clean," and lo, it finds itself renewed as with the life of a little child, "clean, every whit." The mighty deed is done.

When God's Word brings us to the promise: *"I will sprinkle clean water upon you, and ye shall be clean; from all your filthiness will I cleanse you,"* it is nothing but unbelief that holds us back. Let us believe that a simple determined surrender of the whole will to God's promise will indeed bring the heart cleansing we need. "There is a river, the streams whereof make glad the city of God." It flows from under the throne of God and the Lamb, through the channels of a thousand precious promises, and at each step the word is heard: "Wash, and be clean." Christ cleanses "by the washing of water with the word." Every promise is a call: "Wash, and be clean"; and Christ will speak: *"Ye are clean through the word that I have spoken unto you"*—clean, every whit.

March 11

Faith in Christ

Ye believe in God, believe also in me.—John 14:1

In the farewell discourse (John 14-17), when Christ was about to leave His disciples, He taught them that they were to believe in Him with the same perfect confidence which they had reposed in God. "Ye believe in God, *believe also in me.*" "*Believe me*, that I am in the Father. "*He that believeth on me*, the works that I do shall he do also." Here on earth He had not been able to make himself fully known to His disciples. But in heaven the fullness of God's power would be His; and He would, in and through His disciples, do greater things than He had ever done upon earth.

This faith must fix itself first of all on the person of Christ in His union with the Father. They were to have the perfect confidence that all that God had done could now be done by Jesus too. The deity of Christ is the rock on which our faith depends. Christ as man, partaker of our nature, is in very deed true God. As the divine power has worked in Christ even to the resurrection from the dead, so Christ can also, in His divine omnipotence, work in us all that we need.

Dear Christians, do you not see of what deep importance it is that you take time to worship Jesus in His divine omnipotence as one with the Father? That will teach you to count on Him in His sufficiency to work in us all we can desire. This faith must so possess us that every thought of Christ will be filled with the consciousness of His presence as an almighty Redeemer, able to save and sanctify and empower us to the very uttermost.

Child of God, bow in deep humility before this blessed Lord Jesus, and worship Him: my Lord and my God! Take time until you come under the full consciousness of an assured faith that as the Almighty God, Christ will work for you and in you and through you all that God desires and all that you can need.

The Savior was about to leave the world. In His farewell charge on the last night He begins by telling them that everything would depend through their whole life on simply believing Him. By that they would even do greater things than He had ever done. And at the close of His address He repeats again: "Be of good cheer, I have overcome the world." Our one need is a direct, definite, unceasing faith in the mighty power of Christ working in us.

March 12

Christ's Life in Us

Because I live, ye shall live also.—John 14:19

There is a great difference in the teaching of the three first evangelists and that of John. John was the bosom friend of Jesus. He could understand the Master better than the others, and has recorded Christ's teaching, of which they say nothing. This makes John 13-17 the inmost sanctuary of the New Testament. The others could speak of repentance and the pardon of sin as the first great gift of the New Testament. But of the new life which the new covenant was to bring, with the new heart in which the law had been put as a living power, they say little.

It is, John records, what Christ taught about His very own life really becoming ours, and our being united with Him just as He was with the Father. The other evangelists speak of Christ as the Shepherd seeking and saving the lost. John speaks of Him as the Shepherd who so gives His life for the sheep that His very life becomes theirs. "I came that they may have life, and may have it abundantly" (John 10:10).

And so Christ says here, "I live, and ye shall live also." The disciples were to receive from Him, not the life He then had, but the resurrection life in the power of its victory over death, and of His exaltation to the right hand of God. He would from thenceforth ever dwell in them, a new, a heavenly, an eternal life; the life of Jesus himself would fill them. And this promise is to all who will accept it in faith.

Alas, how many there are who are content with the beginnings of the Christian life, but never long to have it in its fullness the more abundant life! They do not believe in it; they are not ready for the sacrifice implied in being wholly filled with the life of Jesus. Child of God, the message comes again to you: *"The things that are impossible with men are possible with God."*

I pray you, do take time, and let Christ's wonderful promise take possession of your heart. Be content with nothing less than a full salvation, *Christ living in you, and you living in Christ.* Be assured that it is meant for everyone who will take time to listen to Christ's promises, and will believe that the almighty power of God will work in him the mighty wonder of His grace—Christ dwelling in the heart by faith.

March 13

The Obedience of Love

If ye keep my commandments, ye shall abide in my love.—John 15:10

The question is often asked: How can I come to abide in Christ always? To live wholly for Him? such is my desire and fervent prayer. In our text the Lord gives the simple but far-reaching answer: "Keep my commandments." This is the only, the sure, the blessed way of abiding in Him. "If ye keep my commandments, ye shall abide in my love; even as I have kept my Father's commandments and abide in his love." Loving obedience is the way to the enjoyment of His love.

Notice how often the Lord speaks of this in the last night. "*If ye love me, ye will keep* my commandments" (14:15). And then again twice over: "He that hath my commandments, and keepeth them, *he it is that loveth me*; and he that loveth me shall be loved of my Father, and I will love him." "If a man love me, *he will keep my word*; and my Father will love him, and we will come unto him, and make our abode with him." And so also three times in chapter 15, "*If my words abide* in you, ask whatsoever ye will, and it shall be done unto you." "*If ye keep my commandments*, ye shall abide in my love." "Ye are my friends, *if ye do the things which I command you.*"

Six times over the Lord connects the keeping of the commandments with loving Him, and with the promise of the great blessing following on it, the indwelling of the Father and the Son in the heart. The love that keeps His commandments is the only way to abide in His love. In our whole relation to Christ, love is everything; Christ's love to us, our love to Him, proved in our love to the brethren.

How little believers have accepted this teaching. How content many are with the thought that it is impossible. They do not believe that through the grace of God we can be kept from sin. They do not believe in the promise of the new covenant (Ezek. 36:27): "I will put my Spirit within you, *and cause you to walk in my statutes, and ye shall keep my judgments.*" They have no conception how to a heart fully surrendered and given over to Christ alone He will make possible what otherwise appears beyond our reach: loving Him, keeping His commandments, abiding in His love.

March 14

The Promise of the Spirit

If I go not away, the Comforter will not come unto you.... He shall glorify me: for he shall receive of mine, and shall show it unto you.—John 16:7, 14

The crucified Christ was to be glorified on the throne of heaven. And out of that glory He would send down the Holy Spirit into the hearts of His disciples to glorify Him in them. The Spirit of the crucified and glorified Christ would be their life in fellowship with Him, and their power for His service. The Spirit comes to us as the Spirit of the divine glory; as such we are to welcome Him and yield ourselves to Him.

Yes, the Spirit that searches the deep things of God, that dwells in the very roots of the Divine Being, that had been with Christ through all His life, and in His death upon the cross, the Spirit of the Father and the Son, was to come and dwell in them and make them the conscious possessors of the presence of the glorified Christ. It was this blessed Spirit who was to be their power for a life of loving obedience, to be their Teacher and Leader in praying down from heaven the blessing they needed. And it was in His power they were to conquer God's enemies and carry the gospel worldwide.

It is this Spirit of God and of Christ the church lacks so sadly; it is this Spirit she grieves so unceasingly. It is due to this that her work is so often feeble and fruitless. And what can be the reason of this?

The Spirit is God. He claims as God to have possession of our whole being. We have thought too much of Him as our help in the Christian life; we have not known that heart and life are to be entirely and unceasingly under His control; we are to be led by the Spirit every day and every hour. In His power our life is to be a direct and continual abiding in the love and fellowship of Jesus. No wonder we have not believed in the great promise that, in a love that keeps the commandments, we can always abide in Christ's love. No wonder we have not the courage to believe that Christ's mighty power will work in us and through us. No wonder that His divine prayer-promises are beyond our reach. The Spirit that searches the deep things of God claims the very depths of our being, there to reveal Christ as Lord and Ruler.

The promise waits for its fulfillment in our life: *"He shall glorify me; for he shall take of mine, and shall declare it unto you."* Let us this very day yield ourselves to believe the promise at once and with our whole heart.

March 15

In Christ

At that day ye shall know that I am in my Father, and ye in me, and I in you. —John 14:20

Our Lord had spoken of His life in the Father: "Believe me that I am in the Father, and the Father in me." He and the Father were not two persons next to each other; they were in each other; though on earth as man, He lived in the Father. All He did was what the Father did in Him.

This divine life of heaven, of Christ in God, and God in Christ, is the picture and the pledge of what our life in Christ is to be here upon earth. It is in the very nature of the divine life that the Son is in the Father. Even so we must know and ever live in the faith that we are in Christ. Then we will learn that even as the Father worked in Christ, so Christ will also work in us if we but believe we are in Him and yield ourselves to His power.

And even as the Son waited on the Father, and the Father worked through Him, so the disciples would make known to Him in prayer what they wanted done on earth, and He would do it. Their life in Him was to be the reflection of His life in the Father. *As the Father worked in Him, because He lived in the Father, so Christ would work in them.*

But this would not be until the Holy Spirit came. It was for this they had to wait until they were endued with the power from on high. It was for this they would abide in Him by daily fellowship and prayer that He might so do in them the greater works He had promised.

How little the church understands the secret of her power is to be found in nothing less than where Christ found it, abiding in the Father and His love. If anyone asks what the lost secret of the pulpit is, we have it here: *"In that day"*—when the Spirit fills your heart—"ye shall know that I am in my Father and ye in me."

March 16

Abiding in Christ

Abide in me, and I in you.—John 15:4

What our Lord had taught in John 14, of the union with Him in the likeness of His being in the Father, He seeks to enforce and illustrate by the wonderful parable of the Branch and the Vine. And all for the sake of bringing home to the apostles, and to all His servants in the gospel, the absolute necessity of a life daily in full communion with Him.

On the one hand He points to himself and to the Father: Just as truly and fully as I am in the Father, *so you are in Me;* and then, pointing to the vine: Just as truly as the branch is in the vine, *you are in Me.* And now, just as the Father abides in Me, and works in Me, and I work out what He works in Me; and just as truly as the branch abides in the vine, and the vine gives its life and strength to the branch, and the branch receives it and puts it forth in fruit—even so do you abide in Me, and receive My strength; and I will work with an almighty power My work in and through you.

Dear child of God, you have often meditated on this blessed passage. But do you not feel how much there is still to learn if you are to have Christ's almighty power working in you as He would wish you to have? The great need is to take time in waiting on the Lord Jesus in the power of His Spirit until the two great truths get complete mastery of your being: As Christ is in God—this is the testimony from heaven; as the branch is in the vine—this is the testimony of all nature: the law of heaven and the law of earth combine in calling to us: "Abide in Christ." *"He that abideth in me, bringeth forth much fruit."* Fruit, more fruit, much fruit, is what Christ seeks, is what He works, is what He will assuredly give to the soul who trusts Him.

To the feeblest of God's children Christ says: *Ye are in Me.* "Abide in me. Ye shall bear much fruit." To the strongest of His messengers He still has the word, there can be nothing higher: "Abide in me, and ye shall bear much fruit." To one and all the message comes: Daily, continuous, unbroken abiding in Christ Jesus, is the one condition of a life of power and of blessing. Take time and let the Holy Spirit so renew in you the secret abiding in Him that you may understand His meaning: "These things have I spoken unto you that my joy might remain in you, and that your joy might be full."

March 17

The Power of Prayer

If ye abide in me, and my words abide in you, ye shall ask what ye will, and it shall be done unto you. —John 15:7

Before our Lord went to heaven He taught His disciples two great lessons in regard to their relation to Him in the great work they had to do.

The one was that in heaven He would have much more power than He had upon earth, and that He would use that power for the salvation of men, solely through them, their word and their work.

The other was that without Him they could do nothing, but that they could count upon Him to work in them and through them, and so carry out His purpose. Their first and chief work would therefore be to bring everything they wanted done, to Him in prayer. In the farewell discourse He repeats the promise seven times: "Abide in me, pray in my name"; you can count upon it, "you can ask what you will; it shall be done to you."

With these two truths written in their heart, He sent them out into the world. They could confidently undertake their work. The almighty, glorified Jesus, ready to do in and with and through them greater things than He himself had ever done upon earth. The impotent, helpless disciples on earth unceasingly looking up to Him in prayer, with the full confidence that He would hear that prayer. The first and only condition was an unflinching confidence in the power of His promise. The chief thing in all their life and in the work of their ministry was to be the maintenance of a spirit of prayer.

Alas, how little the church has understood and believed this! Why? Simply because believers live so little in the daily abiding in Christ that they are powerless in believing His great and precious promises. Let us learn the lesson, both for our life and work, that as the members of Christ's body, the chief thing every day must be that close abiding fellowship with Christ, which ever first takes its place of deep dependence and unceasing supplication. Only then can we do our work in the full assurance He has heard our prayer and will be faithful in doing His part, in giving the power from on high, as the source of strength and abundant blessing.

March 18

The Mystery of Love

I pray that they may be one; as thou, Father, art in me, and I in thee, that they may be one, even as we are one; I in them, and thou in me.—John 17:21-23

The last evening Christ was with His disciples, He specially pressed the thought of their being in Him and abiding in Him. He also mentioned His *being in them*, but did not give such prominence to this as the first thought, their being in Him. But in His prayer as High Priest, He gives larger place to the thought of His *being in them*, just as the Father was in Him. "That they may be one, even as we are one; *I in them, and thou in me*, that they may be perfected into one; that the world may know that thou didst send me, and lovedst them, even as thou lovedst me."

The power to convince the world that God loved the disciples as He loved His Son could only come as believers lived out their life of having Christ in them, and proving it by loving their brethren as Christ loved them. The feebleness of the church is because our life in Christ, and His life in us, is not known, and not proved to the world by the living unity in which our love manifests that Christ is in us. Nothing less than this is needed: such an indwelling of Christ in the heart, such a binding together of believers because they know and see and love each other as those who together have Christ dwelling in them. As we have it in the very last words of the prayer, "I have made known thy name, that the love wherewith thou lovest me may be in them, and I in them." The divine indwelling has its chief glory in that it is the manifestation of divine love. The Father's love to Christ, brought by Christ to us, flowing out from us to the brethren, and to all men.

Christ had given (John 14:21, 23) the great promise to the loving, obedient disciple, "My Father will love him, and I will love him, and we will come and make our abode with him." It is to live this life of love to Christ and the brethren, that the Holy Spirit, in whom the Father and the Son are one, longs to live in our heart. Let nothing less than this be what you seek, what you believe, what you claim with your whole heart and strength—the indwelling of the Lord Jesus in the "love that passeth knowledge," with which He can fill your heart. So will the world indeed be constrained by the love God's children bear to each other to acknowledge that the word is being fulfilled.

March 19

Christ Our Righteousness

Justified freely by his grace through the redemption that is in Christ Jesus.—Romans 3:24

The first three evangelists spoke of redemption as a pardon of sin, or justification. John spoke of it as a life which Christ is to live in us, or regeneration. In Paul we find both truths in their beautiful connection and harmony.

So in Romans he first speaks of justification (Rom. 3:21-5:11). Then he goes on from 5:12 to 8:39 to speak of the life that there is in union with Christ. In Romans 4 he tells us that we find both these things in Abraham. First (vv. 3-5), "Abraham believed God, him that *justifieth the ungodly*; his faith is reckoned for righteousness." Then (v. 17), "Abraham believed God, who *quickeneth the dead.*" Just as God first of all counted to Abraham his faith as righteousness, and then led him on to believe in Him as the God who can give life to the dead, even so with the believer.

Justification comes at the commencement full and complete, as the eye of faith is fixed upon Christ. But that is only the beginning. Gradually the believer begins to understand that he was at the same time born again, *that he has Christ in him, and that his calling now is to abide in Christ, and let Christ abide and live and work in him.*

Most Christians strive by holding fast their faith in justification to stir and strengthen themselves for a life of gratitude and obedience. But they fail sadly because they do not know, do not in full faith yield themselves to Christ, to maintain His life in them. They have learned from Abraham the first lesson, to believe in God who justifies the ungodly. But they have not gone on to the second great lesson, to believe in God who quickeneth the dead, and daily renews that life through Christ, who lives in them and in whose life alone there is strength and fullness of blessing.

The Christian life must be "from faith to faith." The grace of pardon is but the beginning; growing in grace leads on to the fuller insight and experience of what it is to be in Christ—to live in Him and to grow up in Him in all things as the Head.

March 20

Christ Our Life

Much more they which receive abundance of grace and of the gift of righteousness shall reign in life by one, Jesus Christ.—Romans 5:17

Reckon ye also yourselves to be dead unto sin, but alive unto God through [in] Christ Jesus.—Romans 6:11

We said that Paul teaches us now that our faith in Christ as our righteousness is to be followed by our faith in Him as our life from the dead. He asks (Rom. 6:3), "Know ye not that all we who were baptized into Christ Jesus were baptized *into his death?*" We were buried with Him, and raised from the dead with Him. Just as in Adam all his children died, so all believers in Christ actually died too in Him. "Our old man was crucified with him," with Him we were raised from the dead. And now we are to count ourselves as actually "dead to sin and alive unto God."

In very deed, just as the new life in us is an actual participation in and experience of the risen life of Christ, so our death to sin in Christ is also an actual spiritual reality. It is when, by the power of the Holy Ghost, we are enabled to see how really we were one with Christ on the cross in His death, and in His resurrection, that we will understand that in Him sin has no power over us. We present ourselves unto God "as alive from the dead."

Just as the old Adam lives in the sinner, even in the believer, too, who does not know of the new death in Christ which he has died, even so the man who knows that he died in Christ and now is alive in Him can confidently count upon the word, "sin shall not have dominion over you"—not even for a single moment. *Reckon yourselves indeed dead to sin, and alive to God in Christ Jesus.* This is the true life of faith.

As what our Lord said about our being in Him and having Him living His life in us, could only come true as the full power of the Holy Spirit is experienced, so it is here, too. Paul says (Rom. 8:2), "The law of the Spirit of life in Christ Jesus hath made me free from the law of sin and death," of which he had been complaining that it had kept him in captivity. And he then adds "that the requirements of the law might be fulfilled in us who walk not after the flesh, but after the Spirit." Through the Spirit we enter into the glorious liberty of the children of God.

March 21

Crucified with Christ

I am crucified with Christ: nevertheless I live; yet not I, but Christ liveth in me. —Galatians 2:20

As in Adam we died out of the life and the will of God into sin and corruption, so in Christ we are made partakers of a new spiritual death, a death to sin and into the will and the life of God. Such was the death Christ died; such is the death we are made partakers of in Him. To Paul this was such a reality that he was able to say: "I am crucified with Christ; nevertheless I live; yet not I, but Christ liveth in me." The death with Christ had had such power that he no longer lived his own life; Christ lived His life in him. He had indeed died to the old nature and to sin, and been raised up into the power of the living Christ dwelling in him.

It was the crucified Christ who lived in him, and made him partaker of all that the cross had meant to Christ himself. The very mind that was in Christ, with His self-emptying and taking the form of a servant, His humbling himself to become obedient unto death—these inclinations worked in him because the crucified Christ lived in him. He lives in very deed as a crucified man.

Christ's death on the cross was His highest exhibition of His holiness and victory over sin. And the believer who receives Christ is made partaker of all the power and blessing the crucified Lord has won. As the believer learns to accept this by faith, he yields himself as now crucified to the world and dead to its pleasure and pride, its lust and self-pleasing. He learns that the mystery of the cross, as the crucified Lord reveals its power in him, opens the entrance into the fullest fellowship with Christ and the conformity to His sufferings. And so he learns, in the full depth of its meaning, what the Word has said: "Christ crucified, the power of God and the wisdom of God." He grows into a fuller apprehension of the blessedness of those who dare to say: *"I am crucified with Christ; I live no more; Christ the crucified liveth in me."*

Oh, the blessedness of the power of the God-given faith that enables a man to live all the day yielding himself to God, counting himself as indeed dead to sin and alive to God in Christ Jesus.

March 22

The Faith Life

That life which I now live in the flesh I live by faith of the Son of God, who loved me, and gave himself for me.—Galatians 2:20

If we were to ask Paul what he meant by saying he no longer lives but that Christ lives in him, what now is his part in living that life, he would give us the answer: *"The life that I now live in the flesh is a life of faith in the Son of God, who loved me and gave himself up for me."* His whole life, day by day and all the day, was an unceasing faith in the wonderful love that had given itself for him. Faith was the power that possessed and permeated his whole being and his every action.

Here we have the simple but full statement of the secret of the true Christian life. It is not faith only in certain promises of God, or in certain blessings received from Christ. It is a faith that has a vision of how entirely Christ gives himself to the soul to be, in the very deepest and fullest sense of the word, his life and all that implies for every moment of the day. As essential as continuous breathing is to the support of our physical life is the unceasing faith in which the soul trusts Christ and counts upon Him to maintain the life of the Spirit within us. Faith ever rests on that infinite love in which Christ gave himself wholly for us, to be ours in the deepest meaning of the word, and to live His life over again in us. In virtue of His divine omnipresence, whereby He filled all things, He can be to each what He is to all—a complete and perfect Savior, an abiding Guest, in very deed taking charge and maintaining our life in us and for us, as if each of us were the only one in whom He lives. *Just as truly as the Father lived in Him, and worked in Him all that He was to work out, just as truly will Christ live and work in each one of us.*

Faith, led and taught by God's Holy Spirit, gets such a confidence in the omnipotence and the omnipresence of Christ that it carries in the depth of the heart the abiding unbroken assurance all the day: He that loved me, and gave himself for me, He lives in me; He is in very deed my life and my all. *"I can do all things through Christ who strengtheneth me."* May God reveal to us that inseparable union between Christ and us in which the consciousness of Christ's presence may become as natural to us as the consciousness of our existence.

March 23

Full Consecration

Yea, verily, and I count all things to be loss for the excellency of the knowledge of Christ Jesus my Lord. —Philippians 3:8

In studying the promises Jesus gave to His disciples in the last night, the question comes, What was it that made just these men fit and worthy of the high honor of being baptized with the Holy Ghost from heaven? The answer is simple. When Christ called them, they forsook all and followed Him. They denied themselves, even to the hating of their own life, and gave themselves to obey His commands. They followed Him to Calvary, and amid its suffering and death their hearts clung to Him alone. It was this that prepared them for receiving a share in His resurrection life, and so becoming fitted here on earth to be filled with that Spirit, even as He received the fullness of the Spirit from the Father in glory.

Just as Jesus Christ had to sacrifice all to be wholly an offering to God, so all His people, from Abraham and Jacob, and Joseph downward to His twelve disciples, have had to be men who had given up all to follow the divine leading, and lived separated unto God, before the divine power could fulfill His purpose through them.

It was thus with Paul, too. To count all things but loss for Christ was the keynote of His life, as it must be of ours, if we are to share fully in the power of His resurrection. But how little the church understands that we have been entirely redeemed from the world to live wholly and only for God and His love. As the merchantman who found the treasure in the field had to sell all he had to purchase it, Christ claims the whole heart and the whole life and the whole strength if we are indeed to share with Him in the victory through the power of the Holy Spirit. The law of the kingdom is unchangeable: *all things loss for the excellence of the knowledge of Christ Jesus my Lord.*

The disciples had to spend years with Christ to be prepared for Pentecost. Christ calls us to walk every day in the closest union with himself, to abide in Him without ceasing, and so to live as those who are not their own, but wholly His. It is in this we will find the path to the fullness of the Spirit.

Let our faith boldly believe that such a life is meant for us. Let our heart's fervent desire reach out after nothing less than this. Let us love the Lord our God and Christ our Savior with our whole heart. We will be more than conquerors through Him that loved us.

March 24

Entire Sanctification

And the God of peace himself sanctify you wholly; and may your spirit and soul and body be preserved entire, without blame at the coming of our Lord Jesus Christ. Faithful is he that calleth you, who will also do it.—1 Thessalonians 5:23, 24

What a promise! One would expect to see all God's children clinging to it, claiming its fulfillment. Alas, unbelief does not know what to think of it, and but few count it their treasure and joy.

Just listen. God, the God of peace—the peace He made by the blood of the cross, the peace that passeth all understanding, keeping our hearts and thoughts in Christ Jesus—none other but himself can and will do it. This God of peace *himself* promises to sanctify us, to sanctify us wholly, in Christ our sanctification, in the sanctification of the Spirit. It is God who is doing the work. It is in close, personal fellowship with God himself that we become holy.

Ought not each of us to rejoice with exceeding joy at the prospect? But it is as if the promise is too great, and so it is repeated and amplified. *May your spirit*—the inmost part of our being, created for fellowship with God—*and your soul*, the seat of the life and all its powers—*and body*, through which sin entered, in which sin proved its power even unto death, but which has been redeemed in Christ: *spirit, soul, and body be preserved entire, without blame, at the coming of our Lord Jesus Christ.*

To prevent the possibility of any misconception, as if it is too great to be literally true, the words are added: *"Faithful is he that calleth you, who will also do it."* Yes, He has said: "I the Lord have spoken it; and I, in Christ and through the Holy Spirit, will do it." All He asks is that we will come and abide in close fellowship with Him every day. As the heat of the sun shines on the body and warms it, the fire of His holiness will burn in us and make us holy. Child of God, beware of unbelief. It dishonors God; it robs your soul of its heritage. Take refuge in the word: *"Faithful is he that calleth you, who will also do it."* Yes, He will do it; and He will give me grace so to abide in His nearness that I can ever be under the cover of His perfect peace, and of the holiness which He alone can give. Oh, my soul, *He will do it.*

March 25

The Exceeding Greatness of His Power

I cease not to make mention of you in my prayers; that the God of our Lord Jesus Christ, the Father of glory, may give unto you a spirit of wisdom and revelation; having the eyes of your heart enlightened, that ye may know what is the exceeding greatness of his power to us-ward who believe, according to that working of the strength of his might which he wrought in Christ, when he raised him from the dead. —Ephesians 1:16-20

Here we have again one of the great faith texts—words that will make our faith large and strong and bold. Paul is writing to men who had been sealed with the Holy Spirit. And yet he felt the need of unceasing prayer for the enlightening of the Spirit, that they might know in truth what the mighty power of God was that was working in them. It was nothing less than the very same power, the working of the strength of His might, by which He raised Christ from the dead.

Christ died on the tree under the weight of the sin of the world and its curse. When He descended into the grave it was under the weight of all that sin and the power of that death which had apparently mastered Him. What a mighty working of the power of God, to raise that Man out of the grave to the power and the glory of His throne. Now the very same power, in exceeding greatness of it toward us who believe, by the teaching of the Holy Spirit, we are to know as working in us every day of our life. The Lord who said to Abraham, "I am God Almighty, nothing is too hard for me," comes to us with the message that what He did, not only in Abraham, but in Christ Jesus, is *the pledge of what He is doing every moment in our hearts and will do effectually if we but learn to trust Him.*

It is by that Almighty power that the risen and exalted Christ can be revealed in our hearts as our life and our strength. How little believers *believe this*! Oh, let us cry to God, let us trust God for His Holy Spirit to enable us to claim nothing less every day than the exceeding greatness of this resurrection power working in us.

And let us very specifically pray for all believers around us and throughout the church that they may have their eyes opened to the wonderful vision of God's almighty resurrection power working in them.

March 26

The Indwelling Christ

That Christ may dwell in your heart by faith.—Ephesians 3:14-19

The great privilege that separated Israel from other nations was this: they had God dwelling among them, His home in the Holiest of all, in the tabernacle and the temple. The New Testament is the dispensation of the indwelling God in the heart of His people. As Christ said (John 14:21, 23), "If a man keep my words, he it is that loveth me; and my Father will love him, and I will love him, and we will come to him, and make our abode with him." This is what Paul calls "the riches of the glory of this mystery among the Gentiles, which is Christ in you, the hope of glory." Or as he says of himself, "Christ liveth in me."

The gospel—the dispensation of the indwelling Christ. How few Christians there are who believe or experience it! Come and let us listen to Paul's teaching as to the way into the experience of this crowning blessing of the Christian life.

1. *"I bow my knees to the Father, that he would grant you."* The blessing must come from the Father to the supplicant on the bended knee, for himself or for those for whom he labors. It is to be found in much prayer.

2. *"That he would grant you according to the riches of his glory"*—something very special and divine—*"to be strengthened with might by his Spirit in the inner man,"* to separate from sin and the world, to yield to Christ as Lord and Master, and to live that life of love to Christ and keeping His commandments to which the promise has been given: "The Father and I will come to him, and make our abode with him."

3. *"That Christ may dwell in your heart by faith."* It is in the very nature of Christ, in His divine omnipresence and love, to long for the heart to dwell in. As faith sees this and bows the knee and pleads with God for this great blessing, it receives grace to believe that the prayer is answered; and in that faith accepts the wonderful gift, so long thirsted for—Christ dwelling in the heart by faith.

4. *"That ye being rooted and grounded in love may be filled with all the fulness of God,"* as far as it is possible for man to experience it.

Child of God, feed on the words the Holy Spirit has given here. Meditate, with strong desire and childlike faith, on what the Father and the Son and the Holy Spirit have undertaken to work in you. Hold fast the confident assurance that God will do abundantly above what we can ask or think.

March 27

Christian Perfection

The God of peace make you perfect in every good work to do his will, working in you that which is well-pleasing in his sight, through Jesus Christ.—Hebrews 13:20, 21

Prepare your heart for a large and strong faith, here again to take in one of those promises of God, as high above all our thoughts as the heaven is above the earth.

You know what a wonderful exposition we have in the Epistle to the Hebrews of that eternal redemption which Christ our great High Priest, the Mediator of the new covenant, worked out for us through the shedding of His precious blood. The writer of the epistle closes his whole argument, and all its deep spiritual teaching with the benediction—"The God of peace"—listen, "make you perfect in every good work to do his will." Does not that include everything? Can we desire more? Yes, listen—"working in you that which is well-pleasing in his sight," and that through Jesus Christ.

The great thought here is that all Christ had done for our redemption, and all that God had done in raising Him from the dead, was just with the one object that He might now have free scope for working out in us that everlasting redemption which Christ had brought in. He himself as God the Omnipotent ever working will make us perfect in every good work. And if we want to know in what way, we have the answer: by His working within us that which is well-pleasing in His sight. And that through Jesus Christ.

All we have been taught about the completeness of the salvation in Christ, and our call to look on Him, to follow Him, is here crowned and finds its consummation in the blessed assurance that God himself takes such entire charge of the man who really trusts Him that He himself will through Jesus Christ work all that is well pleasing in His sight.

The thought is too high, the promise is too large; we cannot attain to it. And yet there it is, claiming, stimulating our faith. It calls us just to take hold of the one truth—the everlasting God works in me every hour of the day through Jesus Christ. I have just one thing to do: to yield myself into God's hands for Him to work. I am not to hinder Him by my working, but in a silent adoring faith to be assured that He himself through Jesus Christ will work in me all that is well pleasing in His sight. "Lord, increase our faith!"

March 28

The God of all Grace

The God of all grace, who called you unto his eternal glory in Christ, shall himself perfect, stablish, strengthen you, after ye have suffered a little while. —1 Peter 5:10

We know how the Epistle to the Hebrews gathers up all its teaching in that wonderful promise: "The God of peace perfect you in every good work." Peter does the same thing here: "The God of all grace perfect, stablish, strengthen you." God himself is to be the one object of our trust, day by day; as we think of our work, of our needs, of our life and all our hearts' desire, God himself must be the one object of our hope and trust.

Just as God is the center of the universe, the one source of its strength, the one Guide who orders and controls its movements, so God must have the same place in the life of the believer. With every new day, the first and chief thought ought to be—God, God alone, can fit me this day to live as He would have me.

And what is now to be our position toward this God? Do we not feel that the first thought of every day ought to be the humble placing of ourselves in His hands to confess our absolute helplessness, and to yield ourselves in childlike surrender to receive from Him the fulfillment of such promises as these: *"the God of peace perfecting you in every good work"*; *"the God of all grace perfecting, stablishing, strengthening you"*?

It is absolutely indispensable to meet God every morning and give Him time to reveal himself and to take charge of our life for the day. Is not this just what we have to do with these wonderful words of Peter? Until it be an understood thing between God and ourselves: Blessed Father, in view of the life and work of this new day, my heart is resting on Thee; my hope is in Thy Word: *"The God of peace perfect you in every good work"*; *"the God of all grace perfect, stablish, strengthen you."*

By Thy grace may this henceforth be the spirit in which I awake every morning to go out to my work, humbly trusting in the word: *"God shall himself perfect you. The Lord will perfect that which concerneth me."*

March 29

Not Sinning

Ye know that he was manifested to take away sins; and in him is no sin. Whosoever abideth in him sinneth not.—1 John 3:5, 6

John had taken deep into his heart and life the words on abiding in Him that Christ had spoken in the last night. He ever remembered how the Lord had six times over spoken of loving Him and keeping His commandments as the way to abiding in His love, and receiving the indwelling of the Father and the Son. And so as he writes this epistle in his old age, the abiding in Christ is one of the key words of the life it promises (John 2:2, 24, 28; 3:6, 24; 4:13, 16).

In our text John teaches how we can be kept from sinning: "He that abideth in Christ sinneth not." Though there be sin in our nature, the abiding in Christ, in whom is no sin, does indeed free us from the power of sin and enables us day by day to live so as to please God. Of the Lord Jesus it is written that He had said of the Father (John 8:29): "I do always those things that please him."

And so John writes in the epistle: "Beloved, if our heart condemn us not, we have boldness toward God; and whatsoever we ask, we receive of him, *because we keep his commandments and do the things that are pleasing in his sight.*"

Let the soul who longs to be free from the power of sin take these simple but far-reaching words: "In him is no sin" and "of God I am in him." "He that establisheth us in Christ is God." As I seek to abide in Him in whom there is no sin, Christ will indeed live out His own life in me in the power of the Holy Spirit, and fit me for a life in which I always do the things that are pleasing in His sight.

Dear child of God, you are called to a life in which faith, great faith, strong faith, continuous and unbroken faith, in the almighty power of God is your one hope. As you day by day take time and yield yourself to the God of peace, who perfects you in every good work to do His will, you will experience that what the heart has not conceived is what God indeed works in them that wait for Him.

"He that abideth in him sinneth not." The promise is sure: God the Almighty is pledged that He will work in you what is well pleasing in His sight, through Christ Jesus. In that faith, abide in Him.

March 30

Overcoming the World

Who is he that overcometh the world, but he that believeth that Jesus is the Son of God. —1 John 5:5

Christ had spoken strongly of the world hating Him. His kingdom and the kingdom of this world were in deadly hostility. John had understood the lesson, and summed up all in the words: "We know that we are of God, and the whole world lieth in wickedness." "Love not the world, nor the things that are of the world. If any man love the world, the love of the Father is not in him."

John also teaches us what the real nature and power of the world is: *the lust of the flesh*, with its self-pleasing; *the lust of the eyes*, with its seeing and seeking what there is in the glory of the world; and *the pride of life*, with its self-exaltation. We find these three marks of what the world is, in Eve in Paradise. She "saw that the tree was good for food, and that it was pleasant to the eyes, and a tree to be desired to make one wise." Through the body, and the eyes, and the pride of wisdom, the world acquired the mastery over her and over us.

The world still exerts a terrible influence over the Christian who does not know that in Christ he has been crucified to the world. In the pleasure of eating and drinking, in the love and enjoyment of what there is to be seen of its glory, and in all that constitutes the pride of life, the power of this world proves itself. And most Christians are either utterly ignorant of the danger of a worldly spirit, or feel themselves utterly impotent to conquer it.

Christ left us with the great far-reaching promise: "Be of good cheer, I have overcome the world." As the child of God abides in Christ and seeks to live the heavenly life in the power of the Holy Spirit, he may confidently count on the power to overcome the world. "Who is he that overcometh the world, but he that believeth that Jesus is the Son of God?" "I live by the faith of the Son of God, who loved me, and gave himself for me"; this is the secret of daily, hourly victory over the world and all its secret, subtle temptation. But it needs a heart and a life entirely possessed by the faith of Jesus Christ to maintain the victor's attitude at all times. Put your trust in the mighty power of God, in the abiding presence of Jesus, as the only pledge of certain and continual victory.

"Believest thou this?" Yea, Lord, I believe.

March 31

Jesus the Author and Perfecter of Our Faith

Lord, I believe; help thou mine unbelief.—Mark 9:24

What a treasure of encouragement these words contain. Our Lord had said to the father of the possessed child, who had asked for His help: "If thou canst believe, all things are possible to him that believeth." The father felt that Christ was throwing the responsibility on him. If he believed, the child could be healed. And he felt as if he did not have such faith. But as he looked in the face of Christ, he felt assured that the love which was willing to heal, would also be ready to help with his faith and graciously accept even its feeble beginnings. And he cried with tears: "Lord, I believe; help thou mine unbelief." Christ heard the prayer, and the child was healed.

What a lesson for us who have so often felt, as we listened to the wonderful promises of God, that our faith was too feeble to grasp the precious gift. And here we receive the assurance that the Christ who waits for our faith to do its work is a Savior *who himself will care for our faith*. Let us come, however feeble our faith may be, and though it be with tears, cry: "Lord, I believe; help thou mine unbelief." Christ will accept the prayer that puts its trust in Him. Let us bring it into exercise, even though it be but as a mustard seed; in contact with Christ the feeblest faith is made strong and bold. Jesus Christ is the Author and Perfecter of our faith.

Dear Christian, I pray you, as you read God's wonderful promises and long to have them fulfilled, remember the grain of mustard seed. However small, if it be put into the ground and allowed to grow, it becomes a great tree. Take the hidden feeble seed of the little faith you have, with the Word of promise on which you are resting; plant it in your heart. Give utterance to it in the contact with Jesus Christ and fervent prayer to Him; He will in very deed accept the feeble trembling faith that clings to Him and will not let Him go. A feeble faith in an almighty Christ will become the great faith that can remove the mountain.

We saw in Abraham how God took charge of his faith and trained him to become strong in faith, giving glory to God. Count most confidently on the desire of Christ to strengthen your faith. And in answer to the question that each time comes again, "Believest thou that I can do this?" let your heart confidently say: "Yea, Lord, I do believe."

April

The Secret of Adoration

April 1

True Worship

Worship God.—Revelation 22:9

Those who have thought on it have doubtless more than once asked: "What may be the reason that prayer and intercession are not a greater joy and delight? And is there any way in which we may become fitted to make fellowship with God our chief joy, and as intercessors to bring down His power and blessing on those for whom we pray?"

There may be more than one answer to the question. But the chief answer is undoubtedly: *We know God too little.* In our prayer, His presence is not waited for as the chief thing on which our heart is set. And yet it should be so. We think mostly of ourselves, our need and weakness, our desire and prayer. But we forget that in every prayer *God must be first, must be all.* To seek Him, to find Him, to tarry in His presence, to be assured *that His holy presence rests upon us*, that He actually listens to what we say, and is working in us— it is this alone that gives us the inspiration to make prayer as natural and easy to us as is the conversation of a child with his father.

And how is one to attain this nearness to God and fellowship with Him? The answer is simple: *We must give God time to make himself known to us.* Believe with your whole heart that just as you present yourself to God as a supplicant, *so God presents himself to you as the hearer of prayer.* But you cannot realize this except as you give Him time and quiet. It is not in the multitude or the earnestness of your words that prayer has its power, but in the living faith that *God himself is taking you and your prayer into His loving heart.* He himself will give the assurance that in His time your prayer will be heard.

The object of this series of meditations is to help you know the way thus to meet God in every prayer. We will seek to give you each day one or more texts with which your heart can bow before God, waiting on Him to make them living and true in your experience.

Begin this day with the word: *"Unto thee, O Lord, do I lift up my soul."* Bow before Him in stillness, believing that He looks on you and will reveal His presence.

"My soul thirsteth for God, for the living God."

April 2

God Is a Spirit

God is a Spirit: and they that worship him must worship him in spirit and in truth. —John 4:24

When God created man and breathed into him of His own Spirit, man became a living soul. The soul stood midway between the spirit and the body, and had either to yield to the spirit to be lifted up to God, or to the flesh and its lusts. In the Fall, man refused to listen to the spirit, and became the slave of the body. The spirit in man became utterly darkened.

In regeneration this spirit is quickened and born again from above. In the regenerate life and in the fellowship with God it is the spirit of man that has ever to yield itself to the Spirit of God. The spirit is the deepest, inward part of the human being. As we read in Psalm 51: "Thou desirest truth in the *inward parts;* and in *the hidden part* thou shalt make me to know wisdom"; or in Jeremiah 31: "I will put my law in *their inward parts.*"

It is of this also that Isaiah says: "With my soul have I desired thee in the night; yea, *with my spirit within me* will I seek thee early." The soul must sink down into the depths of the hidden spirit, and call upon that to stir itself to seek God.

God is a Spirit, most holy and most glorious. He gave us a spirit with the one object *of holding fellowship with himself.* Through sin that power has been darkened and well-nigh quenched. There is no way for its restoration but by presenting the soul in stillness before God for the working of His Holy Spirit in our spirit. Deeper than our thoughts and feelings, God will in our inward part, in our spirits within us, teach us to worship Him in spirit and in truth.

"The Father seeketh such to worship him." He himself by His Holy Spirit will teach us this if we wait upon Him. In this quiet hour, be still before God and yield yourself with the whole heart to believe in and to receive the gentle working of His Spirit. And breathe out such words as these:

"My soul, be thou silent unto God."

"With my soul have I desired thee in the night, yea, with my spirit within me I seek thee early."

"On thee, O God, do I wait."

April 3

Intercession and Adoration

Worship the Lord in the beauty of holiness.—Psalm 96:9

The better we know God the more wonderful becomes our insight into the power of intercession. We begin to understand that it is the great means by which man can take part in the carrying out of God's purpose. God has entrusted the whole of His redemption in Christ to His people to make known and to communicate to men. In all this, intercession is the chief and essential element; because it is in it that His servants enter into the full fellowship with Christ, and receive the power of the Spirit and of heaven as their power for service.

It is easy to see why God had so ordered it. In very deed God desires to renew us after His image and likeness. And there is no other way to do this but by our making His desires our own, so that we breathe His disposition; and in love sacrifice ourselves, so that we may become, in a measure, even like Christ, "ever living to make intercession." Such can be the life of the consecrated believer.

The clearer our insight into this great purpose of God, the more will the need be felt to enter very truly into God's presence in the spirit of humble worship and holy adoration. The more we thus take time to abide in God's presence, to enter fully into His mind and will, to get our whole soul possessed by the thought of His glorious purpose, the stronger will our faith become that God himself will work out all the good pleasure of His will through our prayers. As the glory of God shines upon us, we will become conscious of the depths of our helplessness; and so rise up into the faith that believes God will do more than we can ask or think.

Intercession will lead to the feeling of the need of a deeper adoration. Adoration will give new power for intercession. A true intercession and a deeper adoration will ever be found to be inseparable.

The secret of true adoration can only be known by the soul that gives time to tarry in God's presence, and that yields itself to God for Him to reveal himself. Adoration will indeed fit us for the great work of making God's glory known.

"Oh, come let us worship and bow down, let us kneel before the Lord our maker; for he is our God."

"Give unto the Lord the glory due unto his name."

April 4

The Desire for God

With my soul have I desired thee in the night.—Isaiah 26:9

What is the chief thing, the greatest and most glorious, that man can see or find upon earth? *Nothing less than God himself.*

And what is the chief and the best and the most glorious thing a man needs every day and can do every day? Nothing less than to seek and to know, and to love and to praise this glorious God. As glorious as God is, so is the glory which begins to work in the heart and life of the man who gives himself to live for God.

Have you learned what is the first and the greatest thing you have to do every day? Nothing less and nothing greater than to seek this God, to meet Him, to worship Him, to live for Him and for His glory. It is a great step in advance in the life of a Christian when he truly sees this and yields himself *to consider fellowship with God every day as the chief end of his life.*

Take time and ask whether this be not the truth, the highest wisdom and the one thing for which a Christian is above all to live—*to know his God aright, and to love Him with his whole heart.* Do believe that it is not only in very deed true, but that God himself desires that you should live thus with Him, and will, in answer to prayer, enable you to do so.

Begin today and take a word from God's Book to speak to Him in stillness of soul.

"O God, thou art my God; early will I seek thee: my soul thirsteth for thee, my flesh longeth for thee, . . . my soul followeth hard after thee" (Ps. 63:1, 8).

"I seek thee with my whole heart" (see Ps. 119:2).

Repeat these words in deep reverence and childlike longing till their spirit and power enter your heart; and wait upon God till you begin to realize what the blessedness is of thus meeting with Him. As you persevere you will learn to expect that the fear and the presence of God can abide with you through all the day.

"I waited patiently for the Lord; and he inclined unto me, and heard my cry" (Ps. 40:1).

April 5

Silent Adoration

My soul is silent unto God. . . . My soul, be thou silent unto God; for my expectation is from him.—Psalm 62:1, 5

When man in his littleness and God in His glory meet, we all understand that what God says has infinitely more worth than what man says. And yet our prayer so often consists in the utterance *of our thoughts* of what we need that we give God no time to speak to us. Our prayers are often so indefinite and vague. We have a great lesson to learn: to be silent unto God is the secret of true adoration. Let us remember the promise, "In quietness and confidence shall be your strength."

"My soul, wait thou only upon God; for my expectation is from him."

"I will wait for the Lord; my soul doth wait, and in his word do I hope."

It is as the soul bows itself before Him to remember His greatness and His holiness, His power and His love, and seeks to give Him the honor and the reverence and the worship that are His due, that the heart will be opened to receive the divine impression of the nearness of God and of the working of His power.

O Christian, do believe that such worship of God—in which you bow low and ever lower in your nothingness, and lift up your thoughts to realize God's presence, as He gives himself to you in Christ Jesus—is the sure way to give Him the glory that is His due, and will lead to the highest blessedness to be found in prayer.

Do not imagine it is time lost. Do not turn from it if at first it appears difficult or fruitless. Be assured that it brings you into the right relation to God. It opens the way to fellowship with Him. It leads to the blessed assurance that He is looking on you in tender love and working in you with a secret but divine power. And as at length you become more accustomed to it, it will give you the sense of His presence abiding with you all the day. It will make you strong to testify for God. Someone has said, "No one is able to influence others for goodness and holiness, beyond the amount that there is of God in him." Men will begin to feel that you have been with God.

"The Lord is in his holy temple; be silent before him, all the earth" (Hab. 2:20).

April 6

The Light of God's Countenance

God is light.—1 John 1:5

The Lord is my light.—Psalm 27:1

Every morning the sun rises, and we walk in its light and perform our daily duties with gladness. Whether we think of it or not, the light of the sun shines on us all day.

Every morning the light of God shines upon His children. But to enjoy the light of God's countenance, the soul must turn to God and trust Him to let His light shine in upon it.

When there is a shipwreck at midnight, with what longing the sailors look for the morning! How often the sigh goes up. When will the day break? Even so must the Christian wait upon God and rest patiently until His light shines upon him.

"My soul waiteth for the Lord more than they that watch for the morning" (Ps. 130:6).

O my soul, begin each day with one of the prayers:

"Make thy face to shine upon thy servant" (Ps. 31:16).

"Lord, lift thou up the light of thy countenance upon us" (Ps. 4:6).

"Cause thy face to shine; and we shall be saved" (Ps. 80:3, 7, 19).

Do not rest until you know that the light of His countenance and His blessing is resting on you. Then you will experience the truth of the word: "They walk in the light of thy countenance; in thy name do they rejoice all the day" (Ps. 89:15, 16).

Children of God, do believe that it is the ardent longing of your Father that you should dwell and rejoice in His light all the day. Just as you need the light of the sun each hour, so the heavenly light, the light of the countenance of the Father, is indispensable. As sure as it is that we receive and enjoy the light of the sun, so confidently may we count on it that God is longing to let His light shine on us.

Even when there are clouds, we still have the sun. So in the midst of difficulties the light of God will rest upon you without ceasing. If you are sure the sun has risen, you count upon the light all the day. *Make sure that the light of God shines upon you in the morning,* and you can count upon that light being with you all day.

"The Lord is my light and my salvation" (Ps. 27:1).

April 7

Faith in God

Jesus said unto them: Have faith in God. —Mark 11:22

As the eye is the organ by which we see the light and rejoice in it, *so faith is the power by which we see the light of God and walk in it.*

Man was made for God, in His likeness; his whole being was formed after the divine pattern. Just think of his wonderful power of thinking out all the thoughts of God hidden in nature. Think of the heart, with its unlimited powers of self-sacrifice and love. Man was made for God, to seek Him, to find Him, to grow up into His likeness and show forth His glory; in the fullest sense to be His dwelling. And faith is the eye which, turning away from the world and self, looks up to God and in His light sees light. To faith God reveals himself.

How often we toil and try to waken thoughts and feelings concerning God, which are but a faint shadow, and we forget "to gaze on the Incomparable Original."

Could we but realize it, in the depth of our soul God reveals himself.

Without faith it is impossible to please God or to know Him. In our quiet time we have to pray to our Father which is in secret. There "he hides us in the secret of his pavilion." And there, as we wait and worship before Him, He will in very deed, just as the light by its very nature reveals itself, let His light shine into our hearts.

Let our one desire be to take time and be still before God, believing with an unbounded faith in His desire to make himself known to us. Let us feed on God's Word to make us strong in faith. Let that faith have large thoughts of what God's glory is, of what His power is to reveal himself to us, of what His longing love is to get complete possession of us.

Such faith, exercised and strengthened day by day in secret fellowship with God, will become the habit of our life, keeping us ever in the enjoyment of His presence and the experience of His saving power.

"Abraham was strong in faith, giving glory to God; being fully persuaded that, what he had promised, he was able also to perform" (Rom. 4:20, 21).

"I believe God, that it shall be even as it was told me" (Acts 27:25).

"Wait on the Lord: be of good courage, and he shall strengthen thine heart: wait, I say, on the Lord" (Ps. 27:14).

April 8

Alone with God

And it came to pass, as he was alone praying.—Luke 9:18

He departed again into a mountain, himself alone.—John 6:15

Man needs God. God made him for Himself, to find his life and happiness in God alone.

Man needs to be alone with God. His fall consisted in his being brought, through the lust of the flesh and the world, under the power of things visible and temporal. His restoration is meant to bring him back to the Father's house, the Father's presence, the Father's love and fellowship. *Salvation means being brought to love and to delight in the presence of God.*

Man needs to be alone with God. Without this, God cannot have the opportunity to shine into his heart, to transform his nature by His divine working, to take possession and to fill him with the fullness of God.

Man needs to be alone with God, to yield himself to the presence and the power of His holiness, of His life and of His love. Christ on earth needed it; He could not live the life of a Son here in the flesh without at times separating himself entirely from His surroundings and being alone with God. How much more must this be indispensable to us!

When our Lord Jesus gave us the blessed command to enter our inner chamber, to shut the door, to pray to our Father in secret, all alone, He gave us the promise that the Father would hear such prayers and mightily answer them in our life before men.

Alone with God—that is the secret of true prayer, of true power in prayer, of real, living, face-to-face fellowship with God, and of power for service. There is no true, deep conversion, no true, deep holiness, no clothing with the Holy Spirit and with power, no abiding peace or joy, *without being daily alone with God.* "There is no path to holiness, but in being *much and long alone with God."*

What an inestimable privilege is the institution of daily secret prayer to begin every morning. Let it be the one thing our hearts are set on—*seeking, and finding, and meeting God.*

"Hearken unto the voice of my cry, my King and my God; for unto thee will I pray" (Ps. 5:2).

"My voice shalt thou hear in the morning, O Lord; in the morning will I direct my prayer unto thee, and will look up" (Ps. 5:3).

April 9

Wholly for God

Whom have I in heaven but thee? and there is none upon earth that I desire beside thee.—Psalm 73:25

Alone with God—this is a word of the deepest importance. May we seek grace from God to reach its depths. Then shall we learn that there is another word of equally deep significance—*wholly for God.*

As we find that it is not easy to persevere in this being *"alone with God,"* we begin to realize that it is because the other is lacking: we are not *"wholly for God."* Because He is the only God, and He alone the Adorable One, God has a right to demand *that He should have us wholly for himself.* Without this surrender He cannot make His power known. We read in the Old Testament that His servants, Abraham, Moses, Elijah, and David, gave themselves wholly and unreservedly to God so that He could work out His plans through them. It is only the fully surrendered heart that can fully trust God for all He has promised.

Nature teaches us that if anyone desires to do a great work, he must give himself wholly to it. This law is especially true of the love of a mother for her child. She gives herself wholly to the little one whom she loves. And is it reasonable that the great God of Love should have us wholly for himself? And shouldn't we have the watchword, "Wholly for God," as the keynote for our devotions every morning as we rise? *As wholly as God gives himself to us, so wholly He desires that we give ourselves to Him.*

Let us in the inner chamber meditate on these things alone with God, and with earnest desire ask Him by His almighty power to work in us all that is pleasing in His sight.

Wholly for God! What a privilege. What wonderful grace to fit us for it. Wholly for God! What separation from men, and work, and all that might draw us away. Wholly for God! What ineffable blessedness as the soul learns what it means, and what God gives with it.

"Thou shalt love the Lord thy God with all thine heart, and with all thy soul, and with all thy mind" (Deut. 6:5; Matt. 22:37).

"They sought him with their whole desire, and he was found of them" (2 Chron. 15:15).

"With my whole heart have I sought thee" (Ps. 119:10).

April 10

The Knowledge of God

This is life eternal, that they might know thee.—John 17:3

The knowledge of God is absolutely necessary for the spiritual life. *It is life eternal.* Not the intellectual knowledge we receive from others, or through our own power of thought, but the living, experimental knowledge *in which God makes himself known to the soul.* Just as the rays of the sun on a cold winter's day warm the body, imparting its heat to us, *so the living God sheds the life-giving rays of His holiness and love into the heart that waits on Him.*

How is it we so seldom experience this life-giving power of the true knowledge of God? *Because we do not give God time enough to reveal himself to us.* When we pray, we think we know well enough how to speak to God. And we forget that one of the very first things in prayer is to be silent before God that He may reveal himself. By His hidden but mighty power, God will manifest His presence, resting on us and working in us. To know God in the personal experience of His presence and love is life indeed.

Brother Lawrence had a great longing to know God, and for this purpose went into a monastery. His spiritual advisers gave him prayer books to use, but he put them aside. It helps little to pray, he said, *if I do not know the God to whom I pray.* And he believed that God would reveal himself. He remained a long time in silent adoration, to come under the full influence of the presence of this great and holy Being. He continued in this practice, until later he lived consciously and constantly in God's presence and experienced His blessed nearness and keeping power. As the sun rising each morning is the pledge of light through the day, so the quiet time waiting upon God, to yield ourselves for Him to shine on us, will be the pledge of His presence and His power resting with us all the day. Be sure that the sun has risen upon your soul.

Learn this great lesson that the sun each day proclaims: As the sun on a cold day shines on us and imparts its warmth, *believe that the living God will work in you with His love and His almighty power.* God will reveal himself as life and light and joy and strength to the soul that waits upon Him.

"Lord, lift thou up the light of thy countenance upon us" (Ps. 4:6).

"Be still, and know that I am God" (Ps. 46:10).

April 11

God the Father

Baptizing them in the name of the Father, and of the Son, and of the Holy Ghost. —Matthew 28:19

It is well we should remember that the doctrine of the Holy Trinity has a deep devotional aspect. As we think of God we remember the inconceivable distance separating Him in His holiness from sinful men, and we bow in deep contrition and holy fear. As we think of Christ the Son, we remember the inconceivable nearness in which He came to be born of a woman, a daughter of Adam, and to die the accursed death, and so to be inseparably joined to us for all eternity. And as we think of the Holy Spirit we remember the inconceivable blessedness of God having His abode in us, and making us His home and His temple through eternity.

When Christ taught us to say, "Our Father, which art in heaven," He immediately added, "Hallowed be thy name." As God is holy, so we are to be holy too. And there is no way of becoming holy but by counting that name most holy, and drawing nigh to Him in prayer.

How often we speak that name without any sense of the unspeakable privilege of our relationship to God. If we would just take time to come into contact with God and to worship Him in His Father love, how the inner chamber would become to us the gate of heaven.

Child of God, if you pray to your Father in secret, bow very low before Him, and seek to adore His name as most holy. Remember that this is the highest blessedness of prayer.

"Pray to thy Father who is in secret; and thy Father who seeth in secret shall reward thee openly" (Matt. 6:6).

What an unspeakable privilege to be alone with God in secret and to say, "My Father," to have the assurance that He has indeed seen me in secret, and will reward me openly.

April 12

God the Son

Grace to you and peace from God our Father, and the Lord Jesus Christ. —Romans 1:7

It is remarkable that the apostle Paul in each of his thirteen epistles writes: "Grace to you and peace from God our Father, *and the Lord Jesus Christ.*" He had such a deep sense of the inseparable oneness of the Father and the Son in the work of grace that in each opening benediction he refers to both.

This is a lesson of the utmost importance for us. There may be times in the Christian life when one thinks chiefly of God the Father, and prays to Him. But later on we realize that it may cause spiritual loss if we do not grasp the truth that each day and each hour it is only through faith in Christ and *in living union with Him* that we can enjoy a full and abiding fellowship with God.

Remember what we read of the Lamb in the midst of the throne. John had seen One sitting on a throne. "And the four living creatures rest not day and night, saying, Holy, holy, holy, Lord God Almighty, which was, and is, and is to come" (Rev. 4:3, 8).

Later (Rev. 5:6) he sees "in the midst of the throne, a Lamb as it had been slain." Of all the worshipping multitude none could see God, but he first saw Christ the Lamb of God. And none could see Christ without seeing the glory of God, the Father and Son inseparably One.

O Christian, if you would know and worship God aright, seek Him and worship Him *in Christ.* And if you seek Christ, seek Him and worship Him *in God.* Then you will understand what it is to have "your life *hid with Christ in God,*" and you will experience that the fellowship and adoration of Christ is indispensable to the full knowledge of the love and holiness of God.

Be still, O soul, and speak these words in deepest reverence: "Grace and peace"—all I can desire—*"from God the Father and the Lord Jesus Christ."*

Take time to meditate, and believe, to expect all from God the Father who sits upon the throne, and from the Lord Jesus Christ, the Lamb in the midst of the throne. Then you will learn truly to worship God. Return frequently to this sacred scene to give "glory to him that sitteth upon the throne, and to the Lamb" (Rev. 5:13).

April 13

God the Holy Spirit

Through him we both have access by one Spirit unto the Father.
—Ephesians 2:18

In our communion with God in the inner chamber, we must guard against the danger of seeking to know God and Christ in the power of the intellect or the emotions. *The Holy Spirit has been given for the express purpose that "by him we may have access to the Father through the Son."* Let us beware lest our labor be in vain, because we do not wait for the teaching of the Spirit.

Christ taught His disciples this truth in the last night. Speaking of the coming of the Comforter, He says: "In that day ye shall ask the Father in my name; ask, and ye shall receive, that your joy may be full." Hold fast the truth that the Holy Spirit was given with *the one great object of teaching us to pray.* He makes the fellowship with the Father and the Son a blessed reality. Be strong in the faith that He is working secretly in you. As you enter the inner chamber, give yourself wholly to His guidance as your Teacher in all your intercession and adoration.

When Christ said to the disciples on the evening of the resurrection day, "Receive ye the Holy Ghost," it was, for one thing, to strengthen and fit them for the ten days of prayer and their receiving the fullness of the Spirit. This suggests to us three things we ought to remember when we draw nigh to God in prayer:

First, we must pray in the confidence that the Holy Spirit dwells in us, and yield ourselves, in stillness of soul, definitely to His leading. Take time for this.

Second, we must believe that the "greater works" of the Spirit for the enlightening and strengthening of the spiritual life—the fullness of the Spirit—will be given in answer to prayer.

Third, we must believe that through the Spirit, in unity with all God's children, we may ask and expect the mighty workings of that Spirit on His church and people.

"He that believeth on me, as the Scripture hath said, out of his belly shall flow rivers of living water" (John 7:18).

"Believest thou this?"

April 14

The Secret of the Lord

Enter into thy closet, and when thou hast shut thy door, pray to thy Father which is in secret; and thy Father which seeth in secret shall reward thee openly.—Matthew 6:6

Christ longed greatly that His disciples should know God as their Father, and that they should have secret fellowship with Him. In His own life He found it not only indispensable but the highest happiness to meet the Father in secret. And He would have us realize that it is impossible to be true, wholehearted disciples *without daily conversation with the Father in heaven*, who waits for us in secret.

God is a God who hides himself from the world and all that is of the world. God would draw us away from the world and from ourselves. He offers us instead the blessedness of close, intimate communion with himself. Oh, that God's children would understand this!

Believers in the Old Testament enjoyed this experience. "Thou art my hiding-place." "He that dwelleth in the secret place of the Most High shall abide under the shadow of the Almighty." "The secret of the Lord is with them that fear him."

How much more ought Christians in the New Covenant to value this secret relationship with God. We read: "Ye are dead, and your life is *hid with Christ in God.*" If we really believe this, we will have the joyful assurance that our life, hid with Christ in God in such divine keeping, is safe and beyond the reach of every foe. We should day by day confidently seek the renewal of our spiritual life in prayer to our Father who is in secret.

Because we are dead with Christ, one plant with Him in the likeness of His death, and of His resurrection too, we know that, as the roots of a tree are hidden under the earth, so the roots of our daily life are hidden deep in God.

O soul, take time to realize: "Thou shalt hide me in the secret of thy presence" (Ps. 31:20).

Our first thought in prayer should be: I must know that I am alone with God, and that God is with me. "In the secret of his tabernacle shall he hide me" (Ps. 27:5).

April 15

Half an Hour Silence in Heaven

And there was silence in heaven about the space of half an hour. And another angel came and stood at the altar; and there was given unto him much incense that he should offer it with the prayers of all saints upon the golden altar. And the smoke of the incense, which came with the prayers of the saints, ascended up before God.—Revelation 8:1, 3, 4

There was silence in heaven about the space of half an hour—to bring the prayers of the saints before God, before the first angel sounded his trumpet. And so ten thousands of God's children have felt the absolute need of silence and retirement from the things of earth for half an hour, to present their prayers before God, and in fellowship with Him be strengthened for their daily work.

How often the complaint is heard that there is no time for prayer. And often the confession is made that, even if time could be found, one feels unable to spend the time in real conversation with God. No one need ask what it is that hinders growth in the spiritual life. *The secret of strength can be found only in living contact with God.*

If you would only obey Christ when He says: "When thou hast shut thy door, pray to thy Father which is in secret," and have the courage to be alone with God for half an hour. Do not think, I will not know how to spend the time. Just believe that if you begin and are faithful and bow in silence before God, He will reveal himself to you.

If you need help, read some passage of Scripture, and let God's Word speak to you. Then bow in deepest humility before God and wait on Him. *He will work within you.* Read Psalm 61, 62 or 63, and speak the words out before God. Then begin to pray.

God longs to bless you. Is it not worth the trouble to take half an hour alone with God? In heaven itself there was need for half an hour's silence to present the prayers of the saints before God. If you persevere, you may find that the half hour that seems the most difficult in the whole day may at length become the most blessed in your whole life.

"My soul is silent unto God.... My soul, be thou silent unto God; for my expectation is from him" (Ps. 62:1, 5).

April 16

God's Greatness

Thou art great, and doest wondrous things; thou art God alone.—
Psalm 86:10

When one begins an important work, he takes time to consider the greatness of his undertaking. Men of science, in studying nature, require years of labor to grasp the magnitude of, for instance, the sun and the heavenly bodies.

And is not our glorious God worthy that we should take time rightly to know and adore His greatness?

Yet how superficial is our knowledge of God's greatness. We do not allow ourselves time to bow before Him, and so come under the deep impression of His incomprehensible majesty and glory.

Meditate on the following texts until you are filled with some sense of what a glorious being God is.

"Great is the Lord, and greatly to be praised, and his greatness is unsearchable.... I will declare thy greatness.... They shall abundantly utter the memory of thy great goodness" (Ps. 145:3, 6, 7).

Do not imagine that it is easy to grasp the meaning of these words. Take time for them to master the heart until you bow, it may be, in speechless adoration before God.

"Ah Lord God!... there is nothing too hard for thee, the Great, the Mighty God ... great in counsel, and mighty in work" (Jer. 32:17-19).

And hear God's answer (v. 27): "Behold, I am the Lord, the God of all flesh; is there anything too hard for me?"

The right comprehension of God's greatness will take time. But if we give God the honor that is His due, and if our faith grows strong in the knowledge of what a great and powerful God we have, we will be drawn to tarry in the inner chamber to bow in humble worship before this great and mighty God. In His abundant mercy He will teach us through the Holy Spirit to say:

"The Lord is a great God. O come, let us worship and bow down: let us kneel before the Lord our maker" (Ps. 95:3, 6).

"The Lord is a great God, and a great King above all gods" (Ps. 95:3).

April 17

A Perfect Heart

For the eyes of the Lord run to and fro throughout the whole earth, to show himself strong in behalf of them whose heart is perfect toward him.—2 Chronicles 16:9

In worldly matters we know how important it is that work should be done with the whole heart. In the spiritual region this rule still holds good inexorably. God has given the commandment: "Thou shalt love the Lord thy God *with all thine heart and with all thy soul, and with all thy might*" (Deut. 6:5). And in Jeremiah 29:13, "Ye shall seek me, and find me, when ye shall search for me *with all your heart.*"

It is amazing that earnest Christians, who attend to their daily work with all their hearts, are so content to take things easy in the service of God. They do not realize that if anywhere, they should give themselves to God's service with all the power of their will.

In the words of our text we get an insight into the absolute necessity of seeking God with a perfect heart. "*The eyes of the Lord run to and fro throughout the whole earth, to show himself strong* in behalf of them whose heart is perfect toward him."

What an encouragement this should be to us to humbly wait upon God with an upright heart. We may be assured that His eye will be upon us, and He will show forth His mighty power in us and in our work.

O Christian, have you learned this lesson in your worship of God—to yield yourself each morning with your whole heart to do God's will? Pray each prayer with a perfect heart, in true wholehearted devotion to Him; and then in faith expect the power of God to work in you and through you.

Remember that to come to this, you must begin by being silent before God till you realize that He is indeed working in secret in your heart.

"I wait for my God" (Ps. 69:3). "In the secret of his tabernacle shall he hide me" (Ps. 27:5).

April 18

The Omnipotence of God

I am the Almighty God.—Genesis 17:1

When Abraham heard these words, he fell on his face; and God spoke to him, and filled his heart with the faith in what God would do for him. O Christian, have you bowed in deep humility before God until you felt that you were in living contact with the Almighty; until your heart has been filled with the faith that the mighty God is working in you and will perfect His work in you?

Read in the Psalms how the saints of old gloried in God and in His strength.

"I will love thee, O Lord, my strength" (Ps. 18:1).

"The Lord is the strength of my life" (Ps. 27:1).

"God is the strength of my heart" (Ps. 73:26).

"Thou strengthenedst me with strength in my soul" (Ps. 138:3).

(See Psalms 18:32; 46:1; 68:28; 68:35; 59:17; 89:17.)

Take time to appropriate these words and to adore God as the Almighty One, *your strength.*

Christ taught us that salvation is the work of God, and quite impossible to man. When the disciples asked, "Who then can be saved?" His answer was, "With men this is impossible, but with God all things are possible." If we firmly believe this, we will have courage to believe that God is working in us all that is well pleasing in His sight.

Think how Paul prays for the Ephesians that through the enlightening of the Spirit they might know "the exceeding greatness of his power to us-ward who believe, according to the working of his mighty power." And (Col. 1:11): "Strengthened with all might, according to his glorious power." When a man fully believes *that the mighty power of God is working without ceasing within him,* he can joyfully say, "God is the strength of my life."

Do you wonder that many Christians complain of weakness and shortcomings? They do not understand that the Almighty God must work in them every hour of the day. That is the secret of the true life of faith.

Do not rest until you can say to God, "I will love thee, O Lord, my strength." Let God have complete possession of you, and you will be able to say with all God's people, "Thou art the glory of their strength."

April 19

The Fear of God

Blessed is the man that feareth the Lord, that delighteth greatly in his commandments.—Psalm 112:1; 128:1, 4

The fear of God—these words characterize the religion of the Old Testament and the foundation which it laid for the more abundant life of the New. "The gift of holy fear" is ever still the great desire of the child of God, and an essential part of a life that is to make a real impression on the world around. It is one of the great promises of the new covenant in Jeremiah: "I will make an everlasting covenant with them; *and I will put my fear in their hearts, that they shall not depart from me.*"

We find the perfect combination of the two in Acts 9:31: "The churches had peace, being edified, and walking in the fear of the Lord, and in the comfort of the Holy Ghost, were multiplied." And Paul more than once gives fear a high place in the Christian life. "Work out your own salvation with fear and trembling, for it is God that worketh in you." "Perfecting holiness in the fear of God" (2 Cor. 7:1).

It has often been said that the lack of the fear of God is one of the things in which our modern times cannot compare favorably with the times of the Puritans and the Covenanters. No wonder, then, that there is so much cause of complaint in regard to the reading of God's Word, of the worship in His House, and the absence of that spirit of continuous prayer which marked the early church. We need texts like the one at the head of this reading, and the young converts fully instructed in the need and the blessedness of a deep fear of God, leading to an unceasing prayerfulness as one of the essential elements of the life of faith.

Let us in the inner chamber earnestly cultivate this grace. Let us hear the word coming out of the very heavens:

"Who shall not fear thee, O Lord, and glorify thy name? for thou only art holy."

"*Let us have grace whereby we may serve God acceptably* with reverence and godly fear."

As we take the word, "*Blessed is the man that feareth the Lord,*" into our hearts and believe that here is one of the deepest secrets of blessedness, we will seek in every approach to God, in His fear to worship toward His holy temple.

"*Serve the Lord with fear, and rejoice with trembling.*"

April 20

God Incomprehensible

Behold, God is great, and we know him not. The Almighty, we cannot find him out: he is excellent in power. —Job 36:26; 37:23

This attribute of God as a Spirit whose being and glory are entirely beyond our power of apprehension is one we ponder all too little. And yet in the spiritual life it is of the utmost importance to feel deeply that, as the heavens are high above the earth, so God's thoughts and ways are infinitely exalted beyond all our thought.

With what deep humility and holy reverence it becomes us to look up to God, and then with childlike simplicity to yield ourselves to the teaching of His Holy Spirit.

"Oh the depth of the riches both of the wisdom and knowledge of God! How unsearchable are his judgments, and his ways past finding out" (Rom. 11:33).

Let our hearts respond, "O Lord, O God of gods, how wonderful art thou in all thy thoughts, and thy purposes how deep." The study of what God is ought ever to fill us with holy awe and the sacred longing to know and honor Him as He deserves.

Just think—

His greatness—incomprehensible.
His might—incomprehensible.
His omnipresence—incomprehensible.
His wisdom—incomprehensible.
His holiness—incomprehensible.
His mercy—incomprehensible.
His love—incomprehensible.

As we worship, let us cry out, "What an inconceivable glory is in this great being who is my God and Father!" Confess with shame how little you have sought to know Him correctly, or to wait upon Him to reveal himself. Begin in faith to trust that in a way passing all understanding, this incomprehensible and all-glorious God will work in your heart and life and give you in ever-growing measure to know Him as He is.

"Mine eyes are unto thee, O God the Lord: in thee is my trust" (Ps. 141:8).

"Be still, and know that I am God" (Ps. 46:10).

April 21

The Holiness of God (O.T.)

Be holy, for I am holy.... I am the Lord, that make you holy.—
Leviticus 11:45; 19:2; 20:7, 8; 21:8, 15, 23; 22:9, 16

Nine times these words are repeated in Leviticus. Israel
had to learn that as holiness is the highest and most glorious
attribute of God, so it must be the marked characteristic of
His people. He who would know God as He is, and meet Him
in secret, must above all desire to be holy as He is holy.
The priests who were to have access to God had to be set
apart for a life of holiness.

Even so also the prophet who was to speak for Him (Isa.
6). Listen. "I saw the Lord sitting upon a throne, high and
lifted up. And the seraphs cried one unto another: 'Holy, holy,
holy is the Lord of Hosts.' " The voice of adoration.

"Then said I: *'Woe is me, for I am undone; for mine eyes
have seen the King, the Lord of Hosts.' "* The voice of a broken,
contrite heart.

"Then one of the seraphim touched his mouth with a live
coal from off the altar, and said: *'Lo, thine iniquity is taken
from thee, and thy sin is purged.' "* The voice of grace
and full redemption.

Then follows the voice of God: *"Whom shall I send?"*
And the willing answer is, "Here am I, send me." Pause
with holy fear and ask God to reveal himself as the Holy
One.

"Thus saith the high and lofty One, that inhabiteth eternity,
whose name is Holy: 'I dwell in the high and holy place,
with him also that is of a contrite and humble spirit" (Isa.
57:15).

Be still and take time and worship God in His great glory,
and in that deep condescension in which He longs and offers
to dwell with us and in us.

Child of God, if you would meet your Father in secret,
bow low and worship Him in the glory of His holiness. Give
Him time to make himself known to you.

It is indeed an unspeakable grace to know God as the Holy
One.

"Ye shall be holy: for I the Lord your God am holy."

"Holy, holy, holy is the Lord of Hosts."

"Worship the Lord in the beauty of holiness."

"Let the beauty of the Lord our God be upon us" (Ps.
90:17).

April 22

The Holiness of God (N.T.)

Holy Father, keep through thine own name those whom thou hast given me. Sanctify them. For their sakes I sanctify myself, that they also might be sanctified through the truth. —John 17:11, 17, 19

Christ ever liveth to pray this great prayer. Expect and appropriate God's answer.

Hear the words of Paul in 1 Thessalonians: "Night and day praying exceedingly that the Lord may stablish your hearts unblameable in holiness before God" (3:10-13).

"The very God of peace sanctify you wholly" (5:23).

"Who also will do it" (5:24).

Ponder deeply these words as you read them, and use them as a prayer to God: "Blessed Lord, strengthen my heart to be unblameable in holiness. God himself sanctify me wholly. God is faithful, who also will do it."

What a privilege to commune with God in secret, to speak these words in prayer and then to wait upon Him until through the working of the Spirit, they live in our hearts and we begin to know something of the holiness of God.

"Unto the church of God which is at Corinth, *to them that are sanctified in Christ Jesus, called to be saints*" (1 Cor. 1:2).

God's holiness has been revealed in the Old Testament. In the New, we find the holiness of God's people in Christ, through the sanctification of the Spirit. Oh, that we understood the blessedness of saying: "Be ye holy, for I am holy."

"With you, O my children, as with Me, holiness should be the chief thing." For this purpose the Thrice Holy One has revealed himself to us through the Son and the Holy Spirit. Let us use the word "holy" with great reverence of God, and then with holy desire, for ourselves. Worship the God who says: *"I am the Lord which hallow you."*

Bow before Him in holy fear and strong desire, and then, in the fullness of faith, listen to the prayer promise: "God himself sanctify you wholly, who also will do it."

April 23

Sin

The chief of sinners.... And the grace of our Lord was exceeding abundant with faith and love which is in Christ Jesus.—1 Timothy 1:14, 15

Never forget for a moment, as you enter the secret chamber, that your whole relation to God depends on what you think of sin and of yourself as a redeemed sinner.

It is sin that makes God's holiness so awful. It is sin that makes God's holiness so glorious, because He has said: "Be ye holy. I am holy. I am the Lord which makes you holy" (Lev. 20:7, 8).

It is sin that called forth the wonderful love of God in not sparing His Son. It was sin that nailed Jesus to the cross and revealed the depth and the power of the love with which He loved. Through all eternity in the glory of heaven, it is our being redeemed sinners that will tune our praise.

Never for a moment forget that it is sin that has led to the great transaction between you and Christ Jesus; and that each day in your fellowship with God His one aim is to deliver and keep you fully from its power, and lift you up into His likeness and His infinite love.

It is the thought of sin that will keep you low at His feet and give the deep undertone to all your adoration.

It is the thought of sin, ever surrounding you and seeking to tempt you, that will give fervency to your prayer and urgency to the faith that hides itself in Christ.

It is the thought of sin that makes Christ so unspeakably precious, that keeps you every moment dependent on His grace, and gives you the claim to be more than conqueror through Him that loved us.

It is the thought of sin that calls to us to thank God with the broken and contrite heart, which God will not despise, that works in us that contrite and humble spirit in which He delights to dwell.

It is in the inner chamber, in secret with the Father, that sin can be conquered, the holiness of Christ can be imparted, and the Spirit of holiness take possession of our lives.

It is in the inner chamber that we will learn to know and to experience fully the divine power of the precious words of promise: "The blood of Jesus Christ cleanseth us from all sin." "He that abideth in him sinneth not" (1 John 1:7; 3:6).

April 24

The Mercy of God

Oh, give thanks unto the Lord; for he is good: for his mercy endureth for ever.—Psalm 136:1

This Psalm is wholly devoted to the praise of God's mercy. In each of the twenty-six verses we have the expression: "His mercy endureth for ever." The psalmist was full of this glad thought. Our hearts too should be filled with the blessed assurance. The everlasting, unchangeable mercy of God is cause for unceasing praise and thanksgiving.

Let us read what is said about God's mercy in the well-known Psalm 103:

"Bless the Lord, O my soul: who crowneth thee with lovingkindness and tender mercies" (v. 4).

Of all God's other attributes, mercy is the crown. May it be a crown upon my head and in my life!

"The lord is merciful and gracious, and plenteous in mercy" (v. 8). As wonderful as God's greatness is, so infinite is His mercy.

"As the heaven is high above the earth, so great is his mercy toward them that fear him" (v. 11).

What a thought! *As high as the heaven is above the earth*, so immeasurably and inconceivably great is the mercy of God waiting to bestow His richest blessing.

"The mercy of the Lord is from everlasting to everlasting upon them that fear him" (v. 17). Here again the psalmist speaks of God's boundless lovingkindness and mercy.

O my soul, how frequently we have read these familiar words without the least thought of their immeasurable greatness! Be still, and meditate until the heart responds in the words of Psalm 36:

"Thy mercy, O Lord, is in the heavens."

"How excellent is thy lovingkindness, O God! therefore the children of men put their trust under the shadow of thy wings."

"Oh, continue thy lovingkindness unto them that know thee."

O child of God, take time to thank God with great joy for the wonderful mercy with which He crowns your life, and say: "Thy lovingkindness is better than life."

April 25

The Word of God

The Word of God is quick and powerful.—Hebrews 4:12

For conversation with God, His Word and prayer are both indispensable; and in the inner chamber they should not be separated. In His Word, God speaks to me; in prayer, I speak to God.

The Word teaches me to know the God to whom I pray; it teaches me how He would have me pray. It gives me precious promises to encourage me in prayer. It often gives me wonderful answers to prayer.

The Word comes from God's heart and brings His thoughts and His love into my heart. And then the Word goes back from my heart into His great heart of love, and prayer is the means of fellowship between God's heart and mine.

The Word teaches me God's will—the will of His promises as to what He will do for me, as food for my faith, and also the will of His commands, to which I surrender myself in loving obedience.

The more I pray, the more I feel my need of the Word, and rejoice in it. The more I read God's Word, the more I have to pray about, and the more power I have in prayer. One great cause of prayerlessness is that we read God's Word too little, or only superficially, or in the light of human wisdom.

It is the Holy Spirit through whom the Word has been spoken, who is also the Spirit of prayer. He will teach me how to receive the Word and how to approach God.

How blessed would the inner chamber be, what a power and an inspiration in our worship, if we only took God's Word as from himself, turning it into prayer and definitely expecting an answer. It is in the inner chamber, in the secret of God's presence, that by the Holy Spirit God's Word will become our delight and our strength.

God's Word in deepest reverence in our hearts, on our lips, and in our lives will be a never-failing fountain of strength and blessing.

Let us believe that God's Word is indeed full of a quickening power that will make us strong, gladly to expect and receive great things from God. Above all, it will give us the daily blessed fellowship with Him as the living God.

"Blessed is the man whose delight is in the law of the Lord; in his law doth he meditate day and night" (Ps. 1:1, 2).

April 26

The Psalms

How sweet are thy words unto my taste! yea, sweeter than honey to my mouth!—Psalm 119:103

These devotionals seek to help us to worship God. Of the sixty-six books in the Bible, the Book of Psalms is given us specially for this purpose. The other books are historical, or doctrinal, or practical. But the Psalms take us into the inner sanctuary of God's holy presence, to enjoy the blessedness of fellowship with Him. It is a book of devotions inspired by the Holy Spirit.

If you would each morning truly meet God and worship Him in spirit and in truth, *then let your heart be filled with the Word of God in the Psalms.*

As you read the Psalms, underline the word "Lord" or "God," wherever it occurs, and also the pronouns referring to God, "I," "Thou," "He." This will help to connect the contents of the Psalm with God, who is the object of all prayer. When you have taken the trouble to mark the different names of God, you will find that more than one difficult Psalm will have light shed upon it. These underlined words will make God the central thought, and lead you to a new worship of Him. Take them upon your lips and speak them out before Him. Your faith will anew be strengthened to realize how God is your strength and help in all circumstances of life.

The Psalms, as the Holy Spirit of old taught God's people to pray, will, by the power of that Spirit, teach us, too, ever to abide in God's presence.

Then take Psalm 119. Every time the word "Lord," or "Thou," or "Thy" occurs, underline it. You will be surprised to find that each verse contains these words once, or more than once. Meditate on the thought that the God who is found throughout the whole Psalm is the same God who gives us His law, and will enable us to keep it.

The Psalm will soon become one of the most beloved, and you will find its prayers and its teaching concerning God's Word drawing you continually up to God, in the blessed consciousness of His power and love.

"Oh, how love I thy law! It is my meditation all the day" (Ps. 119:97).

April 27

The Glory of God

Unto him be glory throughout all ages.—Ephesians 3:21

God himself must reveal His glory to us; then alone are we able to know and glorify Him properly.

There is no more wonderful image in nature of the glory of God than we find in the starry heavens. The telescopes, which are continually made more powerful, have long proclaimed the wonders of God's universe. And by means of photography, new wonders of that glory have been revealed. A photographic plate fixed below the telescope will reveal millions of stars, which could never have been seen by the eye through the best telescope. Man must step on one side, and allow the glory of the heavens to reveal itself; and the stars, at first wholly invisible and at immense distances, will leave their image upon the plate.

What a lesson for the soul that longs to see the glory of God in His Word. Put aside your own efforts and thoughts. Let your heart be as a photographic plate that waits for God's glory to be revealed. The plate must be rightly prepared and clean; let your heart be prepared and purified by God's Spirit.

"Blessed are the pure in heart, for they shall see God." The plate must be immovable; let your heart be still before God. The plate must be exposed sometimes for seven or eight hours to receive the full impression of the farthest stars; let your heart take time in silent waiting upon God, and He will reveal His glory.

If you keep silence before God and give Him time, He will put thoughts into your heart that may be of unspeakable blessing to yourself and others. He will create within you desires and dispositions that will indeed be as the rays of His glory shining in you.

Put this to the proof today. Offer your spirit to Him in deep humility, and have faith that God will reveal himself in His holy love. His glory will descend upon you. You will yourself feel the need of giving Him full time to do His blessed work.

"The Lord is in his holy temple; let all the earth keep silence before him."

"My soul, wait thou only upon God; for my expectation is from him."

"God hath shined in our hearts, to give the light of the knowledge of the glory of God in the face of Christ Jesus" (2 Cor. 4:6).

"Be still, and know that I am God."

April 28

The Holy Trinity

Elect according to the foreknowledge of God the Father, through sanctification of the Spirit, unto obedience and sprinkling of the blood of Jesus Christ. —1 Peter 1:2

Here we have one of the texts in which the great truth of the blessed Trinity is seen to lie at the very root of our spiritual life. In this series we have spoken specially of the adoration of God the Father, and the need of time, sufficient time each day, to worship Him in some of His glorious attributes. But we must remind ourselves that, for all our contact with God, the presence and the power of the Son and the Spirit are absolutely necessary.

What a field this opens for us in the inner chamber. We need time to realize how all our conversation with the Father is conditioned by the active and personal presence and working of the Lord Jesus. It takes time to become fully conscious of what need I have of Him in every approach to God, what confidence I may have in the work that He is doing for me and in me, and what the holy and intimate love is in which I may count upon His presence and all-prevailing intercession. But oh to learn the lesson that it takes time, and that that time will be most blessedly rewarded!

Even so, too, with the divine and almighty power of the Holy Spirit working in the depth of my heart, as the One who alone is able to reveal the Son within me. Through Him alone I have the power to know what and how to pray; above all, how to plead the name of Jesus, and to receive the assurance that my prayer has been accepted.

Have you not felt more than once that it was as it were a mockery to speak of five minutes to be alone with God, to come under the impression of His glory? And now does not the thought of the true worship of God in Christ Jesus through the Holy Spirit make you feel more than ever that it requires time to enter into such Holy alliance with God as to keep the heart and mind all day in His peace and presence? *It is in tarrying in the secret of God's presence that you receive grace to abide in Christ, and all the day to be led by His Spirit.*

Just pause and think: "Elect according to the foreknowledge of God the Father, through sanctification of the Spirit, unto obedience and sprinkling of the blood of Jesus Christ!" What food for thought—and worship!

April 29

The Love of God

God is love; and he that dwelleth in love dwelleth in God, and God in him. —1 John 4:16

The best and most wonderful word in heaven is love. For God is love. And the best and most wonderful word in the inner chamber must be love. For the God who meets us there is love.

What is love? The deep desire to give itself for the beloved. Love finds its joy in imparting all that it has to make the loved one happy. And the Heavenly Father, who offers to meet us in the inner chamber—let there be no doubt of this in our minds—has no other object than to fill our hearts with His love.

All the other attributes of God which have been mentioned find in love their highest glory. The true and full blessing of the inner chamber is nothing less than a life in the abundant love of God.

Because of this, our first and chief thought in the inner chamber should be faith in the love of God. Seek, as you set yourself to pray, to exercise great and unbounded faith in the love of God.

Take time, O my soul, in silence to meditate on the wonderful revelation of God's love in Christ until you are filled with the spirit of worship and wonder and longing desire. Take time to believe the precious truth: *"The love of God is shed abroad in our hearts by the Holy Ghost which is given unto us."*

Let us remember with shame how little we have believed in, and sought after, this love. And as we pray, let us hold fast this assurance: I am confident that my Heavenly Father longs to manifest His love to me. I am deeply convinced of the truth: He will and can do it.

"Yea, I have loved thee with an everlasting love" (Jer. 31:3).

"That ye, being rooted and grounded in love, may be able to comprehend with all saints what is the breadth, and length, and depth, and height; and to know the love of Christ, which passeth knowledge" (Eph. 3:17, 18, 19).

"Behold what manner of love the Father hath bestowed upon us" (1 John 3:1).

April 30

The Praise of God

Praise is comely for the upright.—Psalm 33:1

Praise will ever be a part of adoration. Adoration, when it has entered God's presence, and had fellowship with Him, will ever lead to the praise of His name. Let praise be a part of the incense we bring before God in our quiet time.

It was when the children of Israel, at their birth as the people of God at the Red Sea, had been delivered from the power of Egypt that in the song of Moses the joy of redemption burst forth in praise: "Who is like unto thee, O lord, among the gods? Who is like thee, glorious in holiness, fearful in praises, doing wonders?"

In the Psalms we see what a large place praise ought to have in the spiritual life. There are more than sixty Psalms of praise, becoming more frequent as the book draws to its close. See Psalms 90-101, 103-107, 111-118, 136-138, 144-150. The last five are all hallelujah psalms, with the words "Praise ye the Lord" as the beginning and the ending. And the very last repeats "praise him," twice in every verse, and ends, "Let everything that hath breath praise the Lord."

Let us take time to study this until our whole heart and life be one continual song of praise.

May

The Secret of the Abiding Presence

May 1

The Abiding Presence

Lo, I am with you alway, even unto the end of the world.—Matthew 28:20

When the Lord chose His twelve disciples, it was "that they should be with him, and that he might send them forth to preach" (Mark 3:14). A life in fellowship with the Lord was to be their preparation and their fitness for the work of preaching.

So deeply were the disciples conscious of this having been their great privilege that when Christ spoke of His leaving them to go to the Father, their hearts were filled with great sorrow. The presence of Christ had become indispensable to them; they could not think of living without Him. To comfort them, Christ gave them the promise of the Holy Spirit, with the assurance that they then would have Him in His heavenly presence, in a sense far deeper and more intimate than they ever had known on earth. The law of their first vocation remained unchanged: to be with Him, to live in unbroken fellowship with Him, would be the secret of power to preach and to testify of Him.

When Christ gave them the Great Commission to go into all the world and to preach the gospel to every creature, He added the words: "Lo, I am with you alway, even unto the end of the world."

For all time the principle is to hold good for all His servants that without the experience of His presence ever abiding with them, their preaching would have no power. The secret of their strength would be the living testimony that Jesus Christ was every moment with them, inspiring and directing and strengthening them. It was this that made them so bold in preaching Him as the Crucified One in the midst of His enemies. They never for a moment regretted His bodily absence; they had Him with them, and in them, in the divine power of the Holy Spirit.

In all work of the minister and the missionary, everything depends on the consciousness, through a living faith, of the abiding presence of the Lord with His servant, the living experience of the presence of Jesus as an essential element in preaching the gospel. If this be clouded, work becomes a human effort, without the freshness and the power of the heavenly life. Nothing can bring back the power and the blessing but a return to the Master's feet: "Lo, I am with you alway!"

May 2

The Omnipotence of Christ

All power is given unto me in heaven and on earth.—Matthew 28:19

Before Christ gave His disciples their Great Commission to begin that great world conquest which should aim at bringing His gospel to every creature, He first revealed himself in His divine power as a partner with God himself, the Almighty One. It was the faith of this that enabled the disciples to undertake the work in all simplicity and boldness. They had begun to know Him in that mighty resurrection power which had conquered sin and death; there was nothing too great for Him to command or for them to undertake.

Every disciple of Jesus Christ who desires to take part in the victory that overcomes the world needs time, and faith, and the Holy Spirit to come under the full conviction that it is as the servant of the omnipotent Lord Jesus that he is to take his part in the work. He is to count literally upon the daily experience of being "strong in the Lord and in the power of his might." The word of promise gives the courage to obey implicitly the word of command.

Just think of what the disciples had learned to know of the power of Christ Jesus here on earth. And yet that was but a little thing as compared with the greater works that He was now to do in and through them. He has the power to work even in the feeblest of His servants with the strength of the almighty God. He has power even to use their apparent impotence to carry out His purposes. He has the power over every enemy and every human heart, over every difficulty and danger.

But let us remember that this power is never meant to be experienced as if it were our own. It is only as Jesus Christ as a living person dwells and works with His divine energy in our own heart and life that there can be a power in our preaching as a personal testimony. It was when Christ had said to Paul, "My strength is made perfect in weakness," that he could say what he had never learned to say before, "When I am weak, then am I strong." It is the disciple of Christ who understands aright that all the power has been entrusted to Him, to be received from Him hour by hour, who will feel the need and experience the power of that precious word: "Lo, I am with you alway," the Almighty One.

May 3

The Omnipresence of Christ

Certainly, I will be with thee.—Exodus 3:12

The first thought of man in his conception of a God is that of power, however limited. The first thought of the true God is His omnipotence: "I am God Almighty." The second thought in Scripture is His omnipresence. God ever gave His servants the promise of His unseen presence with them. To His "I am with thee," their faith responded: "Thou art with me."

When Christ had said to His disciples, "All power is given unto me in heaven and on earth," the promise immediately follows, "I am with you alway." The Omnipotent One is surely the Omnipresent One.

The writer of Psalm 139 speaks of God's omnipresence as something beyond his comprehension: "Such knowledge is too wonderful for me; it is high, I cannot attain unto it."

The revelation of God's omnipresence in the man Christ Jesus makes the mystery still deeper. It also makes the grace that enables us to claim this presence as our strength and our joy something unexpressibly blessed. And yet how many a servant of Christ, when the promise is given him, finds it difficult to understand all that is implied in it, and how it can become the practical experience of his daily life.

Here, as elsewhere in the spiritual life, everything depends upon faith accepting Christ's word as a divine reality, and trusting the Holy Spirit to make it true to us from moment to moment. When Christ says "always" (Gr. "all the days"), He means to give us the assurance that there is not to be a day of our life in which that blessed presence is not to be with us. And that "all the days" implies "all the day." There need not be a moment in which that presence cannot be our experience. It does not depend upon us, but upon what He undertakes to do. The omnipotent Christ is the omnipresent Christ, the ever-present is the everlasting, the unchangeable One. As sure as He is the unchangeable One will His presence, as the power of an endless life, be with each of His servants who trusts Him for it.

"Lo, I am with you alway." Let our faith in Christ, the Omnipresent One, be in the quiet confidence that He will every day and every moment keep us in perfect peace, and in the sure experience of all the light and the strength we need in His service.

May 4

Christ, the Savior of the World

This is indeed the Christ, the Savior of the world.—John 4:42

Omnipotence and omnipresence are what are called natural attributes of God. They have their true worth only when linked to and inspired by His moral attributes, holiness and love. When our Lord spoke of the omnipotence having been given to Him— all power on earth and in heaven—and the omnipresence—His presence with each of His disciples—His words pointed to that which lies at the root of all—His divine glory as the Savior of the world and Redeemer of men.

It was because He humbled himself and became obedient to death, the death of the cross, that God so highly exalted Him. His share as the man Christ Jesus in the attributes of God was due to the work He had done in His perfect obedience to the will of God and the finished redemption He had accomplished for the salvation of men.

This gives meaning and worth to what He says of himself as the omnipotent and omnipresent One. Between His mention of these two attributes He gives His command that they should go out into all the world and preach the gospel, and teach men to obey all that He has commanded. It is as the Redeemer who saves and keeps from sin, as the Lord Christ who claims obedience to all He has commanded, that He promises His divine presence to be with His servants.

It follows as a matter of necessity that it is only when His servants in their lives show that they obey Him in all His commands, that they can expect the fullness of His power and His presence to be with them. It is only when they themselves are living witnesses to the reality of His power to save and to keep from sin that they can expect the full experience of His abiding presence, and that they will have power to train others to the life of obedience that He asks.

Yes, it is Jesus Christ who saves His people from their sin, who rules over a people willing in the day of His power, and proves in them that He enables them to say, "I delight to do thy will, O my God," who says, "Lo, I am with you alway." The abiding presence of the Savior from sin is promised to all who have accepted Him in the fullness of His redeeming power, and who preach by their lives as well as by their words what a wonderful Savior He is.

May 5

Christ Crucified

God forbid that I should glory, save in the cross of our Lord Jesus Christ, through which the world hath been crucified unto me, and I unto the world.—Galatians 6:14

Christ's highest glory is His cross. It was in this that He glorified the Father, and the Father glorified Him. As the Lamb slain in the midst of the throne in Revelation 5, He receives the worship of the ransomed and the angels and all creation. And it is as the Crucified One that His servants have learned to say: "God forbid that I should glory save in the cross of our Lord Jesus Christ, through which I am crucified to the world." Is it not reasonable that Christ's highest glory should be our only glory too?

When the Lord Jesus said to His disciples, "Lo, I am with you alway," it was as the Crucified One, who had shown them His hands and His feet, that He gave the promise. And to each one who seeks to claim the promise, it is of the first importance that he should realize: it is the crucified Jesus who promises, who offers, to be with me every day.

May not this be one reason why we find it so difficult to expect and enjoy the abiding presence—because we do not glory in the cross by which we are crucified to the world? We have been crucified with Christ; our "old man was crucified with him"; "they that are Christ's have crucified the flesh with its affections and lusts." Yet how little we have learned that the world has been crucified to us and that we are free from its power.

How little we have learned, as those who are crucified with Christ, to deny ourselves, to have the mind that was in Christ when He emptied himself and took the form of a servant and humbled himself and became obedient even to the death of the cross.

Oh, let us learn the lesson, it is the crucified Christ who comes to walk with us every day, and in whose power we, too, are to live the life that can say: "I have been crucified with Christ"; "Christ crucified lives in me."

May 6

Christ Glorified

The Lamb which is in the midst of the throne shall be their shepherd.
These are they which follow the Lamb whithersoever he goeth.—Revelation 7:17; 14:4

"Lo, I am with you alway." Who is this who thus speaks?
We must take time to know Him well if we are to understand
what we may expect from Him as He offers to be with us
all the day. Who is He? None other than the Lamb who had
been slain in the midst of the throne! The Lamb in His deepest
humiliation enthroned in the glory of God. This is He who
speaks and invites me to the closest fellowship and likeness
to himself.

It needs time and deep reverence and adoring worship to
come under the full impression that He who dwelleth in the
glory of the Father, before whom all heaven bows in prostrate
adoration, is none other than He who offers to be my companion, to lead me like a shepherd, who cares for each individual sheep, and so to make me one of those who follow the
Lamb wherever He goes.

Read often that wonderful fifth chapter of Revelation until
your heart is possessed by the one great thought of how all
heaven falls prostrate, the elders cast their crowns before the
throne, and the Lamb reigns amid the praises and the love
of His ransomed ones and the praises of all creation. And if
this is He who comes to me in my daily life, and offers to
walk with me, and to be my strength and my joy and my
almighty Keeper, surely I cannot expect Him to abide with
me except as my heart bows, if possible, in a still deeper reverence and in a surrender to a life of praise and service such
as may be worthy of the love that has redeemed me.

O Christian, do believe that the Lamb in the midst of the
throne is in very deed the embodiment of the omnipotent glory
of the everlasting God and of His love. And do believe that
to have this Lamb of God as your almighty Shepherd and your
faithful Keeper does indeed make it possible that the thoughts
and the cares of earth shall not be able to separate you from
His love for a single moment.

May 7

The Great Question

Believe ye that I am able to do this? They said unto him, Yea, Lord.
—Matthew 9:28

"If thou canst believe, all things are possible to him that believeth. And straightway the father of the child said with tears: Lord, I believe, help thou mine unbelief" (Mark 9:23, 24). "Jesus said, He that believeth in me, though he were dead, yet shall he live. Believest thou this? She saith unto him, Yea, Lord, I believe" (John 11:25, 26, 27).

To what we have seen and heard of Christ Jesus, our heart is ready to say with Martha, in answer to Christ's question: "Yea, Lord, I have believed that thou art the Christ, the Son of God." But when it comes to the point of believing that what Christ promises us of the power of the resurrection life, of His abiding presence every day and all the day, we do not find it so easy to say, "I do believe that this omnipotent, omnipresent, unchangeable Christ, our Redeemer God, will in very deed walk with me all the day, and give me the unceasing consciousness of His holy presence"—it almost looks too much to venture. And yet it is just this faith for which Christ asks and is waiting to work within us.

It is well that we understand clearly what the conditions are on which Christ offers to reveal to us in experience the secret of His abiding presence. God cannot force His blessings on us against our will. He seeks in every possible way to stir our desire and to help us realize He is able and most willing to make His promises true. The resurrection of Christ from the dead is His great plea, His all-prevailing argument. If He could raise that dead Christ who had died under the burden of all our sin and curse, surely He can, now that Christ has conquered death and is to us the Resurrection and the Life, fulfill in our hearts His promise that Christ can be so with us, and so in us that He himself should be our life all the day.

And now the great question comes, whether in view of what we have said and seen about Christ as our Lord, as our redeeming God, whether we are willing to take His word in all simplicity in its divine fullness of meaning, and to rest in the promise: "Lo, I am with you all the day." Christ's question comes to us: "Believest thou this?" Let us not rest until we have bowed before Him and said: "Yea, Lord, I do believe."

May 8

Christ Manifesting Himself

He that hath my commandments, and keepeth them, he it is that loveth me; and he that loveth me shall be loved of my Father, and I will love him, and will manifest myself unto him.—John 14:21

Christ had promised the disciples that the Holy Spirit would come to reveal His presence as ever with them. When the Spirit thus came, He through the Spirit, would manifest himself to them. They should know Him in a new, divine, spiritual way; in the power of the Spirit they should know Him, and have Him far more intimately and unceasingly with them than they ever had upon earth.

The condition of this revelation of himself is comprised in the one word—love: "He that keepeth my commandments, he it is that loveth me; and he that loveth me shall be loved of my Father, and I will love him." It is to be the meeting of divine and human love. The love with which Christ had loved them had taken possession of their hearts, and would show itself in the love of a full and absolute obedience. The Father would see this, and His love would rest upon the soul; Christ would love him with the special love drawn out by the loving heart, and would manifest himself. The love of heaven shed abroad in the heart would be met by the new and blessed revelation of Christ himself.

But this is not all. When the question was asked, "What is it, that thou wilt thus manifest thyself?" the answer came in the repetition of the words, "If a man love me, he will keep my word"; and then again, "My Father will love him, and we will come unto him and make our abode with him." In the heart thus prepared by the Holy Spirit, showing itself in the obedience of love in a fully surrendered heart, the Father and the Son will take up their abode.

And now, nothing less is what Christ promises them: "Lo, I am with you alway." That "with" implies "in"—Christ with the Father, dwelling in the heart by faith. Oh, that everyone who would enter into the secret of the abiding presence—"Lo, I am with you alway"—would study, and believe, and claim in childlike simplicity the blessed promise: "I will manifest myself unto him."

May 9

Mary: The Morning Watch

Jesus saith unto her, Mary. She turned herself, and saith unto him, Rabboni; which is to say, Master.—John 20:16

Here we have the first manifestation of the risen Savior to Mary Magdalene, the woman who loved much.

Think of what the morning watch meant to Mary. Is it not a proof of the intense longing of a love that would not rest until it had found the Lord it sought? It meant many things: A separation from all else, even from the chief of the apostles, in her longing to find Christ. The struggle of fear against a faith that refused to let go its hold of its wonderful promise. Christ's coming and fulfilling the promise: "If a man love me, he will keep my words, and I will love him and manifest myself to him." Her love was met by the love of Jesus, and she found Him, the living Lord, in all the power of His resurrection life. She now understood what He had said about ascending to the Father, to the life of divine and omnipotent glory. It meant, finally, that she received her commission from her Lord to go and tell His brethren of what she had heard from Him.

That first morning watch, waiting for the risen Lord to reveal himself, what a prophecy and a pledge of what the morning watch has been to thousands of souls! In fear and doubt, and yet with a burning love and strong hope, they waited until He of whom they had known but little, by reason of their human feeble apprehension, should breathe upon them in the power of His resurrection life and reveal himself as the Lord of glory. And there they learned, not in words or thought, but in the reality of a divine experience, what it was that He, to whom all power had been given on earth and in heaven, had now taken them up into the keeping of His abiding presence.

And what are we now to learn? That there is nothing that can prove a greater attraction to our Lord than the love that sacrifices everything and rests satisfied with nothing less than himself. It is to such a love that Christ manifests himself. He loved us and gave himself for us. Christ's love needs our love in which to reveal itself: It is to our love that He speaks the word: "Lo, I am with you alway." It is love that accepts and rejoices in and lives in that word.

May 10

Emmaus: The Evening Prayer

They constrained him, saying, Abide with us.... And he went in to tarry with them. And... as he sat at meat with them... their eyes were opened, and they knew him.—Luke 24:29-31

If Mary teaches us what the morning watch can be for the revelation of Jesus to the soul, Emmaus reminds us of the place that the evening prayer may have in preparing for the full revelation of Christ in the soul.

To the two disciples the day had begun in thick darkness. When at length the women told of the angel who had said that He was alive, they knew not what to think. When "Jesus himself drew near," their eyes were blind, and they knew Him not. How often Jesus does come near with the one object of manifesting himself, but is hindered because we are so slow of heart to believe what the Word has spoken. But as the Lord spake with them, their hearts began to burn within them, and yet there never was a thought that it might be himself. It is often so even now. The Word becomes precious to us in the fellowship of the saints; our hearts are stirred with the new vision of what Christ's presence may be, and yet—the eyes are blind and we see Him not.

When the Lord made as though to go farther, their prayer, "Abide with us," constrained Him. Christ had given in the last night a new meaning to the word "abide." They did not yet understand that, but in the use of it received far more than they expected, a foretaste of that life of abiding which the resurrection had now made possible. Let us learn the lesson of how necessary it is that toward the close of the day there should be a pause, perhaps in fellowship with others, when the whole heart takes up anew the promise of the abiding presence and prays with the urgency that constrains Him: "Abide, abide with us."

And what is now the chief lesson of the story? What was it that led our Lord to reveal himself to these two men? Nothing less than this: their intense devotion to their Lord. There may be much ignorance and unbelief, but if there be a burning desire that above everything longs for Him, a desire that is ever fostered as the Word is heard or spoken, we may count upon it, He will make himself known to us. To such intense devotion and constraining prayer, our Lord's message will be given in power: "Lo, I am with you alway"; our eyes will be opened, and we will know Him and the blessed secret of the abiding presence always.

May 11

The Disciples: Their Divine Mission

The same day at evening... when the doors were shut where the disciples were assembled for fear of the Jews, came Jesus and stood in the midst, and saith unto them, Peace be unto you.—John 20:19

The disciples had received the message of Mary. Peter had told them he had seen the Lord. Late in the evening the men from Emmaus told how He had been made known to them. Their hearts were prepared for what now came, when Jesus stood in the midst of them and said, "Peace be unto you," and showed them His hands and His feet. This was not only to be a sign of recognition, but the deep eternal mystery of what would be seen in heaven when He was in the midst of the throne, "a Lamb as it had been slain."

"Then were the disciples glad when they saw the Lord." And He spoke again: "Peace be unto you! As the Father sent me, so send I you." With Mary He revealed himself to the fervent love that could not rest without Him. With the men at Emmaus it was their constraining prayer that received the revelation. Here He meets the willing servants whom He had trained for His service, and hands over to them the work He had done on earth. He changes their fear into the boldness of peace and gladness. He ascends to the Father; the work the Father had given Him to do He now entrusts to them. The divine mission is now theirs to make known and carry out to victory.

For this divine work they need nothing less than divine power. He breathes upon them the resurrection life He had won by His death. He fulfills the promise He gave: "I live, and ye shall live also." The mighty power of God by which He raised Christ from the dead, none other than that spirit of holiness by which He, as the Son of God, was raised from the dead, will henceforth work in them. And all that was bound or loosed in that power would be bound in heaven.

The story comes to every messenger of the gospel with wonderful power. To us, too, the word is spoken: "As the Father sent me, so send I you." For us, too, is the word: "Receive ye the Holy Ghost." For us, too, the personal manifestation of Jesus as the Living One, with the pierced hands and feet. If our hearts are set on nothing less than the presence of the living Lord, we may be confident it will be given us. Jesus never sends His servants out without the promise of His abiding presence and His almighty power.

May 12

Thomas: The Blessedness of Believing

Jesus saith unto him, Thomas, because thou hast seen me, thou hast believed: blessed are they that have not seen, and yet have believed.
—John 20:29

We all count the blessedness of Thomas as something astonishing: Christ showing himself and allowing Thomas to touch His hands and His side. No wonder that this blessedness can find no words but those of holy adoration: "My Lord and my God." Has there ever been higher expression of the overwhelming nearness and glory of God?

And yet Christ said: "Because thou hast seen me, thou hast believed: blessed are they that have not seen, and yet have believed." True, living faith gives a sense of Christ's divine nearness far deeper and more intimate than even the joy that filled the heart of Thomas. Here, even now, after the lapse of all these centuries, we may have experienced the presence and power of Christ in a far deeper reality than Thomas did. To those who see not, yet believe, simply, only, truly, fully believe in what Christ is and can be to them every moment, He has promised He will manifest himself, and that the Father and He will come and dwell in them.

Have we not often been inclined to think of this full life of faith as something far beyond our reach? Such a thought robs us of the power to believe. Let us turn to take hold of Christ's word: "Blessed are they that have not seen, and yet believe." This is indeed the heavenly blessing, filling the whole heart and life, the faith that receives the love and the presence of the living Lord.

You ask how to come to this childlike faith. The answer is simple. Where Jesus Christ is the one object of our desire and our confidence, He will reveal himself in divine power. Thomas had proved his intense devotion to Christ when he said, "Let us go, that we may die with him." To such a love, even when it is struggling with unbelief, Jesus Christ will reveal himself. He will make His holy promise an actual reality in our conscious experience: "I am with you alway." Let us see to it that our faith in His blessed word, in His divine power, in His holy abiding presence, be the one thing that masters our whole being—Christ will in very deed show himself, abide with us, and dwell in our heart as His home.

May 13

Peter: The Greatness of Love

Peter was grieved because he said unto him the third time, Lovest thou me? He said unto him, Lord, thou knowest all things; thou knowest that I love thee. Jesus saith unto him, Feed my sheep.— John 21:17

It was to Mary who loved much that Christ first revealed himself. Then in Peter's first vision of the Lord, in His making himself known in the supper room at Emmaus, in His appearance to the ten, and in the revelation of himself to Thomas, it was ever to the intense devotion of the prepared heart that Christ revealed himself. And now in His manifestation of himself to Peter, it is again love that is the keynote.

We can easily understand why Christ three times asked the question, "Lovest thou me?" It was to remind Peter of the terrible self-confidence in which he had said: "Though I should die with thee, I will not deny thee"; of the need of quiet, deep heart-searching before he could be sure that his love was real and true; of the need for deep penitence in the consciousness of how little he could trust himself; and then of love being the one thing essential for the full restoration to his place in the heart of Jesus, the first and highest condition for feeding His sheep and caring for His lambs.

God is love. Christ is the Son of His love. Having loved His own, He loved them to the uttermost, and said: "As the Father loved me, so love I you." He asked that they should prove their love to Him by keeping His commandments and loving each other with His love. In heaven and on earth, in the Father and in the Son, and in us, and in all our work for Him and our care for souls, the greatest thing is love.

To everyone who longs to have Jesus show himself—"I am with you alway"—the essential requisite is love. Peter teaches us that such love it is not the power of man to offer. But such love came to him through the power of Christ's death to sin, and that power of His resurrection life, of which Peter became partaker. As he puts it in his first epistle: "Whom having not seen, we love; in whom, though now ye see him not, yet believing, ye rejoice with joy unspeakable and full of glory." Thank God, if Peter the self-confident could be so changed, can we not believe that Christ will work in us the wondrous change, too, and show himself to a loving heart in all the fullness of His precious word: "Lo, I am with you alway"? It is to love that Christ will reveal himself.

May 14

John: Life from the Dead

And when I saw him, I fell at his feet as dead. And he laid his right hand upon me, saying, Fear not; I am the first and the last, I am he that liveth, and was dead, and behold, I am alive for evermore.—Revelation 1:17, 18

Here we have, sixty or more years after the resurrection, Christ revealing himself to the beloved disciple. John fell as dead at His feet. God had said to Moses, in answer to his prayer, "Show me thy glory": "Thou canst not see my face: for man cannot see me and live." Man's sinful nature cannot receive the vision of the divine glory and live; it requires the death of the natural life for the life of God in glory to enter in. When John fell as dead at Christ's feet, it proved how little he could endure the wonderful heavenly vision.

When Christ laid His right hand upon him and said, "Fear not; I am he that liveth, and was dead, and behold, I am alive for evermore," He reminded him that He himself had passed through death before He could rise to the life and the glory of God. For the Master himself and for every disciple, for Moses and for John, there is only one way to the glory of God—death to the sinful nature that cannot enter heaven.

The lesson is a deep and necessary one to all who long that Jesus will reveal himself unto them. The knowledge of Jesus, fellowship with Him, and the experience of His power is not possible without the sacrifice of all that there is in us of the world and its spirit. The disciples had experience of this. Christ had spoken about forsaking father and mother, about taking up the cross, about losing our life for His sake, down to the days before His death, when He said: "Except a corn of wheat die, it abideth alone, but if it die, it bringeth forth much fruit"; "He that loveth his life shall lose it." He made this the one great charge: Deny self; bear the cross, and follow Me.

We are seeking to find out the secret of getting into such touch with the Lord Jesus that His abiding presence will be ours every day. Let us accept the lesson—through death to life. In the power of Christ Jesus, with whom we have been crucified, and whose death now works in us, if we will yield ourselves to it, death to sin, death to the world with all its self-pleasing and self-exaltation, is to be the deepest law of our spiritual life. Peter said to Christ: "Spare thyself" (Matt. 16:22 marg.); Jesus said to him: "Deny thyself." The disciples had followed Christ even to the cross. That was what fitted them to receive His word: "Lo, I am with you alway."

May 15

Paul: Christ Revealed in Him

It was the good pleasure of God ... to reveal his Son in me.—Galatians 1:15, 16

In all our study and worship of Christ we find our thoughts ever gathering round these five points: The incarnate Christ, the crucified Christ, the enthroned Christ, the indwelling Christ, and Christ coming in glory. If the first be the seed, the second is the seed cast into the ground, and the third the seed growing up to the very heaven. Then follows the fruit through the Holy Spirit, Christ dwelling in the heart; and then the gathering of the fruit into the garner when Christ appears.

Paul tells us that it pleased God to reveal His Son in him. And he gives his testimony to the result of that revelation: "Christ liveth in me" (Gal. 2:20). Of that life he says its chief mark is that he is crucified with Christ. It is this that enables him to say, "I live no longer"; in Christ he had found the death of self. Just as the cross is the chief characteristic of Christ himself—"A lamb as it had been slain in the midst of the throne"—so the life of Christ in Paul made him inseparably one with his crucified Lord. So completely was this the case that he could say: "Far be it from me to glory save in the cross of our Lord Jesus Christ, through which I am crucified to the world."

If you had asked Paul, if Christ so actually lived in him that he no longer lived, what became of his responsibility? the answer was ready and clear: "I live by the faith of the Son of God, who loved me and gave himself for me." His life was every moment a life of faith in Him who had loved him and given himself so completely that He had undertaken at all times to be the life of His willing disciple.

This was the sum and substance of all Paul's preaching. He asks for intercession that he might speak "the mystery of Christ"; "even the riches of the glory of this mystery among the Gentiles, which is Christ in you, the hope of glory" (Col. 2:2; 1:27). The indwelling Christ was the secret of his life of faith, the one power, the one aim of all his life and work, the hope of glory. Let us believe in the abiding presence of Christ as the sure gift to each one who trusts Him fully.

May 16

Why Could We Not?

The disciples came to Jesus apart, and said, Why could not we cast it out? He saith unto them, Because of your little faith. Howbeit this kind goeth not out but by prayer and fasting.—Matthew 17:19-21

The disciples had often cast out devils. But here they had been impotent. They asked the Lord what the reason might be. His answer is simple: "Because of your little faith."

We have here the reply to the great question so often asked, How is it that we cannot live that life of unbroken fellowship with Christ which the Scripture promises? Simply because of our unbelief. We do not realize that faith must accept and expect that God will, by His almighty power, fulfill every promise He has made. We do not live in that utter helplessness and dependence on God alone which is the very essence of faith. We are not strong in the faith, fully persuaded that what God has promised He is able and willing to perform. We do not give ourselves with our whole heart simply to believe that God by His almighty power will work wonders in our hearts.

But what can be the reason that this faith is so often lacking? "Howbeit this kind goeth not out but by prayer and fasting." To have a strong faith in God needs a life in close touch with Him by persistent prayer. We cannot call up faith at our bidding; it needs close communion with God. It needs not only prayer, but fasting, too, in the larger and deeper meaning of that word. It needs the denial of self, the sacrifice of that pleasing of the flesh and the eye and the pride of life which is the essence of a worldly spirit. To gain the prizes of the heavenly life here on earth demands the sacrifice of all that earth can offer. Just as it needs God to satisfy the human heart, and work His mighty miracles in it, it needs the whole man, utterly given up to God, to have the power of that faith which can cast out every evil spirit. "Prayer and fasting" are essential.

May 17

The Power of Obedience

He that hath sent me is with me; he hath not left me alone; for I do always the things that are pleasing to him.—John 8:29

In these words Christ not only tells what His life with the Father was, but reveals at the same time the law of all communion with God—simple obedience.

How strongly He insisted upon it we see in the farewell discourse. In John 14 He says three times: "If ye love me, keep my commandments. And then I will pray the Father, and he will give you the Holy Spirit and the Father will love you, and I will love you and manifest myself to you, and then we will make our abode with you." And so three times over in John 15: "If my words abide with you, ye shall ask what ye will, and it shall be done unto you"; "If ye keep my commandments, ye shall abide in my love; even as I kept my Father's commandments and abide in his love"; "Ye are my friends, if ye do the things which I command you."

Obedience is the proof and the exercise of the love of God shed abroad in our hearts by the Holy Spirit. It comes from love and leads to love, a deeper and fuller experience of God's love and indwelling. It assures us that what we ask will be given us. It assures us that we are abiding in the love of Christ. It seals our claim to be called the friends of Christ. And so it is not only a proof of love but of faith, too, as assuring us that we "ask and receive because we keep His commandments, and do the things that are pleasing in his sight."

For the abiding enjoyment of the holy presence, simple, full obedience is necessary. The New Covenant has made full provision for this: "I will write my law in their hearts; I will put my fear in their heart, that they may not depart from me"; "I will cause them to walk in my statutes and to keep them."

Blessed obedience, that enables us to abide in His love and gives the full experience of His unbroken presence. Christ did not speak of an impossibility; He saw what in the power of the Spirit we might confidently expect. Let the thought take deep hold of us. It is to the obedient that the word comes, "Lo, I am with you alway," and to whom all the fullness of its meaning will be revealed.

May 18

The Power of Intercession

We will continue steadfastly in prayer.—Acts 6:4

Prayer was made earnestly of the church unto God for him.—Acts 12:5

J. R. Mott urges us to believe in the unlimited power of united intercession. Traveling in Asia, he was charged by men who have penetrated most deeply into the heart of the problem to press upon the missionary societies the *imperative need of more intercession—above all, of united intercession.* "We can in no way better serve the deepest interest of the churches than by multiplying the number of real intercessors, and by focusing the prayers of Christendom upon those great situations which demand the almighty working of the Spirit of God. Far more important and vital than any service we can render to missions is that of helping to release the superhuman energy of prayer, and, through uniting in this holy ministry true intercessors of all lands, to help the ushering in of a new era abounding in signs and wonders characteristic of the working of the living Christ.

"Immeasurably more important than any other work is the linking of all we do to the fountain of divine life and energy. The Christian world has not only a right to expect mission leaders to set forth the facts and methods of the work, but also a larger discovery of superhuman resources and a greater irradiation of spiritual power."

And where is there a greater need of focusing the united intercession of Christendom than on the great army of missionaries representing Jesus Christ around the world? They confess the need of the presence and the power of God's Spirit in their life and work. They long for the experience of the abiding presence and power of Christ every day. They need it; they have a right to it. Shall we not be a part of the great army that pleads with God for that enduement of power which is so absolutely necessary for effective work? Shall we not, like the early apostles, "continue steadfastly in prayer," until God sends an abundant answer? As we give ourselves continually to prayer, the power of the promise, "Lo, I am with you alway," will be proved in our lives.

May 19

The Power of Time

My times are in thy hand.—Psalm 31:15

The plural implies the singular: "My time is in Thy hand. It belongs to Thee; Thou alone hast a right to command it. I yield it wholly and gladly to Thy disposal." What mighty power time can exert if wholly given up to God!

Time is lord of all things. What is all the history of the world but a proof of how, slowly but surely, time has made man what he is today? All around us we see the proofs. In the growth of the child to manhood, both physically and mentally, in the success in every pursuit, in all our labors and all our attainments, it is under the law of time and its inconceivable power that we spend our lives.

This is particularly true in religion and communion with God. Time here, too, is master. What fellowship with God! What holiness and blessedness! What likeness to His image, and what power in His service for blessing to men!—all on the one condition: that we have sufficient time with God for His holiness to shine on us with its light and its heat, and to make us partakers of His Spirit and His life. The very essence of religion lies in the thought: *Time with God.*

And yet how many of God's servants there are who, while giving their lives to His service, frankly confess the feebleness of their spiritual life as missionaries, and the inadequate results of mission work as a whole. These are due to the failure to make time for, and, when secured, rightly use it, daily communion with God.

What can be the reason behind this sad confession? Nothing but a lack of faith in the God-given assurance that time spent alone with God will indeed bring into the lives of His servants the power to enable them so to use all their time in His fellowship that His abiding presence will be with them all the day.

Oh, you, who complain that overwork, or too much zeal in doing the work, is hindering your spiritual efficiency, do you not see that if you would but submit your timetable to the inspection of Christ and His Holy Spirit, you would find that a new life would be yours if you fully believed and put into daily practice the word: "My *time* is in thy hand"?

May 20

The Power of Faith

All things are possible to him that believeth.—Mark 9:23

Scripture teaches us that there is not one truth on which Christ insisted more frequently, both with His disciples and with those who came seeking His help, than the absolute necessity of faith and its unlimited possibilities. And experience has taught us that there is nothing in which we come so short as the simple and absolute trust in God to fulfill literally in us all He has promised. A life in the abiding presence must of necessity be a life of unceasing faith.

Think for a moment of the marks of true faith. First of all, faith counts upon God to do all He has promised, as the only measure of its expectation. It does not rest content with taking some of the promises; it seeks nothing less than to claim every promise that God has made, in its largest and fullest meaning. Under a sense of its own nothingness and utter impotence, it trusts the power of an almighty God to work wonders in the heart in which He dwells.

It does this with the whole heart and all its strength. Faith yields itself to the promise that God will take full possession, and all through the day and night inspire its hope and expectation. It recognizes the inseparable link uniting God's promises and His commands, and yields itself to do the one as fully as it trusts the other.

In the pursuit of the power which such a life of faith can give, there is often a faith that seeks and strives, but cannot grasp. This is followed by a faith that begins to see that waiting on God is needed, and that quietly rests in the hope of what God will do. This should lead on to an act of decision, in which the soul takes God at His word, and claims the fulfillment of the promise, and then looks to Him, even in utter darkness, to perform what He has spoken.

The life of faith to which the abiding presence will be granted must have complete mastery of the whole being. Christ's presence actually keeping us all day in its blessed experience is a wonderful privilege. We need to give up much that was formerly thought lawful, if He is indeed to be Lord of all, the blessed Friend who companies with us, the joy and light of our life. This faith will be able to claim and to experience the words of the Master: "Lo, I am with you alway."

May 21

John's Missionary Message

That which we have seen and heard declare we unto you, that ye also may have fellowship with us: and truly our fellowship is with the Father, and with his Son Jesus Christ.—1 John 1:3

What a revelation of the calling of the preacher of the gospel! His message is nothing less than to proclaim that Christ has opened the way for us simple men to have, day by day, living, loving fellowship with the holy God. He is to preach this as a witness to the life he himself lives in all its blessed experience. In the power of that testimony, he is to prove its reality, and to show how a sinful man upon earth can indeed live in fellowship with the Father and the Son.

The message suggests to us that the very first duty of the minister or the missionary every day of his life is to maintain such close communion with God that he can preach the truth in the fullness of joy and with the consciousness that his life and conversation are the proof that his preaching is true, so that his words appeal with power to the heart: "These things write we unto you that your joy may be full."

The substance of Keswick teaching on missions is given in these words: "It points to a life of communion with God through Christ as a reality to be entered upon, and constantly maintained, by the unconditional and habitual surrender of the whole personality to Christ's control and government, in the assurance that the living Christ will take possession of the life thus yielded to Him." It is such teaching, revealing the infinite claim and power of Christ's love as maintained by the power of the Holy Spirit, that will encourage and compel men to make the measure of Christ's surrender for them the only measure of their surrender to Him and His service.

It is this intimate fellowship with Christ as the secret of daily service and testimony that has power to make Christ known as the deliverer from sin and the inspiration of a life of wholehearted devotion to His service.

It is this intimate and abiding fellowship with Christ that the promise, "I am with you alway," assures to us. This is what every missionary and Christian needs, what every Christian has a right to claim, and by which alone he maintains that spiritual efficiency that will influence the workers and the converts with whom he comes in contact.

May 22

Paul's Missionary Message

Continue in prayer... withal praying also for us, that God would open unto us a door of utterance, to speak the mystery of Christ... that I may make it manifest, as I ought to speak.—Colossians 4:2-4

The mystery now made manifest to his saints: to whom God would make known what is the riches of the glory of this mystery among the Gentiles; which is Christ in you, the hope of glory.—Colossians 1:26, 27

To Paul's mind, the very center and substance of his gospel was the indwelling Christ. He spoke of the "riches of the glory of this mystery—Christ in you, the hope of glory." Though he had been so many years a preacher of this gospel, he still asked for prayer that he might properly make known that mystery.

The complaint is often made in regard to new Christians, that after a time there appears to be no further growth, and very little of the joy and power for bearing witness to Christ Jesus. The question comes whether the church at home is living in the experience of this indwelling Christ, so that the sons and daughters whom she sends out know the secret and make it the substance of their teaching and preaching.

Some years ago one of our ministers went to the foreign mission field to do deputation work. Before he left there was a little gathering for prayer, at which he asked what his message should be. The thought was expressed that in speaking to Christians it was desirable that a message of a full salvation should be pressed home, and the hearts roused to believe in and to accept the concept of an indwelling Christ. On his return he told with what deep interest the presentation of this truth had been received, many saying that they had never before understood this correctly.

Dr. Maclaren said many years ago that it seemed as if the church had lost the truth of the indwelling Christ. We speak of Paul's missionary methods, but is there not a greater need of Paul's missionary message as it culminates in the one word: "Christ in you, the hope of glory"? Paul felt the need of much prayer to enable him to give this message. We should make it a matter of first importance to obtain the power, and from a living experience to lead other Christians into the enjoyment of their rightful heritage. We need to restore to its rightful place this truth: "Christ in you, the hope of glory."

May 23

The Missionary's Life

Ye are witnesses, and God also, how holily and righteously and un-blameably we behaved ourselves toward you that believe.—1 Thessalonians 2:10

Paul more than once appeals to what his converts had seen of his own life. So he says (2 Cor. 1:12): "Our glorying is this, the testimony of our conscience, that in holiness and sincerity of God, not in fleshly wisdom but in the grace of God, we behaved ourselves in the world, and more abundantly to youward." Christ had taught His disciples as much by His life as by His teaching. Paul had sought to be a living witness to the truth of all that he had preached about Christ—as able to save and to keep from sin, as renewing the whole nature by the power of His Holy Spirit, as himself becoming the life of those who believe in Him.

A missionary report pointed out: "It has come to pass that our representatives on the field, just because they are what we have made them, have far too often hidden the Christ whom they are giving their lives to reveal. It is only in proportion as the missionary can manifest the character of Christ in and through his own life that he can gain a hearing for the gospel. Only as far as he can live Christ before their eyes can he help them to understand his message."

See how Paul's appeal to his life, as holy and righteous and unblameable, gave him courage to put a high standard before his converts. In the same epistle he calls them to trust God, to establish their hearts unblameable in holiness before God (1 Thess. 3:13). And later in the epistle (5:23, 24): "The God of peace himself sanctify you wholly, who also will do it." In Philippians 4:9 he writes: "The things which ye both heard and saw in me, these things do, and the God of peace shall be with you." And in 1 Timothy 1:14-16: "The grace of our Lord abounded exceedingly with faith and love which is in Christ Jesus, . . . for an ensample of them which should hereafter believe on him unto eternal life."

Let us believe that when Paul said, "Christ liveth in me," "I live no more," he spoke of an actual, divine, unceasing, abiding of Christ in him, working in him from hour to hour all that was well-pleasing to the Father. And let us not rest until we can say, "The Christ of Paul is my Christ! His missionary enduement is mine too."

May 24

The Holy Spirit

The Comforter shall glorify me: for he shall receive of mine, and shall show it unto you.—John 16:14

When our Lord spoke the words to the disciples, "Lo, I am with you alway," they did not at first understand or experience their full meaning.

At Pentecost they were filled with the Holy Spirit. That Spirit from heaven brought down into their hearts the glorified Lord Jesus, and they began the new life in the joy of the abiding presence. All our attempts to live that life of continuous, unbroken communion, will be in vain unless we too yield ourselves wholly to the power and the indwelling of the ever blessed Spirit.

Throughout the church of Christ a lack of faith is apparent in what the Spirit is as God, and of what He can enable us to be, and of how completely He demands full and undisturbed possession of our whole being. All our faith in the fulfillment of Christ's glorious promises that Father and Son will make their abode in us is subject to the one essential and indispensable condition—a life utterly and unceasingly yielded to the rule and leading of the Spirit of Christ.

Let no one say: "The experience of Christ's being with us every day and all the day is impossible." Christ meant His word to be a simple and eternal reality. He meant the promises to be accepted—"He that loveth me shall be loved of my Father, and I will love him, and will manifest myself to him," and "We will come unto him and make our abode with him"—as absolute divine truth. But this truth could only be experienced where the Spirit, in His power as God, was known and believed in and obeyed. What Christ speaks of in John 14 is what Paul testifies to when he says, "Christ liveth in me," or, as John expresses it, "Hereby know we that we abide in him and he in us, because he hath given us of his Spirit."

Christ came as God to make known the Father, and the Spirit came as God to make known the Son in us. We need to understand that the Spirit as God claims absolute subjection and is willing to take possession of our whole being and enable us to fulfill all that Christ asks of us. It is the Spirit who can deliver us from all the power of the flesh, who can conquer the power of the world. It is the Spirit through whom Christ Jesus will reveal himself to us in nothing less than His abiding presence: "Lo, I am with you alway."

May 25

Filled with the Spirit

Be filled with the Spirit; speaking one to another in psalms and hymns and spiritual songs, singing and making melody with your heart to the Lord; giving thanks always for all things.—Ephesians 5:18-20

If we had the expression "filled with the Spirit" only in regard to the story of Pentecost, we might naturally think it was something special, and not meant for ordinary life. But our text teaches that it is meant for every Christian and for everyday life.

To realize this more fully, think of what the Holy Spirit was in Christ Jesus, and what the conditions were under which He, as man, was filled with the Spirit. He received the Spirit when He was praying, and had yielded himself as a sacrifice to God in going down into the sinner's baptism. Full of the Holy Spirit, He was led to the forty days' fasting, sacrificing the needs of the body to be free for fellowship with the Father and the victory over Satan. He even refused, when He was hungry, to listen to the temptation of the Evil One to use His power to make bread to supply His hunger.

So He was led by the eternal Spirit, offered himself without blemish unto God. In Christ the Spirit meant prayer, obedience, and sacrifice.

Even so we, if we are to follow Christ, to have His mind in us, to live out His life, we must seek to regard the fullness of the Spirit as a daily supply, as a daily provision, if we are to live the life of obedience, of joy, of self-sacrifice, and of power for service. There may be occasions when that fullness of the Spirit will become unusually evident, but every day and all the day it is only as we are led by the Spirit that we can abide in Christ Jesus, conquer the flesh and the world, and live the life with God in prayer, and with our fellowmen in humble, holy, fruitful service.

Above all, it is only as we are filled with the Spirit that the words of Jesus can be fully understood and experienced: "Lo, I am with you alway." Let no one think this is too high, this is impossible. "Impossible with men, possible with God!" "Lo, I am with you alway" was meant for daily life, and that not without but with the sure and all-sufficient aid of that blessed Spirit of whom Jesus said: "He that believeth in me, out of him shall flow rivers of living water." Our faith in Christ will be the measure of our fullness of the Spirit. The measure of the power of the Spirit in us will be the measure of our experience of the presence of Christ.

May 26

The Christ Life

Christ liveth in me.—Galatians 2:20

Christ is our life.—Colossians 3:4

Christ's life was more than His teaching, more than His work, more even than His death. It was His life in the sight of God and man that gave value to what He said and did and suffered. And it is this life, glorified in the resurrection, that He imparts to His people, and enables them to live out before men.

"Hereby shall all men know that ye are my disciples, if ye love one another." It was the life in the new brotherhood of the Holy Spirit that made both Jews and Greeks feel there was some superhuman power about Christ's disciples; they gave living proof of the truth of what they said, that God's love had come down and taken possession of them.

It has often been said of the missionary, that unless he lives out the Christ life on an entirely different level from that on which other men live, he misses the deepest secret of power and success in his work. When Christ sent His disciples forth, it was with the command: "Tarry till ye be endued with power from on high." "Wait, and ye shall receive the power of the Holy Ghost, and be my witnesses to the ends of the earth." Many a missionary has felt that it is not learning and not zeal, and not the willingness for self-sacrifice in Christ's service, but the secret experience of the life hid with Christ in God that enables him to meet and overcome every difficulty.

Everything depends upon the life with God in Christ being right. It was so with Christ, with the disciples, and with Paul. It is the simplicity and intensity of our life in Christ Jesus, and of the life of Christ Jesus in us, that sustains a man in the daily drudgery of work that makes him conqueror over self and everything that could hinder the Christ life, and gives the victory over the powers of evil and over the hearts from which the evil spirits have to be cast out.

The life is everything. It was so in Christ Jesus. It must be so in His servants. It can be so, because Christ himself will live in us. When He spoke the word, "Lo, I am with you alway," He meant nothing less than this: "Every day and all the day I am with you, the secret of your life, your joy, and your strength."

Oh, to learn what hidden treasures are contained in the blessed words we love to repeat: "Lo, I am with you all the days."

May 27

The Christlike Life

Have this mind in you, which was also in Christ Jesus.—Philippians 2:5

What was the mind that was in Christ Jesus? "Being in the form of God, he emptied himself, taking the form of a servant, being made in the likeness of men; he humbled himself, becoming obedient even unto death, yea, the death of the cross." Self-emptying and self-sacrifice, obedience to God's will, and love to men, even unto the death of the cross—such was the character of Christ for which God so highly exalted Him. Such is the character of Christ that we are to imitate. He was made in the likeness of men that we might be conformed into the likeness of God.

Self-effacement, self-sacrifice, that God's will might be done and that man might be saved—such was the life of Christ. "Love seeketh not its own." This was His life; He lived only to please God and to bless men.

Let no one say that this is an impossibility. "What is impossible with men is possible with God." We are called to work out this salvation of a Christlike character with fear and trembling; for "it is God that worketh in us both to will and to do of his good pleasure." He of whom Christ said, "It is the Father in me that doeth the works," is He who works in us to will and to do.

It has been said that the "missionary who is to commend the gospel must first embody it in a character fully conformed to the likeness of Jesus Christ. It is only as far as he can live Christ before the eyes of the converts that he can help them to understand his message. It has at times come to pass that our representatives on the field, just because they are what we have made them, have far too often hidden the Christ whom they are giving their lives to reveal."

As the church aims at making some marked degree of likeness to Christ's character the standard for Christian teachers, our missionaries will be able to pass this on to their converts, and say to them: "Be ye followers of us, even as we are of Christ."

Let us not rest until our faith lays hold of the promise, "It is God that worketh in us." The confidence will be aroused, that as the character of Christ is the revelation with which every missionary has been entrusted, so the power will be given to fulfill this high and holy calling.

May 28

Christ, the Nearness of God

Draw nigh to God, and he will draw nigh to you. —James 4:8

It has been said that the holiness of God is the union of God's infinite nearness in His redeeming grace. Faith must ever seek to realize both the distance and the nearness.

In Christ God has come near, so very near to man, and now the command comes: If you would have God come still nearer, you must draw nigh to Him. The promised nearness of Christ Jesus expressed in the promise, "Lo, I am with you alway," can only be experienced as we draw near to Him.

That means, first of all, at the beginning of each day afresh to yield ourselves for His holy presence to rest upon us. It means a voluntary, intentional, and wholehearted turning away from the world, to wait on God to make himself known to our souls. It means giving time, and all our heart and strength, to allow Him to reveal himself. It is impossible to expect the abiding presence of Christ with us through the day unless there be the definite daily exercise of strong desire and childlike trust in His word: "Draw nigh to God, and he will draw nigh to you."

And that means, further, the simple, childlike offering of ourselves and our lives in everything to do His will alone, and to seek above everything to please Him. His promise is sure: "If a man love me he will keep my words, and my Father will love him, and we will make our abode in him."

Then comes the quiet assurance of faith, even if there is not much feeling or sense of His presence, that God is with us, and that as we go out to do His will He will watch over us, and keep us, and, what is more, strengthen us in the inner man with divine strength for the work we have to do for Him.

Child of God, let these words come to you with a new meaning each morning: "Draw nigh to God, and he will draw nigh to you." Wait patiently, and He will speak in divine power: "Lo, I am with you alway."

May 29

Love

Jesus, having loved his own which were in the world, loved them unto the end. —John 13:1

These are the opening words of that holy, confidential talk of Christ with His disciples, as out of the depths of eternity He discoursed with them in the last hours before He went to Gethsemane (John 13-17). They are the revelation and full display of that divine love which was manifested in His death on the cross.

He begins with the new commandment: "That ye love one another as I have loved you" (John 13:34). A little later follows: "If ye love me, keep my commandments. . . . He that loveth me shall be loved of my Father, and I will love him, and will manifest myself unto him . . . and we will come unto him, and make our abode with him" (John 14:15, 21, 23). The new life, the heavenly life in Christ Jesus, is to be the unfolding of God's love in Christ. Then, farther on: "As the Father hath loved me, so have I loved you: continue ye in my love. If ye keep my commandments, ye shall abide in my love. . . . This is my commandment, That ye love one another, as I have loved you. Greater love hath no man than this, that a man lay down his life for his friends" (John 15:9-13); "that the world may know that thou hast sent me, and hast loved them, as thou hast loved me. . . . I have declared unto them thy name . . . that the love wherewith thou hast loved me may be in them and I in them" (John 17:23, 26).

Can words make it plainer that God's love to Christ is given to pass into us and to become our life, that the love wherewith the Father loved the Son is to be in us? If the Lord Jesus is to manifest himself to us, it can only be to the loving heart. If we are to claim His daily presence with us, it can only be as a relationship of infinite tender love between Him and us, love rooted in the faith of God's love to Christ coming into our hearts, and showing itself in obedience to His commandments and in love to one another.

We see how in the early church the first love was forsaken after a time, and confidence was put in all the activities of service (Rev. 2:2-4).

It is only in the atmosphere of a holy, living love that the abiding presence of the loving Christ can be known, and the depth of the divine love expressed in Christ's promise, "Lo, I am with you alway," will be realized.

The Trial and Triumph of Faith

Jesus said unto him, If thou canst believe, all things are possible to him that believeth. And straightway the father of the child cried out, and said with tears, Lord, I believe; help thou mine unbelief.
—Mark 9:23, 24

What a glorious promise: "All things are possible to him that believeth"! And yet it is just the greatness of the promise that constitutes the trial of faith. At first we do not really believe its truth. But when we have grasped it, then comes the real trial in the thought: Such a wonder-working faith is utterly beyond my reach.

But what constitutes the trial of faith soon becomes its triumph. How can this be? When Christ said to the father of the child, "If thou canst believe, all things are possible to him that believeth," he felt that this was only casting him into deeper despair. How could his faith be able to work the miracle? But as he looked into the face of Christ, and the love of His tender eye touched his heart, he felt sure that this blessed Man not only had the power to heal his child, but the power also to inspire him with the needed faith. The impression Christ produced upon him made not only the one miracle of the healing possible, but the second miracle, too, that he should have so great a faith. And with tears he cried, "Lord, I believe; help thou mine unbelief." The very greatness of faith's trial was the greatness of faith's triumph.

What a lesson! Of all things that are possible to faith, the most impossible is that I should be able to exercise such faith. The abiding presence of Christ is possible to faith. And this faith is possible to the soul that clings to Christ and trusts Him. As surely as He will lead us into His abiding presence all the day, so surely will He strengthen us with divine power for the faith that claims and receives the promise. Blessed the hour when the believer sees how entirely he is dependent on Christ for the faith as well as the blessing, and, in the consciousness of the unbelief that is still struggling within, he casts himself on the power and the love of Jesus: "Lord, I believe; Lord, I believe."

Through such trial and through such triumph, sometimes the triumph of despair, we enter upon our inheritance, the abiding presence of Him who speaks to us now: "Lo, I am with you alway." Let us wait at His feet until we know He has blessed us. "I can do all things through Christ which strengtheneth me" (Phil. 4:13).

May 31

Exceeding Abundantly

Now unto him that is able to do exceeding abundantly above all that we ask or think, according to the power that worketh in us, unto him be glory in the church by Christ Jesus throughout all ages, world without end. Amen.—Ephesians 3:20, 21

In the great prayer which Paul had just indited, he had apparently reached the highest expression possible of the life to which God's mighty power could bring the believer. But Paul is not content. In this doxology he rises still higher and lifts us up to give glory to God as "able to do exceeding abundantly above all that we can ask or think." Pause a moment to think what that "exceeding abundantly" means.

Think of the words, "the exceeding great and precious promises." This of "the exceeding greatness of his power toward us who believe, according to the working of the strength of his might which he wrought in Christ when he raised him from the dead." Think of the grace of our Lord as exceeding abundant with faith and love which is in Christ Jesus, so that where sin abounded grace did abound more exceedingly. He lifts our hearts to give glory to God as able to do "exceeding abundantly above all that we ask or think," according to the greatness of that power which worketh in us, nothing less than the exceeding greatness of the power that raised Christ from the dead. And as our hearts begin to feel that here is a prospect of something that God will work in us beyond all our imagination, He lifts our hearts to join in the universal chorus: "Unto him be the glory in the church and in Christ Jesus, unto all generations, for ever and ever. Amen."

As we worship and adore, the call comes to believe in this almighty God, who is working in our hearts, according to His mighty power, able and willing to fulfill every one of His exceeding great and precious promises, and, where sin abounded, to prove that grace abounds more exceedingly.

Paul began his great prayer, "I bow my knees to the Father." He ends it by bringing us to our knees, to give glory to Him as able to fulfill every promise, to reveal Christ dwelling in our hearts, and keep us in that life of love which leads to being filled with all the fullness of God.

June

The Secret of United Prayer

June 1

The Lost Secret

Wait for the promise of the Father. Ye shall be baptized with the Holy Ghost not many days hence.—Acts 1:4, 5

After our Lord had given the great command: "Go into all the world and preach the gospel to every creature," He added another, His very last command: "Tarry till ye be endued with power from on high." "Wait for the promise of the Father." "Ye shall be baptized with the Holy Ghost not many days hence."

All Christians agree that the great command to preach the gospel to every creature was not only for the disciples, but is binding on us, too. But all do not appear to consider that the very last command, not to preach until they had received the power from on high, is equally binding on us as it was on the disciples. The church appears to have lost possession of what ought to be to her a secret of secrets—the abiding consciousness, day by day, that only as she lives in the power of the Holy Spirit can she preach the gospel in demonstration of the Spirit and of power. It is because of this that there is so much preaching and working with so little of spiritual result. It is owing to nothing but this that the universal complaint is heard that there is so little prayer, and especially that there is so little of that much-availing prayer that brings down the power from on high on her ministrations.

In this series we will study the secret of Pentecost as it is to be found in the words and the deeds of our blessed Master, and in the words and the deeds of His disciples as they took Him at His word. They continued with one accord in prayer and supplication until the promise was fulfilled, and they became full of the Holy Ghost, proving what the mighty power of their God could do through them.

Let us seek earnestly the grace of the Holy Spirit, who alone can himself reveal to us what eye hath not seen, nor ear heard, nor hath entered into the heart of man to conceive—the things which God has done and loves to do for them that wait upon Him. Let us pray that the lost secret may be found—the sure promise that in answer to fervent prayer the power of the Holy Spirit will indeed be given.

June 2

The Kingdom of God

Jesus showed himself to his apostles, being seen of them forty days, and speaking of the things pertaining to the kingdom of God.—Acts 1:3

When Christ began to preach, He took up the message of John: "The kingdom of heaven is at hand." Later on He spoke: "There be some of them that stand here which shall not taste of death till they have seen the kingdom of God come with power." That could not be until the King had ascended His throne. Then first He and His disciples were ready to receive from the Father the great gift of the Holy Spirit, bringing down the kingdom of God in its heavenly power into their hearts.

Our text tells us that all the teaching of Jesus, during the forty days after the Resurrection, dealt with the kingdom of God, and it is remarkable how Luke, in the last verses of Acts, sums up all the teaching of Paul at Rome; he testified to the kingdom of God, he preached the kingdom of God (Acts 28:23, 31).

Christ seated upon the throne of God was now King and Lord of all. To His disciples He had entrusted the announcement of the kingdom, which is righteousness and peace and joy in the Holy Spirit. The prayer He had taught them: "Our Father, which art in heaven, thy kingdom come," had now for them a new meaning. The rule of God as seen in heaven came down in the power of the Spirit, and the disciples were full of the one thought—to preach the coming of the Spirit into the hearts of men. There was now on earth good tidings of the kingdom of God, a kingdom of God ruling and dwelling with men, even as in heaven.

In the last command our Lord gave to His disciples (Acts 1:4, 8), we will find the great essential characteristics of the kingdom put in great power:

1. The King—the crucified Christ. 2. The disciples—His faithful followers. 3. The power for their service—the Holy Spirit. 4. Their work—testifying for Christ as His witnesses. 5. Their aim—the ends of the earth. 6. Their first duty—waiting on God in united unceasing prayer.

If we are to take up and continue the prayer of the disciples, it is essential to have a clear and full impression of all that Christ spoke to them in that last moment, and what it meant for their inner life and all their service.

June 3

Christ As King

And he said: "Verily, I say unto you, that there be some of them which stand here, which shall not taste of death, till they have seen the kingdom of God come with power."—Mark 9:1

The first mark of the church is *Christ as King.*

Christ and John had both preached that the kingdom of God was at hand. In our text Christ said it would be in the lifetime of some who heard Him that the kingdom would come in power. This could mean nothing else but that when He, as King, had ascended the throne of the Father, the kingdom would be revealed in the hearts of His disciples by the power of the Holy Spirit. In the kingdom of heaven, God's will was always being done. In the power of the Holy Spirit, Christ's disciples would do His will even as it was done in heaven.

The mark of what a kingdom is, is to be seen in *the King.* Christ now reigns as God and man on the throne of the Father. On earth there is no embodiment or external manifestation of the kingdom; its power is seen in the lives of those in whom it rules. It is only in the church, the members of Christ, that the united Body can be seen and known. Christ lives and dwells and rules in their hearts. Our Lord himself taught how close the relationship would be. "In that day ye shall know that I am in my Father, and ye in me, and I in you." Next to the faith of His oneness with God, and His omnipotent power, would be the knowledge that they lived in Him and He in them.

This must be our first lesson if we are to follow in the steps of the disciples and share their blessing: that we must know Christ actually as King, dwelling and ruling in our hearts. We must know we live in Him, and in His power are able to accomplish all He would have us do. Our whole life is to be devoted to our King and the service of His kingdom.

This blessed relationship to Christ will mean above all a daily fellowship with Him in prayer. The prayer life is to be a continuous and unbroken exercise. Thus His people can rejoice in their King, and in Him can be more than conquerors.

June 4

Jesus the Crucified

God hath made that same Jesus, whom ye have crucified, both Lord and Christ.—Acts 2:36

We have spoken of Christ as King in more than one respect. But there is one word more that needs to be said. This King is none other than *the crucified Jesus*. All that we have to say of Him, His divine power, His abiding presence, His wonderful love, does not teach us really to know Him unless we maintain the deep consciousness: *This our King is the crucified Jesus*. God has placed Him in the midst of His throne as a Lamb, as it had been slain, and it is thus the hosts of heaven adore Him. It is thus we worship Him as a King.

Christ's cross is His highest glory. It is through this He has conquered every enemy and gained His place on the throne of God. And it is this He will impart to us, too, if we are to know fully what the victory over sin is to mean.

When Paul wrote: "I have been crucified with Christ, Christ liveth in me," he taught us it was as the Crucified One Christ ruled on the throne of His heart, and that the spirit of the cross would triumph over us as it did in Him.

This was true of the disciples. This was their deepest preparation for receiving the Holy Spirit. They had with their Lord been crucified to the world. The old man had been crucified: in Him they were dead to sin and their life was hid with Christ in God. Each one of us needs to experience this fellowship with Christ in His cross if the Spirit of Pentecost is really to take possession of us.

Through the eternal Spirit Christ gave himself a sacrifice and became the King on the throne of God. It is as we become "conformable to his death," in the entire surrender of our will, in the entire self-denial of our old nature, in the entire separation from the spirit of this world, that we can become the worthy servants of a crucified King, and our hearts the worthy temples of His glory.

June 5

The Apostles

Being assembled together with them, he charged them not to depart from Jerusalem, but to wait for the promise of the Father.—Acts 1:4

The second mark of the church is to be found in *the disciples* whom the Lord had prepared to receive His Spirit and to be His witnesses.

If we would properly understand the outpouring of the Spirit in answer to the prayer of the disciples, we must above all ask: What was there in these men which fitted them for such powerful, effectual prayer, and the wonderful fulfillment of the promise that came to them? They were simple, unlearned men with many faults, whom the Lord had called to forsake all and follow Him.

They had done this, as far as they could; they followed Him in the life He led and the work He did. Though there was much sin in them, and they had as yet no power fully to deny themselves, their hearts clung to Him in deep sincerity.

In the midst of much stumbling they yet followed Him to the cross. They shared with Him His death; unconsciously, but most really, they died with Him to sin, and were raised with Him in the power of a new life. It was this that fitted them for power in prayer, and being clothed with the power from on high.

Let this be the test by which we try ourselves, whether we have indeed surrendered to the fellowship of Christ's sufferings and death, and whether we have hated our own life and crucified it, and have received the power of Christ's life in us. This will give us liberty to believe that God will hear our prayer, too, and give us His Holy Spirit to work in us what we and He desire, if we are indeed with one accord to take up the disciples' prayer, and to share in the answer. We must, like them, be willing learners in the school of Jesus, and seek above everything that intimate fellowship with Him, which will fit us for praying the prayer of Pentecost, and receiving its answer.

June 6

Not of This World

They are not of the world, even as I am not of the world.—John 17:14, 16

In the last night our Lord took pains to make clear to His disciples the impassable gulf between Him and the world, and between them and the world, too (John 16:16-21). He had said of the Spirit: "The world cannot receive him, because it seeth him not, neither knoweth him." "Because ye are not of the world, therefore the world hateth you."

One great mark of the disciples was thus to be that as little as Christ was of the world, so little were they to be of the world. Christ and they had become united in the cross and the resurrection; they both belonged to another world— the kingdom of heaven. This separation from the world is to be the mark of all disciples who long to be filled with the Spirit.

How is it that faith in the Holy Spirit is so little preached and practiced in the church today? The world rules too much in the life of Christians. Christians live too little the heavenly life to which they are called in Christ Jesus. The "love of the world" (1 John 2:15, 16); "The lust of the flesh," pleasure in eating and drinking, in ease and comfort; "The lust of the eyes," delight in all the world offers of beauty and possession; the vain glory of life, the self-exaltation in what the wisdom and power of man has accomplished—all this robs the heart of its susceptibility and desire for true self-denial that fits for receiving the Holy Spirit.

Let each one who would take up the Pentecostal prayer for the power of the Holy Spirit examine himself whether the spirit of the world is not the secret of that lack of love of prayer which is absolutely necessary in all who would plead the promise of the Father. May the Lord write this deep in every heart: the world cannot receive the Holy Spirit! "Ye are not of the world, even as I am not of the world."

June 7

Obedience

If ye love me, ye will keep my commandments. And I will pray the Father, and he shall give you another Comforter.—John 14:15, 16

We have learned to know the disciples in their training for the baptism of the Spirit, and seen what was needed for their continuing "with one accord" in the prayer for the power of the Spirit. Christ was everything to them. Even before the cross, but much more after it, and with the resurrection, He was literally their life, their one thought, their only desire.

Such devotion to Christ, was this something special and not to be expected of all? Or was it indeed something the Lord asked from all who desired to be filled with the Spirit? God expects it of all His children; the Lord has need of such now, as much as then, to receive His Spirit and His power, to minister them here on earth, and, as intercessors, to link the world to the throne of God.

Is Christ something, or nothing, or everything, to us? For the unconverted, Christ is nothing; for the half converted— the average Christian—Christ is something; for the true Christian, Christ is all. Each one who prays for the power of the Spirit must be ready to say: "I yield myself with my whole heart this day to the leading of the Spirit"; a full surrender is the question of life or death, an absolute necessity.

You have heard the word of our text: "If ye love me, *keep my commandments.*" The surrender to live every day, all the day, abiding in Christ, and keeping His commandments, is to be the one mark of your discipleship. It is when the child of God learns it is only as the heart longs in everything to do God's will that the Father's love and Spirit can rest upon it. This was the spirit in which the disciples continued with one accord in prayer. This will be the secret of power in our intercession as we plead for the church and the world.

June 8

The Holy Spirit

Ye shall be baptized with the Holy Ghost. Ye shall receive power when the Holy Ghost is come upon you. —Acts 1:5, 8

The third mark of the church is *the power for service through the Holy Spirit.* Since the time of Adam's fall when he lost the spirit God had breathed into him, God's Spirit had striven with men, and worked in some with power, but He had never been able to find His permanent home in them.

It was only when Christ had come, and by His death had broken the power of sin and had won, in the resurrection, a new life for men to live in himself that the Spirit of God could come and take possession of the whole heart and make it a dwelling for Christ and for God.

Nothing less than this could be the power in the disciples and in us by which sin could be overcome and the prisoners set free. This Spirit is the *Holy Spirit.* In the Old Testament He was called the Spirit of God. But now that in the cross of Christ the holiness of God had been magnified, and Christ had sanctified us that we might be sanctified like Him, the Spirit of God's holiness descends to dwell in men and take possession of them as God's holy temple.

He is *the Spirit of the Son.* On earth He led the Son first into the desert to be tempted of Satan, then to the synagogue in Nazareth to proclaim himself as the fulfillment of what the prophets had spoken (Isa. 61:1; Luke 4:18). And so on to the cross, Christ yielded himself implicitly to the leading of the Spirit.

The Spirit now reveals Christ in us first of all as our life, and then as our strength, for a perfect obedience and the preaching of the Word in the power of God.

Amazing mystery! The Spirit of God, our life; the Spirit of Christ, our light and strength. It is as men and women who are led by this Spirit of the first disciples that we shall have the power to pray the effectual prayer of the righteous man.

June 9

The Power from on High

Tarry ye until ye be clothed with power from on high. —Luke 24:49

The Lord had said to the disciples: "Without me ye can do nothing." And now, why is it that He has chosen these impotent, helpless men to send them out to conquer the world for Him? It was that in their feebleness they might yield themselves and give Him as Lord, the opportunity on His throne, to show His power working through them. As the Father had done all the work in Christ when He was upon earth, so Christ in heaven would now be the great worker, proving in them that all power had been given to Him in heaven and on earth. Their place would be to pray, to believe, and yield themselves to the mighty power of Christ.

The Holy Spirit would not be in them as a power of which they could have possession. But He would possess *them*, and their work would be in very deed the work of the almighty Christ. Their whole posture each day would be that of unceasing dependence and prayer and of confident expectation.

The apostles had indeed learned to know Christ intimately. They had seen all His mighty works; they had received His teaching; they had gone with Him through all His sufferings, even to the death of the cross. And they had not only seen Him but known Him in the power of His resurrection and the experience of that resurrection life in their own hearts. Yet they were not capable of making Him known until He himself, from the throne of heaven, had taken possession of them by His Spirit dwelling in them.

Everything calls the gospel witness to rest content with nothing less than the indwelling life and power of the Holy Spirit revealing Jesus in the heart as the only fitness for preaching the gospel in power. Nothing less than having Christ speaking through us in the power of His omnipotence will make us able ministers of the New Testament.

June 10

My Witnesses

Ye shall be my witnesses.—Acts 1:8

The fourth mark of Christ's church is that *His servants are to be witnesses to Him*, ever testifying of His wonderful love, of His power to redeem, of His continual abiding presence, and of His wonderful power to work in them.

This is the only weapon the King allows His redeemed ones to use. Without claiming authority or power, without wisdom or eloquence, without influence or position, each one is called, not only by his words, but by his life and action, to be a living *proof and witness of what Jesus can do.*

This is to be the only weapon we are to use in conquering men and bringing them to the feet of Christ. This is what the first disciples did. When they were filled with the Spirit, they began to speak of the mighty things Christ had done.

It was in this power that those who were scattered abroad by persecution went forth, even as far as Antioch, preaching in the name of Jesus, so that a multitude of the heathen believed. They had no commission from the apostles; they had no special gifts or training, but out of the fullness of the heart they spoke of Jesus Christ. They could not be silent; they were filled with the life and the love of Christ, and could not but witness to Him.

It was this that gave the gospel its power of increase; every new convert became a witness for Christ.

A heathen writer tells later in regard to the persecutions that if the Christians were only content to keep the worship of Jesus to themselves, they would not have to suffer. But in their zeal they wanted Christ to rule over all.

Here we have the secret of a flourishing church: *every believer a witness for Jesus.* Here we have the cause of the weakness of the church: so few who are willing in daily life to testify that Jesus is Lord.

What a call to prayer! Lord, teach us the blessedness of so knowing Jesus and the power of His love that we may find our highest joy in witnessing to what He is and has done for us.

June 11

The Gospel Ministry

The Spirit of truth, he shall testify of me, and ye shall also bear witness, because ye have been with me from the beginning.—John 15:26, 27

My witness—that not only refers to all believers, but particularly to all ministers of the gospel. This is the high calling, and also the only power of the preacher of the gospel—in everything to be *a witness for Jesus.*

This gives us two great truths. The first, that with all that the preacher teaches from the Word of God, or according to the need of his congregation, he must first of all place *the preaching of Christ himself.* This is what the first disciples did. "They ceased not in every house to teach and to preach Jesus Christ." This was what Philip did at Samaria. "He preached Christ unto them." And so Paul writes: "I determined not to know anything among you, save Jesus Christ and him crucified."

The minister of the gospel may never forget that it is especially for this that he has been set apart, to be with the Holy Spirit a witness for Christ. It is as he does this that sinners will find salvation, that God's children will be sanctified and fitted for His service. It is thus alone that Christ can have His place in the heart of His people and in the world around.

But there is a second thought of no less importance. And it is that the teaching must ever be a personal testimony from experience to what Christ is and can do. As this note is sounded, the Holy Spirit carries the message as a living reality to the heart. This will build up believers so that they can walk in such fellowship with Jesus Christ that He can reveal himself through them. And it is this that will lead them to the knowledge of the indispensable secret of spiritual health —the prayer life in daily fellowship, in childlike love, and true consecration with the Father and the Son.

What abundant matter for a prayer union, to cultivate among believers and ministers that joy of the Holy Spirit in which, out of the abundance of the heart, the mouth speaks to the praise and glory of our ever-blessed Redeemer, Jesus Christ our Lord.

June 12

The Whole World

My witnesses unto the uttermost parts of the earth. —Acts 1:8

Here we have the fifth mark of Christ's church—*the whole world.*

What words are these for the man who in his absolute impotence had been crucified by His enemies, speaking of *the ends of the earth as His dominion.* What folly on the part of those who speak of Christ as being nothing but a man. How could it have entered the mind of any writer to venture the prophecy that a Jew who had been crucified, whose whole life had been proved by that cross to be an utter failure, and whose disciples had at the last utterly forsaken Him—that by them He should conquer the world? No human mind could have formed such a conception. It is the thought of God; He alone could plan and execute such a purpose.

The word that Jesus spoke to His disciples: "Ye shall receive power after that the Holy Ghost is come upon you," gives them the assurance that the Holy Spirit would maintain in them Christ's divine power. As Christ did His works only because the Father worked in Him, so Christ assured His disciples that He himself from the throne of heaven would work all their works in them. They might ask what they would and it should be done unto them. In the strength of that promise the church of Christ can make the ends of the earth its one aim.

Oh, that Christian people might understand that the extension of God's kingdom can only be effected by the united continued prayer of men and women who give their hearts wholly to wait upon Christ in the assurance that He will do for them what they desire.

Oh, that God would grant that His children proved their faith in Christ by making His aim their aim, and yielding themselves to be His witnesses in united persevering prayer, waiting upon Him in the full assurance that He will most surely and most gloriously give all that they can ask.

My reader, do become one of those intercessors who really believe the crucified Jesus will do far more than you can ask or think in answer to your prayer.

June 13

The Whole Earth Filled with His Glory

Blessed be his glorious name for ever: and let the whole earth be filled with his glory; Amen, and Amen. —Psalm 72:19

What a prospect! This earth now under the power of the evil one, renewed and *filled with the glory of God*—a new earth in which righteousness dwells. Though we believe it so little, it will surely come to pass; God's Word is the pledge of it. God's Son by His blood and death conquered the power of sin, and through the eternal Spirit the power of God is working out His purpose. What a vision—the whole earth filled with His glory!

But what a great and difficult work! It is nearly two thousand years since Christ gave the promise and ascended the throne, and yet more than one-half of the human race has never learned to know even the name of Jesus. And of the other half, what millions are called by His name, yet know Him not!

This great work of bringing the knowledge of Christ to every creature has been entrusted to a church that thinks little of her responsibility and of what the consequence of her neglect will be. We may indeed ask: Will the work ever be done? Blessed be His name, His power and His faithfulness are pledges that one day we shall see it, the whole earth filled with the glory of God.

What a wonderful prayer! For in our text it is a prayer— "Let the whole earth be filled with his glory; Amen, and Amen." Every believer is called to this prayer, and he can count upon the Holy Spirit to inspire and to strengthen him. By this prayer we desire to strengthen each other, so that every day of our life, with all the power there is in us, we with one accord and continually, desire to pray in the faith of the name of Jesus and the power of His Spirit.

What blessedness to know that true prayer will indeed help, and be answered! What blessedness every day of our lives to seek God's face, with confidence to lay hold of Him and give Him no rest till the earth is full of His glory! Once again, what blessedness to unite with all God's willing children in this the day of His power, who are seeking to prepare the way for our King!

June 14

The First Prayer Meeting

These all with one accord continued steadfastly in prayer, with the women. —Acts 1:14

The sixth mark of the early church—*waiting on the promise of the Father in united prayer.*

It is difficult to form a right conception of the unspeakable importance of this first prayer meeting in the history of the kingdom, a prayer meeting which was the simple fulfilling of the command of Christ. It was to be for all time the indication of the one condition on which His presence and Spirit would be known in power. In it we have the secret key that opens the storehouse of heaven with all its blessings.

Christ had prayed for the disciples to be one, even as He and the Father were one—perfect in one—that the world might know God loved them as He loved Christ. How far the disciples were from such a state when Christ prayed the prayer, we see in the strife among them at the Lord's table as to who would be chief. It was only after the resurrection, and after Christ had gone to heaven, that they would be brought, in the ten days of united supplication, to the holy unity of love and of purpose which would make them the one Body of Christ prepared to receive the Spirit in all His power.

What a prayer meeting! The fruit of Christ's training during His three years' association with them. Adam's body was first created before God breathed His Spirit into him. And so the Body of Christ had first to be formed before the Spirit took possession.

This prayer meeting gives us the law of the kingdom for all time. Where Christ's disciples are linked to each other in love, and yield themselves wholly to Him in undivided consecration, the Spirit will be given from heaven, as the seal of God's approval, and Christ will show His mighty power. One of the great marks of the new dispensation is the united unceasing prayer "that availeth much," and is crowned with the power of the Holy Spirit. Have we not here the reason why: if our prayers are confined in great measure to our own church or interests, the answer cannot come in such power as we expected?

June 15

The Unity of the Spirit

Endeavouring to keep the unity of the Spirit. There is one body and one Spirit.—Ephesians 4:3, 4

We learn from Paul how the Christian communities in different places ought to remember each other in the fellowship of prayer. He points out how in such prayer God is glorified. So he writes more than once (2 Cor. 1:11, 4:15, 9:12, 13) of how the ministry of intercession abounds to the glory of God.

Today there is great need for the children of God throughout the world to be drawn close together in the consciousness of their being chosen by God to be a holy priesthood ministering continually the sacrifice of praise and prayer. There is too little distinction between the world and the Body of Christ; in the life of many of God's children there is little difference from what the world is. It is a question of the deepest importance: What can be done to foster the unity of the Spirit?

Nothing will help so much as the separation to a life of more prayer, with the definite intercession that God's people may prove their unity in a life of holiness and love. That will be a living testimony to the world of what it means to live for God. When Paul wrote: "Praying always with all prayer and supplication in the Spirit, and watching thereunto with all perseverance and supplication for all saints," he names one of the essential characteristics of the difference between God's people and the world.

You say you long to bear this mark of the children of God, and to be able so to pray for them that you may prove to yourself and to others you are indeed not of the world. Resolve in your life to bear about with you this one great distinctive feature of the true Christian—a life of prayer and intercession. Join with God's children who are seeking with one accord and unceasingly so to maintain the unity of the Spirit and the Body of Christ that they may be strong in the Lord and in the power of His might to pray down a blessing upon His church.

Let none of us think it too much to give a quarter of an hour every day for meditation on some word of God connected with His promises to His church—and then to plead with Him for its fulfillment. Slowly, quietly, and yet surely, you will taste the blessedness of being one, heart and soul, with God's people, and receive the power to pray the effectual prayer that "availeth much."

June 16

Union Is Strength

And when they had prayed, they were all filled with the Holy Ghost, and they spake the word of God with boldness. And the multitude of them that believed were of one heart and one soul.—Acts 4:31, 32

We see the power of union everywhere in nature. How feeble is a drop of rain as it falls to earth. But when the many drops are united in one stream, and thus become one body, how speedily the power is irresistible. Such is the power of true union in prayer. In Psalm 34:5 the English margin has, instead of "they looked unto him," "they flowed unto him." The Dutch translation is, "They rushed toward him like a stream of water." Such was the prayer in the upper room. And such can our prayer be if we united all our forces in pleading the promise of the Father. And when the world "comes in like a flood," it can be overcome in the power of united prayer.

In Natal, owing to the many mountains, the streams often flow down with great force. The Zulus are accustomed, when they wish to pass through a stream, to join hands. The leader has a strong stick in his right hand, and gives his left to some strong man who comes behind him. So they form a chain of twelve or twenty, and help each other to stem and cross the current. When in spirit God's people reach out their hands to each other, there will be power to resist the terrible influence that the world can exert. And in that unity God's children, when they have overcome the power of the world and the flesh, will have power to prevail with God.

They stayed in the upper room the ten days until they had truly become one heart and one soul. When the Spirit of God descended, He not only filled each individual, but took possession of the whole company as the Body of Christ.

Do believe, O Christians, that in this twentieth century the prayer of our Lord Jesus is still being offered: "Father, that they may be one as we are one." It is in the fellowship of loving and believing prayer that our hearts can be melted into one, and that we will become strong in faith to believe and to accept what God has promised us.

June 17

Prayer in the Name of Christ

Whatsoever ye shall ask in my name, that will I do, that the Father
may be glorified in the Son.—John 14:13

How wonderful the link between our prayers and Christ's
glorifying the Father in heaven. Much prayer on earth brings
Him much glory in heaven. Little prayer means, as far as
we are concerned, little glory to the Father. What an incentive to much prayer, to unceasing intercession. Our prayer
is indispensable to the glorifying of the Father.

So deep was the desire of Christ in the last night that His
disciples should learn to believe in the power of His name,
and to avail themselves of His promise of a sure and abundant answer, that we find the promise repeated seven times
over. He knew how slow men are to believe in the wonderful
promise of answer to prayer in His name. He longs to rouse
a large and confident faith, and to free our prayer from every
shadow of a doubt, and to teach us to look upon intercession
as the most certain and most blessed way of bringing glory
to God, joy to our own souls, and blessing to the perishing
world around us.

If the thought comes to us that such prayer is not easy
of attainment, we only need to remember what Christ told
His disciples. *It was when the Holy Spirit came that they*
would have power thus to pray. As we yield ourselves fully
to the control of the blessed Spirit, He holds out to us the
precious promise, "Ask and ye shall receive, that your joy
may be full." As we believe in the power of the Spirit working in us in full measure, intercession will become to us the
joy and the strength of all our service.

When Paul wrote (Col. 3:17), "Whatsoever you do in word
or deed, do all in the name of the Lord Jesus," he reminds
us how in daily life everything is to bear the signature of the
name of Jesus. As we learn to do this, we will have the confidence to say to the Father that as we live in that name before
men we come to Him with the full confidence our prayer in
that name will be answered. The life in fellowship with
men is to be one with the life in fellowship with God. When
the name of Jesus rules all in our life, it will give power to
our prayer, too.

June 18

Your Heavenly Father

Our Father which art in heaven.—Luke 11:2

How simple, how beautiful, this invocation which Christ puts upon our lips! And yet how inconceivably rich in its meaning, in the fullness of the love and blessing it contains.

Just think what a book could be written of all the memories there have been on earth of wise and loving fathers. Think of what this world owes to the fathers who have made their children strong and happy in giving their lives to seek the welfare of their fellowmen. And then think how all this is but a shadow—a shadow of exquisite beauty, but still but a shadow of what the Father in heaven is to His children on earth.

What a gift Christ bestowed on us when He gave us the right to say: "Father!" "The Father of Christ," "Our Father," "My Father."

And then, "Our Father in heaven," our Heavenly Father. We count it a great privilege as we bow in worship to know the Father comes near to us where we are upon earth. But we soon begin to feel the need of rising up to enter into His holy presence in heaven, to breathe its atmosphere, to drink in its spirit, and to become truly heavenly-minded. As we in the power of thought and imagination leave earth behind, and in the power of the Holy Spirit enter the holiest of all, where the seraphs worship, the word "Heavenly Father" takes on a new meaning, and our hearts come under an eternal influence.

As we then gather up our thoughts of what fatherhood on earth has meant, and hear the voice of Christ saying, "How much more," we feel the distance there is between the earthly picture and the heavenly reality, and can only bow in lowly, loving adoration, "Father, our Father, my Father." And only thus can full joy and power come to us as we rest rejoicingly in the word: "How much more shall your heavenly Father give the Holy Spirit to them that ask him?"

Oh, for grace to cultivate a heavenly spirit, and daily to prove we are children who have a Father in heaven, and who love day by day to dwell in His holy presence!

June 19

The Power of Prayer

The effectual fervent prayer of a righteous man availeth much.—
James 5:16

Prayer "availeth much." It avails much with God. It avails much in the history of His church and people. Prayer is the one great power which the church can exercise in securing the working of God's omnipotence in the world.

The prayer *of a righteous man* availeth much. That is, a man who has the righteousness of Christ, not only as a garment covering him, but as a life-power inspiring him, as a new man "created in righteousness and true holiness" (Eph. 4:24). A man who lives as "the servant to righteousness" (Rom. 6:16, 19). These are the righteous whom the Lord loveth and whose prayer hath power (Ps. 66:18, 19; 1 John 3:22). When Christ gave His great prayer promises in the last night, it was to those who keep His commandments. "If ye love me, ye will keep my commandments; and I will pray the Father, and he will give you another Comforter" (John 14:15, 16). "If ye keep my commandments, ye shall abide in my love; and ye shall ask whatsoever ye will, and it shall be done unto you" (15:7, 10).

"The *effectual fervent prayer* of a righteous man availeth much." It is only when the righteous man stirs up himself and rouses his whole being to take hold of God that the prayer availeth much. As Jacob said: "I will not let thee go"; as the importunate widow gave the just judge no rest, so it is that the effectual fervent prayer effects great things.

And then comes the effectual fervent prayer of many righteous. When two or three agree, there is the promise of an answer. How much more when hundreds and thousands unite with one accord to cry to God to display His mighty power on behalf of His people!

Let us join those who have united themselves to call upon God for the mighty power of His Holy Spirit in His church. What a great and blessed work, and what a sure prospect, in God's time, of an abundant answer! Let us pray God individually and unitedly for the grace of the effectual fervent prayer which availeth much.

June 20

Prayer and Sacrifice

I would that ye knew what great conflict I have for you.—Colossians 2:1

As men who are undertaking a great thing have to prepare themselves and summon all their powers to their aid, so Christians need to prepare themselves to pray, "with their whole heart and strength." This is the law of the kingdom. Prayer needs sacrifice of ease, of time, of self. The secret of powerful prayer is sacrifice.

It was thus with Christ Jesus, the great Intercessor. It is written of Him, "When thou shalt *make his soul an offering for sin*, he shall see his seed." "He shall see the *travail of his soul.*" "He shall divide the spoil with the strong, because he hath poured out his soul under death." In Gethsemane "he offered up prayers and supplications with strong crying and tears." Prayer is sacrifice. David said: "Let my prayer be set forth before me as incense; and the lifting up of my hands as the evening sacrifice."

Prayer is sacrifice. Our prayer has its worth alone from being rooted in the sacrifice of Jesus Christ. As He gave up everything in His prayer "Thy will be done," our posture and propensity must ever be the offering up of everything to God and His service.

A pious Welsh miner had a relative whom the doctor ordered to Madeira. But there was no money. The miner resolved to take the little money he had, and dared to spend it all. He procured a comfortable lodging at ten pounds per day for the invalid. He was content with an out-room for himself, and lived on tenpence a day. He spent much time in prayer until he got the assurance that the invalid would recover. On the last day of the month the sick one was well. When the miner reached home he said he had now learned more than ever that the secret law and the hidden power of prayer lay in self-sacrifice.

Need we wonder at the lack of power in our prayer where there is so much reluctance to make the needful sacrifice in waiting upon God? Christ, the Christ we trust in, the Christ who lives in us, offered himself a sacrifice to God. It is as this spirit lives and rules in us, that we will receive power from Him as intercessors to pray the effectual prayer that availeth much.

June 21

The Intercession of the Spirit
for the Saints

He that searcheth the hearts knoweth what is the mind of the Spirit,
because he maketh intercession for the saints according to the will
of God.—Romans 8:27

What a light these words cast upon the life of prayer in
the hearts of the saints! We don't know how to pray as we
should. How often this hinders our prayer or hinders the
faith that is essential to its success. But here we are told for
our encouragement, that the Holy Spirit maketh intercession
for us with groanings that cannot be uttered: "He maketh
intercession for the saints according to the will of God."

What a prospect is here opened up to us! Where and how
does the Spirit make intercession for the saints? In no other
way than that, in the heart which knows not what to pray,
He secretly and effectually prays what is according to the
will of God. This, of course, implies that we trust Him to do
His work in us, and that we wait before God even when we
know not what to pray, in the assurance that the Holy Spirit
is praying in us. This implies further that we take time to
wait in God's presence, that we exercise an unbounded dependence upon the Holy Spirit who has been given us to cry,
"Abba Father" within us, even when we have nothing to
offer but groanings and sighs that cannot be uttered.

What a difference it would make in the life of many of
God's saints if they realized this! They not only have Jesus
the Son of God, the great High Priest, ever living to intercede
for them; they have not only the liberty of asking in faith
what they desire, and the promise it will be given them, but
they have actually and in very deed the Holy Spirit, "the Spirit
of grace and supplication," to carry on, in the depths of their
being, His work of interceding for them according to the will
of God.

What a call to separate ourselves from the world, to yield
ourselves wholeheartedly to the leading and praying of the
Spirit within us, deeper than all our thoughts or expectations!
What a call to surrender ourselves in stillness of soul, resting
in the Lord and waiting patiently for Him, as the Holy Spirit
prays within us not only for ourselves, but specifically for all
saints according to the will of God.

June 22

That They All May Be One

*Holy Father, keep them in thy name which thou hast given me,
THAT THEY MAY BE ONE, even as we are. Neither pray I
for these alone; but for them also which believe on me through
their word; THAT THEY MAY ALL BE ONE, even as thou,
Father, art in me, and I in thee, THAT THEY ALSO MAY BE
ONE IN US. And the glory which thou hast given me I have
given unto them; THAT THEY MAY BE ONE, even as WE
ARE ONE; I in them, and thou in me, THAT THEY MAY BE
PERFECTED INTO ONE; that the world may know that thou
didst send me.* —John 17:11, 20-23

Notice carefully how the Lord uses the expression "that
they may be one" five times over. It is as if He felt the need
of laying the emphasis strongly upon these words, if we are
really to realize the chief thought of His High Priestly prayer.
He wants the words and the thought to have the same place
in our hearts that they have in His. As He was on the way
to go to the Father through the cross, He would have us understand He took the thought and the desire with Him to heaven,
to make it the object of His unceasing intercession there.
And He entrusted the words to us that we should take them
into the world with us and make them the object of our unceasing intercession, too. That alone would enable us to fulfill
the last, the new command, which He gave—that we should
love the brethren as He loved us that our joy might be full.

How little the church has understood this. How little its
different branches are marked by a fervent, affectionate love
to all the saints of whatever name or denomination. Shall we
not welcome heartily the invitation to make this prayer
"*that they may be one*" a chief part of our daily fellowship
with God?

How simple it would be when once we connected the
two words "Our Father" with all the children of God throughout the world. Each time we used these sacred words we would
only have to expand this little word "*our*" into all the large-
ness and riches of God's Father love, and our hearts would
soon learn as naturally as we say "Father" with the thought
of His infinite love and our love to Him, to say "our" with
the childlike affection to all the saints of God, whoever and
wherever they be.

The prayer that "*they may be one*" would then become
a joy and a strength, a deeper bond of fellowship with Christ
Jesus and all His saints, and an offering of a sweet savor to
the Father of love.

June 23

The Disciples' Prayer

These all continued with one accord in prayer and supplication.—
Acts 1:14

*They continued stedfastly in fellowship and in prayers.—*Acts 2:42

What a lesson it would be to us in the school of prayer
to have a clear apprehension of what this continuing with one
accord in prayer meant to the disciples.

Just think of the object of their desire. However defective
the thoughts were that they had of the blessed Spirit, this
they knew, from the words of Jesus, "It is expedient for you
that I go away," that the Spirit would give the glorified
Christ into their very hearts in a way they had never known
Him before. And it would be He himself, in the mighty power
of God's Spirit, who would be their strength for the work to
which He had called them.

With what confidence they expected the fulfillment of the
promise. Had not the Master, who had loved them so well,
given them the assurance of what He would send upon them
from the throne of the Father in heaven?

And with what intensity and persistency they pleaded. In
the midst of their praise and thanksgiving, they worshiped
their Lord in heaven, remembering all He had taught them
about importunity. They had the full assurance that however
long the answer might be delayed, He would most assuredly
fulfill their desires. Let us nourish our hearts with thoughts
such as these until we realize the very same promise given
to the disciples is given to us, and that we, too, even though
we have to cry day and night to God, can count upon the
Father to answer our prayers.

One final thought, and this is not the least—let us believe
that as they continued with one accord in prayer, we also may
unite as one in presenting our petitions, even though we cannot
be together in one place. We can—in the love wherewith His
Spirit makes us one, and in the experience of our Lord's presence with each one who joins with His brethren in pleading
the blessed name—claim the promise that we, too, shall be
filled with the Holy Ghost.

June 24

Paul's Call to Prayer

With all prayer and supplication, praying at all seasons in the Spirit, and watching thereunto in all perseverance and supplication for all the saints and on my behalf.—Ephesians 6:18, 19

What a sense Paul had of the deep divine unity of the whole Body of Christ and of the actual need of unceasing prayer for all the members of the body by all who belong to it. He did not mean this to be an occasional thing, but the unceasing exercise of the life union in which they were bound together. This is evident from the words he uses, "with *all prayer* and supplication, praying *at all seasons* in the Spirit and watching thereunto, in *all perseverance* and supplication *for all the saints.*"

Paul expects believers to be so filled with the consciousness of their being in Christ, and through Him united consciously to the whole body, that in their daily life and all its involvements, their highest aim would ever be the welfare of the Body of Christ of which they had become members. He counted upon their being filled with the Spirit, so that it would be perfectly natural to them, without the thought of burden or constraint, to pray for all who belong to the Body of Jesus Christ. As natural as it is for each member of my body to be ready every moment to do what is needful for the welfare of the whole, even so, where the Holy Spirit has entire possession, the consciousness of union with Christ will ever be accompanied by consciousness of the union and the joy and the love of all the members.

Is not this just what we need in our daily life, that every believer who has yielded himself undividedly to Christ Jesus will, day by day, every day and all the day, live in the consciousness that he is one with Christ and His Body? The saints of God are to live for Christ their King, and also for all the members of that Body of which He is the Head. May God's people be willing to make this sacrifice of prayer and intercession at all times and for all saints!

June 25

Paul's Request for Prayer

And for me, that utterance may be given unto me, that I may open my mouth boldly, to make known the mystery of the gospel, that therein I may speak boldly, as I ought to speak.—Ephesians 6:19, 20

"And for me"—what light these word's cast on the deep reality of Paul's faith in the absolute necessity and the wonderful power of prayer. Just listen for what he asks them to pray: "That utterance may be given unto me, that I may open my mouth boldly, that therein I may speak boldly as I ought to speak."

Paul had now been a minister of the gospel for more than twenty years. One would say he had such experience of preaching and utterance that it would come naturally for him to speak boldly as he ought to speak. But so deep is his conviction of his own insufficiency and weakness, so absolute is his dependence on divine teaching and power, that he feels he cannot do the work as it ought to be done without the direct help of God. The sense of his total and unalterable dependence upon God, who was with him, teaching him what and how to speak, is the ground of all his confidence and the keynote of his whole life.

But there is more. He had in all these twenty years, times without number, been in circumstances where he had to throw himself upon God alone, with no one to help him in prayer. Yet, such is his deep spiritual insight into the unity of the Body of Christ, and his own actual dependence on the prayers of others, that he pleads for their praying with all prayer and supplication in the Spirit, watching thereunto with all prayer and perseverance, and asks them not to forget to pray for him. As little as a wrestler can afford to dispense with the help of the weakest member of his body in the struggle in which he is engaged, so little could Paul do without the prayers of the believers.

What a call to us in this twentieth century, to realize that Christ, our intercessor in heaven, and all saints here upon earth are engaged in one mighty contest, and that it is our duty to call out and to cultivate the gift of unceasing supplication for the power of God's Spirit in all His servants that all may have divine utterance given them, and that all may speak boldly as they ought to speak.

June 26

Prayer for All Saints

To the saints and faithful brethren in Christ, which are at Colosse. We give thanks to God, praying always for you, since we heard of the love which ye have to all the saints.... Continue in prayer, and watch in the same with thanksgiving, withal praying also for us.—Colossians 1:1-4, 4:2, 3

Prayer for all saints: let this be our first thought. It will need time, and thought, and love, to realize what is included in that simple expression. Think of your own neighborhood and the saints you know; think of your whole country, and praise God for all who are His saints; think of the Christian nations of the world and the saints to be found in each of these; think of all the heathen nations and the saints of God to be found among them in ever-increasing numbers.

Think of all the different circumstances and conditions in which these are to be found, and all the varying needs which call for God's grace and help. Think of many, oh, so many, who are God's saints, and yet through ignorance or laziness, through worldly-mindedness or an evil heart of unbelief, are walking in the dark and bringing no honor to God. Think of so many who are in earnest, and yet conscious of a life of failure, with little or no power to please God or to bless man.

Then think again of those who are to be found everywhere, in solitary places or in companies, whose one aim is to serve the Lord who bought them, and to be the light of those around them. Think of them especially as joining, often unconscious of their relation to the whole Body of Christ, in pleading for the great promise of the Holy Spirit and the love and oneness of heart which He alone can give.

This is not the work of one day or one night. It needs a heart which will set itself from time to time to do serious thinking about the state and the need of that Body of Christ to which we belong. But when once we begin, we will find what abundant reason there is for our persevering and yielding to God's Spirit that He may fit us for the great and blessed work of day by day praying the twofold prayer: for the love of God and Christ to fill the hearts of His people, and for the power of the Holy Ghost to come down and accomplish God's work in this sinful world.

June 27

Prayer by All Saints

We trust in God that he will yet deliver us; you also helping together by prayer for us.—2 Corinthians 1:10, 11

Some preach Christ of contention, supposing to add affliction to my bonds. For I know that this shall turn to my salvation, through your prayer, and the supply of the Spirit of Christ Jesus.—Philippians 1:16, 19

This subject calls us once again to think of all saints throughout the world, but leads us to view them from a different perspective. If we are to ask God to increase the number and the power of those who do pray, we will be led to form some impression of what the hope is that our circle of intercessors may gradually increase in number and power.

Our first thoughts will naturally turn to the multitude of saints who think and know little about the duty or the blessedness of pleading for the Body of Christ, or for all the work which has to be done to perfect its members. We will then have to remember how many there are for whom we may praise God that they do intercede for the power of His Spirit, but their thoughts are chiefly limited to spheres of work with which they are acquainted, or directly interested in.

That will leave us with what is, comparatively. speaking, only a limited number of those who will be ready to take part in the prayer which ought to be sent up by the whole church, for the unity of the Body and the power of the Spirit. And even then the number may be but small who really feel themselves drawn and urged to take part in this daily prayer for the outpouring of the Spirit on all God's people.

And yet many may be feeling this proposal meets a long-felt need, and that it is an unspeakable privilege, whether with few or many, to make Christ's last prayer, "that they may be one," the daily supplication of our faith and love. It may be that in time believers will band together in small circles, or throughout wider districts, to help rouse those around them to take part in the great work that the prayer *for all* saints may become *one by all saints.*

This message is sent out urgently to all hearts who desire to be in touch with it, to seek to prove their consecration to their Lord in the unceasing daily supplication for the power of His love and Spirit to be revealed to all His people.

June 28

Prayer for All the Fullness of the Spirit

Bring ye all the tithes unto mine house, and prove me now therewith, saith the Lord of Hosts, if I will not open you the windows of heaven and pour you out a blessing that there shall not be room enough to receive it.—Malachi 3:10

This last promise in the Old Testament tells us how abundant the blessing is to be. Pentecost was only the beginning of what God was willing to do. The promise of the Father, as Christ gave it, still waits for its perfect fulfillment. Let us try to realize what the liberty is that we have to ask, and expect great things.

Just as the great command to go and preach the gospel was not only meant for the disciples but for us, too, so the very last command, "Tarry till ye be endued with power from on high," "Wait for the promise of the Father," "Ye shall be baptized with the Holy Ghost," is also for us, and is the ground for the confident assurance that our prayer with one accord will be heard.

Take time to think of what a cry of need there is throughout the whole church and throughout all our mission fields. Realize that the only remedy to be found for inefficiency or impotence, to enable us to gain the victory over the powers of this world or of darkness, is in the manifested presence of our Lord in the midst of His hosts and in the power of His Spirit. Let us take time to think of the state of all the churches throughout Christendom until we are brought deeper than ever to the conviction that nothing will avail except the supernatural, almighty intervention of our Lord himself, to rouse His hosts for the great battle against evil. Can anyone conceive or suggest any other matter for prayer that can at all compete with this: for the power of God on the ministers of the gospel, and on all His people, to endue them with power from on high to make the gospel in very deed the power of God unto salvation?

As we connect the prayer for the whole church on earth with the prayer for the whole power of God in heaven, we will feel that the greatest truths of the heavenly world and the Kingdom of God have possession of us, and that we are in very deed asking what God is longing to give, as soon as He finds hearts utterly yielded to himself in faith and obedience.

June 29

Every Day

Give us day by day our daily bread. —Luke 11:3

There are some Christians who are afraid of the thought of a promise to pray every day as altogether beyond them. They could not undertake it, and yet they pray to God to give them their bread day by day. Surely if a child of God has once yielded himself with his whole life to God's love and service, he should count it a privilege to avail himself of any invitation that would help him *every day* to come into God's presence with the great need of His church and kingdom.

Are there not many who profess they desire to live wholly for God? They acknowledge that Christ gave himself for them, and that His love now watches over them and works in them without ceasing. They admit the claim that nothing less than the measure of the love of Christ to us is to be the measure of our love to Him. They feel that if this is indeed to be the standard of their lives, they ought surely to welcome every opportunity to prove it day by day; thus they are devoting their heart's strength to the interests of Christ's kingdom and to the prayer that can bring down God's blessing.

Our invitation to daily united prayer may come to some as a new and perhaps unexpected opportunity of becoming God's remembrancers who cry day and night for His power and blessing on His people and on this needy world. Think of the privilege of being thus allowed to plead every day with God on behalf of His saints, for the outpouring of His Spirit, and for the coming of His kingdom that His will may indeed be done on earth as it is in heaven.

To those who have to confess they have but little understood the high privilege and the solemn duty of waiting on God in prayer for His blessings on the world, the invitation ought to be most welcome. And even to those who have already their special circles of work for which to pray, the enlargement of their vision, and their hearts, to include all God's saints and all the work of His kingdom, and all the promise of an abundant outpouring of His Spirit, should urge them to take part in such a ministry. Their other work will not suffer, but their hearts will be strengthened with a joy and a love and a faith that they have never known before.

June 30

With One Accord

They were all with one accord in one place.... And they were all filled with the Holy Ghost. —Acts 2:1, 4

Our last meditations have opened to us wonderful thoughts of the solidarity of the whole Body of Christ and the need of the deliberate cultivation of the slumbering or buried talents of intercession. We may indeed thank God, for we know of the tens of thousands of His children who in daily prayer are pleading particularly for some portion of the work of God's kingdom in which they are personally interested. But in many cases the prayers are limited to the work that they take an interest in, and there is a lack of that large-hearted and universal love that takes up all the saints of God and their service into its embrace. There is not the boldness and the strength that comes from the consciousness of being part of a large and conquering army under the leadership of our conquering King.

A wrestler gathers up his whole strength and counts upon every member of his body doing its very utmost. In an army at war, with its millions of soldiers, each detachment not only throws its whole heart into the work it has to do, but it is ready to rejoice and take new courage from every example of the bravery and enthusiasm of the far-distant members of the one great army. And is not this what we need in the church of Christ, such an enthusiasm for the King and His kingdom and such a faith in His purpose that His name will be made known to every human being? Should not our prayers rise up every day, with a large-hearted love that grasps the whole body of Christ and pleads for the power of the Holy Spirit on all its members, even to the very weakest?

The strength unity gives is something inconceivable. The power of each individual member is increased to a large degree by the inspiration of fellowship with a large and conquering host. Nothing can so help us to an ever-larger faith as the consciousness of being one body and one spirit in Christ Jesus. It was as the disciples were all with one accord in one place on the Day of Pentecost that they were all filled with the Holy Spirit. United prayer brings the answer to prayer.

July

The Secret of Fellowship

July 1

From Day to Day

The inner man is renewed from day to day.—2 Corinthians 4:16

There is one lesson all young Christians should learn, namely this—*the absolute necessity of fellowship with Jesus each day.* This lesson is not always taught at the beginning of the Christian life, nor is it always understood by the young convert. He should realize that the grace he has received of the forgiveness of sins, of acceptance as God's child, of joy in the Holy Ghost, can only be preserved by the daily renewal in fellowship with Jesus Christ himself.

Many Christians backslide because this truth is not clearly taught. They are unable to stand against the temptations of the world, or of their old nature. They strive to do their best to fight against sin, and to serve God, but they have no strength. They have never really grasped the secret: *The Lord Jesus will every day* from heaven continue His work in me. But on one condition—*the soul must give Him time each day* to impart His love and His grace. Time alone with the Lord Jesus each day is the indispensable condition of growth and power.

Read Matthew 11:25-30. Listen to Christ's word: "Come unto me . . . and I will give you rest. Learn of me, and ye shall find rest unto your souls." The Lord will teach us just how meek and humble He is. Bow before Him, tell Him that you long for Him and His love, and He will let His love rest on you. This is a thought not only for young Christians, but for all who love the Lord; and my purpose in this series is to help those who desire to live this life of fellowship with Christ. We will try to put the message as clearly, as lovingly, as urgently as possible. For Christ's sake, and in order to please Him; for my own sake, and to enable me to enjoy this blessed experience each day, I will learn the lesson, *to spend time each day*—without exception—*in fellowship with my Lord.* So will the inner man be renewed from day to day.

July 2

Fellowship with God

As the Father hath loved me, so have I loved you: continue ye in my love.—John 15:9

The three persons in the Godhead are the Father, the Son, and the Holy Spirit. Each one knows himself as different from the others. God desires to reveal himself as a person. Each one of us is an individual, knowing himself as distinct from others, and standing in certain relations to others. God will reveal himself to us as a person, and it is our holy calling to enter into fellowship with Him.

God greatly desires this relationship with man. But sin has come between man and his God. Even in the Christian, who thinks he knows God, there is often great ignorance and even indifference to this personal relationship of love to God.

People believe that at conversion their sins are forgiven, that God accepts them so that they may go to heaven, and that they should try to do God's will. But the idea is strange to them that even as a father and his child on earth have pleasure in being together, *so they may and must each day have this blessed fellowship with God.*

God gave Christ His Son *to bring us to himself.* But this is only possible when we live in close fellowship with Jesus Christ. Our relationship to Christ rests on His deep, tender love to us. We are not able of ourselves to give Him this love. But the Holy Spirit will do the work in us. For this we need to separate ourselves each day from the world and turn in faith to the Lord Jesus and He may shed abroad His love in our hearts, *so that we may be filled with a great love to Him.*

Dear soul, meditate quietly on this thought. Read the words of Christ in John 14:21, "He that loveth me shall be loved of my Father. I will love him." Take time to believe in this personal fellowship. Tell Him of your love. Say to Him: "Lord, Thou hast loved me dearly; most earnestly do I desire to love Thee above all."

July 3

Jesus

Thou shalt call his name Jesus, for he shall save his people from their sins. —Matthew 1:21

As the Lord Jesus was a person, He had His own individual name. His mother, His disciples, all His friends called Him by this name—Jesus. But they probably thought little of what that name meant. And how little do the majority of Christians know what a treasure is contained in that name—Jesus—*"He shall save his people from their sins."*

Many think of His death on the cross, they think of His work in heaven as Intercessor, but do they, or do we, realize that He is a living person in heaven, who thinks of us each day, and longs to reveal himself? And He desires us each day to bring Him our love and adoration.

Christians pray to Christ to save them from their sins, but they know very little how the blessed work is done. The living Christ reveals himself to us, and through the power of His love the love of sin is expelled. It is *through personal fellowship* with Him that Jesus saves us from our sins. I must come as an individual, with my heart and all the sin that is in it, to Jesus as an almighty personal Savior, in whom God's holiness dwells. And as He and I commune together in the expression of mutual love and desire, by the work of His Holy Spirit in my heart, His love will expel and conquer all the sin.

O Christian, learn the blessedness of each day in fellowship with Jesus, finding the secret of happiness and holiness. Your heart will long for the hour of prayer as the best hour of the day. As you learn to go apart with Him alone each day, you will experience His presence with you, enabling you all through the day to love Him, to serve Him, and to walk in His ways. Through this unbroken fellowship you will learn the secret of the power of a truly godly life.

July 4

The Inner Chamber

When thou prayest, enter into thine inner chamber.—Matthew 6:6

Have you ever thought what a wonderful privilege it is that every one each day and each hour of the day has the liberty of asking God to meet him in the inner chamber and to hear what He has to say? We should imagine that every Christian would use such a privilege gladly and faithfully.

"When thou prayest," says Jesus, "enter into thine inner chamber, and having shut thy door, pray to thy Father which is in secret." That means two things: Shut the world out, withdraw from all worldly thoughts and occupations, and shut yourself in alone with God to pray to Him in secret. Let this be your chief object in prayer: *to realize the presence of your Heavenly Father.* Let your watchword be: alone with God.

This is only the beginning. I must take time to realize His presence with me, and pray to my Father who seeth in secret, in the full assurance that He knows how I long for His help and guidance, and will incline His ear to me.

Then follows the great promise: "Thy Father which seeth in secret shall reward thee openly." My Father will see to it that my prayer is not in vain. All through the occupations of a busy day the answer to my prayer will be granted. *Prayer in secret will be followed by the secret working of God in my heart.*

As the Lord Jesus has given us the promise of His presence, and shows us the way to the inner chamber, He will assuredly be with us to teach us to pray. It is through Him that we have access to the Father. Be childlike and trustful in your fellowship with Christ. Confess each sin, bring your every need. Offer your prayer to the Father in the name of Christ. *Prayer in fellowship with Jesus* cannot be in vain.

July 5

Faith

Only believe.—Mark 5:36

We have here a lesson of the greatest importance—namely this, that when alone in the inner chamber we must send up our petitions, trusting implicitly in the love of God and in the power of the Lord Jesus. Take time to ask yourself the question: Is my heart full of a great and steadfast faith in God's love? If this is not the case, do not begin to pray at once. Faith does not come of itself. Consider quietly how impossible it is for God to lie. He is ready with infinite love to give you a blessing. Take some text of scripture in which God's power and faithfulness and love are revealed. Appropriate the words, and say: "Yes, Lord, I will pray in firm faith in Thee and in Thy great love."

It is a mistake to limit the word "faith" to the forgiveness of sins and to our acceptance as children of God. Faith includes far more. We must have *faith in all that God is willing to do for us*. We must have faith each day according to our special needs. God is infinitely great and powerful, Christ has so much grace for each new day, that our faith must reach out afresh each day according to the need of the day.

When you enter into the inner chamber, even before you begin to pray, ask yourself: "Do I really believe that *God is here with me, and that the Lord Jesus will help me to pray,* and I may expect to spend a blessed time in communion with my God?"

Jesus often taught His disciples how indispensable faith was to true prayer. He will teach us this lesson, too. Remain in fellowship with Him, and ask Him to strengthen your faith in His almighty power. Christ says to you and to me as to Martha: "Said I not unto thee that if thou wouldst believe, thou shouldest see the glory of God?"

July 6

The Word of God

Man shall not live by bread alone, but by every word that proceedeth out of the mouth of God. —Matthew 4:4

The illustration that our Lord uses, in which the Word of God is compared to our daily bread, is most instructive.

Bread is indispensable to life. We all understand this. However strong a person may be, if he takes no nourishment, he will grow weaker and life will become extinct. Even so with the Word of God. It contains a heavenly principle and works powerfully in them that believe.

Bread must be eaten. I may know all about bread. I may have bread, and may give it to others. I may have bread in my house and on my table in great abundance, but that will not help me; if through illness I am unable to eat it, I will die. And so a mere knowledge of God's Word and even the preaching of it to others will not avail me. It is not enough to think about it. I must feed on God's Word and take it into my heart and life. In love and obedience I must appropriate the words of God and let them take full possession of my heart. Then they will indeed be words of life.

Bread must be eaten daily. And the same is true of God's Word. The Psalmist says: "Blessed is the man whose delight is in the law of the Lord; and *in his law doth he meditate day and night."* "O how I love thy law; it is my meditation *all the day."* To secure a strong and powerful spiritual life, God's Word every day is indispensable.

When on earth the Lord Jesus learned, loved, and obeyed the word of the Father. And if you seek fellowship with Him, you will find Him in His Word. Christ will teach you to commune with the Father, through the Word, even as was His custom. You will learn, like Him, to live solely for the glory of God and the fulfillment of His Word.

How to Read God's Word

Blessed is the man whose delight is in the law of the Lord, and in his law doth he meditate day and night.—Psalm 1:1, 2

Here are some simple rules for Bible reading.

Read God's Word with great reverence. Meditate a moment in silence on the thought that the words come from God himself. Bow in deep reverence. Be silent unto God. Let Him reveal His Word in your heart.

Read with careful attention. If you read the words carelessly, thinking that you can grasp their meaning with your human understanding, you will use the words superficially, and not enter into their depths. When someone tries to explain anything wonderful or beautiful to us, we give our entire attention to try to understand what is said. How much higher and deeper are God's thoughts than our thoughts. "As the heaven is higher than the earth, so are my thoughts higher than your thoughts." We need to give our undivided attention to understand even the superficial meaning of the words. How much harder to grasp the spiritual meaning?

Read with the expectation of the guidance of God's Spirit. It is God's Spirit alone that can make the Word a living power in our hearts and lives. Read Psalm 119. Notice how earnestly David prays that God will teach him, and open his eyes, and give him understanding, and incline his heart to God's ways. As you read, remember that God's Word and God's Spirit are inseparable.

Read with the firm purpose of keeping the Word day and night in your heart and in your life. The whole heart and the whole life must come under the influence of the Word. David said: "O how I love thy law, it is my meditation all the day." And so in the midst of his daily work, the believer can cherish God's Word in his heart, and meditate on it. Read Psalm 119 again until you accept God's Word with all your heart. Pray that God may teach you to understand it and to carry out its precepts in your life.

July 8

The Word and Prayer

Quicken me, O Lord, according to thy word.—Psalm 119:107

Prayer and the Word of God are inseparable, and should always go together in the quiet time of the inner chamber. *In His Word God speaks to me; in prayer I speak to God.* If there is to be true conversation, God and I must both take part. If I simply pray without using God's Word, I am apt to use my own words and thoughts. What really gives prayer its power is that I take God's thoughts from His Word and present them before Him. Then I am enabled to pray according to God's Word. How indispensable God's Word is for all true prayer!

When I pray, I must seek to know God aright. It is through the Word that the Holy Spirit gives me right thoughts of Him. The Word will also teach me how wretched and sinful I am. It reveals to me all the wonders God will do for me and the strength He will give me to do His will. The Word teaches me how to pray—with strong desire, with a firm faith, and with constant perseverance. The Word teaches me not only what I am, but what I may become through God's grace. And above all, it reminds me each day that Christ is the great intercessor, and allows me to pray in His name.

O Christian, learn this great lesson, *to renew your strength each day in God's Word, and so pray according to His will.*

Then we turn to the other side—prayer. We need prayer when we read God's Word—prayer to be taught of God to understand His Word, prayer that through the Holy Spirit I may rightly know and use God's Word, prayer that I may see in the Word that Christ is all in all, and will be all in me.

Blessed inner chamber, where I may approach God in Christ through the Word and prayer. There I may offer myself to God and His service, and be strengthened by the Holy Spirit, so that His love may be shed abroad in my heart and I may daily walk in that love.

July 9

Obedience

Obey my voice ... and I will be your God. —Jeremiah 11:4

God gave this command to Israel when He gave them the law. But Israel had no power to keep the law. So God gave them a "new covenant" to enable His people to live a life of obedience. We read: "I will write my law in their hearts" (Jer. 31:33); "I will put my fear in their hearts, that they shall not depart from me" (Jer 32:40); "I will cause you to walk in my statutes" (Ezek. 36:27). These wonderful promises gave the assurance that obedience would be their delight.

Let us listen to what the Lord Jesus says about obedience (John 14:21-23), "He that keepeth my commandments, he it is that loveth me; and he that loveth me shall be loved of my Father, and I will love him, and we will make our abode with him." And in John 15:10, "If ye keep my commandments, ye shall abide in my love." These words are an inexhaustible treasure. Faith can firmly *trust Christ to enable us to live such a life of love and of obedience.*

No father can train his children unless they are obedient. No teacher can teach a child who continues to disobey him. No general can lead his soldiers to victory without prompt obedience. Pray God to imprint this lesson on your heart: *the life of faith is a life of obedience.* As Christ lived in obedience to the Father, so we, too, need obedience for a life in the love of God.

Alas, the thought is too common, "I cannot be obedient, it is quite impossible." Yes, impossible to you, but not to God. He has promised *"to cause you to walk in his statutes."* Pray and meditate on these words, and the Holy Spirit will enlighten your eyes, so that you will have power to do God's will. Let your fellowship with the Father and with the Lord Jesus Christ have as its one aim and object a life of quiet, determined, unquestioning obedience.

July 10

Confession of Sin

If we confess our sins, he is faithful and just to forgive us our sins, and to cleanse us from all unrighteousness. —1 John 1:9

Too often the confession of sin is superficial, and often it is quite neglected. Few Christians realize how necessary it is to be in earnest about the matter, or feel that an honest confession of sin gives power to live the life of victory over sin. *In fellowship with the Lord Jesus we need to confess with a sincere heart every sin that may be a hindrance in our Christian lives.*

Listen to what David says: "I acknowledged my sin unto thee; I said, I will confess my transgression, and thou forgavest the iniquity of my sin. Thou art my hiding-place; thou shalt compass me about with songs of deliverance" (Ps. 32:5-7). David speaks of a time when he was unwilling to confess his sin. "When I kept silence, thy hand was heavy upon me." *But when he had confessed his sin, a wonderful change came.*

Confession means not only that I confess my sin with shame, but that I hand it over to God, trusting Him to take it away. Such a confession implies that I am wholly unable to get rid of my guilt, but by an act of faith I reckon on God to deliver me. This deliverance means, first, that I know my sins are forgiven, and second, that Christ undertakes to cleanse me from the sin and to keep me from its power.

O Christian, if you are seeking to have fellowship with Jesus, do not fear to *confess each sin* in the confident assurance that there is deliverance. Let there be a mutual understanding between the Lord Jesus and yourself that you will confess each sin and obtain forgiveness. Then you will know your Lord as Jesus who saves His people from their sin. Believe that there is great power in the confession of sin, for the burden of sin is borne by our Lord and Savior.

July 11

The First Love

I have somewhat against thee, because thou hast left thy first love.
—Revelation 2:4

In Revelation 2:2-3, eight signs are mentioned showing the zeal and activity of the church at Ephesus. But there was one bad sign, and the Lord said: "Except thou repent, I will come unto thee, and will remove thy candlestick out of his place." And what was this sign? *"Thou hast left thy first love."*

We find the same lack in the church of the present day. There is zeal for the truth, there is continuous and persevering labor, but that which the Lord values most is lacking, *the tender, fervent love to himself.*

This is a thought of great significance: a church or a community or a Christian may be an example in every good work, and yet *the tender love to the Lord Jesus in the inner chamber is missing.*

There is no personal, daily fellowship with Christ, and all the manifold activities with which people satisfy themselves are as nought in the eyes of the Master himself.

This series speaks of the fellowship of love with Christ in the inner chamber. Everything depends on this. Christ came from heaven to love us with the love wherewith the Father loved Him. He suffered and died to win our hearts for this love. *His love can be satisfied with nothing less than a deep, personal love on our part.*

Christ considers this of the first importance. Let us do so, too. Many ministers and missionaries and Christian workers confess with shame that in spite of all their zeal in the Lord's work, their prayer life is defective, because they have left their first love. I pray you, write this down on a piece of paper, and remember it continually: *The love of Jesus must be all*—in the inner chamber, in all my work, in my daily life.

July 12

The Holy Spirit

He shall glorify me; for he shall receive of mine, and shall shew it unto you.—John 16:14

Our Lord, in the last night that He was with His disciples, promised to send the Holy Spirit as a Comforter. Although His bodily presence was removed, His presence would be realized in them and with them in a wonderful way. The Holy Spirit as God would so reveal Christ in their hearts that they would experience His presence with them continually. The Spirit would glorify Christ and would reveal the glorified Christ in heavenly love and power.

How little do Christians understand and believe and experience this glorious truth. We should fail in our duty as ministers if in a series like this, or in our preaching, we encouraged Christians to love the Lord Jesus without at the same time warning them that it is not a duty they can perform in their own strength. No, that is impossible; it is God, the Holy Spirit alone, who will shed abroad His love in our hearts and teach us to love Him fervently. *Through the Holy Spirit we may experience the love and abiding presence of the Lord Jesus all the day.*

But let us remember that the Spirit as God must have entire possession of us. He claims our whole heart and life. He will strengthen us with might in the inner man, so that we have fellowship with Christ, and keep His commandments, and abide in His love.

When once we have grasped this truth, we will begin to feel our deep dependence on the Holy Spirit, and pray the Father to send Him in power into our hearts. The Spirit will teach us to love the Word, to meditate on it and to keep it. He will reveal the love of Christ to us that we may love Him with a pure heart fervently. Then we will begin to see that a life in the love of Christ in the midst of our daily life and distractions is a glorious possibility and a blessed reality.

July 13

Christ's Love to Us

Even as the Father hath loved me, I also have loved you: abide ye in my love. —John 15:9

In communion between friends and relations everything depends on their love to each other. Of what value is abundance of riches if love is lacking between husband and wife, or parents and children? And in our religion, of what value is all knowledge and zeal in God's work without the knowledge and experience of Christ's love? (See 1 Cor. 13:1-3.) O Christians, the one thing needful in the inner chamber is to know by experience how much Christ loves you and to learn how you may abide and continue in that love.

Think of what Christ says: "As the Father hath loved me" —what a divine, everlasting, wonderful love! "Even so have I loved you." It was the same love with which He had loved the Father and that He always bore in His heart, which He now gave into the hearts of His disciples. He yearns that this everlasting love should rest upon us, and work within us, that we may abide in it day by day. What a blessed life! Christ desires every disciple to live in the power of the self-same love of God that He himself experienced. Do you realize that in your fellowship with Christ in secret or in public, you are surrounded by and kept in this heavenly love? Let your desire reach out to this everlasting love. The Christ with whom you desire fellowship longs unspeakably to fill you with His love.

Read from time to time what God's Word says about the love of Christ. Meditate on the words, and let them sink into your heart. Sooner or later you will begin to realize: The greatest happiness of my life is that I am beloved of the Lord Jesus. I may live in fellowship with Him all the day long.

Let your heart continually say: His love to me is unspeakable. He will keep me abiding in His love.

July 14

Our Love to Christ

Jesus Christ, whom not having seen, ye love: in whom, though now ye see him not, yet believing, ye rejoice greatly with joy unspeakable and full of glory.—1 Peter 1:8

What a wonderful description of the Christian life! These were people who had never seen Christ, and yet truly loved Him and believed on Him, so that their hearts were filled with unspeakable joy. Such is the life of a Christian who really loves his Lord.

We have seen that the chief attribute of the Father and of the Son is love to each other and love to man. This should be the chief characteristic of the true Christian. The love of God and of Christ is shed abroad in his heart, and becomes a well of living water, flowing forth as love to the Lord Jesus.

This love is not merely a blessed feeling. It is an active principle. It takes pleasure in doing the will of the beloved Lord. It is joy to keep His commandments. The love of Christ to us was shown by His death on the cross; our love must be exhibited in unselfish, self-sacrificing lives. Oh, that we understood this: *In the Christian life love to Christ is everything.*

Great love will beget great faith. Faith in His love to us, faith in the powerful revelations of His love in our hearts, faith that He through His love will work all His good pleasure in us.

The wings of faith and love will lift us up to heaven, and we will be filled with joy unspeakable. The joy of the Christian is an indispensable witness to the world of the power of Christ to change hearts and to fill them with heavenly love and gladness.

O ye lovers of the Lord Jesus, take time daily in the inner chamber with Him anew to drink in His heavenly love. It will make you strong in faith, and your joy will be full. Love, joy, faith—these will be our life each day through the grace of our Lord Jesus.

July 15

Love to the Brethren

A new commandment I give unto you, that ye love one another, even as I have loved you, that ye also love one another.—John 13:34; 15:12

The Lord Jesus told His disciples that as the Father had loved Him, even so He loved them. And now, following His example, we must love one another with the same love. "By this shall all men know that ye are my disciples, if ye have love one to another" (John 13:35). He had prayed, "That they all may be one, as thou, Father, art in me, and I in thee, that the world may believe that thou hast sent me" (John 17:21). If we exhibit the love that was in God toward Christ, and in Christ to us, the world will be obliged to confess that our Christianity is genuine and from above.

This is what actually happened. The Greeks and Romans, Jews and heathen hated each other. Among all the nations of the world there was hardly a thought of love to each other. The very idea of self-sacrifice was a strange one. When the heathen saw that Christians from different nations, under the powerful working of the Holy Spirit, became one, and loved one another, even to the point of self-sacrifice in time of plague or illness—they were amazed and said: "Behold how these people love one another!"

Among professing Christians there is a certain oneness of belief and feeling of brotherhood, but Christ's heavenly love is often lacking, and we do not bear one another's burdens or love others heartily.

Pray that you may love your fellow believers with the same love with which Christ loved you. If we abide in Christ's love, and let that love fill our hearts, supernatural power will be given us to take all God's children unto our hearts in love. As close as is the bond of love between the Father and the Son, between Christ and His followers, so close must the bond of love be between all God's children.

July 16

Love to Souls

Know that he which converteth a sinner from the error of his way, shall save a soul from death. —James 5:20

What a wonderful thought!—that I may save a soul from everlasting death. How can this be? If I convert him from the error of his ways. This is the calling, not only of the minister, but of every Christian—to work for the salvation of sinners.

When Christ and His love took possession of our hearts, He gave us this love that we might bring others to Him. In this way Christ's kingdom was extended. Everyone who had the love of Christ in his heart was constrained to tell others. This was the case in the early Christian church. After the Day of Pentecost, people went out and told of the love of Christ, which they had themselves experienced. Heathen writers have told us that the rapid spread of Christianity in the first century was due to the fact that each convert, being filled with the love of Christ, tried to bring the good news to others.

What a change has come over the church! Many Christians never try to win others to Christ. Their love is so weak and faint they have no desire to help others. May the time soon come when Christians will feel constrained to tell of the love of Christ. In a revival in Korea years ago, the converts were filled with such a burning love to Christ that they felt bound to tell others of His love. It was even taken as a test of membership that each one should have brought another to the Lord before being admitted to the church.

Let the reader examine himself, and pray that in fellowship with Christ, he may think, not only of his own soul, but having received the gift of God's love, he may pass it on to others. He will then know true happiness, the joy of bringing souls to Christ.

Let us pray earnestly to be so filled with God's love that we may wholeheartedly surrender ourselves to win others for Him.

July 17

The Spirit of Love

The love of God is shed abroad in our hearts, by the Holy Ghost, which is given unto us.—Romans 5:5

The fruit of the Spirit is love.—Galatians 5:22

The thought sometimes arises, as we consider Christ's love to us, our love to Christ, our love to the brethren or to souls around us: the demand is too great, it is unattainable, it is impossible for a Christian to live this life of love, and to show it to the brethren and to needy souls. And because we deem it impossible, and because of our unbelief and lack of faith in God's promises, we make little progress in this spirit of love.

We need continually to remind ourselves that it is not in our own strength, or even by serious thought, that we can attain to the love of Christ. We must realize the truth that the love of God is shed abroad in our hearts, and will daily afresh be poured out by the Spirit of God. It is only as we are wholly surrendered to the leading of the Spirit that we will be able to live according to God's will. When the inner life of love is renewed from day to day we will feel compelled to work for souls.

Here is a prayer that you can offer: "I bow my knees unto the Father, that he would grant you to be strengthened with might by his Spirit in the inner man, that Christ may dwell in your hearts by faith, that ye, *being rooted and grounded in love, may know the love of Christ which passeth knowledge.*" You may be rooted and grounded in this love, and know the love that passeth knowledge on one condition—you must be *strengthened by the Spirit in the inner man, so that Christ may dwell in your heart.* Then you will indeed be rooted and grounded in love.

Christian, take this message from God's Word and let it influence your life. Unless you wait upon God daily on your knees for His Spirit to be revealed in your heart, you cannot live in this love. A life of prayer will make a life in the love of Christ, in the love of the brethren, in love to souls, a blessed reality in your experience.

Put your confidence each day in secret in the Holy Spirit —the Spirit of love which God will give to those who ask in faith.

July 18

Persevering Prayer

Men ought always to pray, and not to faint.—Luke 18:1

Continue in prayer.—Romans 12:12

Pray without ceasing.—1 Thessalonians 5:17

One of the greatest drawbacks to the life of prayer is the fact that the answer does not come as speedily as we expect. We are discouraged by the thought, "Perhaps I do not pray aright," and so we do not persevere in prayer. This was a lesson our Lord taught often and urgently. If we consider the matter we can see that there may be a reason for the delay, and the waiting may bring a blessing to our souls. Our desire must grow deeper and stronger, and we must ask with our whole heart. God puts us into the practicing school of persevering prayer that our weak faith may be strengthened. Do believe that there is a great blessing in the delayed answer to prayer.

Above all, God would draw us into closer fellowship with himself. When our prayers are not answered, we learn to realize that the fellowship and nearness and love of God are more to us than the answers of our petitions, and we continue in prayer. What a blessing Jacob received through the delay in the answer to his prayer! He saw God face to face, and as a prince he had power with God and prevailed.

Christians, listen to this warning. Be not impatient or discouraged if the answer does not come. "Continue in prayer." "Pray without ceasing." You will find it an unspeakable blessing to do so. You will ask whether your prayer is really in accordance with the will of God and the Word of God. You will inquire if it is in the right spirit and in the name of Christ. Keep on praying; you will learn that the delay in the answer to prayer is one of the most precious means of grace God can bestow on you. You will learn, too, that those who have persevered often and long before God, in pleading His promises, are those who have had the greatest power with God in prayer.

July 19

The Prayer Meeting

These all continued with one accord in prayer and supplication. And they were all filled with the Holy Ghost.—Acts 1:14; 2:4 (See also Matthew 18:19, 20.)

Great is the value of a genuine prayer meeting. There God's children meet together, not as in church to listen to one speaker, but to lift up their hearts unitedly to God. By this means Christians are drawn closer to each other. Those who are weak are strengthened and encouraged by the testimony of the older and more experienced members, and even young Christians have the opportunity of telling of the joy of the Lord.

The prayer meeting may become a great power for good in a congregation and a spiritual help to both minister and members. By means of intercession God's blessing is poured out at home and abroad.

But there are also dangers to be considered. Many attend, and are edified, but never learn to pray themselves. Others go for the sake of social and religious fervor, and have a form of godliness, but do not know the hidden life of prayer. Unless there is *much and earnest prayer in the inner chamber*, attendance at a prayer meeting may be a mere form. There should be hearty love and fellowship between the members. It is well to ask: What constitutes a living prayer meeting?

The leaders should realize how great the influence of such a meeting may be, with its roots nourished by the life of prayer in the inner chamber. Prayer should include God's people and His church all over the world. And above all, as on the Day of Pentecost, there must be waiting on God for the filling with the Holy Spirit.

Dear reader, this book aims at helping you in your spiritual life. But remember, you do not live for yourself alone. You are part of the Body of Christ. Your prayer must include in its intercession all Christians. As the roots of the tree hidden deep in the earth and the branches spread out to heaven are one, so the hidden prayer life is inseparably bound up with united prayer.

July 20

Intercession

Praying at all seasons in the Spirit . . . in all perseverance and supplication for all the saints.—Ephesians 6:18

What an unspeakable blessing there is in intercession. That one should pray down heavenly gifts on himself is a wonder of grace, but that he should bring down blessing on others is indeed an inconceivable honor. Will God indeed make the pouring out of blessing on others *dependent on our prayers*? Yes, He makes us His remembrancers and fellow workers. He has taken us into partnership in His work; if we fail in doing our part, others will suffer, and His work will suffer unspeakable loss.

God has appointed intercession as one of the means by which souls will be saved, and saints and ministers of the gospel edified and built up in the faith. Even the ends of the earth will receive life and blessing through our prayers. Should we not expect God's children to strive joyfully and with all their powers, by means of intercession, to bring down blessing on the world?

Christian, begin to use intercession as a means of grace for yourself and for others. Pray for your neighbors. Pray for souls with the definite desire that they may be won for Christ. Pray for your minister, for all ministers and missionaries. Pray for your country and people, for rulers and subjects. Pray for all men. If you surrender yourself to the guidance of the Holy Spirit, and live a life wholly for God, you will realize that the time spent in praying is an offering well pleasing to God, bringing blessing to yourself and power into the lives of those for whom you pray.

Yes, "pray always with all prayer and supplication, watching thereunto with all perseverance and supplication for all saints." And in so doing you will learn the lesson that intercession is the chief means of winning souls and bringing glory to God.

July 21

Prayer and Fasting

And Jesus said unto them, Because of your unbelief. Howbeit this kind goeth not out but by prayer and fasting. —Matthew 17:20, 21

Our Lord here teaches us that a life of faith requires both prayer and fasting. That is, prayer grasps the power of heaven, fasting loosens the hold on earthly pleasure.

Jesus himself fasted to get strength to resist the devil. He taught His disciples that even as with prayer and alms-giving, fasting should be in secret, and the Heavenly Father would reward openly. Abstinence from food, or temperance in taking it, helps to strengthen the soul for communion with God.

Let us learn this great lesson that abstinence, temperance, and self-denial in temporal things is a help to the spiritual life. After having partaken of a hearty meal, one does not feel much desire to pray. To willingly sacrifice our own pleasure, or bodily enjoyment, and to subdue the lust of the flesh and the lust of the eyes will help to set our minds more fully on heavenly things. The very exertion needed in overcoming the desires of the flesh will give us strength to take hold of God in prayer.

The great lesson is this. Our dullness in prayer comes from our fleshly desire of comfort and ease. "Those who are in Christ have crucified the flesh and its desires." Prayer is no easy work. It may easily become a mere form. For the real practice of prayer, and taking hold of God, and having communion with Him, it is necessary that all things pleasing to the flesh must be sacrificed and given over to death.

Beloved Christian, do believe that it is worth any trouble to deny ourselves daily in order to meet the Holy God and receive from Him heavenly blessings.

July 22

The Spirit of Prayer

The Spirit maketh intercession for the saints.—Romans 8:27

"Prayer is not our work, but God's work, that He works within us by His almighty power." As we think of this, our attitude should be one of silent expectation that as we pray, the Holy Spirit may help our infirmities and pray within us with groanings that cannot be uttered.

What a thought! When I feel how defective my prayer is, when I have no strength of my own, I may bow in silence before God in the confidence that His Holy Spirit will teach me to pray. The Spirit is the Spirit of prayer. It is not my work, but God's work in me. My very desire is a sign that God will hear me. When God would grant our requests, He first works the desire in our hearts, and the Spirit will perfect the work, even in our weakness.

We see this in the story of Jacob. The same One who wrestled with him, and seemed to withhold the blessing, was in reality strengthening him to continue and to prevail in prayer. What a wondrous thought!

Prayer is the work of the Triune God: the Father, who wakens the desire, and will give all we need; the Son, who through His intercession teaches us to pray in His name; and the Holy Spirit, who in secret will strengthen our feeble desires.

We have spoken of the Spirit of truth who will glorify Christ in us, and of the Spirit of love, who will shed this love abroad in our hearts. And now we have the Spirit of prayer, through whom our life may be one of continual prayer. *Thank God, the Spirit has been given from heaven to dwell in our hearts and to teach us to pray.*

Christian, listen to the leading of the Spirit. Obey His voice in all things. He will make you a person of prayer. You will then realize the glory of your calling as intercessor, asking great things of God for those around you, for the church, and for the whole heathen world.

July 23

Wholly for Christ

One died for all... that they which live should no longer live unto themselves, but unto him who for their sakes died and rose again.
—2 Corinthians 5:14, 15

Here we have a threefold life described. First, the life of the Christian, who lives according to his old nature: *he lives for himself alone.* Second, the life of the true Christian: *he lives wholly for Christ.* Third, the life of Christ in heaven: *He lives wholly for us.*

Many a Christian needs to be convinced of the folly of living only for himself. At conversion he thinks more of his own salvation and less of the glory of God and the right that Christ, who has redeemed us with His precious blood, has upon him. Many Christians just live for themselves, content with doing a little for the Master. Happy the believer who realizes his high calling and the privilege and blessedness of consecrating his life entirely to God's service.

The great hindrance to such a life is the unbelief which says it is impossible. But when the truth takes hold of us that Christ in heaven lives wholly for me and will impart His life to me and will enable me to live wholly for Him, then we will be able to say joyfully: Dear Lord Jesus, from this moment let my prayer each day be—wholly for Christ, wholly for Christ.

Let nothing less be your earnest desire, your prayer, and your firm expectation: Christ has not only died for me, but also lives in heaven to keep and sanctify me, his purchased possession. Ponder this wonderful thought, that Christ will keep you as a member of His Body, to work and live for Him. Pray for grace to live wholly for God in seeking souls and in serving His people. Take time from day to day to be so united to Christ in the inner man that you can say with all your heart: I live wholly for Him, who gave himself wholly for me and now lives in heaven wholly for me.

July 24

The Cross of Christ

I am crucified with Christ.—Galatians 2:20

The cross of Christ is His greatest glory. Because He humbled himself to the death of the cross, *therefore* God has highly exalted Him. The cross was the power that conquered Satan and sin.

The Christian shares with Christ in the cross. The crucified Christ lives in him through the Holy Spirit, and the spirit of the cross inspires him. He lives as one who has died with Christ. As he realizes the power of Christ's crucifixion, he lives as one who has died to the world and to sin, and the power becomes a reality in his life. It is as the Crucified One that Christ lives in me.

Our Lord said to His disciples: "Take up your cross and follow me." Did they understand this? They had seen men carrying a cross and knew what it meant—a painful death on the cross. And so all His life Christ bore His cross—the death sentence that He should die for the world. And each Christian must bear his cross, acknowledging that he is worthy of death, and believing that he is crucified with Christ, and that the Crucified One lives in him. "Our old man is crucified with Christ." "He that is Christ's hath crucified the flesh with all the lusts thereof." When we have accepted this life of the cross, we will be able to say with Paul: "Far be it from me to glory save in the cross of our Lord Jesus Christ."

This is a deep spiritual truth. Think and pray over it, and the Holy Spirit will teach you. Let the disposition of Christ on the cross, His humility, His sacrifice of all worldly honor, His Spirit of self-denial, take possession of you. The power of His death will work in you, and you will become like Him in His death, and you will know Him and the power of His resurrection. Take time, O soul, that Christ through His Spirit may reveal himself as the Crucified One.

July 25

The World

Love not the world, neither the things that are in the world. If any man love the world, the love of the Father is not in him.—1 John 2:15

John teaches us clearly what he means by the world. He says: "All that is in the world, the lust of the flesh, and the lust of the eyes, and the pride of life, is not of the Father, but is of the world" (1 John 2:16).

The world is that disposition or power under which man has fallen through sin. And the god of this world, to deceive man, conceals himself under the form of what God has created. The world with its pleasures surrounds the Christian each day with temptations.

This was the case with Eve in the Garden of Eden. We find in Genesis 3 the three characteristics which John mentions: (1) The lust of the flesh—"The woman saw the tree that it was good for food." (2) The lust of the eyes—"It was pleasant to the eyes." (3) The pride of life—"A tree to be desired to make one wise." And the world still comes to us offering desirable food and much to please the fleshly appetites. And much that the eye desires, riches and beauty and luxury. And the pride of life, when a man imagines he knows and understands everything, and prides himself on it.

Is our life in the world not full of danger, with the allurements of the flesh—so much to occupy our eyes and our hearts, so much worldly wisdom and knowledge?

So John tells us: "Love not the world, for then the love of the Father is not in you." And our Lord calls us, as He called His disciples of old, to leave all and follow Him.

Christian, you live in a dangerous world. Hold fast to the Lord Jesus. As He teaches you to shun the world and its attractions, your love will go out to Him in loyal-hearted service. But remember—there must be daily fellowship with Jesus. His love alone can expel the love of the world. Take time to be alone with your Lord.

July 26

Put on Christ

As many of you as have been baptized into Christ have put on Christ.—
Galatians 3:27

*Put ye on the Lord Jesus Christ, and make not provision for the flesh, to fulfil the lusts thereof.—*Romans 13:14

The word that is here translated "put on" is the same that is used in regard to putting on clothes. We have put on "the new man," and we have the new nature as a garment that is worn, by means of which all can see who we are. Paul says of the Christian when he has confessed Christ at baptism, that he has put on Christ. As a man may be recognized by the garment he wears, so the Christian is known as one who has put on Christ and exhibits Him in his whole life and character.

And again he says: "Put on the Lord Jesus"—not alone at conversion, but from day to day. As I put on my clothes each day and am seen in them, so the Christian must daily put on the Lord Jesus, so that he no longer lives after the flesh to fulfill its lusts, but shows forth the image of his Lord and the new man formed in His likeness.

Put on Christ! This work must be done each day in the inner chamber. I must put on the Lord, the heavenly Jesus. But I need time to put on Christ. As my garments cover me and protect me from wind and sun, even so Christ Jesus will be my beauty, my defense, and my joy. As I commune with Him in prayer, He imparts himself to me and strengthens me to walk as one who is in Him and bound to Him forever.

O soul, take time to meditate on this wonderful truth. Just as your clothing is a necessity as you go out into the world, let it be equally indispensable for you to put on Jesus Christ, to abide in Him and walk with Him all the day.

You feel that this cannot be done hastily and superficially. It takes time, quiet time in living fellowship with Jesus, to realize that you have put Him on. Take the time and the trouble. Your reward will be great.

The Strength of the Christian

Finally, my brethren, be strong in the Lord, and in the power of his might.—Ephesians 6:10

The apostle has reached the end of his epistle and begins his last division with the words: "Finally, my brethren, be strong in the Lord."

The Christian needs strength. This we all know. The Christian has no strength of his own. This is also true. Where may strength be obtained? Notice the answer: "Be strong *in the Lord* and the power of his might."

Paul had spoken of this power in the earlier part of his epistle (1:17-19). He had prayed God to give them the Spirit that they might know the exceeding greatness of His power according to the working of His mighty power, which He wrought in Christ when He raised Him from the dead. This is the literal truth: *the exceeding greatness of His power,* which raised Christ from the dead, *works in every believer*— in me and in you. We hardly believe it, and still less do we experience it. That is why Paul prays, and we must pray with him, that God through His Spirit would teach us to believe in His almighty power. Pray with all your heart: Father, grant me the Spirit of wisdom that I may experience this power in my life.

In Ephesians 3:16, 17, Paul prays the Father to grant them, according to the riches of His glory, to be strengthened with might by His Spirit in the inner man, that Christ might dwell in their hearts. And then: "Now unto him that is able to do exceeding abundantly above all that we ask or think, *according to the power that worketh in us,* unto him be glory."

Read over these two passages again, and pray for God's Spirit to enlighten your eyes. Believe in the divine power working within you. Pray that the Holy Spirit may reveal it to you, and appropriate the promise that God will manifest His power in your heart, supplying all your needs.

Do you not begin to realize that time is needed, much time in communion with the Father and the Son, if you would experience the power of God within you?

July 28

The Whole Heart

With my whole heart have I sought thee. —Psalm 119:10

Notice how often the Psalmist speaks here of the whole heart. "They that seek him with the whole heart" (v. 2). "I shall observe thy law with my whole heart" (v. 34). "I will keep thy precepts with my whole heart" (v. 69). "I cried with my whole heart" (v. 145). In seeking God, in observing His law, in crying for His help—each time it is with the whole heart.

When we want to make anything a success in worldly affairs, we put our whole heart into it. And is this not much more necessary in the service of a holy God? Is He not worthy? Does not His great holiness and the natural aversion of our hearts from God demand it? The whole heart is needed in the service of God when we worship Him in secret.

And yet how little most Christians think of this. They do not remember how necessary it is—in prayer, in reading God's Word, in striving to do His will—to say continually: *With my whole heart have I sought thee.* Yes, when we pray, and when we try to understand God's Word, and to obey His command, let us say continually: *With my whole heart have I sought thee.* Yes, when we pray, and when we try to understand God's Word, and to obey His commands, let us say: I desire to seek God, to serve Him and to please Him with my whole heart.

"With my whole heart have I sought thee." Dear reader, take this word into your heart. Think over it. Pray over it. Speak it out before God until you feel that you really mean what you say, and you have the assurance that God will hear your prayer. Say it each morning as you approach God in prayer. "I seek Thee with my whole heart." You will, by degrees, feel the need of waiting in holy stillness upon God that He may take possession of your whole heart. You will learn to love Him with your whole heart and with all your strength.

July 29

In Christ

Of God are ye in Christ Jesus.—1 Corinthians 1:30

The expression "in Christ" is often used in the Epistles. The Christian cannot read God's Word correctly, nor experience its full power in his life, until he prayerfully and believingly accepts this truth: *I am in Christ Jesus.*

The Lord Jesus in the last night with His disciples used this word more than once. "In that day"—when the Spirit had been poured out—"ye shall know that I am in the Father, and *ye in me*." And then follows: "Abide *in me*; he that abideth *in me* beareth much fruit." "If ye abide *in me,* ye shall ask what ye will, and it shall be done unto you." But the Christian cannot appropriate these promises unless he first prayerfully accepts the word "in Christ."

Paul expresses the same thought in Romans: "We are buried *with Christ.*" "We are dead indeed unto sin, but alive unto God *through Jesus Christ* our Lord." "There is no condemnation to them which are *in Christ Jesus.*" And in Ephesians: "God has blessed us with all spiritual blessings *in Christ*"; hath chosen us in Him; hath made us accepted in the beloved; in Him we have redemption. And in Colossians: "*In him* dwelleth all the fulness"; we are "perfect *in Christ Jesus.*" "Walk ye *in him.*" "Ye are complete *in him.*"

Let our faith take hold of the words: "It is God that stablisheth us in Christ." "Of God I am in Christ Jesus." The Holy Spirit will make it our experience. Pray earnestly and follow the leading of the Spirit. The word will take root in your heart, and you will realize something of its heavenly power. But remember that abiding in Christ is a matter of the heart. It must be cultivated in a spirit of love. Only as we take time from day to day in fellowship with Christ will the abiding in Christ become a blessed reality and the inner man be renewed from day to day.

July 30

Christ in Me

Know ye not ... how that Jesus Christ is in you?—2 Corinthians 13:5

The apostle would have each Christian live in the full assurance: *Christ is in me.* What a difference it would make in our lives if we could take time every morning to be filled with the thought: Christ is in me. *As assuredly as I am in Christ, Christ is also in me.*

In the last night Christ put it clearly to His disciples that the Spirit would teach them: "In that day ye shall know that I am in the Father, and ye are in me, and *I in you.*" First of all, *Ye in Me.* Through the power of God all we who believe were crucified with Christ and raised again with Him. And as a result *Christ is in us.* But this knowledge does not come easily. Through faith in God's Word the Christian accepts it, and the Holy Spirit will lead us into all truth. Take time this very day to realize and appropriate this blessing in prayer.

How clearly Paul expresses the thought in the prayer of Ephesians 3:16: "That the Father would grant you according to the riches of his glory." Notice that it is not the ordinary gift of grace, but a special revelation of the riches of His love and power. That He grant you to be strengthened with might by His Spirit in the inner man, so that *Christ may dwell in your hearts by faith.* Have you grasped it? The Christian may really have the experience of being filled with the fullness of God.

Dear Christian, Paul said: "I bow my knees unto the Father." That is the only way to obtain the blessing. Take time in the inner chamber to realize: *Christ dwells in me.* Too little have I experienced this in the past, but I will cry to God and wait upon Him to perfect His work in me. Even in the midst of my daily work, I must look upon my heart as the dwelling place of the Son of God, and say: "I am crucified with Christ, I live no more; *Christ liveth in me.*" Thus, only will Christ's words, "Abide in me, and I in you," become my daily experience.

July 31

Christ Is All

Christ is all and in all.—Colossians 3:11

In the eternal counsel of God, in the redemption on the cross, as King on the throne in heaven and on earth—*Christ is all*! In the salvation of sinners, in their justification and sanctification, in the upbuilding of Christ's Body, in the care for individuals, even the most sinful—this word avails, *Christ is all*. Every day and every hour it affords comfort and strength to the child of God, who accepts it in faith—*Christ is all*.

Have you perhaps thought in reading these pages that the full salvation here described is not meant for you? You feel too weak, too unworthy, too untrustworthy. My dear reader, do believe that if you will only accept the Lord Jesus in child-like faith, you have a leader and a guide who will supply all your need. Believe with your whole heart in the word of our Savior, "Lo, I am with you alway," and you will experience His presence each day. However cold and dull your feelings may be, however sinful you are, meet the Lord Jesus in secret and He will reveal himself to you.

Tell Him how wretched you are, and then trust Him to help and sustain you. Wait before Him until by faith you can rejoice in Him. Read this series over again with the thought: *Christ is all*. I have failed to remember this, but each day as I go to secret prayer, let this thought be with me: *Christ is all*.

Let me take it as my motto—to teach me to pray, to strengthen my faith, to give me the assurance of His love, and access to the Father, to make me strong for the work of the day: *Christ is all*.

Yes, Christ, my Christ, is all I need. It will teach me to abide in His love. It will give me the assurance that He dwells in my heart, and I may know the love that passes knowledge. God be praised to all eternity: Christ, my Christ, is my all in all!

August

The Secret of the Cross

August 1

The Redemption of the Cross

Christ redeemed us from the curse of the law, having become a curse for us. —Galatians 3:13

Scripture teaches us that there are two points of view from which we may regard Christ's death upon the cross. The one is *the redemption of the cross:* Christ dying for us as our complete deliverance from the curse of sin. The other, *the fellowship of the cross:* Christ taking us up to die with Him, and making us partakers of the fellowship of His death in our own experience.

In our text we have three great unsearchable thoughts. The law of God has pronounced a curse on all sin and on all that is sinful. Christ took our curse upon Him, yea, became a curse, and so destroyed its power, and in that cross we now have the everlasting redemption from sin and all its power. The cross reveals to us man's sin, as under the curse, Christ becoming a curse and so overcoming it, and our full and everlasting deliverance from the curse.

In these thoughts the lost and most hopeless sinner finds a sure ground of confidence and hope. God had indeed in Paradise pronounced a curse upon this earth and all that belongs to it. On Mount Ebal, in connection with giving the law, half of the people of Israel were twelve times over to pronounce a curse on all sin. And there was to be in their midst a continual reminder of it: "Cursed is every one that hangeth on a tree" (Deut. 21:23; 27:15-20). And yet who could ever have thought that the Son of God himself would die upon the accursed tree and become a curse for us? But such is in very deed the gospel of God's love, and the penitent sinner can now rejoice in the confident assurance that the curse is forever put away from all who believe in Christ Jesus.

The preaching of the redemption of the cross is the foundation and center of the salvation the gospel brings us. To those who believe its full truth it is a cause of unceasing thanksgiving. It gives us boldness to rejoice in God. There is nothing which will keep the heart more tender toward God, enabling us to live in His love and to make Him known to those who have never yet found Him. God be praised for the redemption of the cross!

August 2

The Fellowship of the Cross

Have this mind in you, which was also in Christ Jesus.—Philippians 2:5

Paul here tells us what that mind was in Christ: He emptied himself; He took the form of a servant; He humbled himself, even to the death of the cross. It is this mind that was in Christ, the deep humility that gave up His life to the very death, that is to be the spirit that animates us. It is thus that we shall prove and enjoy the blessed fellowship of His cross.

Paul had said (v. 1): "If there is any comfort in Christ"—the Comforter was come to reveal His real presence in them—"if any fellowship of the Spirit"—it was in this power of the Spirit that they were to breathe the Spirit of the crucified Christ and manifest His disposition in the fellowship of the cross in their lives.

As they strove to do this, they would feel the need of a deeper insight into their real oneness with Christ. They would learn to appreciate the truth that they had been crucified with Christ, that their "old man" had been crucified, and that they had died to sin in Christ's death and were now living to God in His life. They would learn to know what it meant that the crucified Christ lived in them, and that they had crucified the flesh with its affections and lusts. It was because the crucified Jesus lived in them that they could live crucified to the world.

And so they would gradually enter more deeply into the meaning and the power of their high calling to live as those who were dead to sin and the world and self. Each in his own measure would bear about in his life the marks of the cross, with its sentence of death on the flesh, with its hating of the self life and its entire denial of self, with its growing conformity to the crucified Redeemer in His deep humility and entire surrender of His will to the life of God.

It is no easy school and no hurried learning—this school of the cross. But it will lead to a deeper apprehension and a higher appreciation of the redemption of the cross through the personal experience of the fellowship of the cross.

August 3

Crucified with Christ

I have been crucified with Christ; yet I live; and yet no longer I, but Christ liveth in me.—Galatians 2:20

The thought of fellowship with Christ in His bearing the cross has often led to the vain attempt in our own power to follow Him and to bear His image. But this is impossible to man until he first learns to know something of what it means to say, "I have been crucified with Christ."

Let us try to understand this. When Adam died, all his descendants died with him and in him. In his sin in Paradise, and in the spiritual death into which he fell, I had a share; I died in him. And the power of that sin and death, in which all his descendants share, works in every child of Adam every day.

Christ came as the second Adam. In His death on the cross, all who believe in Him had a share. Each one may say in truth, "I have been crucified with Christ." As the representative of His people, He took them up with Him on the cross, and me, too. The life that He gives is the crucified life in which He entered heaven and was exalted to the throne, standing as a Lamb as it had been slain. The power of His death and life work in me, and as I hold fast the truth that I have been crucified with Him and that now I myself live no more but Christ liveth in me, I receive power to conquer sin. The life that I have received from Him is a life that has been crucified and made free from the power of sin.

We have here a deep and precious truth. Most Christians have but little knowledge of it. That knowledge is not gained easily or speedily. It needs a great longing in very deed to be dead to all sin. It needs a strong faith, wrought by the Holy Ghost, that the union with Christ crucified, that the fellowship of His cross, can day by day become our life. The life that He lives in heaven has its strength and its glory in the fact that it is a crucified life. And the life that He imparts to the believing disciple is even so a crucified life with its victory over sin and its power of access into God's presence.

It is in very deed true that I no longer live, but Christ lives in me as the Crucified One. As faith realizes and holds fast the fact that the crucified Christ lives in me, life in the fellowship of the cross becomes a possibility and a blessed experience.

August 4

Crucified to the World

Far be it from me to glory, save in the cross of our Lord Jesus Christ, through which the world hath been crucified unto me, and I unto the world.—Galatians 6:14

What Paul had written in Galatians 2 is here in the end of the epistle confirmed, and expressed still more strongly. He speaks of his only glory being that in Christ he has in very deed been crucified to the world and entirely delivered from its power. When he said: "I have been crucified with Christ," it was not only an inner spiritual truth, but an actual, practical experience in relation to the world and its temptations. Christ had spoken about the world hating Him and His having overcome the world. Paul knows that the world, which nailed Christ to the cross, had in that deed done the same to him. He boasts that he lives as one crucified to the world, and that now the world as an impotent enemy was crucified to him. It was this that made him glory in the cross of Christ. It had wrought out a complete deliverance from the world.

How very different the relation of Christians to the world in our day! They agree that they may not commit the sins that the world allows. But further, they are good friends with the world and have liberty to enjoy as much of it as they can if they only keep from open sin. They do not know that the most dangerous source of sin is the love of the world with its lusts and pleasures.

O Christian, when the world crucified Christ, it crucified you with Him. When Christ overcame the world on the cross, He made you an overcomer, too. He calls you now, at whatever cost of self-denial, to regard the world, in its hostility to God and His kingdom, as a crucified enemy over whom the cross can ever keep you conqueror.

What a different relationship to the pleasures and attractions of the world the Christian has who by the Holy Ghost has learned to say: "I have been crucified with Christ; the crucified Christ liveth in me"! Let us pray God fervently that the Holy Spirit, through whom Christ offered himself on the cross, may reveal to us in power what it means to "glory in the cross of our Lord Jesus Christ, through which the world has been crucified unto me."

August 5

The Flesh Crucified

They that are in Christ Jesus have crucified the flesh with the passions and lusts thereof.—Galatians 5:24

Of the flesh Paul teaches us (Rom. 7:18), "In me, that is, *in my flesh, dwelleth no good thing.*" And again (Rom. 8:7), "The mind of the flesh is *enmity against God; for it is not subject to the law of God, neither indeed can it be.*" When Adam lost the spirit of God, he became flesh. Flesh is the expression for the evil, corrupt nature that we inherit from Adam. Of this flesh it is written, "Our old man was crucified with him" (Rom. 6:6). And Paul puts it here even more strongly, "They that are in Christ Jesus have crucified the flesh."

When the disciples heard and obeyed the call of Jesus to follow Him, they honestly meant to do so; but as He later on taught them what that would imply, they were far from being ready to yield immediate obedience. And even so those who are Christ's and have accepted Him as the Crucified One, little understand what that includes. By that act of surrender they actually have crucified the flesh, and consented to regard it as an accursed thing, nailed to the cross of Christ.

Alas, how many there are who have never for a moment thought of such a thing! It may be that the preaching of Christ crucified has been defective. It may be that the truth of our being crucified with Christ has not been taught. They shrink back from the self-denial that it implies, and as a result, where the flesh is allowed in any measure to have its way, the Spirit of Christ cannot exert His power.

Paul taught the Galatians: "Walk in the Spirit, and ye shall not fulfil the lusts of the flesh." "As many as are led by the Spirit of God, they are the children of God." And the Spirit can alone guide us as the flesh, in living faith and fellowship with Christ Jesus, is kept in the place of crucifixion.

Blessed Lord, how little I understood when I accepted Thee in faith that I crucified once for all the flesh with its passions and lusts! I beseech Thee humbly, teach me so to believe and so to live in Thee, the Crucified One, that with Paul I may ever glory in the cross on which the world and the flesh are crucified.

August 6

Bearing the Cross

He that doth not take his cross and follow after me is not worthy of me. He that loseth his life for my sake shall find it.—Matthew 10:38-39

We have had some of Paul's great words to the Galatians about the cross and our being crucified with Christ. Let us now turn to the Master himself to hear what He has to teach us. We will find that what Paul could teach openly and fully after the crucifixion was given by the Master in words that could at first hardly be understood, and yet contained the seed of the full truth.

It was in the ordination charge, when Christ sent forth His disciples, that He first used the expression that the disciple must take up his cross and follow Him.

The only meaning the disciples could attach to these words was from what they had often seen, when an evil-doer who had been sentenced to death by the cross was led out bearing his cross to the place of execution. In bearing the cross, he acknowledged the sentence of death that was on him. And Christ would have His disciples understand that their nature was so evil and corrupt that it was only in losing their natural life that they could find the true life. Of Jesus it was true. All His life He bore His cross, the sentence of death that He knew to rest upon himself on account of our sins. And so He would have His disciple bear his cross, the sentence of death upon himself and his evil, carnal nature.

The disciples could not at once understand all this. But Christ gave them seed words, which would germinate in their hearts and later on begin to reveal their full meaning. The disciple was not only to carry the sentence of death in himself but to learn that in following the Master to His cross, he would find the power to lose his life and to receive instead of it the life that would come through the cross of Christ.

Christ asks of His disciples that they should forsake all and take up their cross, give up their whole will and life and follow Him. The call comes to us, too, to give up the self life with its self-pleasing and self-exaltation, and bear the cross in fellowship with Him, and we shall be made partakers of His victory.

August 7

Self-Denial

Then said Jesus unto his disciples, "If any man will come after me, let him deny himself, and take up his cross, and follow me."— Matthew 16:24

Christ had for the first time definitely announced that He would have to suffer much and be killed and be raised again. "Peter rebuked him, saying, 'Be it far from thee, Lord: this shall never be unto thee.' " Christ's answer was, "Get thee behind me, Satan." The spirit of Peter, seeking to turn Him away from the cross and its suffering, was nothing but Satan tempting Him to turn aside from the path which God had appointed as our way of salvation.

Christ then adds the words of our text, in which He uses for the second time the words "take up the cross." But with that He uses a most significant expression revealing what is implied in the cross: "If any man come after me, *let him deny himself,* and take up his cross." When Adam sinned, he fell out of the life of heaven and of God into the life of the world and of self. Self-pleasing, self-sufficiency, self-exaltation became the law of his life. When Jesus Christ came to restore man to his original place, "being in the form of God, *he emptied himself,* taking the form of a servant, and *humbled himself* even to the death of the cross." What He himself has done He asks of all who desire to follow Him: "If any man will come after me, let him deny himself."

Instead of denying himself, Peter denied his Lord: "I know not the man." When a man learns to obey Christ's commands, he says of himself: "I know not the man." It is the secret of true discipleship, to bear the cross, to acknowledge the death sentence that has been passed on self, and to deny any right that self has to rule over us.

Death to self, is to be the Christian's watchword. The surrender to Christ is to be so entire, the surrender for Christ's sake to live for those around us so complete, that self is never allowed to come down from the cross to which it has been crucified, but is ever kept in the place of death.

Let us listen to the voice of Jesus: "Deny self"; and ask that by the grace of the Holy Spirit, as the disciples of a Christ who denied himself for us, we may ever live as those in whom self has been crucified with Christ, and in whom the crucified Christ now lives as Lord and Master.

August 8

He Cannot Be My Disciple

If any man cometh unto me, and hateth not his own life, he cannot be my disciple. Whosoever doth not bear his own cross, and come after me, cannot be my disciple. Whosoever he be of you that renounceth not all that he hath, he cannot be my disciple.—Luke 14:26-33

For the third time Christ speaks about bearing the cross. He gives new meaning to it when He says that a man must hate his own life and renounce all that he has. Three times over He solemnly repeats the words that without this a man cannot be His disciple.

"If a man hate not his own life." And why does Christ make such an exacting demand the condition of discipleship? Because the sinful nature we have inherited from Adam is indeed so vile and full of sin, that if our eyes were only opened to see it in its true nature, we would flee from it as loathsome and incurably evil. "The flesh is enmity against God"; the soul that seeks to love God cannot but hate the "old man" which is corrupt through its whole being. Nothing less than this, the hating of our own life, will make us willing to bear the cross and carry within us the sentence of death on our evil nature. It is not till we hate this life with a deadly hatred that we will be ready to give up the old nature to die the death that is its due.

Christ has one word more: "He that renounceth not all that he hath," whether in property or character, "cannot be my disciple." Christ claims all. Christ undertakes to satisfy every need and to give a hundredfold more than we give up. It is when by faith we become conscious of what it means to know Christ, and to love Him and to receive from Him what can in very deed enrich and satisfy our immortal spirits, that we shall count the surrender of what at first appeared so difficult, our highest privilege. As we learn what it means that Christ is our life, we shall count all things but loss for the excellency of the knowledge of Christ Jesus our Lord. In the path of following Him, and ever learning to know and to love Him better, we shall willingly sacrifice all, self with its life, to make room for Him who is more than all.

August 9

Follow Me

Then Jesus, beholding him, loved him, and said: "One thing thou lackest: go thy way, sell whatsoever thou hast, and come, take up the cross, and follow me."—Mark 10:21

When Christ spoke these words to the young ruler, the young man went away grieved. Jesus said: "How hardly shall they that have riches enter into the kingdom of God!" The disciples were astonished at His words. When Christ repeated once again what He had said, they were astonished and asked, "Who then can be saved?"

"Jesus looking upon them said, 'With men it is impossible, but not with God; for with God all things are possible.'"

Christ had spoken about bearing the cross from the human side, as the one condition of discipleship. Here with the rich young ruler He reveals from the side of God what is needed to give men the will and the power thus to sacrifice all if they were to enter the kingdom. He said to Peter, when he had confessed Him as Christ, the Son of God, that flesh and blood had not revealed it unto him, but his Father in heaven, to remind him and the other disciples that it was only by divine teaching that he could make the confession. So here with the ruler, He unveils the great mystery that it is only by divine power that a man can take up his cross, lose his life, deny himself and hate the life to which he is by nature so attached.

Multitudes have sought to follow Christ and obey His injunction, and have found that they have utterly failed! Multitudes have felt that Christ's claims were beyond their reach and have sought to be Christians without any attempt at the wholehearted devotion and the entire self-denial which Christ asks for!

Let us in our study of what the fellowship of the cross means take today's lesson to heart, and believe that it is only by putting our trust in the living God, and the mighty power in which He is willing to work in the heart, that we can attempt to be disciples who forsake all and follow Christ in the fellowship of His cross.

A Grain of Wheat

Verily, verily, I say unto you, Except a grain of wheat fall into the earth and die, it abideth by itself alone; but if it die, it beareth much fruit. He that loveth his life loseth it; and he that hateth his life in this world shall keep it unto life eternal.—John 12:24, 25

All nature is the parable of how the losing of a life can be the way of securing a truer and a higher life. Every grain of wheat, every seed throughout the world, teaches the lesson that through death lies the path to a beautiful and fruitful life.

It was so with the Son of God. He had to pass through death in all its bitterness and suffering before He could rise to heaven and impart His life to His redeemed people. And here under the shadow of the approaching cross He calls His disciples: "If any man will serve me, let him follow me." He repeats the words: "He that hateth his life in this world shall keep it unto life eternal."

One might have thought that Christ did not need to lose His holy life before He could find it again. But so it was: God had laid upon Him the iniquity of us all, and He yielded to the inexorable law: Through death to life and to fruit.

How much more ought we, in the consciousness of that evil nature, and that death which we inherited in Adam, be willing, yea, most grateful, that there is a way open to us by which, in the fellowship of Christ and His cross, we can die to this accursed self! With what gratitude ought we to listen to the call to bear our cross, to yield our "old man" as crucified with Christ daily to that death which he deserves! Surely the thought that the power of the eternal life is working in us ought to make us willing and glad to die the death that brings us into the fellowship and the power of life in a risen Christ.

How little this is understood! Let us believe that what is impossible to man is possible to God. Let us believe that the law of the Spirit of Christ Jesus, the risen Lord, can in very deed make His death and His life the daily experience of our souls.

August 11

Thy Will Be Done

O my Father, if it be possible, let this cup pass away from me: nevertheless, not as I will, but as thou wilt.—Matthew 26:39

The death of Christ on the cross is the highest and the holiest that can be known of Him even in the glory of heaven. And the highest and the holiest the Holy Spirit can work in us is to take us up and to keep us in the fellowship of the cross of Christ. We need to enter deeply into the truth that Christ the beloved Son of the Father could not return to the glory of heaven until He had first given himself over unto death. As this great truth opens up to us, it will help us to understand how in our life, and in our fellowship with Christ, it is impossible for us to share His life until we have first in very deed surrendered ourselves every day to die to sin and the world, and so to abide in the unbroken fellowship with our crucified Lord.

And it is from Christ alone we can learn what it means to have fellowship with His sufferings, and to be made conformable unto His death. In the agony of Gethsemane He looked forward to what a death on the cross would be: There He had a vision of what it meant to die the accursed death under the power of sin, with God's countenance so turned from Him that not a single ray of its light could penetrate the darkness. There he prayed that the cup might pass from Him. But when no answer came, and He understood that the Father could not allow the cup to pass by, He yielded up His whole will and life in the prayer: "Thy will be done."

O Christian, in this word of your Lord in His agony, you can enter into fellowship with Him, and in His strength your heart will be made strong to believe most confidently that God in His omnipotence will enable you in very deed with Christ to yield up everything because you have in very deed been crucified with Him.

"Thy will be done"—let this be the deepest and the highest word in your life. In the power of Christ with whom you have been crucified, and in the power of His Spirit, the definite daily surrender to the ever-blessed will of God will become the joy and strength of your life.

August 12

The Love of the Cross

Then said Jesus: "Father, forgive them; for they know not what they do."—Luke 23:34

The seven words on the cross reveal what the mind of Christ is, and show the dispositions that become His disciples. His first three words are the expression of His wonderful love.

1. "Father, forgive them, for they know not what they do." He prays for His enemies. In the hour of their triumph over Him, and of the shame and suffering which they delight in showering on Him, He pours out His love in prayer for them. It is the call to everyone who believes in a crucified Christ to go and do likewise, even as He has said, "Love your enemies, bless them that curse you, do good to them that hate you, and pray for them which persecute you." The law of the Master is the law for the disciple; the love of the crucified Jesus, the only rule for those who believe in Him.

2. "Woman, behold thy son!" "Behold thy mother!" The love that cared for His enemies, cared too for His friends. Jesus felt what the anguish must be in the heart of His widowed mother, and commits her to the care of the beloved disciple. He knew that for John there could be no higher privilege and no more blessed service than that of taking His place in the care of Mary. Even so we who are the disciples of Christ must not only pray for His enemies, but prove our love to Him, and to all who belong to Him, by seeing to it that every solitary one is comforted, and that every loving heart has some work to do in caring for those who belong to the blessed Master.

3. "Verily I say unto thee, today shalt thou be with me in Paradise." The penitent thief had appealed to Christ's mercy to remember him. With what readiness of joy and love Christ gives the immediate answer to his prayer! Whether it was the love that prays for His enemies, or the love that cares for His friends, or the love that rejoices over the penitent sinner who was being cast out by man—in all Christ proves that the cross is a cross of love, that the Crucified One is the embodiment of a love that passes knowledge.

With every thought of what we owe to that love, with every act of faith in which we rejoice in its redemption, let us prove that the mind of the crucified Christ is our mind, and we trust in His love not only for ourselves, but it guides us in our loving relationships with the world around us.

August 13

The Sacrifice of the Cross

My God, my God, why hast thou forsaken me?—I thirst.—It is finished.—Matthew 27:46; John 19:28, 30

The first three words on the cross reveal love in its outflow to men. The next three reveal love in the tremendous sacrifice that it brought, to deliver us from our sins and give the victory over every foe. These words still reveal the very mind which was in Christ, and that is to be in us as the disposition of our whole life.

"My God, my God, why hast thou forsaken me?" How deep must have been the darkness that overshadowed Him, when not one ray of light could pierce, and He could not say, "My Father"! It was this awful desertion breaking in upon that life of childlike fellowship with the Father in which He had always walked that caused Him the agony and the bloody sweat in Gethsemane. "O my Father, let this cup pass from me"—but it could not be, and He bowed His head in submission: "Thy will be done." It was His love to God and love to man, yielding himself to the very uttermost. It is as we learn to believe and to worship that love that we, too, will learn to say: "Abba, Father, Thy will be done."

"I thirst." The body now gives expression to the terrible experience of what it passed through when the fire of God's wrath against sin came upon Christ in the hour of His desertion. He had spoken of Dives crying: "I am tormented in this flame." Christ utters His complaint of what He had suffered. Physicians tell us that, in crucifixion the whole body is in agony with a terrible fever and pain. Our Lord endured it all and cried: "I thirst"; soul and body was the sacrifice He brought the Father.

Then comes the great word: "It is finished." All that there was to suffer and endure had been brought a willing sacrifice; He had finished the work the Father gave Him to do. His love held nothing back. He gave himself an offering and a sacrifice. Such was the mind of Christ, and such must be the disposition of everyone who owes himself and his life to that sacrifice. The mind that was in Christ must be in us ready to say: "I am come to do the will of Him that sent me, and to finish His work." Every day that our confidence grows fuller in Christ's finished work must see our heart more entirely yielding itself like Him, a whole burnt offering in the service of God and His love.

August 14

The Death of the Cross

"Father, into thy hands I commit my spirit." And having said this, he gave up the ghost. —Luke 23:46

Like David (Ps. 31:5), Christ had often committed His spirit into the hands of His Father for His daily life and need. But here is something new and very special. He gives up His spirit into the power of death, gives up all control over it, to sink down into the darkness and death of the grave, where He can neither think, nor pray, nor will. He surrenders himself to the utmost into the Father's hands, trusting Him to care for Him in the dark, and in due time to raise Him up again.

If we have indeed died in Christ, and are now in faith every day to carry about with us the death of our Lord Jesus, this word is exactly what we need. Just think once again what Christ meant when He said we must hate and lose our life.

We died in Adam; the life we receive from him is death; there is nothing good or heavenly in us by nature. It is to this inward evil nature, to all the life we have from this world, that we must die. There cannot be any thought of any real holiness without totally dying to this self or "old man." Many deceive themselves because they seek to be alive in God before they are dead to their own nature: a thing as impossible as it is for a grain of wheat to be alive before it dies. This total dying to self lies at the root of all true piety. The spiritual life must grow out of death.

If we ask how we can do this, we find the answer in the mind in which Christ died. Like Him we cast ourselves upon God, without knowing how the new life is to be attained; but as we in fellowship with Jesus say, "Father, into Thy hands I commit my spirit," and depend simply and absolutely upon God to raise us up into the new life, there will be fulfilled in us the wonderful promise of God's Word, concerning the exceeding greatness of His power in us who believe. This operates according to the mighty power which He wrought in Christ when He raised Him from the dead.

This indeed is the true test of faith that lives every day and every hour in the absolute dependence upon the continual and immediate quickening of the divine life in us by God himself through the Holy Spirit.

August 15

It Is Finished

When Jesus had received the vinegar, he said: "It is finished."—John 19:30

The seven words of our Lord on the cross reveal to us His mind and disposition. At the beginning of His ministry He said (John 4:34): "My meat is to do the will of him that sent me, and *to finish his work.*" In all things, the small as well as the great, He accomplished God's work. In the High-Priestly prayer at the end of the three years' ministry, He could say (John 17:4): "I have glorified thee on the earth. *I have finished the work* which thou gavest me to do." He sacrificed all, and in dying on the cross could in truth say: "It is finished."

With that word to the Father He laid down His life. With that word He was strengthened, after the terrible agony on the cross, in the knowledge that all was now fulfilled. And with that word He uttered the truth of the gospel of our redemption: all that was needed for man's salvation had been accomplished on the cross.

This disposition should characterize every follower of Christ. The mind that was in Him must be in us—it must be our meat, the strength of our life, *to do the will of God in all things, and to finish His work.* There may be small things about which we are not conscientious, and so we bring harm to ourselves and to God's work. Or we draw back before some great thing which demands too much sacrifice. In every case we may find strength to perform our duty in Christ's word: "It is finished." His finished work secured the victory over every foe. By faith we may appropriate that dying word of Christ on the cross and find the power for daily living and dying in the fellowship of the crucified Christ.

Child of God, study the inexhaustible treasure contained in this word: "It is finished." Faith in what Christ accomplished on the cross will enable you to show in your daily life the spirit of the cross.

August 16

Dead to Sin

We who died to sin, how shall we any longer live therein?—Romans 6:2

After having, in the first section of the Epistle to the Romans (1:16-5:11), expounded the great doctrine of justification by faith, Paul proceeds, in the second section (5:12-8:39), to unfold the related doctrine of the new life by faith in Christ. Taking Adam as a figure of Christ, he teaches that just as we all really and actually died in Adam, so that his death reigns in our nature, even so, in Christ, those who believe in Him, actually and effectually died to sin, were set free from it and became partakers of the new holy life of Christ.

He asks the question: "We who died to sin, how shall we any longer live therein?" In these words we have the deep spiritual truth that our death to sin in Christ delivers us from its power, so that we no longer may or need to live in it. The secret of true and full holiness is by faith and in the power of the Holy Spirit to live in the consciousness that *I am dead to sin.*

In expounding this truth he reminds them that they were baptized *into the death of Christ.* We were buried with Him through baptism into death. We became *united with Him* by the likeness of His death. Our "old man" was crucified with Him that the body of sin might be done away—rendered void and powerless. Take time and quietly (asking for the teaching of the Holy Spirit) ponder these words until the truth masters you: I am indeed dead to sin in Christ Jesus. As we grow in the consciousness of our union with the crucified Christ, we will experience that the power of His life in us has made us free from the power of sin.

Romans 6 is one of the most blessed portions of the New Testament of our Lord Jesus, teaching us that our "old man," the old nature that is in us, was actually crucified with Him, so that now we need no longer be in bondage to sin. But remember it is only as the Holy Spirit makes Christ's death a reality within us, that we shall know, not by force of argument or conviction, but in the reality of the power of a divine life, that we are in very deed dead to sin. It only needs the continual living in Christ Jesus.

August 17

The Righteousness of God

Abraham believed God, and it was counted unto him for righteousness.
He believed God, who quickeneth the dead. —Romans 4:3, 17

Let us now, after listening to the words of our Lord Jesus about our fellowship with Him in the cross, turn to Paul and see how through the Holy Spirit he gives the deeper insight into what our death in Christ means.

You know how the first section of Romans is devoted to the doctrine of justification by faith in Christ. After speaking (1:18-32) of the awful sin of the heathen, and then (2:1-29) of the sin of the Jew, he points out how Jew and Gentile are "guilty before God." "All have sinned and come short." And then he sets forth that free grace which he points to Abraham as having, when he believed, understood that God justified him freely by His grace, and not for anything that he had done.

Abraham had not only believed this, but something more. "He believed in God, who quickeneth the dead, and calleth the things that are not, as though they were." The two expressions are most significant, as indicating the two essential needs there are in the redemption of man in Christ Jesus. There is the need of justification by faith to restore man to the favor of God. But there is more needed. He must also be quickened to a new life. Just as justification is by faith alone, so is regeneration also. Christ died for our sins; He was raised again out of, or through, our justification.

In the first section (down to 5:11) Paul deals exclusively with the great thought of our justification. But in the second section (5:12-8:39) he expounds that wonderful union with Christ through faith—by which we died with Him, by which we live in Him, and by which, through the Holy Spirit, we are made free, not only from the punishment, but also from the power of sin, and are enabled to live the life of righteousness, obedience, and sanctification.

August 18

Dead with Christ

If we died with Christ, we believe that we shall also live with him. —
Romans 6:8

The reason God's children live so little in the power of the resurrection life of Christ is that they have so little understanding of or faith in their death with Christ. How clearly this appears from what Paul says: "If we died with Christ, we believe that we shall also live with him"; it is the knowledge and experience that gives us the assurance of the power of His resurrection in us. "Christ died unto sin once; but the life that he liveth, he liveth unto God" (v. 10). It is only because and as we know we are dead with Him that we can live with Him.

On the strength of this, Paul now appeals to his readers. "Even so reckon ye also yourselves to be dead unto sin, but alive unto God in Christ Jesus" (v. 11). The words "even so reckon yourselves" are a call to an act of bold and confident faith. Reckon yourselves to be indeed dead unto sin, as much as Christ is, and alive to God in Christ Jesus. The word gives us a divine assurance of what we actually are and have in Christ. And this not only as a truth that our minds can master and appropriate, but a reality which the Holy Spirit will reveal within us. In His power we accept our death with Christ on the cross as the power of our daily life.

Then we are able to accept and obey the command: "Let not sin reign in your mortal body; but present yourselves unto God, as alive from the dead; for sin shall not have dominion over you" (vv. 12, 13, 14). "Being made free from sin, ye became servants of righteousness; present your members as servants to righteousness unto sanctification. Being now made free from sin, ye have your fruit unto sanctification" (vv. 18, 19, 22).

The whole chapter is a wonderful revelation of the deep meaning of its opening words: "How shall we, *who died to sin*, live any more therein?" Everything depends upon our acceptance of the divine assurance: If we died with Christ, as He died and now lives to God, we too have the assurance that in Him we have the power to live unto God.

August 19

Dead to the Law

Ye were made dead to the law, through the body of Christ. Having died to that wherein we were holden, so that we serve in newness of the spirit.—Romans 7:4, 6

The believer is not only dead to sin, but dead to the law. This is a deeper truth, giving us deliverance from the thought of a life of effort and failure, and opening the way to life in the power of the Holy Spirit. "Thou shalt" is done away with; the power of the Spirit takes its place.

In the remainder of this chapter (7:7-24) we have a description of the Christian as he still tries to obey the law, but utterly fails. He experiences that "in him, that is in his flesh, dwelleth no good thing." He finds that the law of sin, notwithstanding his utmost efforts, continually brings him into captivity, and compels the cry: "O wretched man that I am, who shall deliver me from the body of this death?"

In the whole passage, it is everywhere "I," without any thought of the Spirit's help. It is only when he has given utterance to his cry of despair that he is brought to see that he is no longer under the law, but under the rule of the Holy Spirit (8:1, 2). "There is therefore now no condemnation," such as he had experienced in his attempt to obey the law, "to them that are in Christ Jesus. For the law of the Spirit of life in Christ Jesus has made me free from the law of sin and death."

As chapter 7 gives us the experience that leads to being a captive under the power of sin, chapter 8 reveals the experience of the life of a man in Christ Jesus, who has now been made free from the law of sin and death. In the former we have the life of the ordinary Christian doing his utmost to keep the commandments of the law, and to walk in His ways, but ever finding how much there is of failure and shortcoming. In the latter we have the man who knows that he is in Christ Jesus, dead to sin and alive to God, and by the Spirit has been *made* free and is *kept* free from the bondage of sin and of death.

Oh, that men understood what the deep meaning is of Romans 7, where a man learns that in him, that is in his flesh, there is no good thing, and that there is no deliverance from this state but by yielding to the power of the Spirit making free from the power and bondage of the flesh, and so fulfilling the righteousness of the law in the power of the life of Christ!

August 20

The Flesh Condemned on the Cross

What the law could not do, in that it was weak through the flesh, God, sending his own Son in the likeness of sinful flesh, and for sin, condemned sin in the flesh.—Romans 8:3

In Romans 8:7 Paul writes: "The mind of the flesh is enmity against God; for it is not subject to the law of God, neither indeed can it be." Here Paul opens up the depth of sin that there is in the flesh. In chapter 7 he had said that in the flesh there is no good thing. Here he goes deeper, and tells us that the flesh is enmity against God; it hates God and His law. It was on this account that God condemned sin in the flesh on the cross; all the curse that there is upon sin is upon the flesh in which sin dwells. As the believer understands this, he will cease from any attempt at seeking to perfect in the flesh what is begun in the Spirit. The two are at deadly, irreconcilable enmity.

See how this lies at the very root of the true Christian life (vv. 3, 4): "God condemned sin in the flesh, that the righteousness of the law might be fulfilled in us who walk, not after the flesh, but after the Spirit." All the requirements of God's law will be fulfilled, not in those who strive to keep and fulfill that law—an utterly impossible accomplishment—but who walk by the Spirit, and in His power live out the life that Christ won for us on the cross and imparted to us in the resurrection.

Would God His children might learn the double lesson. In me, that is in my flesh, in the old nature which I have from Adam, there dwells literally no good thing that can satisfy the eye of a holy God! And that flesh can never by any process of discipline, or struggling, or prayer, be made better than it is! But the Son of God in the likeness of sinful flesh—in the form of a man—condemned sin on the cross. "There is therefore now no condemnation to them which are in Christ Jesus, who walk not after the flesh, but after the Spirit."

August 21

Jesus Christ and Him Crucified

I determined not to know anything among you, save Jesus Christ and him crucified. And my preaching was in demonstration of the Spirit and of power.—1 Corinthians 2:2, 4

This text is very often understood as presenting Paul's purpose in his preaching to know nothing but Jesus Christ and Him crucified. But it contains a far deeper thought. He speaks of his purpose, not only in the matter of his preaching, but in his whole spirit and life to prove how he in everything seeks to act in conformity to the crucified Christ. Thus he writes (2 Cor. 12:4, 5): "Christ was crucified through weakness, yet he liveth through the power of God. For we also are weak in him, but we shall live with him through the power of God toward you." His whole ministry and conversation bore the mark of Christ's likeness—crucified through weakness, yet living by the power of God.

Just before the words of our text Paul had written (1:17-24): "The word of the cross is to them that are perishing foolishness; but unto us which are being saved it is the power of God." It was not only in his preaching, but in his whole disposition and deportment that he sought to act in harmony with that weakness in which Christ was crucified. He had so identified himself with the weakness of the cross, and its shame that in his whole life and conduct he would prove that in everything he sought to show forth the likeness and the spirit of the crucified Jesus. Hence he says (2:3): "I was with you in weakness, and in fear, and in much trembling."

It is on this account he spoke so strongly: "Christ sent me to preach the gospel, not in wisdom of words, lest the cross of Christ should be made void" (1:17); "My preaching was not with enticing words of man's wisdom, but in demonstration of the Spirit and of power" (2:4).

Have we not here the great reason why the power of God is so little manifested in the preaching of the gospel? Christ crucified may be the subject of preaching; yet there may be such confidence in human learning and eloquence that there is nothing to be seen of that likeness of the crucified Jesus which alone gives preaching its supernatural, divine power.

God help us to understand how the life of every minister and of every believer must bear the hallmark, the stamp of the sanctuary—nothing but Jesus Christ, and Him crucified.

August 22

Temperate in All Things

Every man that striveth in the games is temperate in all things. I buffet my body, and bring it into bondage.—1 Corinthians 9:25, 27

Paul here reminds us of the well-known principle that anyone competing for a prize in the public games is "temperate in all things." Everything, however attractive, that might be a hindrance in the race is given up or set aside. And this is done to obtain an earthly prize. And shall we, who strive for an incorruptible crown and that Christ may be Lord of all, not be temperate in all things that could in the very least prevent our following the Lord Jesus with an undivided heart?

Paul says: "I buffet my body, and bring it into bondage." He would allow nothing to hinder him. He tells us: "This one thing I do; I press towards the mark for the prize." No self-pleasing in eating and drinking, no comfort or ease, should for a moment keep him from showing the spirit of the cross in his daily life, or from sacrificing all, as his Master did. Read the following four passages which comprise Paul's life history: 1 Corinthians 4:11-13; 2 Corinthians 4:8-12, 6:4-10, 11:23-27. The cross was not only the theme of his preaching, but the rule of his life in all its details.

We need to pray God that this disposition may be found in all Christians and preachers of the gospel, through the power of the Holy Spirit. When the death of Christ works with power in the preacher, then Christ's life will be known among the people. Let us pray that the fellowship of the cross may regain its old place, and that God's children may obey the injunction: "Let this mind be in you that was in Christ Jesus." He humbled himself and became obedient unto the death of the cross. For, "if we have been planted together in the likeness of his death, we shall be also in the likeness of his resurrection" (Rom. 6:5).

August 23

The Dying of the Lord Jesus

Always bearing about in the body the dying of Jesus, that the life also of Jesus may be manifested in our body. So then death worketh in us, but life in you.—2 Corinthians 4:10, 12

Paul here is very bold in speaking of the intimate union there was between Christ living in him, and the life he lived in the flesh, with all its suffering. He had spoken (Gal. 2:20) of his being crucified with Christ, and Christ living in him. Here he tells how he was always bearing about in the body the dying of Jesus; it was through this that the life also of Jesus was manifested in his body. And he says that it was because the death of Christ was thus working in and through him that Christ's life could work in them.

We often speak of our abiding in Christ. But we forget that this means the abiding in a crucified Christ. Many believers appear to think that when once they have claimed Christ's death in the fellowship of the cross, and have counted themselves as crucified with Him, they may now consider it as past and accomplished. They do not understand it is in the crucified Christ, and in the fellowship of His death, that they are to abide daily and unceasingly. The fellowship of the cross is to be the life of a daily experience. The self-emptying of our Lord, His taking the form of a servant, His humbling himself and becoming obedient unto death, even the death of the cross—this mind that was in Christ is to be the disposition that marks our daily life.

"Always bearing about in the body the dying of Jesus." This is what we are called to as much as Paul. If we are indeed to live for the welfare of men around us, if we are to sacrifice our ease and pleasure to win souls for our Lord, it will be true of us as of Paul that we are able to say: Death worketh in us, but life in those for whom we pray and labor. It is in the fellowship of the sufferings of Christ that the crucified Lord can live and work out His life in us and through us.

Let us learn the lesson, that the abiding in Christ Jesus, for which we have so often prayed and striven, is nothing less than the abiding of the Crucified in us and we in Him.

The Cross and the Spirit

How much more shall the blood of Christ, who through the eternal Spirit offered himself without blemish unto God, cleanse your conscience?—Hebrews 9:14

The cross is Christ's highest glory. The glory which He received from the Father was entirely due to His having humbled himself to the death of the cross. "Wherefore also God highly exalted him." The greatest work the Holy Spirit could ever do in the Son of God was when He enabled Him to yield himself a sacrifice and an offering for a sweet-smelling savor. And the Holy Spirit can now do nothing greater or more glorious for us than to lead us into the fellowship and likeness of that crucified life of our Lord.

Have we not here the reason our prayers for the mighty working of the Holy Spirit are not more abundantly answered? We have prayed too little that the Holy Spirit might glorify Christ in us in the fellowship with and the conformity to His sufferings. The Spirit, who led Christ to the cross, is longing and is able to maintain in us the life of abiding in the crucified Jesus.

The Spirit and the cross are inseparable. The Spirit led Christ to the cross; the cross brought Christ to the throne to receive the fullness of the Spirit to impart to His people. The Spirit taught Peter at once to preach Christ crucified; it was through that preaching the three thousand received the Spirit. In the preaching of the gospel, in the Christian life, as in Christ, so in us, the Spirit and the cross are inseparable.

It is the sad lack of the mind and disposition of the crucified Christ, sacrificing self and the world to win life for the dying, that is one great cause of the feebleness of the church. Let us beseech God fervently to teach us to say: We have been crucified with Christ; in Him we have died to sin; "always bearing about in the body the dying of Jesus." So shall we be prepared for that fullness of the Spirit which the Father longs to bestow.

August 25

The Veil of the Flesh

Having therefore, brethren, boldness to enter into the holy place by the blood of Jesus, by the way which he dedicated for us, a new and living way, through the veil, that is to say, his flesh.— Hebrews 10:19, 20

In the temple there was a veil between the holy place and the most holy. At the altar in the court the blood of the sacrifice was sprinkled for forgiveness of sins. That gave the priest entrance into the holy place to offer God the incense as part of a holy worship. But into the most holy, behind the veil, the high priest alone might enter once a year, That veil was the type of sinful human nature; even though it had received the forgiveness of sin, full access and fellowship with God was impossible.

When Christ died, the veil was rent. Christ dedicated a new and living way to God through the rent veil of His flesh. This new way, by which we now can enter into the holiest of all, ever passes through the rent veil of the flesh. Every believer "has crucified the flesh with the passions and the lusts thereof" (Gal. 5:24). Every step on the new and living way for entering into God's holy presence maintains the fellowship with the cross of Christ. The rent veil of the flesh has reference, not only to Christ and His sufferings, but to our experience in the likeness of His sufferings.

Do we not have here the reason why many Christians can never attain to close fellowship with God? They have never yielded the flesh as an accursed thing to the condemnation of the cross. they desire to enter into the holiest of all, and yet allow the flesh with its desires and pleasures to rule over them. God grant that we may rightly understand, in the power of the Holy Spirit, that Christ has called us to hate our life, to lose our life, to be dead with Him to sin that we may live to God with Him. There is no way to a full abiding fellowship with God but through the rent veil of the flesh, through a life with the flesh crucified in Christ Jesus. God be praised that the Holy Spirit ever dwells in us to keep the flesh in its place of crucifixion and condemnation, and to give us the abiding victory over all temptations.

August 26

Looking unto Jesus

Let us run with patience the race that is set before us, looking unto Jesus, the Author and Perfecter of our faith, who for the joy that was set before him endured the cross, despising the shame.—Hebrews 12:1, 2

In running a race the eye and heart are ever set upon the goal and the prize. The Christian is here called to keep his eye fixed on Jesus enduring the cross, as the one object of limitation and desire. In our whole life we are ever to be animated by His Spirit as He bore the cross. This was the way that led to the throne and the glory of God. This is the new and living way which He opened for us through the veil of the flesh. As we study and realize it was for His bearing the cross that God so highly exalted Him, we will walk in His footsteps bearing our cross after Him with the flesh condemned and crucified.

The impotence of the church is largely due to the fact that this cross-bearing mind of Jesus is so little preached and practiced. Most Christians think that as long as they do not commit actual sin, they are at liberty to possess and enjoy as much of the world as they please. There is so little insight into the deep truth that the world, and the flesh that loves the world, is enmity against God. Hence it comes that many Christians seek and pray for years for conformity to the image of Jesus, and yet fail so entirely. They do not know, they do not seek with the whole heart to know, what it is to die to self and the world.

It was for the joy set before Him that Christ endured the cross—the joy of pleasing and glorifying the Father, the joy of loving and winning souls for himself. We have indeed need of a new crusade with the proclamation: This is the will of God, that as Christ found His highest happiness, and received from the Father the fullness of the Spirit to pour down on His people, through His endurance of the cross, so it is only *in our fellowship of the cross* that we can really become conformed to the image of God's Son. As believers awake to this blessed truth and run the race ever looking to the crucified Jesus, they will receive power to win for Christ the souls He has purchased on the cross.

August 27

Without the Gate

The bodies of those beasts, whose blood is brought into the holy place, are burned without the camp. Wherefore Jesus also, that he might sanctify the people through his own blood, suffered without the gate. Let us go forth therefore unto him without the camp, bearing his reproach.—Hebrews 13:11-13

The blood of the sin offering was brought into the Holy Place; the body of the sacrifice was burned without the camp. Even so with Christ, His blood was presented to the Father, but His body was cast out as an accursed thing, without the camp.

And so we read in Hebrews 10: "Let us enter into the Holy Place by the blood of Jesus." And in our text: "Let us go forth unto him without the camp, bearing his reproach." The deeper my insight is into the boldness which His blood gives me in God's presence, so much greater will be the joy with which I enter the Holy Place. And the deeper my insight is into the shame of the cross which He on my behalf bore without the camp, the more willing will I be, in the fellowship of His cross, to follow Him without the camp, bearing His reproach.

There are many Christians who love to hear of the boldness with which we can enter into the Holy Place through His blood, who yet have little desire for the fellowship of His reproach, and are unwilling to separate themselves from the world with the same boldness with which they think to enter the sanctuary. The Christian suffers inconceivable loss when he thinks of entering into the Holy Place in faith and prayer, and then feels himself free to enjoy the friendship of the world, so long as he does nothing actually sinful. But the Word of God has said: "Know ye not that the friendship of the world is enmity against God?" "Love not the world, neither the things that are in the world; if any man love the world, the love of the Father is not in him." "Be not conformed to this world."

To be a follower of Christ implies a heart given up to testify for Christ in the midst of the world, if by any means some may be won. To be a follower of Christ means to be like Him in His love of the cross and His will to sacrifice self that the Father may be glorified and men may be saved.

August 28

Alive unto Righteousness

Who his own self bare our sins in his own body on the tree, that we, having died unto sins, might live unto righteousness.—1 Peter 2:24

Here we have in the Epistle of Peter the same lessons that Paul has taught us. First, *the atonement of the cross*: "Who his own self bare our sins in his body upon the tree." And then, *the fellowship of the cross*: "That we, having died unto sins, might live unto righteousness."

In this last expression we have the great thought that a Christian cannot live unto righteousness, except as he knows he has died to sin. We need the Holy Spirit to make our death to sin in Christ such a reality that we know ourselves to be forever free from its power, and so yield our members to God as instruments of righteousness. The words give us a short summary of the blessed teaching of Romans 6.

Dear Christian, it cost Christ much to bear the cross, and then to yield himself for it to bear Him. It cost Him much when He cried: "Now is my soul troubled, and what shall I say? Father, save me from this hour. But for this cause came I unto this hour."

Let us not imagine that the fellowship of the cross, of which Peter speaks here, "that we, having died to sins, might live unto righteousness," is easily understood or experienced. It means the Holy Spirit will teach us what it is to be identified with Christ in His cross. It means we realize by faith how actually we shared with Christ in His death, and now, as He lives in us, abide in unceasing fellowship with Him, the Crucified One. This costs self-sacrifice; it costs earnest prayer; it costs a wholehearted surrender to God and His will and the cross of Jesus; it costs abiding in Christ and unceasing fellowship with Him.

Followers of the Cross

Hereby know we love, because he laid down his life for us: and we ought to lay down our lives for the brethren.—1 John 3:16

"Greater love hath no man than this, that a man lay down his life for his friend." Here our Lord reveals to us the inconceivable love that moved Him to die for us. And now under the influence and in the power of that love dwelling in us, comes the message: *"We ought to lay down our lives for the brethren."* Nothing less is expected of us than a Christlike life, and a Christlike love, proving itself in all our relationships with our brethren.

The cross of Christ is the measure by which we know how much Christ loves us. That cross is the measure, too, of the love which we owe to the brethren around us. It is only as the love of Christ on the cross possesses our hearts, and daily animates our whole being, that we will be able to love the brethren. Our fellowship in the cross of Christ is to manifest itself in our sacrifice of love, not only to Christ himself, but to all who belong to Him.

The life to which John calls us here is something entirely supernatural and divine. It is only the faith of Christ himself living in us that can enable us to accept this great command in the assurance that Christ himself will work it out in us. It is He himself who calls us: "If any man will come after me, let him deny himself, and take up his cross, and follow me." Nothing less than this, a dying to our own nature, a faith that our "old man," our flesh, has been crucified with Christ, so that we no longer need to sin—nothing less than this can enable us to say: We love His commandments; this commandment, too, is not grievous.

But for such fellowship and conformity to the death of Christ, nothing will avail but the daily, unbroken abiding in Christ Jesus which He has promised us. By the Holy Spirit revealing and glorifying Christ in us, we may trust Christ himself to live out His life in us. He who proved His love on the cross of Calvary, He himself, He alone can enable us to say in truth: He laid down His life for us; we ought to lay down our lives for the brethren. It is only as the great truth of the indwelling Christ obtains a place in the faith of the church which it has not now that the Christlike love to the brethren will become the mark of true Christianity, by which all men will know we are Christ's disciples.

August 30

Following the Lamb

These are they which follow the Lamb whithersoever he goeth.—Revelation 14:4

It may not be easy to say exactly what is implied in this following of the Lamb in the heavenly vision. But of that we may be sure, that it will be the counterpart in glory of what it is to follow in the footsteps of the Lamb here upon earth. As the Lamb on earth reveals what the Lamb in heaven would be, so His followers on earth can show forth something of the glory of what it is to follow Him in heaven.

And how may the footsteps of the Lamb be known? "He humbled himself." "As a Lamb that is led to the slaughter, he opened not his mouth" (Isa. 53:7). It is the meekness and gentleness and humility that marked Him which calls for His followers to walk in His footsteps.

Our Lord himself said: "Learn of me, that I am meek and lowly of heart, and ye shall find rest unto your souls." Paul writes: "Have this mind in you, which was also in Christ Jesus" (Phil. 2:5). And then he teaches us in what that mind consisted: Being in the form of God, He emptied himself; He was made in the likeness of men; He took the form of a servant; He humbled himself; He became obedient unto death, even the death of the cross. The Lamb is our Lord and Lawgiver. He opened the only path that leads to the throne of God. It is as we learn from Him what it means to be meek and lowly, what it means to empty ourselves, to choose the place of the servant, to humble ourselves and become obedient, even unto death, the death of the cross, that we will find the new and living way that leads us through the rent veil into the Holiest of All.

"Wherefore also God highly exalted him, and gave unto him the name which is above every name" (v. 9). It is because Christians so little bear the mark of this self-emptying and humiliation even unto death that the world refuses to believe in the possibility of a Christ-filled life.

Children of God, come and study the Lamb who is to be your model and your Savior. Let Paul's words be the keynote of your life: "I am crucified with Christ: nevertheless I live; yet not I, but Christ liveth in me." Here you have the way to follow the Lamb even to the glory of the throne of God in heaven.

August 31

To Him Be the Glory

Unto him that loved us, and washed us from our sins in his own blood, and hath made us kings and priests unto God and his Father; to him be glory and dominion for ever and ever. Amen.—Revelation 1:5, 6

Some may feel that it is not easy to understand the lesson of the cross, or to carry it out in their lives. Do not think of it as a heavy burden or yoke that you have to bear. Christ says: "My yoke is easy, and my burden is light." *Love makes everything easy.* Do not think of your love to Him, but of His great love to you, given through the Holy Spirit. Meditate on this day and night until you have the assurance: He loves me unspeakably. It is through the love of Christ on the cross that souls are drawn to Him.

We have here the answer as to what will enable us to love the fellowship of the crucified Jesus. Nothing less than His love poured out through the continual inspiration of the Holy Spirit into the heart of every child of God.

"Unto him that loved us."—Be still, O my soul, and think what this everlasting love is that seeks to take possession of you and fill you with joy unspeakable.

"And washed us from our sins in his own blood."—Is that not proof enough that He will never reject me; that I am precious in His sight, and through the power of His blood am well pleasing to God?

"And hath made us kings and priests unto God and his Father."—He now preserves us by His power, and will strengthen us through His Spirit to reign as kings over sin and the world, and to appear as priests before God in intercession for others. O Christian, learn this wonderful song, and repeat it until your heart is filled with love and joy and courage, and turns to Him in glad surrender day by day: "To him be glory and dominion for ever and ever. Amen."

Yes, to Him, who has loved me, and washed me from my sins in His blood, and made me a king and a priest—*to Him be the glory in all ages.* Amen.

September

The Secret of Brotherly Love

September 1

Love and Faith

This is his commandment, that we should believe in the name of his Son Jesus Christ, and love one another, even as he gave us commandment.—1 John 3:23

At a Bible conference I attended, the closing service was to be held on Sunday night. At the afternoon meeting we decided to take, as subject, the five great lessons to be learned from the parable of the Vine and Branches in John 15. The subject of brotherly love fell to the lot of a certain minister. But he hesitated, saying: "I cannot speak on that subject, and I have never yet preached on it." In explanation he said: "You know that I studied in Holland, and when there the subject of love was left to the liberal section. They did not believe in God's stern justice, nor in the redemption through Christ. God was love; that was enough. The orthodox party were not allowed to suggest that their opponents should be put out of the church. No, all should be borne in love! And so it came to pass that the orthodox party were strong in preaching faith, but left the preaching of love to the liberal section."

The church must learn not only to preach the love of God in redemption; it must go further and teach Christians to show that the love of Christ is in their hearts, by love shown to the brethren. Our Lord called this a new commandment: a badge by which the world should recognize His disciples!

There is great need for this preaching of love. God sometimes allows bitterness to arise between Christians that they may view the terrible power of sin in their hearts and shrink back at the sight. How greatly a minister and his people should feel the importance of Christ's command: "Love one another." A life of great holiness will result if we really love each other as Christ loves us.

May the reading of this meditation help us to understand the two manifestations of love: the wonderful love of God in Christ to us, and the wonderful love in us, through the Holy Spirit, to Him and to our brethren.

September 2

Faith and Love

And the grace of our Lord abounded exceedingly with faith and love.—
1 Timothy 1:14

*Your work of faith and labor of love.—*1 Thessalonians 1:3

*The breastplate of faith and love.—*1 Thessalonians 5:8

*Your faith groweth exceedingly, and the love of each of you all toward one another aboundeth.—*2 Thessalonians 1:3

These expressions of the apostle Paul show us the true connection between faith and love in the life of the Christian. Faith always comes first; it roots itself deeply in the love of God and bears fruit in love to the brethren. As in nature the root and the fruit are inseparable, so is it with faith and love in the realm of grace.

Too often the two are separated. On the Day of Pentecost they were one. There was a powerful faith toward the Lord Jesus, with a fervent love to the brethren. The sum of the preaching on that day was: Believe in the name of Jesus Christ, and ye shall receive the gift of the Holy Ghost. And the natural result followed: "And all that believed were together, and had all things common." "And the multitude of them that believed were of one heart and of one soul."

It is too bad that this should not have been wholly the case at the Reformation. A powerful reformation took place in regard to the doctrine of faith, but at the same time what a lack of love there was between the preachers and the leaders in that faith! So the world was not taught the lesson that God's love was all-powerful to sanctify the whole life of man!

Let this thought sink deep into our hearts: "The grace of our Lord abounded exceedingly with faith and love." As we cultivate *faith in God's love,* our hearts will be *filled with love to the brethren.* The genuineness of our faith in the love of God must be shown by love in our daily lives at home.

May God help us from day to day by faith to be rooted in this love that we may at all times be living examples of its truth and power, and so become a blessing to others.

September 3

The Love of God

God is love, and he that dwelleth in love dwelleth in God, and God in him.—1 John 4:16

May God through His Holy Spirit grant us grace rightly to understand this unfathomable mystery.

Jesus said: "None is good save one, even God." The glory of God in heaven is that He has a will to all that is good. That includes the two meanings of the word *good*: (1) all that is right and perfect; (2) all that makes happy.

The God who wills nothing but good is a God of love. He does not seek His own: He does not live for himself, but pours out His love on all living creatures. All created things share in this love, to the end that they may be satisfied with that which is good.

The characteristic of love is that she "seeketh not her own." She finds her happiness in giving to others; she sacrifices herself wholly for others. Even so God offered himself to mankind in the person of His Son, and the Son offered himself upon the cross to bring that love to men, and to win their hearts. The everlasting love with which the Father loved the Son is the same love with which the Son has loved us. This self-same love of God, Christ has poured into our hearts through the Holy Spirit, so that our whole life may be permeated with its vital power.

The love of God to His Son, the love of the Son to us, the love with which we love the Son, the love with which we, in obedience to His command, love the brethren, and try to love all men and win them for Christ—all is the same eternal, incomprehensible, almighty love of God. Love is the power of the Godhead—in the Father, Son and Holy Ghost. This love is the possession of all who are members of the Body of Christ and streams forth from them to take the whole world within its embrace.

Unsearchable, adorable wonder of love! "He that abideth in love, abideth in God, and God in him." O my soul, meditate on this wondrous love, and adore the great God of love!

September 4

The Love of Christ

The love of Christ constraineth us. —2 Corinthians 5:14

God sent His Son into the world to make known His everlasting love, even as it was known in heaven. God's existence there is in the glory of that love; all His angels are as tongues of fire overflowing with praise and worship through the power of the love that fills them. God's desire is that on this sinful earth, likewise, His love should take possession of the hearts of men.

And how was this accomplished? By sending Christ, the Son of His love, to earth to reveal as Man the love of the Father, and win our hearts to himself. The Lord Jesus became man and made himself of no reputation. In His dealings with the poor and needy, and those who were unbelieving and rebellious, and through His miracles, He poured out His love into the hearts of sinful men.

With the same purpose our Lord chose the disciples to be always with Him and to be filled with His love. With this purpose He gave on the cross the greatest proof of love the world has ever seen. He took our sins upon Him; He bore the suffering, and the scorn of His enemies that friend and foe alike might know God's eternal love.

And then, after He had ascended to heaven, He gave the Holy Spirit, to shed abroad this love in our hearts. The disciples, impelled by the love of Christ, in turn offered their lives to make it known to others.

O Christians, think this over: God longs to have our hearts wholly filled with His love. Then He will be able to use us as channels for this love to flow out to our fellowmen. Let us say with the apostle Paul: "The love of Christ constraineth me" (Dutch version—'urges'). I can be satisfied with nothing less. I will sacrifice everything to secure a place for this great love in the hearts of the children of men.

September 5

The Love of the Spirit

The love of God hath been shed abroad in our hearts through the Holy Ghost, which was given unto us.—Romans 5:5

How many a Christian must confess all his life long that he knows very little of a fervent, childlike love to his Heavenly Father! He realizes, too, that he cannot keep Christ's second great commandment, to love his neighbor as himself. The thought of this lack of a joyful love the the Lord Jesus, or of a continual love to the brethren, is a great source of shame and sorrow.

What is the cause of this failure? Has the Heavenly Father made no provision for His children on earth, enabling them to prove their love to Him and to each other? Certainly He has. But God's children have not learned the lesson that there must be a constant renewal of faith in what God is able to do. One tries to stir up love toward God in his heart, yet is conscious all the time that in his own strength one cannot awaken the slightest love to God. O Christian, *believe that the love of God will work in your heart as a vital power to enable you to love God and to love the brethren.*

Cease to expect the least love in yourself. Believe in the power of God's love, resting on you, and abiding in you; teaching you to love God and the brethren with His own love.

Learn the lesson of our text: "The love of God hath been shed abroad in our hearts, through the Holy Ghost." The Spirit will enable us to love God, and our brethren, and even our enemies. Be assured of two things. First, that in your own strength you cannot love God, or the brethren. And, second, that the Holy Spirit is within you every day and every hour, seeking to fill you with the Spirit of love. Each morning as you commit yourself into the keeping of the Holy Spirit for the day, let this prayer arise: Grant me the assurance that Thou wilt pour forth the love of Christ into my own heart, and then let it stream forth to all around me!

September 6

The Power of Love

We are more than conquerors through him that loved us.—Romans 8:37

In days of unrest and strong racial feeling, we need above all a new discovery, and living experience, of the love of God. Let us anchor our hope in the thought, "God is love." God's power, by which He rules and guides the world, is the power of an undying, persistent love. He works through the hearts, spirits, and wills of men and women who are wholly yielded to Him and His service. He waits for them to open their hearts to Him in love, and then, full of courage, to become witnesses for Him.

When this has been achieved, Christ's kingdom is manifested, and His reign of love on earth begun. Christ died to establish this kingdom. The only means He used to gain influence was through the manifestation of a great serving, suffering love. He saw the possibility of redemption in the hearts of even the worst of men. He knew that men's hearts could never resist the steady, continuous influence of love; and that unbounded faith in God's love would be our strength and stay. It was in the fire and the fervor of that love that the disciples were able to expect, and to do, the impossible.

The spirit of hatred and bitterness can never be overcome by argument, or by reproaches. Some think things can never be different, but if we really believe in the omnipotence of God's love, we may not distrust His power. God's children must learn to accept His love, not only for themselves individually, but for the life of others. Gradually, better feelings will prevail if believers will yield themselves unreservedly for God to work through them.

Our faith in love as the greatest power in the world should prepare us for a life in communion with God in prayer and for a life of unselfish service among our fellowmen. Let each Christian examine his life, and pray for grace, as a servant of that all-powerful love, to live for those around him.

September 7

The Sign of a True Church

By this shall all men know that ye are my disciples, if ye have love one to another.—John 13:35

We are taught in most of our creeds that the true church is to be found where God's Word is rightly preached and the holy sacraments dispensed, as instituted by Christ. Christ himself took a much broader view. Not merely what the church teaches through her ministers was, to Him, the distinguishing mark of His followers, but a life lived in love to the brethren.

It is most important that we should understand this. In God, love reaches its highest point, and is the culmination of His glory. In the man Christ Jesus on the cross, love is at its highest. We owe everything to this love. Love is the power that moved Christ to die for us. In love, God highly exalted Him as Lord and Christ. Love is the power that broke our hearts, and love is the power that heals them. Love is the power through which Christ dwells in us, and works in us. Love can change my whole nature, and enable me to surrender all to God. It gives me strength to live a holy, joyous life, full of blessing to others. Every Christian should show forth, as in a mirror, the love of God.

How seldom do Christians realize this, however. They seek, in the power of human love, to love Christ and the brethren. And then they fail. They are sure it is impossible to lead such a life, and they do not even greatly desire it, or pray for it. They do not understand that we may and can love with God's own love, which is poured forth into our hearts by the Holy Spirit.

Oh, that this great truth might possess us: *the love of God is shed abroad in our hearts by the Holy Spirit.* If we fully believe that the Holy Spirit, dwelling within us, will maintain this heavenly love from hour to hour, we shall be able to understand the word of Christ: "All things are possible to him that believeth," and to love God and Christ with all our hearts; and, what is even harder, to love our brethren, and even our enemies, while love flows from us as a stream of living water, "through the Holy Spirit."

September 8

Race-Hatred

For we also were sometimes foolish, living in malice and envy, hateful, and hating one another.—Titus 3:3

What a dark picture of the state of human nature and of human society! From where does such a sad condition of things come, worse even than we see among animals? The answer is: "From Adam's fall." Just think how Cain, the first child born on earth, born of man whom God had created, shed the blood of his brother Abel. Yes, the first child born on earth was the murderer of his own brother, and came under the power of the devil, who "was a murderer from the beginning." "God saw that the wickedness of man was great on the earth, and that every imagination of the thoughts of his heart was only evil continually." No wonder He destroyed mankind by a flood. Yet soon after the flood there were signs that man was still under the power of sin.

No wonder that man's love of his own people, implanted in his heart by nature, soon changed to hatred of other peoples. Love of country became the fruitful source of race-hatred, war, and bloodshed. Note how, in many parts of the world, God has placed the two races side by side, as in a school, to see if our Christianity will enable us to overcome race hatred, and in the power of Christ's love, prove that "in the new creature there is neither Greek nor Jew, barbarian nor Scythian, bond nor free, but are all one in Christ Jesus."

What an opening there is for the church of Christ and her ministers to preach and proclaim the love of God, and to prove its might to change race-hatred into brotherly love! God has abundant power to bring this to pass.

What a call to every Christian to pray for himself and his brethren that we may not make the Word of God of none effect by our unbelief!

O God, make known to us Thy love in heavenly power, and let it take full possession of our lives!

September 9

Love your Enemies

Ye have heard that it hath been said: Thou shalt love thy neighbor and hate thine enemy.—Matthew 5:43

It was the Jewish rabbis in Christ's earthly day who said this. They deemed they had a right to say it because of what was written in Leviticus 19:17, 18: "Thou shalt not hate thy brother in thine heart; thou shalt not bear any grudge against the children of thy people; but thou shalt love thy neighbor as thyself." From this they argued that it was only the children of their own people whom they might not hate; it was all right to hate their enemies. But our Lord said: "Love your enemies: bless them that curse you."

How often the Christian follows the example of the Jewish teachers! The command of our Lord is too strict and narrow for him; he has not yielded himself to God in obedience to the new commandment to love his brethren with Christ's love, believing that this love will flow out to all around, even to those who hate us. This will require much grace, and will cost time, trouble, and much earnest prayer.

When I was a minister in Cape Town, I met a German deaconess, who was working in connection with the English Church at Woodstock. She had a class every evening for ten or twelve Kaffirs, who were preparing for admission to the church. One evening she spoke about loving our enemies. She asked one man if his people had enemies. "Oh yes!" "Who were they?" "The Fingoes." (The Kaffirs count the Fingoes as dogs.) She asked the man if he could love a Fingo. His answer was quite decided: "Me no' love Fingo. Me no' love Fingo." It was an indisputable fact; there could be no question about it. He could not love a Fingo. She told him that in that case he could not go to the Communion. He went home very thoughtful, and the next evening at class seemed very downcast. But he still had only one answer: "Me no' love Fingo." He was not received into the church with the others, but continued to attend the class. He was always in earnest, and there was evidently a struggle going on; until one evening he appeared with a bright face, and said: "Me *now* love Fingo." He had prayed about it, and God had heard his prayer. There is only one way to love our enemies: by the love of Christ, sought and found in prayer.

September 10

Forgive, but Not Forget

I will forgive their iniquity, and I will remember their sin no more.—
Jeremiah 31:34

Many years ago at the unveiling of the Women's Monument at Bloemfontein, I happened to be sitting in the front row on the platform at the foot of the monument. After a while the sun became very hot. Suddenly I noticed that someone behind me was holding an umbrella over my head. When the speaker had finished, I asked my nephew beside me: "Who is so friendly as to hold an umbrella over my head?" His answer was: "General de Wet." I was surprised, and turning round, thanked him heartily. My nephew told me afterwards that he had said: "But I would gladly have paid for the privilege of doing it." I thought, what a generous nature to speak in that way.

Presently the general's turn came to give an address. I could agree with all he said, except his last words, which were: "Forgive—yes, but forget—never." When the ceremony was over, and I shook hands with him again, it was in my heart to say to him: "You say, 'I can never forget.' Be careful to what that may lead."

Many a one has allowed himself to be deceived by these words. On the farms, I have often seen a dog come in at the front door to seek coolness and shade. He would be driven out, and the door closed. Then he would go through the back door, and would soon be inside the house again. The front door is, "I will forgive." One wishes to put away all thought of hatred or ill-feeling. But see how quickly and quietly these evil thoughts come back through the back door of "I will never forget." Many trust in God's forgiving love, but do not remember that when God forgives, He forgets. "I will forgive their iniquity, and will remember their sins no more." And Paul gives us the advice in Colossians 3:13: "Forgiving one another, even as Christ forgave you, so also do ye."

September 11

As God Forgives

And forgive us our sins; for we also forgive every one that is indebted to us.—Luke 11:4

The forgiveness of sins is the great all-embracing gift by which, in His mercy, God sets the sinner free and receives him back into His love and favor. The forgiveness of sins gives us boldness toward God and is the source of our salvation. The forgiveness of sins gives us cause for thankfulness every day of our lives. It is God's will, and our souls feel the need of it, that we should each day walk with Him as those whose sins are forgiven and who are living in the light of His countenance.

As we walk with God in the full assurance of sins forgiven, He desires that, in our contacts with our fellowmen, too, we should live as those who have been freely forgiven. And we can only prove our sincerity by forgiving those who have offended us, as freely and as willingly as God has forgiven us.

How clearly and urgently our Lord speaks upon this! In the Lord's Prayer we are taught to pray each day: "Forgive us our debts, as we forgive our debtors," and then at the end of the chapter we are reminded: "If ye forgive not men their trespasses, neither will your heavenly Father forgive your trespasses" (Matt. 6:15). After the great promise of Mark 11:24, come the words: "And, whensoever ye stand praying, forgive, if ye have aught against any." In Matthew 18:21, we have the question of Peter: "Lord, how oft shall my brother sin against me, and I forgive him?" and our Lord's answer: "Unto seventy times seven." Then follows the parable of the servant whose Lord forgave him his debt, but who would not show compassion on his fellow servant. His Lord's question to him was: "Shouldest not thou also have had mercy on thy fellow-servant, even as I had mercy on thee?" So he was delivered to his tormentors. And our Lord gives the warning: "So shall also my heavenly Father do unto you, if ye forgive not every one his brother from your hearts."

Let us remember to realize daily: As I need God's forgiveness each day, so let me be ready each day to forgive my brother. God grant us grace to do it!

September 12

The Preaching of Love

The greatest of these is love.—1 Corinthians 13:13

During the Boer War, when there was much unrest in the country, a certain minister asked his brother-minister, who was a leader in the church, to do his best to calm the minds of those around him. His answer was: "I have enough trouble with myself; my own mind is unsettled. How can I quiet others?" If there were a revival of the preaching of love, more than one of our ministers would have to say: "There is such a lack of love in my own heart; how can I teach others?"

Yet there is a remedy. Let me tell you what I have learned from John Wesley. During the first fourteen years of his ministry he had no insight into what a free and full salvation by faith meant. After he had been convicted of the sin of unbelief, by means of a conversation with one of the Moravian brethren, he began to preach with such power that many were converted.

But he felt that it was too much a matter of the intellect; he had not yet experienced the full joy and love which the Moravian possessed. He asked the brother what he should do. The answer was: "Preach it because you believe that it is what God's Word teaches. You will soon find what you are seeking, and will then preach it because you possess it."

This has been my own experience. Often in preaching, or in writing, I have asked myself: But do you possess what you preach to others? And I have followed the advice: *Preach it because you believe it to be the teaching of God's Word, and heartily desire it.* Preach the truth by faith, and the experience will follow. Let the minister who feels impelled to preach about love, not hesitate to do so, and he will soon be able to preach it because he himself has received that which he commends.

September 13

The Two Leaders

I exhort, therefore, that first of all supplications, prayers, intercessions, thanksgivings, be made for all men; for kings and all that are in authority, that we may lead a quiet and peaceable life in all godliness and honesty.—1 Timothy 2:1, 2

At the time of the unveiling of the Women's Monument at Bloemfontein, before the procession took place, I spoke a few words about the suffering, praying, all-conquering love of these women, who, they say, prayed earnestly that God would keep them from hatred, or want of love toward their enemies. I expressed the hope that this prayerful love might be ours, and that nothing might be done to disturb the feeling of peace and unity. I said that there were some who feared disunion, not only between the two races in the country, but between those who were fellow countrymen. Not long after, we heard that there had been a breach between the leaders of the two parties.

I felt impelled to write an article on the question: "For whom do you pray?" Someone answered: "I pray for the man at the head of the government, and who, under God's guidance, has now become the leader of the whole country. I pray for him." And another: "I pray especially for the man who has been influential in bringing the interests of his people into the foreground."

Would it not be sad if we came into God's presence divided into two camps, praying one against the other? No, we must pray for both our leaders and for *all* who are in authority. As leaders of the people, their influence, for good or evil, is inexpressible. Their hearts are in God's hands, and He can turn them withersoever He wills. Let our prayers ascend to God in all sincerity and He will hear and grant that which is good for the whole land. Let us pray: "Lord, the hearts of rulers are in Thy hands; teach them to do Thy will."

September 14

Unfeigned Love of the Brethren

Seeing ye have purified your souls through the Spirit, unto unfeigned love of the brethren, see that ye love one another with a pure heart fervently.—1 Peter 1:22

In the beginning of this chapter, Peter had expressed a wonderful truth about our love to Christ: "Whom having not seen, ye love; in whom ye rejoice with joy unspeakable and full of glory" (v. 8). This was the fruit of the Spirit.

In our text he speaks of "the love of the brethren." "Ye have purified your souls in obeying the truth through the Spirit unto the unfeigned love of the brethren." In the days of the early church it was clearly understood at conversion that, in confessing Christ, the new convert also promised unfeigned love to the brethren. So Peter continues: "See that ye love one another with a pure heart fervently." Unfeigned, fervent love through the Spirit should be the chief token of a true conversion.

We see how much stress Peter lays on this point in the next three chapters, as he returns to the subject each time (2:17), "Love the brotherhood. Fear God. Honor the king." (3:8), "Finally, be ye all like minded, compassionate, loving as brethren, tender-hearted, humble-minded." These are all signs of the life of God in the soul. And then (4:7, 8), "Watch unto prayer, above all things being fervent in your love among yourselves; for love covereth a multitude of sins." Unfeigned, fervent love of the brethren was the indispensable sign of true godliness.

God's Word is a mirror into which the church and each individual member must look, to see that we are truly Christian, showing by our conduct that we take God's Word as our rule of life. If our hearts condemn us, we must turn at once to God, confessing our sin. Let us believe that *the Spirit of love does indeed dwell in us* and will shed abroad God's love in our hearts and purify us from all hatred and selfishness, *restoring the image of Christ within us.* Let us not rest content until we have surrendered ourselves wholly to God that His Spirit of love may reign and rule within us.

September 15

The Spirit of Love

The fruit of the Spirit is love.—Galatians 5:22

God hath given us the spirit of love.—2 Timothy 1:7

Our love, which is the fruit of the Spirit, does not consist merely in the knowledge of, and faith in, God's love as revealed in our redemption. No, the matter goes far deeper. Our love has its origin in the fact that the love of God has been shed abroad in our hearts by the Holy Spirit, not only as an experience or feeling, but the spirit of love takes possession of us and directs and controls and inspires.

This love becomes a heavenly life-power, a disposition of the soul, whereby man tastes and knows that God is good. The Spirit gives to love such a form that it contains the commands of the divine love within itself, and thus can keep the commandments without difficulty. "This is the love of God, that we keep his commandments, and his commandments are not grievous" (1 John 5:3).

When God, according to promise, writes His law in our hearts, the summing up of that law is love. It governs the life of the man wholly devoted to God, and controls his thoughts and actions. This divine love in the heart of man is as a little sanctuary, whence the child of God receives power, in obedience to the inner law of love, to live always in the love of God. This holy love includes fellowship with God, union with Christ, and love to the brethren.

How can we attain to this experience? Through faith alone. The chief sign of faith in the blind and the lepers who came to Christ to be healed was the knowledge of their own impotence and inability to help themselves. When our eyes have been opened, and we realize that the love of God has already been shed abroad in our hearts by His Spirit, enabling us to keep His commandments and to love the brethren—then let us bow in stillness of soul before God and adore the love which has taken possession of our hearts until our faith can firmly say: God has indeed given me the spirit of love in my heart. *In the power of the Spirit I can and will love God and my fellowmen.*

September 16

A Song of Love

But now abideth faith, hope, love, these three; and the greatest of these is love.—1 Corinthians 13:13

This chapter is wholly devoted to the praise of love. The first three verses speak of the absolute necessity of love as the chief thing in our Christian faith. "If I speak with the tongues of angels, if I have the gift of prophecy, if I have all faith, so as to remove mountains, and if I bestow all my goods on the poor, and if I give my body to burned, but have not love"; then, three times repeated, "I am becoming sounding brass, I am nothing, it profiteth me nothing." *If I have not love, it all profiteth me nothing.*

Then follows the Song of Love (vv. 4-8). There are fifteen things said about love—what it is and what it is not. In this description one sentence sums up the whole nature of love: "It seeketh not its own." And again: "Love never faileth." Prophecies, tongues, and knowledge will vanish away. Even faith and hope will be changed into sight. But love abides to all eternity, as long as God endures. *Love is the greatest thing* in the world.

We should read this chapter more often than we do, and commit the song to memory; so that the great words are imprinted on our hearts: "Love seeketh not her own." Think over it and pray over it. "Love never faileth." Consider all that means. "The greatest of these is love." Let this love rule in your life.

God is love. "He that dwelleth in love, dwelleth in God, and God in him." O Christian, are you living in a world that is uncharitable and selfish, or full of bitterness and hatred? Take refuge under the wings of this everlasting love. Let your heart be filled with it, so that by God's almighty power you may be a witness to the transforming power of love. Thus you will be a fountain of blessing to all around you.

Live each day in fellowship with the triune love of Father, Son and Holy Spirit, and you will learn the secret of how to love.

September 17

The Obedience of Love

If ye love me, ye will keep my commandments.—John 14:15

The love with which the Father loved the Son was a wonderful, never-ending love. All that the Father was and had He gave to the Son. The Son responded to this love by giving the Father all. Cost what it might, He kept the Father's commandments and abode in His love.

Christ, in His great love to us, sacrificed all; His life and death were wholly at our service, and He asks of us that which is only reasonable: that we, out of love, should keep His commandments. Read verses 15, 21, 23, and see how the words are repeated three times, together with the great promise that follows. And chapter 15, verses 7, 10, 14 speak three times of the rich blessing connected with the keeping of the commandments.

"If ye love me, keep my commandments." This precept loses its power because Christians say: "It is quite impossible: I cannot always keep His commandments." And so conscience is quieted, and the commands are not kept. Yet our Lord really meant it, for in the last night with His disciples He promised them definitely a new life, in which the power of the Spirit would enable them to live a life of obedience.

"But what becomes of man's sinful nature?" you ask. Man keeps his sinful nature to the end of his life. "In me, that is, in my flesh, dwelleth no good thing." The Holy Spirit is the power of God that works within us, both to will and to do, and so prevents the flesh from gaining the upper hand. Think of the text in Hebrews (13:20, 21), "The God of peace . . . make you perfect in every good thing to do his will, working in you that which is well-pleasing, through Jesus Christ."

These are no mere idle words: "If ye love me, keep my commandments," and "My Father will love him, and we will make our abode with him." Believe that the Holy Spirit will cause the love of Christ to work in your heart in such power that you will be able to abide in the love of Jesus the whole day, and to keep His words with great joy. Then you will understand the saying: "This is the love of God, that we keep his commandments; and his commandments are not grievous." Only believe that the Holy Spirit will endue you with power to live this life of perfect love.

September 18

Love and Prayer

Be sober, and watch unto prayer, above all things being fervent in your love among yourselves. —1 Peter 4:7, 8

In our text, watching unto prayer and fervent love are closely linked. This is true, too, in the spiritual life. The man who prays only for himself will not find it easy to be in the right attitude towards God. But where the heart is filled with fervent love to others, prayer will continually rise to God for those whom we love, and even for those with whom we do not agree.

There would be a great defect in our look at brotherly love if we neglected to indicate what an important place prayer holds in the life of love. These two fruits of the Spirit are inseparably connected. If you wish your love to grow and increase, forget yourself, and pray, pray earnestly, for God's children and His church. And if you would *increase in prayerfulness*, give yourself in fervent love to the service of those around you, helping to bear their burdens.

What a great need there is, at this time, of earnest, powerful intercessors! Let those who complain that there is so little love among Christians acknowledge that one of the chief signs of love is lacking in themselves, if they do not *pray much and often for their brethren.*

I am deeply convinced that God desires His children, as members of one body, to present themselves each day before the throne of grace to pray down the power of the Spirit upon all believers. Union is strength. This is true in regard to the kingdom of heaven. Real spiritual unity will help us to forget ourselves, to live unselfishly, wholly for God and our fellow-men. And the word of Peter will be applied to our lives— "watching in prayer—fervent in love."

There can be no surer way of growing in the spirit of love than by uniting daily at the throne of grace, and finding our joy and life in the oneness of Spirit with the whole Body of Christ.

Let this discussion of love be also a book on prayer. As we meditate on love to the brethren, we shall be constrained to have fellowship with God. And we shall attain this, not by reading or thinking, but by contact with the Father and with the Lord Jesus through the Holy Ghost. Love impels to prayer; to believing prayer is vouchsafed the love of God.

September 19

The First and Great Commandment

The Lord thy God will circumcise thine heart... to love the Lord thy God with all thine heart, and with all thy soul.—Deuteronomy 30:6

God greatly desires our love. It is the nature of all love to long to be acceptable and to meet with response. Yes, God longs with a never-ending fervent desire to have our love, the love of the whole heart.

But how can I attain such a condition? Just in the same way that I receive salvation—through faith alone. Paul says: "I live through the faith of the Son of God, who loved me." When we take time to wait upon God, and remember with what a burning desire God sought to win our love through the gift of His Son, we shall be able to realize that God has a strong and never-ceasing longing for the love of our heart.

Our hearts are blind and dark, and we are apt to forget that God longs each day for the love of His child. If I once begin to believe it, I shall feel constrained to tarry before God, and ask Him to let His light shine into my heart. Just as the sun is willing to give me its light and heat, if I will receive them, God is a thousand times more willing to give me the light and glow of His love.

In the Old Testament God gave us the promise of the new covenant (Ezek. 36:25, 26), "I will cleanse you, a new heart will I give you, and put within you a new spirit." He gave His Son to die for us to win our love. Take time, O my soul, to grasp this, and wait silently upon God, and become strong in the assurance of faith: God, who longs for my love, is almighty and will shed abroad His love in my heart through the Holy Spirit now dwelling within me.

Oh, that we could understand that there is nothing on earth to be compared to this experience! Shall I not take time each day and give God His desire and believe with firmer faith? God, who so greatly longs for my love, will work within me by His Spirit, granting the desire to love Him with my whole heart, and enabling me to prove my love by keeping His commandments.

September 20

The Royal Law of Love

If ye fulfill the royal law according to the scripture, Thou shalt love thy neighbor as thyself, ye do well.—James 2:8

When our Lord, in answer to the question, "Master, which is the great commandment in the law?", had answered: "Thou shalt love the Lord thy God with all thy heart," He added: "The second is like unto it, Thou shalt love thy neighbor as thyself." These two commandments both contain the one verb, *love*. In heaven, where God is, and on earth among men, love is the royal law, love is supreme.

The Christian's love for his fellowmen has more than one purpose:

1. It reveals to us our own nature, implanted by God, that we should love ourselves, and it calls us to love our neighbors with the same love. Thus we have in our hearts the law to love our neighbors as ourselves.

2. Christianity teaches us to love our neighbor because God loves him. Every man, however sinful, has a share in God's compassion and love, because he is made in God's image. I ought, then, to love my neighbor, not merely because he is a fellowman, but because I see God's likeness in him and because God loves him. As God loves all men, even His enemies, even so, not more, nor less, I must love all. "Be ye merciful, even as your Father is merciful." From my Father in heaven I must learn how to love.

3. The Christian love of all mankind may rise still higher. In the realm of grace, God has reconciled us to himself so that He can apportion to us His personal love. This is the law for each child of God; he must love his brother with the same love with which Christ has loved him.

4. And then comes the last and the highest thought, that even as Christ, in His great love, redeemed a world dying in misery and sin, so all those who have received this love should give themselves, even as Christ did, to love all men, and devote their lives to making others partakers of this great blessedness.

Child of God, here are four reasons why we should love our neighbors. Have they not a divine authority and irresistible power, which will compel us to manifest this Christian love toward our brethren in fullness of beauty?

May God write the royal law of love deep in our hearts!

September 21

National Feeling

God hath made of one blood all nations of men. —Acts 17:26

A former Prime Minister of England said in regard to the Boer War, that it "served to maintain the principle that the smaller nationalities should not be oppressed. That is to say, that all these precious lives and the treasures of gold were offered up in vindication of nationality, which may be regarded as a gift of God, as the divine right of each nation, according to its special nature, to preserve and develop its individuality in the service of the common life of all the world. This war will develop national feeling more intensely, and will increase a national consciousness, and arouse hope amongst the peoples who have hitherto been considered the most backward in the world. People will slowly learn that national feeling depends on character, and character depends on religion.

"In a struggle such as this we cannot expect the breach to be healed at once; but we can cultivate a spirit of Christian sympathy with those who differ from us, and cease to regard each other with suspicion and distrust. We can trust the honesty of each other's convictions, and take more trouble to understand one another."

This extract speaks most strongly of the divine right of national feeling, yet we must also clearly understand that the feeling, as a merely human force, is under the power of sin. Let us remember "every creature of God is good, for it is sanctified by the word and by prayer." Without that sanctifying process, national feeling may become the prey of ambition, and the source of hatred, and aversion, and contempt for other nations. God has, in Christ, placed all men under the law of heavenly love. It is the holy calling of every Christian, and more especially of every minister of the gospel, under the guidance of the Holy Spirit, to point out to others the way by which national feeling may attain its twofold aim: (1) the development and uplifting of the people themselves, and (2) the right attitude to other peoples in the upbuilding of all mankind.

September 22

One Stream or Two Streams?

The stick of Ephraim, and the stick of Judah, I will make them one stick, and they shall be one in mine hand.—Ezekiel 37:19

If anyone were to ask me: "In which of these two do you believe?" my answer would be: "In both." "And why?" "Because God has so willed it." When the small stream of the Africander people, with less than one million souls, was turned into the mighty stream of the British Empire, with its three hundred millions, it was God's will that this should happen. It was His will that in the great stream there should be two streams, side by side. The two nationalities, the smaller as well as the greater, have each their own history, their own national characteristics, and their own special virtues and shortcomings. In God's plan and council there was room for both.

Why has there been such terrible strife and discord over the question: one stream or two streams? Because people would not accept both viewpoints and accord each its right. They wanted one or the other, exclusively, in the foreground. They forgot that God had said: "What God hath joined together, let not man put asunder." One who is really desirous of knowing and doing God's will—in His dealings with our people —must try to understand his twofold calling: to be faithful in preserving his own nationality; and at the same time to show his love and appreciation of the second nationality, with whom, under God's providence, his lot has been cast.

God has given to His people, in this land, a great and holy calling, in submission to His will and in the power of His love, to prove what it is to be a true Africander, and yet, at the same time, a faithful subject of the British Empire. Our love to God and to our neighbors will supply the right incentive.

When Ephraim and Judah became one in God's hand, the difference between the two was not destroyed. Each kept his own characteristics. But the oneness was that of true unity and mutual love. "Ephraim shall not envy Judah, and Judah shall not vex Ephraim." God will fulfill this promise to us; but on one condition: We must place our people in God's hand by our prayers. "They shall be one in mine hand." Let us, by means of intercession, place our people in God's hand. He can, and will, give the love and mutual forbearance that is needed.

September 23

Pray for Love

The Lord make you to increase and abound in love one toward another, and toward all men, even as we also do toward you; to the end he may stablish your hearts unblameable in holiness.—1 Thessalonians 3:12, 13

What a prayer! That the Lord would make them to abound in love toward each other, even as Paul did toward them: that He would strengthen their hearts to be unblameable in holiness. Without love this was impossible. Their hearts would be strengthened for a life of true holiness through the love of the brethren, by the power of God. Let us use this prayer often, both for ourselves and for those around us. Do you pray for holiness? Then show it by a hearty love to the brethren!

In 2 Thessalonians 3:5 we read: "The Lord direct your hearts into the love of God." Yes, that is what the Lord Jesus will do for us, give us a heart always directed to the love of God.

"Always in every prayer of mine for you all making request with joy. I pray that your love may abound yet more and more in knowledge ... that ye may be filled with the fruits of righteousness" (Phil. 1:4-11). The apostle, in his constant prayer for those in his charge, makes *love the chief thing.* Let us do the same.

"I would that ye knew what great conflict I have for you, that your hearts may be comforted, being knit together in love, unto all riches of understanding" (Col. 2:1, 2). Paul considers it indispensable for their growth in the knowledge of God that the hearts of the believers should be knit together in love. God is love—everlasting, endless love. That love can only be experienced when Christians are knit together in love, and live for others, and not just for themselves.

These four prayers of Paul give us abundant matter for meditation and prayer. Take time to let these heavenly thoughts grow in your heart. As the sun freely gives its light and heat to the grass and grain, that they may grow and bring forth fruit, so God is far more willing to give His love to us in ever-increasing measure.

September 24

Like Christ

I have given you an example, that ye should do as I have done to you.—John 13:15

The love of Christ, manifested in His death on the cross, is the ground, not only of our hope of salvation, but it is *the only rule for our daily life and conduct.* Our Lord says clearly: "Ye should do as I have done." The love of Christ is my only hope of salvation. A walk in that love is the way truly and fully to enjoy that salvation.

"Let each one of us please his neighbor for that which is good, unto edifying; for even Christ pleased not himself. Wherefore receive ye one another, as Christ also received us" (Rom. 15:2, 7). God will work the power within us to "receive one another, as Christ received us." He will do it for every upright soul, and for all who pray in confident faith.

"Be ye followers of God, as dear children; and walk in love, as Christ also hath loved us, and hath given himself for us" (Eph. 5:1, 2). Here, again, love is everything. We must realize that Christ loved us even unto death, and that we are now God's dear children. It follows naturally that we should walk in love. Faith in Christ's wonderful love, and in God's inconceivable love resting upon us, makes it not only possible, but certain, that those who keep close to Christ will walk in love.

"Put on therefore, as God's elect, holy and beloved, a heart of compassion; forbearing one another, and forgiving each other; even as the Lord forgave you, so also do ye. *And above all these things put on love,* which is the bond of perfectness" (Col. 3:12-14). What a blessed life in the love and the power that we have in Christ! What a blessed walk in His fellowship, when we are led by the Holy Spirit and strengthened for a life in His likeness!

September 25

The Power of God's Word

The words that I have spoken unto you they are spirit and they are life.—John 6:63

Ye received the word of God, as it is in truth, the word of God that worketh effectually in you that believe.—1 Thessalonians 2:13

The word of God is living and active.—Hebrews 4:12

The question constantly recurs: Why do God's children so little realize the great value and absolute necessity of brotherly love? One answer is: Because of unbelief. Without faith, great faith, persevering faith, there can be no thought of the power of love within us. But it is a different faith from what we usually mean, when we say we believe in God's Word. This true faith is deeper and higher. It bows before God in the deep realization of His greatness, of His power to work wonders in our hearts, and of His loving care. The word of a king, or a general, has great influence over his soldiers. And how great beyond compare is the Word of the Infinite and Almighty One!

It is necessary to be deeply convinced of our utter inability to produce this love, which is holy, and can conquer sin and unbelief. We need a burning desire to receive this heavenly love into our hearts whatever the cost may be. Then at length we will gain an insight into what God's Word is, as a living power in our hearts. This supernatural power will be the love of God shed abroad in our hearts by the Holy Spirit, living and working within us.

In the next meditation we will consider the verses from the First Epistle of John, in which the love of God is promised to believers. Let each Christian ask himself, is he ready to acknowledge his deep sinfulness and want of power and to yield his heart unreservedly for this love to take possession? And, above all, take time in God's presence to wait on Him in the confidence that His Word will work effectually in us, as a seed of new life. Then we shall love our Lord Jesus and our brethren with a love like that with which God has loved us.

September 26

Perfect Love

These are the true sayings of God.—Revelation 19:9

He that loveth his brother abideth in the light.—1 John 2:10

"Whosoever doeth not righteousness is not of God, neither he that loveth not his brother. For this is the message which ye heard from the beginning, that *we should love one another*" (3:10, 11). "We know that we have passed out of death into life, because we love the brethren" (3:14). "Hereby know we love, because he laid down his life for us: and we ought to lay down our lives for the brethren" (3:16). "And this is his commandment, That we should believe on the name of his Son Jesus Christ, and love one another" (3:23). "Beloved, let us love one another: for love is of God" (4:7). "Beloved, if God so loved us, *we ought also to love one another.* If we love one another, God abideth in us, and His love is perfected in us. We have known and believed the love that God hath to us. God is love; and he that abideth in love abideth in God, and God in him" (4:11, 12, 16). "If a man say, I love God, and hateth his brother, he is a liar: for he that loveth not his brother whom he hath seen, cannot love God whom he hath not seen. And this commandment have we from Him, that *he who loveth God love his brother also*" (4:20, 21).

Each of these words is a living seed. It has within it a divine power which is able to take root and grow and bear fruit in our hearts. But just as the seed requires the soil in which it grows to be kept free of all weeds, so the heart must be wholly surrendered to God and His service that the seed of the Word may bear this heavenly fruit.

Read over again 3:23. As necessary as faith is for our salvation, so necessary is love of the brethren. And (4:21) love to God and love to the brethren are inseparable.

September 27

The Love That Suffers

Walk in love, as Christ also hath loved us, and hath given himself for us.—Ephesians 5:2

Is it not strange that love, which is the source of the greatest happiness, should also be the cause of the most intense suffering? Our life on earth is such that suffering always follows, when love seeks to save the object of its love. Yes, it is only by means of suffering that love can gain its end, and so attain the highest happiness.

What a wonderful thought! Even the almighty power of God's love could not achieve its purpose without suffering that passes understanding. By means of His sufferings, Christ bore and overcame the sins of the whole world, and the hard heart of man was softened and drawn to God. So love in the midst of suffering manifested the greatest glory and attained its end perfectly.

Let no one, with such an example before him, imagine that love is self-sufficient. No; love worthy of the name manifests itself in a life of continual self-sacrifice. Love's strength lies in renunciation. Just think what a mother suffers when a beloved child is ill, or when a son falls into evil ways. Love gives her strength to endure, whatever the circumstances may be. Think, too, what one must undergo who has yielded himself wholeheartedly to work and to pray for others. It may mean tears and heartache and much wrestling in prayer. But love overcomes all obstacles.

O Christian, do you really long to know the love of Christ in all its fullness? Then yield yourself wholly to Him and His blessed service. Regard yourself as a channel through which the highest love can attain its aim. Take the souls around you into a sympathizing, loving heart, and begin to suffer with them and intercede for them. Let it be your chief delight to live and to suffer for others, in the love and fellowship of the Lord Jesus. Then at length you will realize what this life of love is, as a servant of God, and even as God himself and as Christ, to live wholly for the welfare and happiness of others.

O soul, dwell on this wondrous truth, that there can be no real fellowship in the love of Christ, save in unreserved surrender, to seek always the glory of God in the salvation of your fellowmen. "He that dwelleth in love, dwelleth in God, and God in him."

September 28

The Works of the Flesh

The works of the flesh are manifest; witchcraft, hatred, strife, jealous-ies, wrath, envyings, murders, and such like.—Galatians 5:19-21

Paul, in these three verses, mentions seventeen of the terrible "works of the flesh." Nine of these are sins against love. And he says, elsewhere (Eph. 4:31), "Let all bitterness, and wrath, and anger, and clamour, and evil speaking, be put away from you, with all malice." He here answers the question, why there is so little love among Christians, and why it is so hard to arouse such love. All these sins are "works of the flesh."

Even the earnest Christian is still in the flesh. Paul says: "In me, that is in my flesh, dwelleth no good thing . . . because the mind of the flesh is enmity against God." It is quite impossible for a Christian by his own efforts to lead a life of love. Scripture says: "Walk in the Spirit, and ye shall not fulfil the lusts of the flesh." The Spirit will enable us to keep the flesh always in subjection. The "fruit of the Spirit" will be Christ's love poured into our hearts as a fountain of love.

Paul adds to what was quoted above: "The law of the Spirit of life in Christ Jesus hath made me free from the law of sin." The grace of God will enable the Christian to walk, not after the flesh, but after the Spirit.

Learn these three great lessons: (1) The Christian cannot in his own strength love God and his fellowman. (2) The great reason for so much bitterness, and want of love, is that the Christian walks after the flesh. (3) The only sure way to abide in this life of love, to love God, and Christ, with the whole heart, to love the brethren fervently, and to have a tender compassionate love for all who do not yet know Christ—is an absolute surrender to the Holy Spirit, to be led and guided by Him each day of our lives. It is through the Holy Spirit that this love is shed abroad in our hearts.

Child of God, learn the lesson that the Holy Spirit will take entire possession of you and will work continually within you a life of love to Christ and to all men. Pray over this thought until it gains control of your whole being!

September 29

Passing the Love of Women

My brother Jonathan: very pleasant hast thou been unto me: thy love to me was wonderful, passing the love of women.—2 Samuel 1:26

God created man to show what the power of love is when a man strives for the welfare of others, and even gives up his life for them. He created woman to show what tenderness and quiet endurance are when she sacrifices herself for the sake of others. A little child, during the first years of its life, is dependent on the mother. It is not only that the child may learn to love its mother, but that the mother herself may be trained in the school of self-sacrificing love, for her greatest adorning is "the ornament of a meek and quiet spirit, which is in the sight of God of great price" (1 Pet. 3:4).

The tendency nowadays in public life is to place woman on an equal footing with man. This is only right in many cases. But one must not forget that the best ornament of a woman is a meek and quiet spirit, which is of great price in the sight of God, and of man, and which makes her a blessing in her home. It is the suffering, prayerful, all-conquering love of the wife and the mother which secures the happiness of a people.

Dear sisters, preserve as a great treasure the precious jewel which God has entrusted to you—to reflect the love of God in all its tenderness and sympathy. "As one whom his mother comforteth, so will I comfort you." Let each one, as she reads this book, take time to meditate on God's wonderful love and pray for it earnestly in a receptive spirit. This will give her a heavenly influence, and power over her husband and children, and in her dealings with her neighbors she will be a living witness to what the love of God can do.

Think of Mary, the woman who loved much, and the other women to whom the Lord revealed himself on the resurrection morning. It was the love of these women that gave them the right to be the first to meet the Lord and to take the message to the disciples.

God bless the mothers and wives and daughters of our land! May they prove in their lives how beautiful and powerful the love of women is! And the words from the time of David will still be true: "Wonderful as the love of women" is the love of God's children.

September 30

Faith Working Through Love

In Christ Jesus neither circumcision availeth anything, nor uncircumcision; but faith working through love. —Galatians 5:6

Faith is the root; love is the fruit. Faith becomes strong in the love of God and of Christ. Faith in God and love to the brethren must always go hand in hand. Faith in God's wonderful love, shed abroad in our hearts, enables us to live always in love toward our fellowmen. This true faith gives us power for a life of fervent, all-embracing love.

Yet how little the church realizes of all this! How seldom does the preacher lay stress on a Christlike love to the brethren as the fruit and joy of the life of faith!

All of our life—in the home, between father and mother, parents and children, brothers and sisters, friends and servants —should be a life in the love of Christ. Do not say it is impossible. All things are possible to God, who through His Holy Spirit will shed His love in our hearts to be lived out in our daily lives. Let our faith cling to God's Word and to the unseen and wonderful things He will do for us each day. Let these thoughts about love impel us to accept with new and greater faith the love of God, and then dedicate our lives to letting it radiate from us to all men—yes, even to our enemies, and to the heathen at the uttermost parts of the earth.

O Christian, the whole of salvation lies in these two words— faith and love. Let our faith each day take deeper root in God's eternal love. And then each day the fruit of the Spirit will be love in all our contacts with those around us. May God imprint these words deeply in our hearts, and make them a joy and strength to us: In Jesus Christ nothing avails but "love working through faith."

October

The Secret of Power
from on High

October 1

The Dispensation of the Spirit

How much more shall your heavenly Father give the Holy Spirit to them that ask him?—Luke 11:13

The writer of a little book on prayer tells us he has learned through his own experience the secret of a better prayer life, and would gladly pass on that which has helped him. As he was meditating on prayer, the great thought came with power, that we are now living in the dispensation of the Spirit. He says: "I feel deeply that in this time of the working of the Holy Spirit, all we may do in God's service is of little value unless it is inspired by the power of the Holy Spirit. This brought me to the well-known, precious, and inexhaustible text, 'How much more shall your heavenly Father give the Holy Spirit to them that ask him?'"

As I thought on this truth, I felt anew that the main thing for each of us is to receive, afresh from the Father, the Holy Spirit for our daily needs and daily life. Without this we cannot please God, nor can we be of any real help to our fellowmen. This brought the further thought that our prayers, if they are to raise our lives to fulfill God's purpose, must have their origin in God himself, the highest source of power.

Water cannot rise higher than its source. And so it happens that if the Holy Spirit prays through us, as human channels or conduits, our prayers will rise again to God, who is their source; and the prayers will be answered by the divine working in ourselves and in others. "I believe more and more," says the writer, "that the Christian life of each one of us depends chiefly on the quality of our prayers and not on the quantity."

What material for thought is here for deep meditation, for earnest prayer! When you pray today, ask the Heavenly Father to give you the Holy Spirit afresh for this day. He yearns to do it.

October 2

The Fruit of the Spirit

The fruit of the Spirit is love, joy, peace, longsuffering, gentleness, goodness, faith, meekness, temperance.—Galatians 5:22, 23

Here are two lessons on prayer: We must pray the Father every morning to give us the Spirit anew, and then pray the Spirit to teach and help us. A third lesson is this: commit to memory the text at the head of this meditation.

Christians often think they have only to ask God to teach them to pray, and He will do it at once. This is not always the case. What the Spirit does is so to strengthen our spiritual lives that we are able to pray better. When we ask Him to teach us, it is important that we open our hearts to His gracious influence, so that our desires are stirred, and we first of all surrender ourselves to the working of the Spirit. This surrender consists in naming before Him the fruit of the Spirit, with the earnest prayer to be filled with this fruit. As we pray for the teaching of the Spirit, we may say: "Here is my heart; fill it with the fruit of the Spirit."

Think of the first three: *love, joy, peace,* the three chief characteristics of a strong faith life. *Love* to God and to Christ, to the brethren, and to all men. *Joy,* the proof of the perfect fulfillment of every need, of courage and faith for all the work we have to do. *Peace,* the blessed state of undisturbed rest and security in which the peace of God that passes all understanding can keep our hearts and minds.

In the last discourse with His disciples, Christ used these three words, with the word "my" before them. "Abide in *my love.*" "That *my joy* might remain in you." "*My peace* I give unto you." Shall we not lay before the Spirit as the great desire of our hearts that He may make this fruit reach perfection within us? Then at last we shall be able to pray properly, and always ask more and more of our Heavenly Father.

October 3

Led by the Spirit

As many as are led by the Spirit of God, they are the sons of God.—Romans 8:14

Let us now consider four other fruits of the Spirit: *long-suffering, gentleness, goodness, meekness.* These four words all denote attributes of the Godhead. They will reach maturity in us through much prayer for the working of the Holy Spirit. Think of what they mean.

Longsuffering—In the Old Testament, in the time of Moses, God's longsuffering was praised. All Scripture bears witness to the wonderful *patience* with which God dealt with sinful man, until we come to the word in 2 Peter 3:9: "The Lord is longsuffering, not willing that any should perish, but that all should come to repentance." This attribute of God, the Spirit, will make a characteristic of our lives, so that we too may exercise a divine patience with all sin and wrong, so that souls may be saved.

Gentleness—What wonderful things we read in the Psalms about God's goodness and gentleness, which are from ever-lasting to everlasting. "As the heavens are high above the earth, so great is his mercy towards them that fear him." God works in our hearts this same goodness and mercy toward all the sin and wretchedness around us.

Goodness—"There is none good but God." All goodness comes from Him, and He gives to His children according as each heart asks and desires. And this goodness is manifested in sympathy and love to all who are in need.

Meekness—We read in Psalm 18:35, "Thy gentleness hath made me great." But it was chiefly in God's Son that the divine meekness was shown. Jesus says: "Learn of me, for I am meek and lowly of heart." Paul entreats his readers "by the gentleness and meekness of Christ." The Holy Spirit, too, the gentle Dove, longs to impart the ripe fruit of meekness to our hearts.

Is it not a wonderful thought that these four attributes of God, which are the characteristics of God's work among sinners, may be brought to ripeness in our hearts by the Holy Spirit, so that we in all our ways and conversation may be like the Meek and Lowly One?

October 4

The Spirit of Faith

Having the same spirit of faith, we also believe. —2 Corinthians 4:13

Do you begin to realize why it is so important to commit to memory the text, Galatians 5:22? It will strengthen the desire in our hearts to have and to hold the fruit of the Spirit within us. Our expectation of the blessing God will give will be enlarged. Let us pause awhile on the two last fruits of the Spirit—*faith and temperance.*

When the disciples asked the Lord: "Why could we not cast out the evil spirit?" His reply was: "This kind goeth not out but by prayer and fasting." Their faith was not powerful enough, and even if they had prayed, they had not the zeal and self-sacrifice needed for prevailing prayer. Here we see the union of faith and temperance.

Faith is a fruit of the Spirit—and leads the seeking soul to depend on God alone. Faith believes God's Word, and clings to Him, and waits in perfect trust that His power will work within us all He has promised. The whole life of the Christian each day is a faith life.

Let us now think of *temperance.* This refers in the first place to eating and drinking, and leads us to restraint, carefulness, and unselfishness in our conversation, our desires, in all our relationships with one another. Our motto should be: "Forsaking all worldly desires, to live righteously and godly and temperately in all things." Temperate in all our dealings with the world and its temptations. Righteous in the doing of God's will. Devout in the close communion with God himself.

Faith and temperance are both fruits of the Spirit. When we ask the Spirit to teach us to pray, we open our hearts toward Him that He may grant us the fruits of the Spirit, faith and temperance, to influence our daily lives in our relationships with God and man.

Learn this text by heart, and let the promptings of the Spirit in your heart each day lead you to the Father that He may grant the fruit of the Spirit in your inner life, which will be seen in all your actions.

October 5

Worship God in the Spirit

We are the circumcision, which worship God in the Spirit, and rejoice in Christ Jesus, and have no confidence in the flesh.—Philippians 3:3

The foregoing remarks serve as preparatory to the prayer itself. We have come to the Father with the prayer for the Holy Spirit. We have invoked the guidance of the Holy Spirit. Now we begin to pray.

First, we pray to God the Father, thanking Him for all the blessings of this life. We acknowledge our entire dependence and impotence, and express our trust in His love and care for us. We wait before Him until we have the assurance that He sees and hears us. Then we direct our prayer to the Lord Jesus, and ask for grace to abide in Him always, for without Him we can do nothing. We look to Him as our Lord, our preserver, our life, and give ourselves into His keeping for the day. We give utterance to our faith in His infinite love and the reality of His presence with us.

Lastly, we pray to the Holy Spirit. We have already prayed to Him for guidance. We now ask Him to strengthen us in the faith that what we have asked of the Father and the Son may be truly worked out in us. He is the dispenser of the power and gifts of the Father and of the Lord Jesus; all the grace we need must be the result of the working of the Spirit within us.

Our text says: "We serve God in the Spirit, we glory in the Lord Jesus, and have no confidence in the flesh." We have no power to do the thing that is good. We count on the Lord Jesus, through the Holy Spirit, to work within us. Let us take time to think and meditate on these things. It will help to strengthen our faith if we repeat the text of Galatians 5:22, asking God to grant these fruits in our lives. As we surrender ourselves wholly, we shall have boldness by faith to accept the working of the Holy Spirit in our hearts.

October 6

Intercession

Pray one for another.—James 5:16

There is much value in intercession, and it is an indispensable part of prayer. It strengthens our love and faith in what God can do, and is a means of bringing blessing and salvation to others. Let us learn the lesson thoroughly: Prayer should not be for ourselves alone, but chiefly for others. Let us begin by praying for those who are near and dear to us, those with whom we live, that we may be of help, and not a hindrance, to them. Pray for divine wisdom, for thoughtfulness for others, for kindliness, for self-sacrifice on their behalf.

Pray for all your friends, and all with whom you come into contact. Pray that you may watch in prayer for their souls. Pray for all Christians, especially for ministers and those in responsible positions.

Pray for those who do not yet know the Lord as their Savior. Make a list of the names of those whom God has laid upon your heart, and pray for their conversion. You belong to Christ; He needs you to bring to Him in prayer the souls of those around you. The Holy Spirit will strengthen you to an active love in watching for souls. Pray, too, for all poor and neglected ones.

Pray for the heathen and for all mission work. Use a mission calendar, with daily subjects of prayer, and bear on your heart before God the missionaries, evangelists, teachers, and believers among the heathen.

Do you think this will take too much time? Just think what an inconceivable blessing it is to help souls through your prayers; and look to the Holy Spirit for further guidance. If this takes too much time in your morning watch, then take some time later in the day. Cultivate the feeling: "I am saved to serve." You will taste the great joy of knowing you are living even as Jesus Christ lived on earth—to make God's love known to others.

October 7

Time

What, could ye not watch with me one hour?—Matthew 26:40

One who wishes to pray as we have indicated in our previous meditations might say: "I think I could do all that in ten minutes' time." Very well; if ten minutes is all the time you can give, see what you can do in that time. Most people can spare more time. If they will only persevere from day to day, with their hearts set on prayer, time will come of its own accord.

Is it possible that Christians can say they cannot afford to spend a quarter or half an hour alone with God and His Word? When a friend comes to see us, or we have to attend an important meeting, or there is anything to our advantage or pleasure, we find time easily enough.

And God, the great God, who has a right to us and who in His wondrous love longs for us to spend time with Him that He may communicate to us His power and grace—we find no time for fellowship with Him. Even God's own servants, who might consider it their special privilege to be much with Him in prayer to receive the fullness of power—even His servants are so occupied with their own work that they find little time for that which is all-important—waiting on God to receive power from on high.

Dear child of God, let us never say, "I have no time for God." Let the Holy Spirit teach us that the most important, the most blessed, the most profitable time of the whole day is the time we spend alone with God. Pray to the Lord Jesus, who in His earthly life experienced the need of prayer; pray to the Holy Spirit, who will impress upon us this divine truth. As indispensable to me as the bread I eat, and the air I breathe, is communion with God through His Word and prayer. Whatever else is left undone, God has the first and chief right to my time. Then only will my surrender to God's will be full and unreserved.

October 8

The Word of God

The Word of God is living and active. —Hebrews 4:12

I find it a great help to use much of God's Word in my prayers. If the Holy Spirit impresses a certain text upon my mind, I take it to the throne of grace and plead the promise. This habit increases our faith, reminds us of God's promises, and brings us into harmony with God's will. We learn to pray according to God's will, and understand we can expect an answer only when our prayers are in accordance with that will (1 John 5:14).

Prayer is like fire. The fire can burn brightly only if it is supplied with good fuel. That fuel is God's Word, which must not only be studied carefully and prayerfully, but must also be taken into the heart and lived out in the life. The inspiration and powerful working of the Holy Spirit alone can do this.

By thoughts such as these we gain a deeper insight into the value and power of God's Word, as a seed of eternal life. We are all familiar with the characteristics of a seed—a small grain in which the life-power of a whole tree slumbers. If it is placed in the soil it will grow and become a large tree.

Each word or promise of God is a seed containing a divine life in it. If I carry it in my heart by faith, love it and meditate on it, it will slowly but surely spring up and bring forth the fruits of righteousness. Ponder this until you gain the assurance: although my heart seems cold and dead, the Word of God will work within me the disposition He has promised.

The Holy Spirit uses both the Word and prayer. Prayer is the expression of our human need and desire. The Word of God is the means the Holy Spirit teaches us to use as a guide to what God will do for us, and the demonstration of the secret working of the Holy Spirit in our hearts, by which God himself fulfills His promise and gives us what we could not obtain without the help of the Spirit.

October 9

In the Name of Christ

Whatsoever ye do, in word or in deed, do all in the name of the Lord Jesus, giving thanks to God the Father through him.—Colossians 3:17

At the close of your prayer it is always well to add a request for the "spirit of remembrance"; "He shall bring all things to your remembrance" all through the day, so that the prayers of the morning may not be counteracted by the work of the day. Read the text at the head of this passage once more, prayerfully.

Have you ever realized that it is a command? Is it the aim of your life to obey it, and to fulfill its injunctions? This may be difficult, but it is not impossible, or God would not have asked it of us. God's Word has a wonderful power to preserve the spirit of thanksgiving in our lives. When we rise in the morning let us thank God for the rest of the night before in "the name of the Lord Jesus," and in His name let us at night thank Him for the mercies of the day. The ordinary daily life, full of most ordinary duties, will thus be lightened by the thought of what God has done for us for Christ's sake. Each ordinary deed will lead to thankfulness that He has given us the power to perform it.

At first it may seem impossible to remember the Lord Jesus in everything, and to do all in His name; yet the mere endeavor will strengthen us. Even as a mother is conscious of her love for her little child all through the day's hard work, so the love of Christ will enable us to live all day in His presence. We need to completely surrender ourselves to live for God all the day.

I have often spoken and written of what it means to pray in the name of Christ. On reading our text of today I thought: Here we have the right explanation. The man who does all in word and deed, in the name of Jesus, may have the full, childlike confidence that what he asks in that name, he will receive. Take the text into your heart, and you may count on the Holy Spirit to make it true in your life.

October 10

The Spirit Glorifies Christ

He shall glorify me, for he shall take of mine, and shall declare it unto you.—John 16:14

To understand the work of the Holy Spirit, and truly to experience it, one must try to grasp the relationship of the Holy Spirit to the Lord Jesus. Our Lord said definitely, before His departure, that the Spirit would come as a Comforter to the disciples. *The Spirit* would reveal Him in their hearts *in heavenly glory.* The disciples were full of the thought. They would not miss their Lord, but have Him with them always.
This made them pray earnestly for the Holy Spirit, for they longed to have Jesus with them always. This was the promise of the Master: the Spirit should reveal Him to them.

This is the meaning of our text—"The Spirit shall glorify me"; even as I am in the glory of heaven. He will make Me known. "He shall take of mine"—My Love, My Joy, My Peace, and all My life—"and reveal it unto you." Where there is an earnest desire for the glory of Jesus in the heart of the believer, the Holy Spirit will preserve the holy presence of Jesus in our hearts all the day.

We must not weary ourselves with striving after God's presence. We must quietly endeavor to abide in fellowship with Christ always, to love Him and keep His commandments, and to do anything, in word and deed, in the name of Jesus. Then we will be able to count upon the secret but powerful working of the Spirit within us.

We see again the value of remembering and meditating on the text in Galatians 5:22. If our thoughts are always occupied with the Lord Jesus, His love, His joy, His peace—then the Holy Spirit will graciously bring these fruits to ripeness within us.

The great desire of the Holy Spirit and of the Father is that Christ may be glorified in and through us. Let it be the earnest desire and prayer of our lives, too!

October 11

Praying in the Spirit

Praying in the Spirit, keep yourselves in the love of God. —Jude 20, 21

Paul began the last section of the Epistle to the Ephesians with the words: "Be strong in the Lord and the power of his might." He speaks of the whole armor of God, and closes by saying that this armor must be put on with prayer and supplication, "praying always in the Spirit." As the Christian needs to be strong in the Lord all the day, and to wear his armor against the foe the whole day, so he needs to live always praying in the Spirit.

The Holy Spirit will not come to us, nor work within us, just at certain times when we think we need His aid. The Spirit comes to be our life-companion. He wants us wholly in His possession at all times, otherwise He cannot do His work in us. Many Christians do not understand this. They want the Spirit to help and to teach them, but do not grasp the truth that He must dwell in them continually, and have full possession of all their being.

When once this truth is grasped, we will realize that it is possible to live always "praying in the Spirit." By faith we may have the assurance the Spirit will keep us in a prayerful attitude, and make us realize God's presence, so that our prayer will be the continual exercise of fellowship with God and His great love. But as long as we regard the work of the Spirit as restricted to certain times and seasons, it will remain an unsolved mystery, and a possible stone of offense.

The apostle Jude expresses the same thought as Paul when he says: "Praying in the Spirit, keep yourselves in the love of God." This is what each child of God desires, and what the Spirit will do within him, keeping him in the love of God, even as he may keep himself in the sunlight all day long. It is this blessed nearness of God which can enable one to abide in His love at all times, even in the busiest moments of one's life, praying without ceasing, in entire dependence on Him.

October 12

The Temple of God

Know ye not, that ye are the temple of God, and that the Spirit of God dwelleth in you? The temple of God is holy, which temple ye are. —1 Corinthians 3:16, 17

From eternity it was God's desire to create man for a dwelling in which to display His glory. Through man's sin this plan was a seeming failure. In His people Israel God sought a means of carrying out His plan. He would have a house in the midst of His people—first a tabernacle, and then a temple—in which He could dwell. This was but a shadow and image of the true indwelling of God in redeemed mankind, who would be His temple to eternity. So we are built up "into a holy temple, for a habitation of God through the Spirit" (Eph. 2:22).

In the meantime, since the Holy Spirit has been poured forth, He has His dwelling in each heart cleansed and renewed by the Spirit. The message comes to each believer, however feeble he may be: "Know ye not? Know ye not?—that ye are a temple of God?" How little this truth is known or experienced. And yet how true it is, "The temple of God is holy, which temple ye are."

Paul testifies of himself: "Christ liveth in me."

This is the fullness of the gospel which he preached: the riches of the glory of the mystery, Christ in you. This is what he prayed for so earnestly for believers, that God would strengthen them through His Spirit in the inner man; that Christ might dwell in their hearts by faith. Yes, this is what our Lord himself promised: "He that loveth me, and keepeth my words—the Father will love him; and *we will come unto him, and make our abode with him.*" Is it not strange that Christians are so slow to receive and to adore this wonder of grace?

Through the Holy Spirit you will be sanctified into a temple of God, and you will experience that Christ, with the Father, will take up His abode in your heart. Do you desire that the Holy Spirit should teach you to pray? He will do it on this one condition, that you surrender yourself wholly to His guidance.

October 13

The Fellowship of the Spirit

The communion of the Holy Ghost be with you.—2 Corinthians 13:14

In this verse we have one of the chief characteristics and activities of the Holy Spirit. It is the Holy Spirit through whom the Father and Son are one, and through whom they have fellowship with each other in the Godhead. For the Holy Spirit is the true life of the Godhead.

We have fellowship with the Father and the Son through the Spirit. "Our fellowship is with the Father and the Son." "Hereby know we that he abideth in us, by the Spirit which he has given us" (1 John 3:24). Through the Spirit we know and experience the fellowship of love in the life with the Father and Son.

Through the Spirit we, as God's children, have fellowship one with another. In the child of God there should be nothing of the selfishness and self-interest that seeks its own welfare. We are members of one Body. "It is one Body and one Spirit." And through the Spirit the unity of the Body must be maintained.

One reason the Spirit does not work with greater power in the church is that the unity of the Spirit is too little sought after. At Pentecost, after ten days spent in united prayer, the 120 seemed melted together into one body. They received the Spirit in fellowship with one another.

We have the fellowship in the bread and wine when we meet at the communion table; we also have fellowship one with another in the trials of other members of the Body. Always it is: "The fellowship of the Spirit be with you now and evermore." Remember the words of the text in Galatians about the fruit of the Spirit, and present it to the Spirit in prayer, and so we show our love for all God's children.

In heaven there is an eternal fellowship of love between Father and Son through the Spirit. Do we really long to be filled with the Spirit? Let us offer ourselves to God, beseeching Him to grant us the unity and the fellowship of the Spirit with all members of Christ's Body.

October 14

With the Whole Heart

Ye shall seek me, and find me, when ye shall search for me with all your heart.—Jeremiah 29:13

You have often heard it said that if one seeks to perform any great work, he must do it *with his whole heart and with all his powers.* In worldly affairs this is the secret of success and of victory. And above all in divine things it is indispensable, especially in praying for the Holy Spirit.

I cannot too earnestly or too urgently repeat that the Holy Spirit desires to have full possession of you. He can be satisfied with nothing less if He is to show His full power in your life. He has the right. Why? Because He is the Almighty God.

Have you ever realized when you pray for the Holy Spirit *that you are praying for the whole Godhead to take possession of you?* Do you really understand this? Or have your prayers had a wrong motive? Were you expecting that God would do something in your heart, but for the rest you must be free to do your own will? That would be a great mistake. The Holy Spirit must have *full* possession.

You say, that is just the trouble. You do not feel such a burning, urgent desire as you ought, and you do not see any chance of its becoming true in your life. God knows about this impotence of yours; He has ordained in His divine providence that the Holy Spirit shall work within you all you need. What God commands and demands of us, *He will himself work within us.* On our part there must be the earnest prayer to the Father each day, and an acceptance of the Holy Spirit as our leader and guide.

Child of God, the Holy Spirit longs to possess you wholly. Take time in your impotence to give Him your answer. Cast yourself in complete dependence on the word of His promise and on His almighty power at work within you.

October 15

The Love of God in Our Hearts

The love of God hath been shed abroad in our hearts through the Holy Ghost, which is given unto us. —Romans 5:5

The Holy Spirit is shed abroad in our hearts by God the Father. The love of God is shed abroad in our hearts through the Holy Spirit. As truly as God has poured forth the Spirit, so truly is the love of God shed forth by the Spirit.

Why do we seldom experience this? Simply because of our unbelief. It takes time to believe in the divine mighty working of the Holy Spirit through whom our hearts are filled with the love of God. We need time for retirement from the world and its interests, for our souls to bask in the light of God so that the eternal love may take possession of our hearts.

If we believe in the infinite love of God, and the divine power with which He takes possession of the heart, then we will receive what we ask for—the love of God shed abroad in our hearts by the Holy Spirit. God desires His children to love Him with all their hearts and all their strength. He knows how impotent we are. And for that very reason He has given the Spirit, who searches the deep things of God, and in these depths has found the fountain of eternal love to fill our hearts with His love to His Son.

If you long for this, draw nigh to God, and abide with Him in quiet worship and adoration, and you will know the love of God in Christ which passes all knowledge.

The Holy Spirit wants to have all of you. He will teach you each day to dwell with the Father in His great love as a little child, and to abide in the love of Christ each day, and to demonstrate that love to the brethren and a perishing world. He will make your heart a fountain of everlasting love, springing up to life eternal and flowing forth in blessing to all around. Say with a heart full of thanksgiving: the love of God is shed abroad in my heart through the Holy Spirit.

October 16

Walk in the Spirit

Walk in the Spirit.... If we live in the Spirit, let us also walk in the Spirit.—Galatians 5:16, 25

The word "walk" reminds us of daily life with our fellow-men. The Christian in his walk and conversation must follow the leading of the Spirit, and walk by the Spirit. That will be the sign of the spiritual man, one who serves God in the Spirit and does not trust in the flesh.

People speak as though the Spirit were only needed in our communion with God when we pray, or for our work in the service of the kingdom. This is a great mistake. God gives us His Spirit to be in us the whole day. We need Him most in the rush of our daily work, because the world has then such power to lead us away from God. We need to pray the Father every morning for a fresh portion of His Spirit for each day. During the course of the day let us remind ourselves that the Spirit is with us, and lift up our hearts to God, remembering the Spirit abides with us always.

Paul says: "As ye have received Christ Jesus our Lord, so walk ye in him"; and again: "Put on the Lord Jesus Christ." As he puts on his coat when he goes out, so the Christian must put on the Lord Jesus and show by his conduct that Christ lives in Him and that he walks by the Spirit.

"Walk in the Spirit, and ye shall not fulfill the lusts of the flesh." As long as we are not under the guidance of the Holy Spirit, the flesh will rule over us. Oh, that we knew the unspeakable value of the grace God has given! The Spirit of His Son in our hearts will cry "Abba, Father," so that we may walk the whole day in God's presence as His beloved children. Christian, learn this lesson: the Spirit is given you to teach you that you may walk by the Spirit at all times. Thank God continually for this divine leader, who gives us daily renewal from heaven and enables us to walk and to abide in Christ.

October 17

The Spirit Promised to the Obedient

If ye love me, ye will keep my commandments. And I will pray the Father, and he shall give you another Comforter.—John 14:15, 16

Christ would ascend to heaven, and pray the Father to send the Comforter, the Holy Spirit. He would not only do this once, but it would form part of His intercessory work. He would remain "ever living to make intercession." The continual communication of the Spirit of the Father comes through the Son.

The Lord tells us here on what conditions He will send the Spirit. If we love Him and keep His commandments: "I will pray the Father." This is a work of deep meaning, a searching word—a word of greatly needed and blessed teaching. The Holy Spirit is given us to empower us to do the will of the Father. The condition is reasonable and just, that as far as we have kept the commandments through the Spirit, the Spirit will be granted to us in fuller measure. As we heartily accept this truth, and yield ourselves willingly to the Spirit's guidance, we will receive from day to day the fullness of the Spirit. Let us say to God that we accept the condition with all our heart, and will strive to keep His commandments, and ask for power to do His commandments more perfectly.

Do not listen to the whispers of Satan, or give way to unbelief and sloth. Surrender yourself unreservedly to the Lord, who has said: "If ye love me, ye will keep my commandments." Love will enable you to do it. The Lord Jesus does not deceive us with a vain hope in this matter. No, He gives the grace, He gives His own love in our hearts, teaching us to say: "I delight to do Thy will." Let us trust Him with childlike faith, and give ourselves totally—that is all that is necessary—to do His will. Then the beauty of the divine agreement He makes with us will dawn upon us: "If ye keep my commandments, ye shall abide in my love," and the Father will send the Holy Spirit anew each day.

October 18

Spiritual or Carnal?

And I, brethren, could not speak unto you as unto spiritual, but as unto carnal, even as unto babes in Christ.—1 Corinthians 3:1

The apostle here uses three words describing the spiritual condition of a man. There is *the natural man,* in his unconverted state—one who cannot "receive the things of the Spirit of God" (1 Cor. 2:14). There is *"the spiritual man,* who can discern spiritual things" (1 Cor. 2:13, 14). And between the two there is *the carnal man,* who is called "a babe in Christ," and who lives in jealousy and strife (1 Cor. 3:3).

It is important for us to know whether we are carnal Christians, giving way to sin and the lusts of the flesh. With the thought that things cannot be otherwise, we are apt to be content to allow much that is sinful and wrong in our lives. God calls us, and the Spirit draws us to be spiritual men and women—that is to say, people who pray daily to be led and guided each day into a truly spiritual life.

When the Lord Jesus promised the Spirit to His disciples, it was in the full expectation that they *would yield themselves wholly to the leading and power of the Spirit.* And it is in the same expectation that the Spirit will be granted anew each day, if we yield ourselves unreservedly to be sanctified in all our walk and conversation. Oh, that our eyes were open to see how right and how blessed that is!

Many Christians pray for the Holy Spirit, but always with a certain reservation, for they intend in many things still to do their own will. Oh, Christian, when you pray, entrust yourself completely to the guidance of the Holy Spirit for the whole day. If there is true willingness on your part, then the Holy Spirit will take full possession of you, and will preserve and sanctify your life. Do not serve God halfheartedly. Pray for the enlightenment of the Spirit that you may see the possibility and the blessedness of a life wholly surrendered to His service.

October 19

The Spirit of Wisdom

*That the Father may give unto you a spirit of wisdom and revelation
in the knowledge of him, having the eyes of your heart enlightened.—*
Ephesians 1:17, 18

In the Word of God we find a wonderful combination of
the human and the divine. The language is that of a man.
Anyone who has a good understanding can grasp the meaning
of the words and the truths contained in them. Yet this is
all that man, in the power of his human understanding, can
do.

There is a divine side in which the holy God expresses
His deepest thoughts to us. The carnal man cannot attain
to them, or comprehend them, for they must be "spiritually
discerned." Only through the Holy Spirit can the Christian
appropriate the divine truth contained in God's Word. Paul
prays earnestly that God would grant the spirit of wisdom
to his readers, eyes that are enlightened through the Holy
Spirit to understand what is written, and to know the exceeding greatness of His power working in all who believe.

Much of our religion is ineffectual, because people accept
the truths of God's Word with the intellect, and strive to put
them into practice in their own strength, but *it is only the
Holy Spirit who can really reveal divine truth to us.*

A young student in a theological seminary may accept the
truths of God's Word as head knowledge, while the Word has
little power in his heart to lead to a life of joy and peace
in the Lord Jesus. Paul teaches us that when we read God's
Word, or meditate on it, we should pray: *"Father, grant me
the spirit of wisdom and revelation."* As we do this each day
we will find that God's Word is living and powerful, and will
work experience in our hearts: God's commands will be
changed into promises. His commands are not grievous, and
the Holy Spirit will teach us to do lovingly and joyfully all
He has commanded.

October 20

The Spirit of Sanctification

Elect, through sanctification of the Spirit, unto obedience and sprinkling of the blood of Christ.—1 Peter 1:2

In the Old Testament God was revealed as the thrice Holy One. The Spirit is mentioned more than a hundred times, but only three times as the Holy Spirit. But in the New Testament the word "holy" is ascribed to the Holy Spirit, and Christ sanctified himself for us that we might be holy. The great work of the Holy Spirit is to glorify Christ in us as our sanctification.

Has this truth ever taken hold of you—at the pentecostal prayer meetings or in your private devotions—that the great object for which the Holy Spirit is given is to sanctify you? If you do not accept this truth, then the Holy Spirit cannot do His purifying work. If you only want the Spirit to help you to be a little better, and to pray a little more, you will not get very far. But when you once understand He has the name of Holy Spirit in order definitely to impart God's holiness, and will sanctify you wholly, then you will begin to realize that the Holy Spirit dwells in your heart.

And what will be the result? You will feel He must have you totally. He must rule and control the whole day. My whole life and conversation must be in the Spirit. My prayer, my faith, my fellowship with the Father, and all my work in God's service, must be completely under His sway. As the Spirit of holiness, He is the Spirit of my sanctification.

Dear fellow Christian, what I have just said is deep, eternal truth. Even if we are willing to accept this truth, and meditate on it daily, it will be of no value if we do not wait upon God to grant us the Spirit of heavenly wisdom, and a vision of what God has intended for us in His wonderful gift—the Spirit of sanctification. Each morning say slowly and calmly: "Abba, Father, for this new day renew within me the gift of Thy Holy Spirit."

Rivers of Living Water

He that believeth on me, out of [him] shall flow rivers of living water.—John 7:38

Our Lord, in His conversation with the Samaritan woman, said: "The water that I shall give him shall be in him a well of water springing up to eternal life." In our text the promise is even greater: rivers of living waters flowing from him, bringing life and blessing to others. John says further that this refers to the Holy Ghost, who should come when Christ had been glorified, for the Holy Spirit was not yet poured out.

The Spirit of God was mentioned in the Old Testament, but the Holy Spirit had not yet been given. Christ must first be offered through the eternal Spirit (on the cross) (Heb. 9:14), and raised from the dead by the spirit of holiness (Rom. 1:4), and receive from the Father power to send forth the Holy Spirit. Then only would the Christian be able to say: Now the Holy Spirit of Christ is in me.

What do we need in order to experience these two wonderful promises of the well of water, and the rivers of living water? Just one thing—*the inner attachment to Christ, and the unreserved surrender to fellowship with Him, and the firm assurance that His Spirit will work in us what we cannot do.* In one word: *He that believeth on Me.* We need a faith that rejoices in the divine might and love, and depends on Him day by day to grant us grace that living water may flow forth from us.

If the water from a reservoir is to flow into a house all day, one thing is necessary—the connection must be perfect, then the water passes through the pipe of its own accord. So the union between you and Christ must be uninterrupted; your faith must accept Christ and depend on Him to sustain the new life.

Let your faith rejoice that Jesus Christ gives the Holy Spirit, and may you have the assurance that the Holy Spirit is within you as a fountain of blessing.

October 22

Joy in God

For the kingdom of God is righteousness and peace and joy in the Holy Ghost.—Romans 14:17

Now the God of hope fill you with all joy and peace in believing . . . through the power of the Holy Ghost.—Romans 15:13

A Christian man said to me, shortly after his conversion: "I always thought if I became religious, it would be impossible for me to do my worldly business. The two things seemed so contrary. I seemed to be a man trying to dig a vineyard with a bag of sand on his shoulders. But when I found the Lord, I was so filled with joy that I could do my work cheerfully from morning till night. The bag of sand was gone; the joy of the Lord was my strength for all my work."

Truly a significant lesson. Many Christians do not understand that the joy of the Lord will keep them and fit them for their work. Even slaves, when filled with the love of Christ, could testify to the happiness that He gave.

Read the two texts at the heading of this meditation, and see how the kingdom of God is pure joy and peace *through the Holy Spirit,* and how God will "fill us with all joy and peace in believing . . . *through the power of the Holy Ghost."*

Then try to realize that the Holy Spirit will give this joy and peace of Christ in our hearts. To many the thought of the Holy Spirit is a matter of grief and self-reproach, of desire and disappointment, of something too high and holy for them. What a foolish thought, that the great gift of the Father, meant to keep us in the joy and peace of Christ, should be a matter of self-reproach and care!

Remember Galatians 5:22, and listen attentively to the voice of the Spirit each day as He points to Jesus Christ, who offers you this wonderful fruit: "My Love, My Joy, My Peace." "On whom, though now ye see him not, yet believing, ye rejoice greatly with joy unspeakable and full of glory" (1 Peter 1:8). Pray to the Holy Spirit and He will lead you into His joy.

October 23

All the Day—Every Day

Every day will I bless thee.—Psalm 145:2

It is a step forward in the Christian life when one definitely decides to seek to have fellowship with God in His Word each day without fail. His perseverance will be crowned with success if he is really in earnest. His experience may be somewhat as follows:

On waking in the morning God will be his first thought. He must set apart a time for prayer, and resolve to give God time to hear his requests, and to reveal himself to him. Then he may speak out all his desires to God, and expect an answer.

Later on in the day, even if only for a few minutes, he will take time to keep up the fellowship with God. And again in the evening, a quiet period is necessary to review the day's work, and with confession of sin receive the assurance of forgiveness, and dedicate himself afresh to God and His service.

Such a person will gradually get an insight into what is lacking in his life, and will be ready to say: Not only "every day" but "all the day." He will realize that the Holy Spirit is in him unceasingly, just as his breathing is continuous. In the inner chamber he will make it his aim to gain the assurance through faith that the Holy Spirit, and the Lord Jesus, and the Father himself will grant His presence and help all through the day.

All the day! Christian, the Holy Spirit says: "Today." "Behold, now is the accepted time!"

A man who had undergone a serious operation asked his doctor, "How long will I have to lie here?"

The answer came: "Only a day at a time."

And that is the law of the Christian life. God gave the manna daily, the morning and evening sacrifice on the altar—by these God showed that His children should live by the day. Seek this day to trust to the leading of the Holy Spirit for the whole day. You need not care for the morrow, but rest in the assurance that He who has led you today will draw still nearer tomorrow.

October 24

The Spirit and the Cross

The blood of Christ, who through the eternal Spirit offered himself without blemish unto God, shall cleanse your conscience to serve the living God.—Hebrews 9:14

The connection between the cross and the Spirit is inconceivably close and full of meaning. The Spirit brought Christ to the cross and enabled Him to die there. The cross was to Christ and to the Spirit the culminating point of their desire on earth. The cross gave Christ the right to pray down the Holy Spirit on earth, because He had there made reconciliation for sin. The cross gave Christ the right and the power to grant us the power of the Spirit, because on it He freed us from the power of sin.

To put it briefly: Christ could not have attained to the heavenly life, or have poured out the Holy Spirit, if He had not first died to sin, to the world, and to His own life. He died to sin that He might live to God. And that is the way the Holy Spirit brings the cross into our hearts. It is only as those who have been crucified with Christ that we can receive the full power of the Spirit. It is because we do not realize how necessary it is to die to all earthly things that the Spirit cannot gain full possession of us.

How is it so few Christians understand or experience that the fellowship of the Spirit is a fellowship of the cross? Simply because they do not feel the need of praying for the Spirit of wisdom to give them a deep, spiritual insight into the oneness of the Spirit and the cross. They try to use their human understanding, but there is too little waiting upon God to teach them divine truths through the Spirit.

Dear Christian, begin today to ask God to grant you a sight of how the Spirit will take you to the cross of Christ, in fellowship with Him, to die to the world and to sin, so that all things may become new, and you will actually live and walk and work and pray in the Spirit to the glory of God.

October 25

The Spirit and the Blood

There are three who bear witness, the Spirit, and the water, and the blood: and these three agree in one. —1 John 5:8

The water is external, a sign of the renewing and purifying through regeneration used in baptism. The Spirit and the blood are two spiritual expressions, working together in regeneration: the blood for the forgiveness of sins, the Spirit for the renewal of the whole nature. All through life the Spirit and the blood must agree.

The oneness is spiritual and true. Through the blood we obtain the Spirit, as through the blood we are redeemed and purified unto it to receive the Spirit. Only through the blood can we with confidence pray for and receive the Spirit. O Christian, would you have boldness each day to trust to the guidance of the Spirit? Then let your faith in the precious blood be sure and strong.

There may be some sin in your life of which you are hardly conscious, but which grieves the Spirit and drives Him away. The only way to avoid this is to believe that "the blood of Jesus Christ cleanses from all sin." Your only right to approach God is through the blood of the Lamb. Come with every sin, known or unknown, and plead the blood of Christ as your only claim on the love that accepts and forgives.

Nevertheless, do not rest content with the forgiveness of sins, but accept the fullness of the Spirit, to which the blood gives you access. In the Old Testament the priest went into the Holy Place with the blood, and the high priest into the Holiest of All. With the blood Christ entered the heavenly sanctuary and poured out there the Holy Spirit. Do not for a moment doubt that you have a right through the blood to the fullness of the Spirit.

As one who has been redeemed by the blood of Christ, make a complete surrender of yourself to God as His purchased possession, a vessel ready for Him to use, a dwelling place of the Holy Spirit.

October 26

The Spirit in Preacher and Hearer

Our gospel came unto you ... in power, and in the Holy Ghost, and in much assurance.... Having received the Word ... with joy of the Holy Ghost.—1 Thessalonians 1:5, 6 (See also 1 Cor. 2:4, 5.)

Paul more than once reminds his converts that the chief characteristic of his preaching was *the power—the supernatural power of the Holy Ghost.* The Holy Spirit was so imparted to His hearers that they received the word "with joy of the Holy Ghost."

This is one of the most important lessons in the spiritual life. We, as hearers, are so accustomed to listen attentively to the sermon to see what it has to teach us, that we are apt to forget the blessing of our church-going depends on two things. First, the prayer for the preacher that he may speak "in the demonstration of the Spirit and of power," and then the prayer for the congregation and for ourselves, that we may receive the word, not from man, but as it is in truth, God's Word, "which effectually worketh in you that believe" (1 Thess. 2:13).

How often there is no manifestation of the Spirit, when both the speaking and the hearing are mainly the work of human understanding or feeling. So often there is no power that raises the soul with spiritual insight into the life of faith that God has provided for His children.

How earnestly we should ask God to reveal to us all, both minister and people, *"the Spirit of wisdom and revelation"* that we may discover the place the Holy Spirit should have in our lives, and the perfect work that He will do within us! God help us to learn this prayer! Then we will understand what Christ meant when He said: *"Go not, preach not*—but wait for the promise of the Father, and ye shall receive the power of the Spirit, and ye shall be my witnesses unto the uttermost part of the earth" (Acts 1:4, 8).

Pray earnestly that God may teach us to pray down the power of the Holy Spirit upon ministers and missionaries and their congregations, that the preaching may be in the manifestation of the Spirit and of power, for the conversion and sanctification of souls.

October 27

The Full Gospel

Then Peter said: Repent, . . . for the remission of sins, and ye shall receive the gift of the Holy Ghost. —Acts 2:38

When John the Baptist preached, "Repent, for the kingdom of heaven is at hand," he also said: "He that cometh after me shall baptize you with the Holy Ghost and with fire." When Christ preached the gospel of the kingdom, He said: "There are some standing here, who shall not see death till the kingdom of God has come in power." This is what happened at the outpouring of the Holy Spirit. On the day of Pentecost, Peter preached the full gospel of repentance and forgiveness of sins, *and the gift of the Holy Spirit.* This is indispensable in preaching the gospel, for then only is it possible for a Christian to live in the will of God and to please Him in all things. The kingdom of God is righteousness (in Christ), and joy (in God) through the Holy Spirit. The continuous joy of which Christ speaks, "My joy," can only be obtained through the power of the Holy Ghost.

How often only half the gospel is preached—conversion and forgiveness of sins, and souls are led no further into the truth. The knowledge and appropriation of the life of the Spirit within us is not mentioned. No wonder so many Christians fail to understand that they must depend each day on the Spirit for the joy which will be their strength.

Dear Christian, accept this truth for yourself, as well as those among whom you labor—that the daily enjoyment of the leading of God's Spirit is indispensable for a joyous life of faith. If you feel there has been a lack in your spiritual life, then begin at once to pray the Father to grant you the gift of the Holy Spirit anew each day. Then trust yourself to His leading and guidance all the day. Let the remembrance of the text (Gal. 5:22) give you courage for all that the Holy Spirit will do for you. Regard your heart constantly as a garden of the Lord in which the Holy Spirit will bear abundant fruit to the glory of God.

October 28

The Ministry of the Spirit

Ye are an epistle of Christ, ministered by us, written with the Spirit of the living God, in fleshly tables of the heart.—2 Corinthians 3:3

The Corinthian church was a "letter of recommendation" for Paul, showing how much he had done for them. Although he claimed nothing for himself, God had enabled him as a "minister of the Spirit" to write in their hearts "with the Spirit of the living God." He himself declared: "Not that we are sufficient of ourselves to think anything as of ourselves: but our sufficiency is from God; who also made us sufficient as ministers of a new covenant."

What a wonderful presentation of the work of a minister for his people! A preacher prepared to be a minister of the Spirit, with power to write in the hearts of his people the name and the love of Christ. No wonder that Paul (vv. 7-11), speaking of the glory that was upon the face of Moses when he communed with God, says, "The ministration of the Spirit is more glorious by reason of the glory that excelleth." He then (v. 18) speaks of how "we all, with open face reflecting as in a mirror the glory of the Lord, are transformed into the same image from glory to glory, even as from the Lord, the Spirit."

Oh, that God would restore the ministry of the gospel to its original power! Oh, that all ministers and church members would unite in the prayer that God, by the mighty working of His Spirit, would give the ministry of the Spirit its right place, and teach the people to believe that when Christ is preached to them, they are beholding as in a glass the glory of the Lord, and may be changed into the same image by the Spirit of the Lord!

What a call that is for us to persevere in the prayer that the Holy Spirit may again have His rightful place in the ministry of the Word, so that the exceeding and abundant glory of this ministry may be demonstrated.

The Spirit from Heaven

Them that preached the gospel unto you by the Holy Ghost sent down from heaven.—1 Peter 1:12

Christ has taught us to think of God as our own Father in heaven, who is ready to bestow His blessings on His children on earth. Our Lord himself was taken up into the glory of heaven, and we are told that we are seated with Him in the heavenly places in Christ. The Holy Spirit comes to us from heaven to pour into our hearts all the light, and the love, and the joy, and the power of heaven.

Those who are truly filled with the Spirit have a heavenly life in themselves. Their walk and conversation are in heaven. They are in daily fellowship with the Father and with the Son. They seek the things that are above, for their life is hid with Christ in God. Their chief characteristic is heavenly-mindedness. They carry about with them the marks of their eternal, heavenly destiny.

How can one cultivate this heavenly disposition? By allowing the Holy Spirit, sent from heaven, to do His heavenly work in our hearts, and to bring to ripeness in our souls the fruits of the Spirit which grow in the Paradise of God. The Spirit will raise our hearts daily to fellowship with God in heaven, and will teach us to dwell in the heavenlies with Him. The Spirit makes the glorified Christ in heaven present in our hearts and teaches us to dwell in His abiding presence.

O Christian, take time each day to receive from the Father the continual guidance of the Holy Spirit. Let Him overcome the world for you and strengthen you as a child of heaven to walk daily with your God and with the Lord Jesus. Do not be unbelieving. The Holy Spirit will do His part if you in faith surrender yourself to His control. You will learn to speak to others with such heavenly joy that you will draw them, too, to give themselves to the leading of the Spirit and to walk in the heavenly joy of Christ's love.

October 30

The Spirit and Prayer

Verily, verily, I say unto you, If ye shall ask anything of the Father, in my name, he will give it you. —John 16:23

In our Lord's farewell discourse (John 13:17), He presented the life in the dispensation of the Spirit in all its power and attractiveness. One of the most glorious results of the day when the Holy Spirit should come would be: *the new power that man should have* to pray down from heaven the power of God to bless the world. Seven times we have the promise repeated: *"Whatsoever ye shall desire in my name, that will I do"* (John 14:13, 14; 15:7, 16; 16:23, 24, 26). Read these passages over, that you may come to understand fully how urgently and earnestly our Lord repeated the promise.

In the power of the perfect salvation that Christ accomplished, in the power of His glory with the Father, in the power of the outpouring of the third person of the Godhead— the Holy Spirit—to dwell in the hearts of His servants, they would have the unspeakable freedom to ask what they desired of the fullness of the will of God, and it should be done. Everything was included in these few words: *"What ye desire, that will I do."*

During the ten days before Pentecost the disciples put this to the proof. In response to their continuous united prayer, the heavens were opened, and the Spirit of God descended to earth to dwell in their hearts, filling them with His life-power. They received the power of the Spirit that they might impart it to thousands. That power is still *the pledge for all time of what God will do.* If God's children will agree with one accord to wait for the promise of the Father each day, there is no limit to what God will do for them.

O Christian, remember that you are living in the dispensation of the Spirit. That means that the Holy Spirit will dwell in you with heavenly power, enabling you to testify for Him. But it also means you may unite with God's children to ask in prayer greater and more wonderful things than the heart has conceived.

October 31

With One Accord in Prayer

These all with one accord continued stedfastly in prayer.—Acts 1:14

And when the day of Pentecost was now come, ... they were all filled with the Holy Spirit.—Acts 2:1, 4

Our Lord gave the command to His disciples: "Go ye into all the world and preach the gospel to every creature," and He added the promise: "Lo, I am with you always." We may be fully assured that this command and this promise were not meant alone for the disciples, *but also for us, their followers.*

Just before His ascension, Christ gave His very last command, also with a promise attached to it. The command was: "Go not, preach not—*wait* for the promise of the Father." And the promise was: "Ye shall receive power after that the Holy Ghost is come upon you; and ye shall be witnesses to me, unto the uttermost parts of the earth." *This very last command and promise are also meant for us.* As irrevocable as the command: "*Preach* the gospel," with its accompanying promise, is this last command of all, to *wait* for the promise of the Father—"Ye shall receive the power of the Holy Ghost."

For ten days the disciples pled that promise with one accord, and their prayer was wonderfully answered. Unfortunately, the church of our day has tried to carry out the first command, "Preach the gospel," but has too often forgotten the second, "Wait for the promise of the Father." The call comes to each believer to *pray daily with one accord* for this great gift of the Holy Spirit. Many Christians who pray for themselves and their own work forget to pray for the church of Christ. The power of the first disciples lay in the fact that they *as one body* were prepared to forget themselves and to pray for the Holy Spirit over all mankind.

O Christian, whatever you may have learned from reading these meditations, learn one more lesson. *Daily prayer in fellowship with God's children is indispensable*, and it is a sacred duty if the Spirit is again to come in power. Let not your knowledge of the working of God's Holy Spirit be limited to yourself alone, nor even to your church, but in a world-embracing love of Christ, for all God's children, and His kingdom over the whole world, pray for power.

November

The Secret of God's Saving Plan

November 1

God's Plan of Salvation

When Christ, who is our life, shall be manifested, then shall ye also with him be manifested in glory.—Colossians 3:4

After Adam had sinned, and brought death upon himself and his descendants, God gave the promise that a man born of woman should conquer the power of Satan and sin. This Man, who was the Son of God, the Bible calls the Second Adam: "Adam, who is the figure of him that was to come" (Rom. 5:14). The second Adam was in every respect to be like the first.

Adam not only brought the curse of sin and death upon his descendants, but actually bequeathed to them a life which was the cause of their being wholly dominated by evil. In this way, the old sinful nature of Adam survived in his descendants. The old nature lived in them and held sway. Likewise Christ by His death not only delivered us from the power of sin and death, but He himself lives in each of His redeemed ones and is their life.

We are too apt to think of Christ as in heaven, and from there living for and through us; but the last night He was on earth He taught that as His Father lived and worked in Him here on earth, even so would He dwell in us and work in us. The full gospel is contained in these words: "Christ is our life." "Christ lives in me." "Know ye not that Jesus Christ is in you?"

Many Christians forget this. They believe Christ died on the cross for them, and lives in heaven for them, but hardly that Christ is *in* them. The powerlessness of the church is mainly due to this. *We do not realize that the almighty Christ dwells in us.* We must know and experience and testify to this great truth if there is to be a real and lasting revival in the church of Christ. Then we shall know what it means to give ourselves wholly to Christ, always to abide in fellowship with Him, that His work may be accomplished through us. "Christ liveth in me. . . . To me to live is Christ."

November 2

The Twofold Life

I came that they may have life, and may have it abundantly.—John 10:10

Everyone can understand the difference between life that is weak and sickly and life that has abundant vitality. Thus, Paul speaks of the Christian life of the Corinthians as not spiritual but carnal, as of young children in Christ incapable of assimilating strong meat, or of understanding the deeper truths of the gospel (see 1 Cor. 3 and Hebrews 5). There are some, the majority of Christians, who never advance beyond first principles. They are dull of hearing and remain carnal Christians. There are others again, a minority, who indeed show forth the abundant riches of grace. All through the history of the church we find this difference. In our day, too, the number is small of those who seek to live wholly for God, and being spiritually minded have large thoughts of the abundant life there is in Christ. They witness to the glory of Christ "full of grace and truth." "For of his fulness we all received, and grace for grace" (John 1:16).

The preacher's aim should be so to declare the fullness of God's grace in Jesus Christ as to make Christians ashamed of the poverty of their spiritual life, and to encourage them to believe that "life abundant" in the fullness of the Spirit is for them.

Dear reader, ask yourself if you are living such an abundant life as Jesus came to bestow. Is it manifest in your love to the Savior and in the abundant fruit you bear to the glory of God? If not, pray God to strengthen your faith. Ask Him to make all grace abound toward you that you always having all sufficiency may abound in every good work. Let Jesus be precious to you, and daily communion with Him indispensable. He will teach you by His Holy Spirit to honor Him by an abundant life.

November 3

Life Abundant

Where sin abounded, grace did abound more exceedingly; that, as sin reigned in death, even so might grace reign through Jesus Christ our Lord.—Romans 5:20, 21

How little this truth is grasped or understood. That sin abounds we know full well. But do we believe that "grace abounds more exceedingly" and enables us to reign over sin? Yet it is absolutely necessary that we grasp this truth if we would have life abundant in Christ. Read 2 Corinthians 9:8, and observe the words "all" and "every," denoting abundance. "God is able to make *all grace* abound unto you; that ye, having *always* (without exception) *all* sufficiency in *every* thing (every possible need), may abound unto *every* good work." Ask yourself: "Is this abundant all-abounding life for me? Verily, if God is faithful it is possible for me! O God, write this truth upon my heart!"

Now take Paul's prayer in Colossians 1:9-11, so that you may be able to pray it first for yourself and then for others: "We do not cease to pray and make request for you, that ye may be filled with the knowledge of his will in *all* spiritual wisdom and understanding, to walk worthily of the Lord unto *all* pleasing, bearing fruit in *every* good work, strengthened with *all* power, according to the might of his glory, unto *all* patience and longsuffering with joy" (cf. 1 John 3:22). These words of the Holy Spirit are almost beyond our grasp. Let us continually take them to God that He himself through His Holy Spirit may make them live in our hearts. By them we shall attain to a firm and joyous faith. With such a God, with such abounding grace—much more abundant than the easily besetting sin—with such a Lord Jesus to give grace and cause grace to reign—thank God, I may believe that life abundant is for me!

November 4

Christ Liveth in Me

I have been crucified with Christ; yet I live: and yet no longer I, but Christ liveth in me.—Galatians 2:20

In these words Paul expresses three great thoughts: First, "I am crucified with Christ." When Christ died on the cross He identified all God's people with himself in that death. As we all died in Adam, and have inherited Adam's sinful nature, so we all have been crucified with Christ, and the power of His death works in us daily, that having died to sin in Christ we may live unto God. Our union with the crucified Christ is vital and complete. The power of His death and of His life is active in us.

Paul's second thought is, "I live, and yet no longer I." Having actually participated in the death of Christ he could say: "No longer do I live." My life has been yielded to death upon the cross of Christ. By faith I see my life under sentence of death cancelled. It is still mine, in my flesh wherein no good thing dwells, but I am free in Christ so that I no longer serve sin, as long as I abide in Christ.

His third thought, "Christ liveth in me," is the true secret of a Christlike life. Christ was not only crucified for me. He does not live only in heaven to intercede for me. No! *Christ liveth in me.* He himself said that even as His Father dwelt and worked in Him, even so He dwells and works in us. He is truly the life in us by which we live.

Oh, Christian, I beseech you, take time to meditate and adore. Allow the Holy Spirit to make these words live in your heart. This is the work of the Holy Spirit, to manifest Christ in you, to glorify Him in you with the heavenly glory which fills all things. Do not imagine that Christ's life can be manifested in us unless we die to the world and to self. Christ had to die. You are crucified with Christ and must experience the crucified life. The rest will follow—"I live no longer, Christ lives in me." "Thanks be to God for His unspeakable gift!"

November 5

The Life of Faith

That life which I now live in the flesh I live in faith, the faith which is in the Son of God, who loved me, and gave himself for me.— Galatians 2:20

These words are Paul's reply to the objection: "If you say, 'Christ lives in me,' where does your will come in?" If Christ does actually live in you, and holds himself responsible for your life, what remains for you to do?

Paul's words contain the secret of the true life of faith. Elsewhere he prays for believers, "that Christ may dwell in your hearts by faith." Here we see the great work that faith has to accomplish in us, and for us, moment by moment, in order to allow the living Lord to work His will in us. Christ will accomplish the work in our hearts.

Because of His divinity, it is natural for the Lord Jesus to fill all things, to be all in all, and especially in the hearts of His children.

Christ's own words to His disciples best explain this. Even as the Father dwelt in Him and worked His work in Him, so our Lord dwells in us and works His work in us. The Son expressed the Father. We are to express Christ. The Father worked in the Son, and the Son worked out what the Father had wrought in Him. Christ works in us and enables us to carry on His work. This is His gift to us.

The only attitude that becomes us is one of trust, strengthening our faith in the assurance that "he loved me and gave himself for me." He and I are eternally and inseparably one. "He lives in me."

This is almost too great to grasp or to believe, and yet it is God's truth. The child of God needs time for meditation and adoration, so that the Spirit of God may reveal to Him how completely He will fill our being, accomplishing the work in us. Oh, the depth of the riches and the wisdom and the knowledge of God! How unsearchable are His judgments, and His ways past finding out! Oh, the depth of the love of God in Christ. Let us sacrifice all that we may know and trust and honor His love.

November 6

The Ever-Abiding Spirit

The Father shall give you another Comforter, that he may be with you for ever.... He abideth with you, and shall be in you.—John 14:16, 17

We usually think of the abiding presence of the Lord Jesus as promised to us. Christ distinctly says, "Abide in me and I in you." "Abide ye in my love" (John 15). In today's text He speaks of "abiding" as evidence of the indwelling and work of the Holy Spirit. Read the text over again, and you will see that Christ abiding in us and our abiding in Him— "ye in me, and I in you"—is altogether dependent upon the indwelling of the Holy Spirit. Therefore it is of the greatest importance that we rightly grasp the fact of the ever-abiding indwelling of the Holy Spirit.

This can only be done each day as we appear in God's presence, by renewing and confessing our faith in the ever-abiding indwelling of the Spirit. It was as the Comforter that He was to compensate the disciples for the absence of Christ's physical presence, and with this heavenly comfort He comforts us each hour. It is through Him we have Christ in our hearts, a living mighty force, animating and enlightening us and filling our lives. This can be ours if we come into touch with God in Christ each day, thus receiving fresh power to influence and bless others.

Oh, my brother! Begin the day with the Triune God. Take time to worship God in Christ. Take time to yield yourself to the Holy Spirit, and to count upon Him to accomplish a great work in you by making Christ ever present in you.

November 7

Christic and the Spirit

He that believeth on me, out of his belly shall flow rivers of living water. This spake he of the Spirit, which they that believed on him were to receive.—John 7:38, 39

Each person of the blessed Trinity gives honor to the other. The Father seeks the honor of the Son, and the Son seeks the honor of the Spirit, and the Spirit honors the Son. So in our text today we hear Christ calling us to *believe in Him*, confident that the Holy Spirit will work powerfully in us according to the measure of our faith in Christ. On the other hand, Christ says, "The Spirit shall not speak from himself; but what things soever he shall hear, these shall he speak. He shall glorify me: for he shall take of mine, and shall declare it unto you" (John 16:13, 14).

Here we learn the important lesson that we must not expect the Holy Spirit always to give us tokens of His presence. He will ever seek to fix our attention upon Christ. The surest way to be filled with the Spirit is wholeheartedly occupying ourselves by faith in Christ. We may rely upon the Holy Spirit to enable us to do this.

Begin every morning in God's presence, and there commit yourself to Christ to accomplish His work in you. Thank the Father for the gift of the Holy Spirit, who enables you to abide in the love and the obedience of the Lord Jesus. Believe firmly that the Triune God works in your heart and has His hidden heaven there, which will be revealed to you as your heart is wholly given to His Son and Spirit. "Through Christ we have access to the Father through the Spirit."

Learn this important lesson: The stronger your faith in Christ the more freely will the Spirit flow from you. The more you believe in the ever-abiding Spirit the more surely you will know that Christ dwells and works within.

November 8

The Spirit and Christ

He shall glorify me; for he shall take of mine, and shall declare it unto you.—John 16:14

We have seen that Christ spoke of the gift of the Spirit as the fruit of faith in Christ. The Spirit would flow as a river from those who believed in Christ. Today we have the other side of the truth; the Spirit flows from Christ; the Spirit reveals Christ and imparts Him. This is a lesson of deep importance. Do you desire the Spirit? Have faith in Christ who bestows His Spirit. Do you desire Christ? Rely upon the Spirit to reveal Christ to you. The Spirit is sent from Christ glorified in heaven to impart Christ glorified to us upon earth, that Christ may be glorified in our hearts.

We have seen that the fullness of the Godhead dwelt in Christ that Christ as the life of God might dwell in us. All the life and love of God which the Spirit imparts to us is in Christ. Our whole life consists in union with Christ. As the branch is in the vine, so are we in Christ and He in us. Our first requirement each new day is to know that Christ lives in us and that the Holy Spirit will make this an abiding reality. Count upon the quiet, unseen working of the Holy Spirit in your heart.

Oh, Christian, this truth so deep and so divine is almost beyond our finite grasp. The Holy Spirit, who is God, will reveal it to us. Cling in childlike trust to Christ, confident that the Holy Spirit is working silently within you, so that Christ may dwell in your heart by faith. Make it a matter of prayer every day that "the Father may grant you to be strengthened with might by his Spirit in the inner man, that Christ may dwell in your heart by faith." Fix your heart upon Christ on the cross, upon Christ on the throne, in childlike trust that while you do so Christ will be revealed in your heart by the Holy Spirit, and you may confidently say: "Christ liveth in me—Christ is my life!"

November 9

Carnal or Spiritual?

And I, brethren, could not speak unto you as unto spiritual, but as unto carnal, as unto babes in Christ.—1 Corinthians 3:1

The difference Paul makes between the two kinds of Christians is of great importance. Man's natural life is altogether carnal. The Christian at his new birth receives the Holy Spirit, and immediately there begins a struggle between flesh and spirit. So long as the Christian allows the Spirit to conquer, and is led by the Spirit, the power of the Spirit over him increases, and he becomes a spiritual man. The flesh is still there, and in the flesh is no good thing, but he learns that it means that his flesh is crucified as something that deserves the accursed death, and he becomes the spiritual man, of whom it may be said: "The spiritual man discerneth all things."

When, on the other hand, the Christian is ignorant about the Spirit, or if informed, disobedient, then the flesh obtains the mastery, and the Christian remains weak; and as there is no spiritual growth, he remains a babe. He may try in his own strength to do better, and what was begun in the Spirit is continued in the flesh—a carnal attempt to become holy (cf. Gal. 3:3). By degrees the flesh triumphs, so that he has no power to resist the works of the flesh or the spirit of this world.

This is the sad condition of the church, that the majority of her members remain carnal. They constantly fall under the power of the flesh, and, as a result, are overcome by envy and anger and uncharitableness. Such Christians have no insight into spiritual truth. If their life in Christ, daily fellowship with Him, and what God promises to do for His children is mentioned, they can hardly understand what is meant.

How earnestly we should pray God to reveal to us what is carnal and what is spiritual, and enable us to yield ourselves completely to the guidance of His Spirit.

November 10

Go On to Perfection

But solid food is for full-grown men.... Wherefore let us cease to speak of the first principles of Christ, and press on unto perfection.
—Hebrews 6:1

In the epistle from which this text is taken we read that the Hebrews had long been Christians, and now ought to be teaching others; instead, they were still as babes needing to be fed on milk (Heb. 5:12-14). The apostle seeks to rouse them "to cease to speak of the first principles of Christ, not laying again a foundation of repentance." They were to go on to perfection, to the status of full-grown men, and be prepared for deeper truths which would be taught to them regarding Christ as the High Priest.

"But he, because he abideth for ever, hath his priesthood unchangeable. Wherefore he is able to save to the uttermost them that draw near unto God through him, seeing he ever liveth to make intercession for them" (7:24, 25). The truth of this ever-abiding unchangeable priesthood and complete salvation is the solid food of the believer, who desires perfection. In chapter 9, we are told of Christ appearing before the face of God for us, and later that we might enter into the Holy Place to live in communion with God (10:19, 20).

It is when he ceases to speak of the first principles of Christ, not laying again a foundation of repentance, that the Christian will grow and be strengthened in grace. He will then actually live in full fellowship with Christ.

Oh, Christian, if up till now you have been content to know that you have repented and believe in God, and so are sure of salvation, I beseech you, do remember this is only the beginning of eternal life. Listen to the call to press on to perfection. This is what God desires and what the Son himself will do for you. Learn to yield yourself fully to Christ and to find daily in Him the hidden life, so that you may grow in grace and God use you as a soul-winner. Nothing less than this conformity to Jesus Christ should satisfy you—a life wholly dedicated to God and to His dear Son.

November 11

The Building and Its Foundation

Let us press on to perfection, not laying again a foundation of repentance from dead works, and of faith toward God.—Hebrews 6:1

The parable of the difference between the foundations and the effect on the houses built on them will teach us important lessons about the two kinds of life. Paul lays the foundation of the house of God in the doctrine of justification by faith in Jesus Christ. That is the one sure, immovable ground upon which a lost sinner finds his eternal salvation (Rom. 5:2).

What is the house built upon this foundation? Read Romans 5:12-18. There the apostle points out that justification and peace with God are not everything; they are only the beginning. Then he goes on to show that as in Adam we died, so in the second Adam, Christ, we receive the abundance of grace whereby we may live through Jesus Christ. That is the life built on the foundation.

He points out in chapter 6 how in Christ we have died unto sin: we are baptized into His death; and as we are united to Him by the likeness of His death, we shall be united by the likeness of His resurrection. If we have died with Christ, we may be sure we really are dead to sin, but alive unto God in Jesus our Lord.

It is union with the crucified and risen Christ that sets us free from the power of sin. This life in Christ is the edifice that must be built upon the foundation of justification.

How little is Romans 6 grasped or appropriated. We are ever ready to lay the foundation and be content with that. No, child of God, our experience must be deeper. We must experience that Christ is our life, that we are crucified with Him, and in Him, and in Him are dead and risen again. That only will enable us to live a holy, godly life in the joy of the Holy Spirit.

November 12

The Reformation

For other foundation can no man lay, than that which is laid, which is Jesus Christ; but let each man take heed how he buildeth thereon.—1 Corinthians 3:10, 11

"Not laying again the foundation"—these words to the Hebrews were certainly not applicable to the Reformation. In the course of centuries the Church of Rome in building had left the true foundation. Instead of justification by faith in Jesus Christ being the foundation of Christian life, the church itself claimed power to forgive sin. Forgiveness could be obtained only through a priest; indeed it might be bought from a priest for money. The great work of Luther and Calvin was to lay anew the foundation of Jesus Christ, to the comfort of thousands of anxious souls. We can never thank God enough for the Reformation, when Jesus was proclaimed anew our righteousness—our peace with God.

That great work of Reformation was not accomplished in a day or a year. It took fifty years to establish the Reformation, and even after that time there were many priests whose conversion did not include the power of a holy life. Calvin himself said the Reformation was more in doctrine than in the lives of the people, and he felt deeply the need of the people to be taught and trained in the paths of righteousness. It was no wonder that so long as the foundation had to be relaid in the full truth of conversion and faith, there was delay in the building itself on the true foundation—a life of sanctification.

The Reformation is sometimes thought of as a return to Pentecost, but it was by no means that. Instead of brotherly love, separation from the world, and earnestness in preaching Christ by all who loved Him, there was much controversy among the Reformers. They trusted too much to the patronage of statesmen where these were kindly disposed toward them, and preaching was the work of ordained priests only, in contrast to the Pentecostal witnessing for Christ by all those who were constrained by His love.

November 13

The Walk in Christ

As therefore ye received Christ Jesus the Lord, so walk in him, rooted and builded up in him, and stablished in your faith, even as ye were taught, abounding in thanksgiving.—Colossians 2:6, 7

Here again we have the two kinds of life. The first is described in the words, "Ye have received Christ Jesus." That includes conversion, forgiveness of sin through the blood of Jesus Christ, and acceptance as a child of God. Then comes the second, the walk in Christ, "rooted in him," as a tree that must each moment receive its life from the earth in order to bear fruit. "Builded up in him," who is the only foundation. "Stablished in your faith and abounding in it," by which each day the Christian in his walk and conversation proves he abides and lives in Christ. As the roots of a tree receive life uninterruptedly from the soil, so the Christian receives his life and power moment by moment from abiding in Christ.

In the Confessions of Faith drawn up by the Reformers, prominence is given to conversion, acceptance of Christ. "Justification" and "justified" are words in frequent use. But the word "sanctification" is rarely found. Emphasis is laid on the doctrine of the forgiveness of sin, of faith in Christ as our righteousness before God, but we find little about Christ living in us, and our life being rooted in Him. The Heidelberg Catechism gives the explanation of the Ten Commandments, but Christ's commands in Matthew 5 and John 13-16 are hardly mentioned.

Let us thank God for the Reformation at a time when the foundation truth of a crucified Savior was laid, but at the same time let us go on to perfection, to a daily uninterrupted walk in Christ wherein we may abound in faith, experiencing the abundance of grace from the fullness there is in Christ for us to enjoy daily. The earliest description of true godliness is in the words: "Enoch walked with God." So Christians must learn to walk in Christ daily, established in the faith and abounding in it.

November 14

The Mediator of a New Covenant

Ye are come to Jesus the mediator of a new covenant, and to the blood of sprinkling. —Hebrews 12:24

The mediator is responsible that both sides will faithfully fulfill the obligations as set forth in the covenant. Jesus is our surety that God will fulfill His promise. He is surety to God for us that we on our part will faithfully perform what God requires of us, and He will enable us to keep the covenant.

It was as Mediator, in the night of the Last Supper, that He gave His disciples the great promise of a New Covenant, the gift of the Holy Spirit as prophesied by Ezekiel.

He also undertook to fulfill the promise, "I will cause you to walk in my statutes, and ye shall keep my judgments, and do them." It was in the fulfillment of this promise that He spoke so definitely to His disciples of the keeping of His commandments being the way by which God's designs would be accomplished. "If ye love me, ye will keep my commandments, and I will pray the Father *and he shall give you another Comforter.*"

"He that hath my commandments, and keepeth them, he it is that loveth me, and he that loveth me shall be loved of my Father, *and I will manifest myself unto him.*"

"If a man love me he will keep my word, and my Father will love him *and we will come unto him and make our abode with him.*"

"If my words abide in you, ask whatsoever ye will, and it shall be done." "If ye keep my commandments, ye shall abide in my love." "Ye are my friends, if ye do the things which I command you."

Would the Lord definitely have said that all these blessings depend upon the keeping of His commandments if it were impossible for His disciples to keep them? Assuredly not. He had given them a pledge that the Holy Spirit would enable them. Meditate on this until you have the assurance that Christ expects His disciples, for love of Him, through the power of the Holy Spirit, to do all that He asks; and through His abiding in their hearts they will unceasingly keep His commands.

November 15

Better Promises

He is the mediator of a better covenant, which hath been enacted upon better promises.—Hebrews 8:6

Ye are come to Jesus the mediator of a new covenant, and to the blood of sprinkling.—Hebrews 12:24

We have here some of the better promises of the New Covenant. Jeremiah 31:33: "This is the covenant: I will put my law in their inward parts, and in their hearts will I write it." Jeremiah 32:40: "I will put my fear in their hearts, and they will not depart from me." Ezekiel 36:25, 27: "From all your filthiness will I cleanse you, and I will give you a new heart, and I will put my Spirit within you and cause you to walk in my statutes, and ye shall keep my judgments to do them." Ezekiel 36:36: "*I the Lord have spoken it, and I will do it.* For this moreover will I be inquired of by the house of Israel to do it for them."

Could there be better or more definite promises than these, that God himself would put His fear into the hearts of His people *so absolutely that they would not depart from Him, and that He would cause them* to keep His judgments and do them?

This is the New Covenant of which Jesus is Mediator. Through the Holy Spirit He dwells in us and will keep us from sin, so that we shall have the desire and the power to do God's will in all things. Think of Zachariah's inspired words as he prophesied the deliverance Christ would bring: "That we being delivered out of the hands of our enemies might serve him without fear, in holiness and righteousness before him, all our days" (Luke 1:74).

These are the words of God and show what He will do for those who inquire of Him. The promises are sure. The Mediator gave first His blood and then His Spirit. He sees to it that the better promises are fulfilled to those who wholeheartedly and confidently desire and claim them from Him. Alas, how seldom is such a life either preached or experienced!

November 16

Fellowship with God

That which we have seen and heard declare we unto you, that ye also may have fellowship with us: yea, and our fellowship is with the Father, and with his Son Jesus Christ.—1 John 1:3

Fellowship with God is the unique blessing of the gospel. Christ died for us "that he might bring us to God," that the prodigal son might return to the father's house and to a life in his father's love. By His blood Christ dedicated for us a new and living way into the Holy Place where we may walk in the light of God. The promise is, "They shall walk, O Lord, in the light of thy countenance. In thy name shall they rejoice *all the day*." Our walk with God may be as natural and as joyful as a walk in the sunshine. A life of unbroken fellowship with God—this is the gospel.

Fellowship with God is the Christian's theme. If Christians are content to speak only of conversion, forgiveness of sin, and safety after death, they will fail grievously in their witness. Christians must be educated to practice the presence of God, to have fellowship with God, thereby ensuring holy living. This was the apostle John's message: Fellowship with the Father and with His Son Jesus Christ.

Fellowship with God is the Christian's only source of power. If fellowship with God is the blessing of the gospel, and the burden of the Christian's witnessing, then it follows the Christian must show in his own life the possibility and blessing of such a walk with God. Experiencing it himself, he is able to tell others of it as most blessed and full of joy. A life of close fellowship with the Father, and with the Son, lived by the Christian, gives him the right to win others to the same joyous fellowship. What God can do for me He can do for you. May fellowship with the Father and with His Son Jesus Christ be our daily life, first in the quiet hour, then in our daily duties, and finally in winning souls for Christ that they too may share this full salvation.

November 17

The Fullness of Christ

And the Word became flesh, and dwelt among us (and we beheld his glory, glory as of the only begotten from the Father), full of grace and truth. For of his fullness we all received, and grace for grace.—John 1:14, 16

Read these words again and again until you come under the impression of the supreme fullness of Christ. Let the Holy Spirit teach you to worship this Christ as the One in whom dwells all the fullness of the Godhead.

I may receive a purse containing very little or nothing at all, or the purse may contain a great deal of money. There is a great difference between the two! And so with us as Christians. Some receive Christ with the forgiveness of sin and the hope of heaven, but know little of the fullness of Christ and all the treasure there is in Him. Other Christians are not satisfied, but sacrifice all things until they can say, "Of His fullness have we received, and grace for grace." Paul said: "I count all things loss for the excellency of the knowledge of Christ Jesus my Lord." He is like the merchant seeking goodly pearls, who when he had found the pearl of great price, sold all that he had in order to buy it. So is the Christian who grasps something of the fullness of Christ, the fullness of love and joy. His holiness and obedience, His utter devotion to the Father and to mankind. That Christian gives up all that he may be united to this Christ. Listen to our Lord's words: "These things have I spoken unto you, that my joy might remain in you, and that your joy might be full." "Your heart shall rejoice and your joy no man taketh away from you." "Ask, and ye shall receive, that your joy may be full."

Dear reader, do you know this Christ in whom all fullness dwells? Or do you live as a pauper, depending in a great measure upon the world for joy? It is God's will that Christ should fill all things, even your heart and its needs. Let the Holy Spirit imprint deeply upon your heart the words of our text in all its fullness.

November 18

The Heavenly Life

Ye died, and your life is hid with Christ in God. Christ is our life.
—Colossians 3:3, 4

It is of the utmost importance for a Christian to know that the new life he receives *actually is the life of Christ which He lives in the Father.* Our life, my life, is hid with Christ in God, and must daily be received anew, and preserved as a holy of holies.

It takes time and quiet thought and prayer in any measure to grasp this great marvel, that the life Christ lives in the Father is the same life He lives in me. Christ does not live one life in the Father and another in me. His words are: "I live and ye shall live." "In that day ye shall know that I am in my Father, and ye in me, and I in you." As He is in the Father, so are we in Him, and He in us. One divine life in the Father and in Christ and in me.

How little have we grasped this! How little trouble do we take to experience it. Here is the secret of the necessity of taking quiet time and prayerful meditation each day, to become deeply impressed with the truth that the Lord Jesus, whose life is hid in God, has also His life hid in me. It is only by taking time to realize that the glorious heavenly Christ lives in my heart that I shall truly live as a child of my Father in heaven.

When we allow God's Holy Spirit daily to keep alive in us that heavenly life in Christ, we will grasp what it means to say, "I died with Christ, and I die daily to sin and self and the world, to make room for that glorious heavenly life that Christ actually lives in me." Then we will experience, "our conversation is in heaven." Thus shall I have courage to believe that Christ lives in me and reigns and works that which is well pleasing to His Father. Thus shall my life be a humble and constant walk with God, in the fellowship of His holiness and His love.

November 19

A Royal Priesthood

Ye are an elect race, a royal priesthood.—1 Peter 2:9

In the Old Testament the thought of the kingdom took the first place; in the New Testament prominence is given to that of priesthood.

One of the chief reasons for the feeble life in the church is the mistaken idea that man's happiness is the main object of God's grace. A fatal error! God's aim is far holier and far higher. He saves men on purpose that they in turn will carry out His purpose in saving their fellowmen. Each believer is appointed to be the means of imparting to others the new life he has received.

Those who are saved have the holy calling of being channels of God's grace to others. The feeble state of the church is largely due to the fact that most Christians imagine their chief concern is to desire and receive sufficient grace to reach heaven after death. The church must so proclaim the gospel that each saved soul will understand its message: "saved to serve," "saved to save others." "Ye are a royal priesthood."

A royal priesthood! The priestly heart is above all things a sympathetic heart, in which the love of Christ constrains us to win souls for Him. And that by virtue of two compelling motives: love to Christ, whom I shall please and honor in winning others to love Him; and love for souls, which will constrain me to sacrifice everything that others may share this heavenly life.

A priestly heart! A heart that has access to God in prayer and intercession for those who are yet unconverted. A priestly heart that, having pleaded in prayer for souls, has courage to speak to them of Christ. A priestly heart—in which the life of Jesus, great High Priest who ever lives to make intercession, is continued, and His power to save to the uttermost is manifested. O Spirit of God, write upon my heart, with indelible letters, "A royal priesthood."

November 20

"Apart from Me—Nothing"

He that abideth in me, and I in him, the same beareth much fruit, for apart from me, ye can do nothing.—John 15:5

The Lord Jesus follows up His great promise that those who abide in Him will bear much fruit with the words, "Apart from me, ye can do nothing."

What a cause for humiliation! The nature we inherit from Adam is so corrupt that in us—that is, in our flesh—dwelleth no good thing. Nay, more, our flesh is at enmity against God. We are under the power of sin to such an extent that we are unable to do anything well pleasing to God.

What a call to repentance! How often we as Christians have thought that we were able to do that which is good. How often we thought we were making ourselves better. Let us remember Christ's words, "Apart from me, ye can do nothing," and henceforth rely only upon Him.

What cause for thanksgiving! Christ has united us to himself and so dwells within us. He may work in and through us each day and all day. This is the secret of the spiritual life: the Lord Jesus working in us, enabling us to do His work.

What cause for joy and encouragement! All that in the Christian life has appeared too high and unattainable for me, all that, Christ will work in me. I have to care for one thing only, that I remain utterly dependent upon Him to care for me and work through me all the day. Whenever I remember, "Apart from me, ye can do nothing," I remember too, "He that abideth in me beareth much fruit."

He himself will see to it that He abides in me and I in Him. This, praise God, is the great work of which the eternal Spirit will make me capable. Thank God for the life of Christ in me. I in Him, He in me, is the work of the Holy Spirit in each soul that humbly and believingly yields itself for such communion with God.

November 21

The Thrice-Holy God

The God of peace himself sanctify you wholly, and may your spirit and soul and body be preserved entire, without blame at the coming of our Lord Jesus Christ. Faithful is he that calleth you, who will also do it.—1 Thessalonians 5:23, 24

What inexhaustible words! The God of peace himself. Yes, He himself, and none other, can and will do the work. And what is this work? To sanctify you wholly. How is this work to be done? Your entire spirit and soul, and even your body, is to be preserved without blame at the coming of our Lord.

This promise is so great it appears incredible. The apostle feels the difficulty and adds the words, "Faithful is he that calleth you, who also will do it." That leaves no room for doubt, but calls us to place our confidence in the faithfulness of God.

This work is accomplished by the Holy Trinity. God the Father says, "Be ye holy, for I am holy. I am the Lord that sanctifieth you." The Son prayed, "For their sakes, I sanctify myself that they also may be sanctified in the truth." And the Holy Spirit is the Spirit of sanctification, through whom the church of God consists of the sanctified ones in Christ Jesus.

How does the thrice-holy God accomplish this great work of sanctifying us wholly? Through His continual indwelling and fellowship and breathing of His holy life into us. As upon a cold day a man may warm himself by standing in the rays of the sun, until its warmth penetrates his body, so the soul who takes time for communion with God becomes permeated with the strength of the Triune holiness.

Oh, what a treasure there is in these words, what cause for adoration, what confidence that God, who is faithful, will do it. What encouragement to wait upon Him, to walk with Him, as Abraham did, knowing God, being fully assured that what He had promised He was able to perform. God grant us a vision of this divine holiness and grace and power, that we may confidently feel that He will sanctify us wholly and preserve spirit, soul, and body without blame.

November 22

The Spirit of His Son

Because ye are sons, God sent forth the Spirit of his Son into our hearts, crying, Abba, Father.—Galatians 4:6

The Spirit that dwells in you, O child of God, is none less than the same Spirit that was in Christ, the Spirit of God's holiness. In Gethsemane He taught Christ to cry, "Abba, Father, thy will be done." He teaches us to know God's father-love, and to respond with childlike love and obedience. He will be in us even as He was in Christ, the Spirit of sonship expressing itself in a life of prayer. I may most assuredly expect of Him that He will impart to me God's love and holiness.

I may also rely upon Him as the Spirit of God's Son to reveal Christ in my heart, and always to keep alive in me Christ's life. All that Christ has said of His abiding in me and I in Him, the Spirit of Christ will work in me. Through the Spirit Christ's indwelling becomes an actual experience, and as a result the mind of Christ and His disposition may be formed in me, and become manifest. I may with certainty expect this of the Holy Spirit.

And furthermore the Holy Spirit will fit me for God's service. As the Spirit that sanctifies He will reveal Christ to me as my sanctification. *The Spirit will enable me to overcome the world and its entanglements, and be a witness to what Christ's life in His child may be.* He will fill me with love to the brethren, with love to those who hate or ignore me, with love to all around me who are not yet saved, so that I will pray for them and be ready to help them. He will give me love to all the world, so that I may labor with enthusiasm for missions that the gospel may be brought to all men. Oh, take time each day with the Lord for your heart to be filled with the confident expectation of what God's Spirit will do for you.

November 23

Ye Are Bought with a Price

Know ye not that your body is a temple of the Holy Spirit which is in you, which ye have from God? and ye are not your own; for ye are bought with a price: glorify God, therefore, in your body.
—1 Corinthians 6:19, 20

Here you have the reply to the question: What does the Spirit expect of me? Your body is His temple. The temple of God is holy, devoted to His service. You are not your own; you have no right to please yourself. You have been dearly bought with the blood of Christ. The Spirit has absolute right to your whole life. Therefore you must glorify God in your body and your spirit, which are God's. The Holy Spirit is the Spirit of God's holiness. He comes to make me holy. He expects me to obey Him fully.

Let me dwell upon these words that I may comprehend clearly what the relationship must be between the Spirit and me, and what it is He has a right to expect of me. *He asks that I, as one dearly bought with the blood of Christ, and no longer my own, will work in all things to please Him and to follow His leading.* All that I owe to God and to the Lord Jesus must be shown in my conduct toward the Holy Spirit. I must in all things be guided by Him, for as God He has absolute right to me. He expects me to say each morning, "Speak, Lord, Thy servant heareth. I yield myself to obey the prompting of Thy voice within me." He expects absolute obedience.

Furthermore, He expects that I will keep in close touch with Him by taking time each day to renew the bond between Him and me. My whole life must be yielded to Him that He may bring to perfection in me all His glorious fruits.

He also expects that in His strength I shall witness for Jesus Christ, and consider it my work to help to bring the souls around me to the Lord Jesus. The Spirit expects that my body, which has been dearly bought, will be a temple of God from which adoration and praise to God the Father and His Son Jesus Christ will continually arise.

November 24

Revival

Turn us again, O Lord God of Hosts. Cause thy face to shine, and we shall be saved. —Psalm 80:19

Israel was in sore need. Their enemies scoffed at them as if God had forsaken them. Three times the Psalmist uses the words of our text to reinforce his prayer, "Stir up thy might, and come and save us."

In our day the enemy rejoices that in spite of our many churches, Christianity is so powerless in overcoming the sins of drunkenness, immorality, worldly-mindedness, and love of money. God's children are asking: "Can nothing be done? Is there no hope of revival?" Is God not willing to lead His people into a fuller, deeper life of victory over sin and all that opposes Christ in Christian and heathen lands? Has not God in His great love promised to give us His Spirit in answer to prayer? Is God not waiting for our prayers to begin the work of revival? A revival is much needed, and it is possible. God is longing for us to claim His promise and exercise our right as members of the Royal Priesthood (1 Pet. 2:9).

Where must the revival begin? *With God's children*, who may offer themselves to God as instruments to be used by the Holy Spirit, separating themselves from sin, and devoting themselves to the work of saving souls. Christians must realize and prove that the object of their life is God's service, and the saving of those for whom Christ shed His blood.

Revival has already begun wherever God's children offer up everything to live and work and suffer as Christ did.

Dear child of God, it means little to desire a deeper or more abundant life unless this is the chief object: to be a witness for Jesus, to win others to His service, and to intercede for them as a labor of love.

November 25

A Threefold Cord

All things whatsoever ye pray and ask for, believe that ye have received them, and ye shall have them. —Mark 11:24

To know, to desire, to will—these are the three chief activities of the soul. When a Christian realizes the fullness there is in Christ and the abundant life He gives, then these three words will show him the way to participate in this fullness.

To know. We must not be content with our own thoughts about growth in grace. We must see to it that we *know clearly what God promises to do in us, and what He requires of us.* God's Word teaches us that if we come honestly, with all our sin and impotence, and sincerely yield to Christ our Lord, He will do in us far above what we dare think. See to it that you know clearly what God says you may ask of Him.

To desire. We must be careful to desire with our whole heart that for which we pray, and be willing to pay the price for it. It may be our desire is faint. God will create the desire in answer to prayer. It may cost us a struggle, and much self-sacrifice, to let go the world and self, but the Spirit will come to our aid. But without strong desire and self-sacrifice progress will not be made.

To will. The will is the most important point: only by firmness will faith have courage to appropriate what God bestows. Often in the midst of fear and struggle, and almost in despair, we *will* to grasp what God offers. Our confidence must be in God alone. Christ Jesus will give us the assurance that He is strengthening us to yield ourselves to the Spirit's guidance. When our desire has developed into a firm will, we will have courage to believe all that God has promised.

Child of God, thousands have by these means come to experience such fullness in Christ as they never thought possible. The more you cast yourself upon the Word of God, and the love and power of Christ, the sooner you will enter into the rest of faith that ceases from works and depends upon God to fulfill His purposes in you.

November 26

The Vine and the Branches

He that abideth in me, and I in him, the same beareth much fruit.
—John 15:5

In this parable we see what the new life is which the Lord promised His disciples for the work of the Holy Spirit. It clearly mirrors the life of faith.

1. "Not fruit," "more fruit," "much fruit," "fruit that abides" (vv. 2, 8, 16): The one object of the life of faith is to bear much fruit to the glory of God the Father.

2. Cleansing (v. 2): The indispensable cleansing through the Word that is sharper than a two-edged sword.

3. "Abide in me": Intimate, continuous fellowship.

4. "I in you": Divine indwelling through the Spirit.

5. "Apart from me ye can do nothing": Complete impotence, deep humility, constant dependence.

6. "My words abide in you," "If ye keep my commandments, ye shall abide in my love," "Ye are my friends, if ye do the things I command you": Indispensable obedience.

7. "If my words abide in you, ye shall ask whatsoever ye will": Limitless confidence of faith.

8. "It shall be done unto you": Powerful answer to prayer.

9. "Even as the Father hath loved me, I also have loved you; abide ye in my love": Life through faith in Him that loved Me.

10. "These things have I spoken unto you that my joy may be in you and that your joy may be fulfilled": Joy full and abiding.

11. "This is my commandment, that ye love one another, even as I have loved you": The new commandment kept through the power of Christ's love in our hearts.

12. "I appointed you that your fruit should abide, that whatsoever ye shall ask of the Father in my name, he will give it you": The all-prevailing name of Christ.

This is the life Christ makes possible for us and works in us through the Holy Spirit. This is the life so sadly wanting, yet so indispensable, in the church. This is the life assured to childlike faith and obedience.

November 27

Give Time to God

To everything there is a season, and a time to every purpose under the sun. —Ecclesiastes 3:1

This is literally true: there is a time for everything. Can it be true, as so many maintain, that there is no time for communion with God? Is not the most important matter for which we must find time, fellowship with God, in which we may experience His love and His power? Give God time, I beseech you.

You need time to feed upon the Word of God and to draw from it life for your soul. Through His Word, His thoughts and His grace enter our hearts and lives. Take time each day to read the Bible, even if it be only a few verses; meditate upon what you have read, and thus assimilate the bread of life. If you do not take the trouble to let God speak to you through His Word, how can you expect to be led by the Spirit?

Meditate upon the Word, and lay it before God in prayer as the pledge of what He will do for you. The Word gives you matter *for* prayer, and courage and power *in* prayer. Our prayers are often futile because we speak our own thoughts and have not taken time to hear what God has to say.

Let the Word of God teach you what God promises, what you need, and in what manner God wishes you to pray. Thus by prayer and the Word your heart will be prepared to have fellowship with God through faith in Christ Jesus.

Dear child of God, it is of little use to speak of the deeper, more abundant life of Christ as our life if we do not daily, above all things, take time for fellowship with our Father in heaven. The life and love and holiness of God cannot be ours amidst the distractions and temptations of the world unless we give God time to reveal himself to us and to take possession of our hearts.

November 28

Deeper Life

And others fell upon the rocky places, where they had not much earth: and straightway they sprang up, because they had no deepness of earth. —Matthew 13:5

The seed sown upon the rocky places where the soil was superficial sprang up quickly, but it withered as quickly because there was no deepness of earth. Here we have a striking picture of so much religion which begins well, but which does not endure. The Christian needs a deeper life.

Let your whole life be an entrance into that love which passeth knowledge. In Ephesians 3:17-19, Paul prays "that Christ may dwell in your hearts through faith, that ye, being rooted and grounded in love, may be strong to apprehend what is the depth, and to know the love of Christ which passeth knowledge, that ye may be filled unto all the fulness of God."

He prays that Christians may stand rooted first in the love of Christ which passes knowledge, realizing and acknowledging that the depth of this love passes knowledge. He believes it possible for the soul of a Christian to be so rooted in this love that he may be filled with all the fullness of God in such measure as may be granted to a saint upon earth.

And how may we attain to this? "I bow my knees unto the Father." The way to remain rooted in love is in humble prayer upon your knees before God. Furthermore, "That he would grant you according to the riches of his glory"—great indeed, and wonderful—"that ye may be strengthened with power through his Spirit in the inward man."

Only in the life that knows the powerful working of the Spirit is such a life rooted in love possible. And yet more: "That Christ may dwell in your hearts by faith." The most important is that Christ in His everlasting love will dwell in you every day, ensuring a life ever more deeply rooted in the love of Him who gave himself for us.

I beseech you, dear child of God, take time to bow before the Lord in prayer, and thus meditate upon, and appropriate, these words. Do not grudge time or trouble. Commune with the Christ who loved you with the same love with which the Father loved Him, that thus you may get an insight into the greatness of the condescension of that love to you.

November 29

Soul-Winning

He that abideth in me, and I in him, beareth much fruit, for apart from me ye can do nothing.... Herein is my Father glorified, that ye bear much fruit.—John 15:5, 8

Fruit is that which a tree or a vine yields for the benefit of its owner. Even so, all that the Lord Jesus has taught us about His abiding in us and we in Him is to make us understand that it is not for our benefit, but for His good pleasure and the honor of the Father. We, as branches of the heavenly Vine, receive and enjoy such astounding grace that we may win souls for Him.

Could this be the reason why you have not enjoyed unbroken fellowship with Christ? You have forgotten that the object of fellowship and communion is fruit-bearing in saving others. Have you not given too much thought to your own sanctification and joy, not remembering that as Christ sought His blessing and glory from the Father in the sacrifice of himself for us, so we too are called to live solely to bring Christ to others? It is for this purpose that we become branches of the heavenly Vine, in order to continue the work that He began, and with the same wholeheartedness.

When Christ was on earth, He said, "I am the light of the world"; but speaking of the time when He should be taken from the earth, He said, "Ye are the light of the world."

How often you have said to the Lord, "I yield myself to Thee for cleansing and keeping and to be made holy," but you have hesitated to add "to be used of Thee for the salvation of others"? Let us acknowledge our failure here and humbly offer ourselves to the Lord for His work. Let us begin by praying for those around us, seeking opportunities of helping them, and not being satisfied until we bear fruit to the glory of the Father.

Christ said, "Apart from me ye can do nothing." He knows our utter weakness. He has promised, "He that abideth in me beareth much fruit." Let all that we learn of the more abundant life and abounding grace constrain us to live to win souls for Jesus.

November 30

Christ Our Life

Ye died, and your life is hid with Christ in God.... Christ is our life.—Colossians 3:3, 4

Paul writes to the Colossians: "Ye died, and your life is hid with Christ in God." Only God's Spirit can enable the believer to grasp and appropriate the truth that he was actually crucified and died with Christ. The new life he receives in Christ through the Spirit is life out of death. In Christ as the Lamb in the midst of the throne, the power of that life is shown as a crucified life in each one who has received it. The Holy Spirit gives me the assurance that I died with Christ, and the power of His death works in me.

And of Christ's life: "Your life is hid with Christ in God." This is what Christ said in the last night: "Ye shall know that I am in the Father and ye in me"—with Him in the Father. My life is safely hid with Christ in God, and from there I each day by faith receive it anew through the working of the Holy Spirit.

Is this not the reason why so many of God's children make so little progress? They do not know that the life of Christ who died on the cross and now lives in heaven is truly *their* life hid in God, and must daily be received afresh from God in the quiet hour. What joy to know my spiritual life is not in my keeping, but is hid in God. Christ and the Holy Spirit will grant to each humble believing child of God to receive this new life.

What joy to know that the new life of God's children around me is also hid with Christ in God! What a bond of union this will be. How sincerely we should love each other and pray for each other.

"Your life is hid with Christ in God. . . . Christ is our life."

December

The Secret of the Throne of Grace

December 1

The Throne of Grace

Unto him that sitteth on the throne, and unto the Lamb, be the blessing, and the honor, and the glory, and the dominion, for ever and ever. —Revelation 5:13

In chapters 4 and 5 of Revelation we are shown the difference between the throne of God the Creator, and the throne of grace. In chapter 4 John saw "a throne set in heaven, and one sitting upon the throne; and he that sat was to look upon like a jasper stone and a sardius." There was no definite form, but the shining light of precious stones. Round about the throne were four beasts, "and they rest not night and day, saying, Holy, holy, holy, Lord God Almighty, which was, and is, and is to come." The four-and-twenty elders fall down before Him, saying, "Worthy art thou, our Lord and our God, to receive the glory and the honor and the power: *for thou didst create all things, and because of thy will they were, and were created.*" Here we have the throne of God, the Almighty Creator!

In chapter 5 we read: "I saw in the midst of the throne a *Lamb* standing, as though it had been slain, and the four living creatures and the four-and-twenty elders fell down before the Lamb, and they sing a new song, saying, Worthy art thou, for thou wast slain, and didst purchase unto God with thy blood men of every tribe, and tongue, and people." Then thousands and thousands of angels cried: "Worthy is the Lamb that hath been slain to receive the power, and riches, and wisdom, and might, and honor, and glory, and blessing. And every created thing, which is in the heaven and on the earth, heard I saying, *Unto him that sitteth on the throne, and unto the Lamb,* be the blessing, and the honor, and the glory, and the dominion, for ever and ever."

There we have the throne of grace, the throne of God and of the Lamb. And the threefold song which we heard is the heavenly chorus which was sung at the dedication of the throne of grace, to the glory of God and of the Lamb. O my soul, bow down and worship and adore. When you draw near to the throne of grace, think of what it cost Christ to found that throne, and what assurance it gives that you will find grace to help in time of need. In deepest humility and with all your heart, worship the Lamb on the throne of grace.

December 2

The Lamb in the Midst of the Throne

Having then a great high priest. . . . Jesus the Son of God. . . . One that hath been in all points tempted like as we are, yet without sin. Let us draw near with boldness unto the throne of grace. —Hebrews 4:14-16

Can you imagine, O child of God, any way by which the Father could have given us greater boldness of access than by giving His only Son as a Lamb upon earth, with His godlike, gentle disposition, to win our hearts to Him? After Jesus had given himself on the cross, a ransom for our sins, God placed Him in the midst of the throne that we as sinners might have perfect boldness through His blood to present our prayers through Him, in full assurance that He, as intercessor, will make them acceptable to the Father.

Truly the holy God has done His utmost to draw us to himself and to grant us heavenly boldness to pray with the assurance that our defective prayers, through the Lamb on the throne, the sympathizing High Priest, will be heard and find acceptance with God the Father.

O my fellow Christian, take time, with the vision of the Lamb on the throne before you to give you boldness—take time in deepest humility and childlike faith, and with all the love of which your heart is capable, to worship Him as your Surety and Intercessor and great High Priest. When the Holy Spirit has given that vision of the Lamb on the throne unto your heart, it will indeed be a throne of grace, and you can do nothing less than fall prostrate before Him in adoration and praise, and give Him the glory to all eternity.

Your heart will then become a true temple of God, where, day by day, even hour by hour, the song will arise: "Salvation be unto our God who sitteth upon the throne, and to the Lamb."

When our hearts are filled with love for the Lamb upon the throne, who makes our prayers acceptable to God the Father, then we shall have the joy and the faith to expect a speedy answer.

December 3

Abundant Grace

The grace of our Lord abounded exceedingly with faith and love which is in Christ Jesus.—1 Timothy 1:14

If we would properly value and love the throne of grace, we must try to understand what it is it provides for our use. Scripture uses great words to reveal this grace to us. It speaks of "the riches of grace," "the glory of grace," "the abundance of grace," "the exceeding riches of grace," "the manifold riches of grace." Let these words sink deep into your hearts as we point to them in God's Word.

"Much more did *the grace of God,* and the gift by the grace of the one man, Jesus Christ, abound unto the many" (Rom. 5:15). "Much more shall they that receive *the abundance of grace* and of the gift of righteousness reign in life through the one, even Jesus Christ" (5:17). "Where sin abounded, *grace did abound more exceedingly*" (5:20).

"By the grace of God, I am what I am: and his grace which was bestowed upon me was not found vain [powerless]; but I laboured more abundantly than they all: yet not I, but the grace of God which was with me" (1 Cor. 15:10). "God is able to make *all grace abound* unto you; that ye, always having all sufficiency in all things, may abound to every good work" (2 Cor. 9:8).

"To the praise of the glory of his grace, which he freely bestowed on us in the beloved: according to *the riches of his grace*" (Eph. 1:6, 7). "But God, being rich in mercy, for his great love wherewith he loved us, quickened us together with Christ; that he might show *the exceeding riches of his grace* in kindness toward us in Christ Jesus" (Eph. 2:4-7).

What treasures are contained in these words! Let the Holy Spirit write them in your heart that you may receive the full impression of the "exceeding riches" and the abundance of the glory of the grace to be received at the throne of grace. Let the thought take possession of you that all day long the abundance of grace will be granted to the soul who approaches with boldness and is ready to receive from the sympathizing High Priest that which He has to give.

December 4

"With All Thy Heart"

Thou shalt love the Lord thy God with all thy heart, and with all thy soul, and with all thy mind, and with all thy strength.—Mark 12:30

In this great command the Lord our God has tried to teach us how greatly He needs us wholly for himself. Our love, our prayers, our consecration, our trust, our obedience—in all these there must be an unreserved surrender to God's will and service.

"With all thy heart"—with its longings, with its affections, with its attachments, with all its desires. "With all thy soul"— with its vital powers, and the will as a royal master in the soul. "With all thy mind"—its faculties of thought, of knowledge, of reasoning, and its powers of memory and imagination. "With all thy strength"—this is nothing less than the sacrifice of everything, and the putting forth of our utmost efforts. All for God, for God alone, and our one desire must be to love and serve Him perfectly.

What a wonderful God it is who has such a right to expect so much from us! Is He not the Creator, who has made us to show forth His glory, and for this purpose must possess us wholly? Is He not the perfect and Glorious One, who is worthy that we should forsake all to follow Him? Is He not the Everlasting Love, and Goodness and Mercy, ever desiring to pour out blessings upon us? Is He not indeed worthy, ten thousand times worthy, that all that is within us shall love and honor Him with all our strength and all our heart?

Think what it would mean in your prayer life if you were strengthened with all might to call upon God each day! Take this commandment into your heart, and make it the rule of your life, and try to realize that God must have all. It will make a great difference in your life, and you will go from strength to strength until you appear before God in Zion.

God will assuredly work in our hearts that which He has promised in this command. We are unable to keep it in our own strength. The Almighty One will, through His Spirit, pour out His love in our hearts. Let us earnestly desire an answer to our prayers, and approach with boldness the throne of grace where this grace may be received.

December 5

The Lamb and Missionary Work

Thou wast slain, and didst purchase unto God with thy blood men of every tribe, and tongue, and people, and nation.—Revelation 5:9

The Song of the Lamb tells us that the redeemed will come from all the different tribes and nations of the whole earth. The many languages into which the Bible has been translated, and the still greater number into which the New Testament or portions of the Bible have been translated, gives us some idea of how strenuous work by missionaires in many lands is making Christ and His gospel known.

Think for a little while of the extent of blessed work done by missionaries all over the earth! Christ came as a propitiation, not for our sins alone, but for the sins of the whole world, and to complete the great work of the redemption of mankind. When He had accomplished His share of the work, He entrusted the rest of the work to His people, trusting them to take the message of redemption to all parts of the world. As holy and divine as was Christ's part, as an indispensable beginning, so equally holy is the second part of the work—to bring souls everywhere to know of and accept this great salvation.

In the Song of the Lamb we find this twofold truth: the Lamb upon the throne has brought salvation to all the nations and tribes of the earth, and to the church of the Lamb has been entrusted the distribution of the salvation by the power of the Holy Spirit. Unspeakably glorious is the task of the missionary!

We will be able to understand this fully only when we have seen the great multitude which no man can number, out of every nation, and of all tribes and peoples, and tongues, standing before the throne and before the Lamb, arrayed in white robes, with palms in their hands; and they cry, saying: "Salvation unto our God which sitteth upon the throne and unto the Lamb."

May the Holy Spirit imprint deeply in our hearts the wonder of missionary work! Just as the Lamb of God gave himself to die that He might send the glad tidings to all, let us so offer ourselves wholly and without reserve to live and to die that souls may be led to join in the Song of the Lamb before the throne of grace.

December 6

The Lamb and His Worshippers

And hast made us unto our God kings and priests: and we shall reign on the earth.—Revelation 5:10

The four-and-twenty elders sang the new song that all those who are redeemed may now join in singing. If we take part with all our hearts in the Song of the Lamb, we will realize that we are priests of the throne of grace. As priests we worship God and the Lamb, and with hearts full of adoration may approach the throne of the Lamb for ourselves and others. As kings we receive the abundance of grace that we may reign in life, over sin and the power of the world, so that we may bring liberty to the captives. Such an overcoming life on earth will form and prepare us for sitting with Christ on His throne (Rev. 3:21).

Let all who read this take to heart the great thought: I come to the throne of grace, not only to receive the abundant grace for my own needs, but to be strengthened and fitted for taking that grace to others. How can God, how can the Lamb, make known the glory of the throne of grace to those who sit in darkness? By means of those who know the throne of grace, and will offer themselves wholly to the service of that throne, and are willing to share their experience with others. The throne of grace will become more precious to us, as we understand that abundant grace will work within us in greater power, when we give our lives to make this salvation known to others.

Then the Song of the Lamb will acquire a new meaning for us; "Unto him that loved us, and washed us from our sins in his own blood, *and hath made us kings and priests unto God;* to him be glory and dominion for ever and ever" (Rev. 1:5, 6). We will realize that it is worthwhile living as men ready to fulfill a heavenly calling.

O fellow Christian, the Lamb on the throne has chosen you to see Him upon the throne, and *to make Him and His love known to others.* Grace demands this of you; grace will strengthen you with heavenly power and joy. Let this grace operating in yourself and others be sufficient for your daily fellowship with the Lamb on the throne!

December 7

The Lamb and the Spirit

I saw ... a Lamb standing, as though it had been slain, having seven horns, and seven eyes, which are the seven Spirits of God, sent forth into all the earth. —Revelation 5:6

In the fourth chapter of Revelation we read that John had seen "seven lamps of fire burning before the throne, which are the seven Spirits of God." In our text we see that these Spirits have been taken up into the life of the Lamb: they are His eyes; and through them He works in all the earth. When the Lamb was upon earth, He was obedient to God's Spirit in all things: "Through the eternal Spirit he offered himself unto God." This is why His blood has such divine power, and why the Father gave Him unlimited power to pour out the Holy Spirit in full measure on whom He would.

Let us learn two great lessons. The *first*, that the Lamb on the throne has power to fill us with the Holy Spirit and enable us to follow Him fully, and so fit us to commune with God in the power of the blood and be more than conquerors. The *second*, that it is only through the Spirit we will understand the glory of the Lamb, and be filled with His love, and so stand firm in the faith of what He can do in us and for us and through us.

Beloved Christian, let the Song of the Lamb ring in your ears continually. The Lamb who was slain is worthy to receive the power and the glory. God has exalted Him to the throne and has put all things under His feet. Do you not long to give Him the place of honor in your heart, and in fervent love submit all you have to Him and His service? The glory of heaven is the worship of the Lamb and of Him that sitteth on the throne. You, too, may experience the glory of redemption as you tarry at the throne of grace. Do not rest until in silent adoration and deep humility the song of the Lamb arises as incense before God. "*Unto him that sitteth on the throne and unto the Lamb, be the blessing and the honor, and the glory, and the dominion for ever and ever.*" Amen.

December 8

The Lamb and Prayer

The four-and-twenty elders fell down before the Lamb, having each one a harp, and golden bowls full of incense, which are the prayers of the saints. —Revelation 5:8

We learn here that the prayers of the saints in the Old Testament concerning the promised redemption were preserved in heaven. Here, where homage is paid to the Lamb on the throne, these prayers are offered as incense that He may take them up and lay them before the Father.

The same thought is to be found in chapter 8 of Revelation. John saw an angel standing by the golden altar before the throne, and much incense was given to him that he should offer it with the prayers of the saints upon the golden altar: "And the smoke of the incense with the prayers of the saints, went up before God, out of the angel's hand" (Rev. 8:4).

What profound and heavenly thoughts do these words awaken within us! The prayers of the saints are not answered at once. Just as men on earth accumulate money and allow it to increase as capital for greater undertakings, so the prayers of the saints are stored up in heaven until the measure is full and the answer can descend.

Remember this: you do not pray alone. All over the world God's children are praying. When with perseverance and faith they entrust their prayers to the Lamb, then in His own time God will graciously send the answer. Do not think your prayer is in vain because you do not at once receive the answer. No, let your faith attach itself all the more firmly to the wonderful truth here revealed, that *the Lamb on the throne keeps our prayers in safety* to lay them before the Father at the right time.

The Lamb is seated on the throne of grace with the purpose of drawing out your prayers and strengthening you through His Spirit for more prayer. Pray for the church of God all over the world, pray for preachers and teachers; pray for all believers. Pray in love and fellowship with others who are also praying. Let your daily communion with God on the throne, and with the Lamb, be a means of receiving from that throne the rich abundant grace for your every need and the need of those around you in the church and the world.

December 9

The Blood of the Lamb

They have washed their robes, and made them white in the blood of the Lamb. Therefore are they before the throne of God, and they serve him day and night in his temple.—Revelation 7:14, 15

When I am to be presented to a king in his palace, my garments must be in accordance with the rules of the Court. What I wear helps to give me liberty to approach an earthly monarch. If I am to appear before God and serve Him day and night in His temple, I must wear "a robe made white in the blood of the Lamb."

What a close relationship to the Lord Jesus it gives me when I know He has bought me with His blood—paid so great a price for me! It gives me the assurance He places a great value upon me and will preserve me so that I may appear in His presence and serve Him day and night in His temple.

What new glory shines from the throne of grace, as the Lamb of God lives each day to make me acceptable to the Father, and I receive the abundant grace that I need to abound in good works! How attractive the inner chamber becomes, when we love and honor the Lamb on the throne, and ask to be fitted for His service!

O Christian, just as you are clothed in suitable garments to meet royalty, so you must each day put on the white robe, which has been washed in the blood of the Lamb. You then become one of the royal priesthood who serve God and intercede for souls and for the whole world. The precious blood of Christ gives us access with boldness into God's presence. It links us closely to the Lord Jesus, and gives us the needed power that we may be a blessing to others. Even here on earth the word may be fulfilled in us: "Therefore are they before the throne of God, and serve him day and night in his temple."

December 10

Following the Lamb

These are they which follow the Lamb whithersoever he goeth. These were purchased from among men, to be the firstfruits unto God and unto the Lamb.—Revelation 14:4

The Lamb is the Leader of whom it was written: "For it became Him . . . in bringing many sons unto glory, to make *the captain of their salvation* perfect through sufferings" (Heb. 2:10). He was "the Author and Perfecter of our faith . . . who endured the cross" (Heb. 12:2).

Let us consider:

The Lamb as our Leader and Example; and His redeemed ones, who follow Him whithersoever He goeth.

The Lamb in His great humility, who says: "Learn of me, for I am meek and lowly of heart."

The Lamb in His perfect innocence and purity.

The Lamb in His patience and silence: "He was brought as a Lamb to the slaughter."

The Lamb who offered himself to God as a burnt offering and sweet-smelling incense.

He is the Captain of our salvation whom the Father has given us to bring many sons to glory, and in whose footsteps we seek to walk.

The Lamb on the throne is my Advocate with the Father, who lives to intercede for me. The Lamb on the throne has power to lead me and fashion me according to His own image. The Lamb on the throne of my heart is willing and able to increase His own meekness and self-sacrifice within me, and His love to the Father and His redeemed ones. "These are they which have washed their robes and made them white in the blood of the Lamb." "*The Lamb which is in the midst of the throne* shall be their Shepherd, and shall guide them to fountains of waters of life" (Rev. 7:17).

Follow the Lamb! Let this be our watchword and prayer each day! The Lamb who was slain for us is now in the fullness of His grace in the midst of the throne, our chief Captain, and the Perfecter of our faith.

December 11

The Victory of the Lamb

They overcame him [the old serpent, the devil], because of the blood of the Lamb, and because of the word of their testimony; and they loved not their life even unto death. —Revelation 12:11

The Lamb is the Lord of Lords and King of Kings, and is the Victor over every enemy; and those who are with Him, the called, the chosen and faithful, reign with Him. They conquered the foe through the blood of the Lamb. Faith in the power of Christ and His blood is the assurance that every foe has been vanquished, and that the blood now makes each one a conqueror in the power of God—this is the secret of victory over sin and the world. The daily fellowship with Christ in the sprinkling of the blood makes us to triumph daily. Christian warrior: remember, there is victory through the blood of the Lamb!

Do not seek only your own salvation or blessedness. Note that *they overcame because of the word of their testimony.* Here is that which Christ promised: "Ye shall receive power, when the Holy Ghost is come upon you; and ye shall be my witnesses" (Acts 1:8). As we make known the love of God, and witness to the power of the blood, and strive ever to bring souls to God, the enemy will be overcome and souls will be rescued from his power.

And then again: "*They loved not their life even unto death.*" This was the way the Chief Captain, the Lamb that was slain, gained the victory and won His place in the midst of the throne. Those who follow the Lamb whithersoever He goeth, follow Him in this particular: they have dedicated themselves wholly to His service and "loved not their life even unto death." As the subjects of an earthly king offer themselves with enthusiasm to his service when needed, so they count nothing too great or too small in the service of the Lamb.

Dear children of God, if you would in the end be crowned as conquerors in life, be faithful followers of the Lamb. Live as He did. Let your trust in the wonderful life-giving power of the blood, and the remembrance of all that He has done for you, be joined to the intense feeling that reckons even life not too precious to be offered up wholly for Him.

December 12

The Marriage of the Lamb

And he saith unto me, Write, Blessed are they which are bidden to the marriage supper of the Lamb.—Revelation 19:9

All who rejoice in salvation are called to the marriage of the Lamb, not merely as spectators, but unitedly they form the bride of the Lamb. We read that when one of the angels said, "Come, and I will show you the bride, the wife of the Lamb," he showed the Holy Jerusalem descending from heaven from God, and she had the glory of God, and the nations who shall be saved, walk in her light. The time of the marriage feast of the Lamb will be when Christ presents His redeemed people as one body to the Father, and they are taken up to sit with Him on the throne eternally.

When the prodigal son returned to his home, his father made a feast, where all rejoiced together over the return of the son who had been dead but now was alive again. What joy there will be when the Everlasting Love that gave itself for us on the cross shall celebrate its triumph and the glory of God, and the revelation of the love of God, that passes all understanding!

When we are invited to the wedding of a distinguished person, we take great care to be arrayed in suitable wedding garments. What concern then, mingled with joy, should there be in the hearts of those who are called to the marriage supper of the Lamb! O child of God, if you really cherish the joyful hope of sitting at the marriage feast of the Lamb, will you not each day make use of the unspeakable privilege of approaching the throne of grace? Will you not entrust yourself, in loving surrender, to Him, and pray for grace that each day the way may be made more ready for the great heavenly marriage feast of the Lamb? Do not only prepare yourself; but seek for grace that you may win others, and bring them as well to partake of the feast of Everlasting Love.

December 13

The Throne of God and of the Lamb

He showed me a river of water of life, bright as crystal, proceeding out of the throne of God and of the Lamb.—Revelation 22:1

What does the river of the water of life signify? Nothing less than the Holy Spirit, which was not given until the Lamb was in the midst of the throne.

Where does the river of the water of life flow? Through the whole earth. It gives us according to our faith and desire what Christ has promised, a fountain springing up to eternal life. It gives streams of living water to each one who believes in Him fully. It surrounds us all, but through slowness and worldliness we are unable to grasp it and enjoy it.

This may be made clear to us by means of a parable. When Marconi discovered the means for wireless telegraphy, he found that waves of ether were streaming through the whole world. He discovered he could entrust a message to these waves, and it would be conveyed to distant places. When he sent his first message from England to Italy, it passed through France, where there were millions of people who had no idea any such message was passing. The message was heard and understood only when it reached the reception station which had been prepared for it in Italy.

Just so are we surrounded by the waves of the river of the water of eternal life without being aware of it. Yes, the waves of heavenly grace, of life and power, of love and joy, surround us, and we don't know it. Marconi spent years trying to learn the secret of wireless telegraphy. Only as we too seek with an undivided heart will our eyes be opened to see that the waves of the life-stream flowing from the throne of God and the Lamb really do surround us and are for our daily use.

O Christian, take time to worship God and the Lamb in the midst of the throne, and to be filled with their glory. You will realize that the Holy Spirit as a stream of living water surrounds you each day, and will be in you a fountain springing up to eternal life, and as a stream flowing from you in blessing to others. How wonderful it will be to see the Lamb in the midst of the throne of God, and the water of life, that flows from beneath the throne.

December 14

The Heavenly Life

The throne of God and of the Lamb shall be therein: and his servants shall do him service; and they shall see his face; and his name shall be on their foreheads.—Revelation 22:3, 4

Many Christians seek the throne of grace that they may find grace sufficient for their need, but they do not linger until the grace from the throne of God and of the Lamb fills their entire life, and enables them to walk night and day in its light, and experience the full impress of its glory.

To those who have faith in the unseen life, and know they have come to the heavenly Jerusalem, and the blood of sprinkling (Heb. 12:22-24)—to them the promises in our text are fulfilled. The earthly life becomes an actual experience of preparation for the heavenly life.

"His servants shall do him service"; at first without the sight of His glory. The faithful soul finds a reward and goes a step farther, *"They shall see his face."* It becomes possible to walk in the light of His countenance, and to rejoice in Him the whole day. The Omni-present One is the Almighty One, and His presence abides with His servant.

There is a further promise—*"His name shall be on their foreheads."* Obedience to God's commandments, the abiding in the light of His countenance, has an influence on the character and even the appearance of the children of God. As the fruit and reward of seeking to do all in the name of Jesus (Col. 3:17), the likeness to His image is seen in them, and His name is visible on their foreheads.

Dear Christian, it is a great thing to approach the throne of grace and to receive grace for each day. But there is a still greater blessing when the face of God and of the Lamb are revealed to our earnest gaze, and we walk each day in their light. When the name of Christ is engraved upon our hearts and upon our foreheads, then we are changed into His image, from glory to glory, as by the Spirit of the Lord.

God grant that we may all know the throne of grace in its holy and sanctifying influence! "His servants shall do him service; and they shall see his face; and his name shall be on their foreheads."

December 15

The Reign of Grace

They that receive the abundance of grace shall reign in life through Jesus Christ.—Romans 5:17

Let us once more think what the throne of grace can be to us. The grace that reigns through Jesus Christ enables us to gain the victory over sin in our life here below.

Salvation does not, as many think, mean a life of falling and rising again. No, it is God's will that His children should be conquerors in their life here upon earth. But on one condition—that they should day by day live in the abundance of grace obtained at the throne of grace. Let us read again the words in which the reign of grace is revealed to us. In the verses which follow our text this point is made clear (Rom. 5:20, 21). "The law came in beside, that the trespass might abound; but where sin abounded, grace did abound more exceedingly." Is it not wonderful, that although sin abounds, grace is always greater and more abundant than sin can ever be! I may, by reading God's Word, have an overpowering sense of the great power of sin, but I have also the assurance that grace, as the life-power of God within me, is far more abundant and powerful.

Then these words follow: "As sin reigned in death, even so might grace reign through righteousness unto eternal life through Jesus Christ our Lord." Whatever I may know or feel of the power of sin in the world, or in myself, I know, too, that grace is stronger, grace always has the victory over sin —"We are more than conquerors through him that loved us." This is a sure word. They that receive the abundance of grace reign already in this life through Jesus Christ.

Do you not see how everything depends on appearing daily before the throne of grace with a deep sense of need, but fully assured that abundant grace, as the power to conquer sin, will be given us? Oh, might God's children realize that the footstool of the throne of grace is the place where each one may experience that "God is able to make all grace abound unto us, that we, always having all sufficiency in everything, may abound unto every good work!"

December 16

Peniel: Face to Face

I have seen God face to face, and my life is preserved.—Genesis 32:30

In these words of Jacob, uttered after he had become Israel, a Prince with God, we find expression of what prayer meant to him. The words show us what each child of God, through the grace of God, and the power of the Holy Ghost, may experience each day. God will cause His face to shine upon us; *we shall see Him face to face*, and be delivered.

How often Christians complain that they have so little experience of what it means to meet with God in prayer, and to feel the light of His countenance upon them. They have done their best, but it seems of no avail. The thoughts of the inner chamber bring a feeling of self-reproach and shame; and yet they feel quite unable to overcome this disappointment.

Dear children of God, I bring you this message: your Father in heaven is not only willing, but greatly desirous, that the light of His countenance shall rest upon you. Perhaps the words of this series may be a help to you, by giving you that assurance. If we can find out why you cannot break through in your prayers to see God face to face, then we will know what you need to make your inner chamber a true Peniel. Only there will you realize what it is to meet with God, to see His face, and to feel how certain and blessed it is that His love rests upon you.

Begin with the prayer: "Turn us again, O Lord God of hosts, cause thy face to shine, and we shall be saved" (Ps. 80:19), and meditate on the words. Believe firmly that you may know the power and truth of this text—only then will you be able to say with Jacob: "I have seen God face to face, and my life is preserved." Remember how Jacob reached this point. He had learned to say: *"I will not let thee go, except thou bless me."* Persevering prayer is needed to bring the soul into the steadfast conviction that God will really make himself known.

December 17

I Am the Lord, and There Is None Else

Jesus answered, The first (of all the commandments) is: "Hear, O Israel! The Lord our God, the Lord is one."—Mark 12:29

The law may command us to love, but it cannot make us love. It is powerless to force us to love God. Love can be called forth only by that which is worthy of love. Love to God can be born only of the knowledge of Him as the one true God, in His excellent greatness and glory, His unspeakable love and compassion. When Moses said, "The Lord our God is one God," he was making known the supreme right that God has to our love. It is when the love of God expressed in these words enters our hearts, "The Lord God, full of compassion and gracious, slow to anger, and plenteous in mercy and truth," that we are willing to accept the truth and love Him wholeheartedly.

We have already referred to God's command that we should love Him with all the heart, and all the soul, and all the mind, and all the strength. The soul that earnestly seeks will soon find the difficulty of continuance in this love unless it has a vision of how worthy God is to be loved with the whole heart. It is no wonder that Christians are afraid of the words "with all thy heart and all thy strength."

It is impossible for anyone unless he has really confessed his sin to understand how abundantly God forgives, and how rich He is in mercy. The heart filled with a burning desire to serve God will say: "God is indeed worthy of my love; I will love Him with my whole heart."

Dear reader, here you have the secret of the prayer-life —to meet God each day, to live in the light of His love, to draw near in an absolute surrender to His will. We will attain to this only as we daily approach the throne of grace with boldness. Let this be the great object of your life. You will find these two thoughts complete each other. God, the only Lord, in the glory of His unspeakable love, giving himself wholly for us, and the soul in true worship and adoration giving itself to God with all the heart and all the strength.

December 18

The Abiding Presence of God

The Lord is nigh unto all them that call upon him, to all that call upon him in truth.—Psalm 145:18

You long to experience continually the nearness of God. Here is the secret: Pray, pray without ceasing. Then you will have the assurance: "The Lord is nigh unto all who call upon him." Prayer has a wonderful power of helping us to draw near to God and to keep us in His presence. God is everywhere, and as the Almighty One is ever ready and able to grant us unbroken fellowship with Him.

Would you know the secret of always abiding in a state of prayerfulness? The answer is clear. Realize first that God is near you and within you; then you will feel how natural it is to talk with Him each moment about your needs and desires. This is the secret of the prayerful life, of which Paul writes: "Night and day praying exceedingly" (1 Thess. 3:10). It is only when you live a life apart from God that you say: "I must take time, I must take trouble first of all to find God before I can pray." But to the true Christian, *life is a constant abiding with the Father.* "In thy name do they rejoice all the day" (Ps. 89:16). The communion between the Father and His children should be continuous. Even so prayer may become a daily life activity, like breathing or sleeping, instead of something brought into use only once a day. The principle of complete dependence on the unseen God, and the holy habit of claiming His presence with us each moment of the day— this is the secret of a life of true godliness.

God is always near, so that you may call upon Him at all times. According to the word of Paul, you will be "anxious for nothing, but in everything by prayer and supplication let your requests be made known unto God, and the peace of God will guard your hearts and minds." Remember these two things: A God always near, with His infinite and abundant grace; and His child in utter weakness, calling upon One who will surely hear and answer.

December 19

Take Time with God

To everything there is a season, and a time to every purpose under the heaven.—Ecclesiastes 3:1

It should be the aim of every Christian to set aside a little time each day for quiet communion with God. A time for everything—and no time to spend in the presence of the Creator of all things? No time to contemplate His will and purposes for us? The holy, loving God is indeed worthy of the best of our time—of all of our time. We should live in constant fellowship with Him, but each day there should be a special time of quiet when we are with Him alone.

We need a period daily for secret fellowship. Time to turn from daily occupation and search our hearts in His presence. Time to study His Word with reverence and godly fear. Time to seek His face and ask Him to make himself known to us. Time to wait until we know that He sees and hears us so that we can make our wants known to Him in words that come from the depth of our hearts. Time to let God deal with our special needs, to let His light shine in our hearts, to let ourselves be filled with His Spirit!

What do you think? Will it be possible to give a quarter of an hour each day for this purpose? If you are unwilling to make such an arrangement, you must not be surprised if your spiritual life is enfeebled and becomes ineffective. Fellowship with God should have a first claim on your time, and if you will only arrange for this brief communion with God, you will soon learn to value it. It will not be long before you feel ashamed there was ever a time when you thought fifteen minutes would suffice.

Everything on earth needs time. Think of the hours per day for so many years that a child spends at school gathering the rudiments of knowledge that he may cope with this life. How much longer then should we spend in learning from God for life everlasting?

O Christian, give the holy, gracious God all the time you can until His light and life and love fill your whole life and you abide in Christ and His love through His Word and through prayer.

December 20

The Will

All Judah rejoiced, for they had sought him with their whole desire; and he was found of them. —2 Chronicles 15:15

The will is the royal faculty of the soul; it rules over the whole man. Many people become the slaves of sin because they do not decide with a firm will to listen to the voice of conscience. Many Christians make no advance in the prayer life because they have not the courage to say with a strong purpose of will: "By God's help I will make time for prayer and quiet fellowship with Him."

In the practice of prayer, it is quite indispensable to say in regard to wandering thoughts, or the brevity and haste of our prayers, or their formality and superficiality, "*I will not* give way to these things, *I will* call upon God with all my heart and strength."

This is not easy. One must face the position calmly and decide to go on praying without any real zeal or earnestness, or else look to God to help him by His Holy Spirit to say: "In the few minutes I spend with God and His Word I am determined to give the time *with an undivided heart.*" Keep on, even though you find it difficult. You will find it easier each time you say to God: "Lord, I can be satisfied with nothing less. *I will seek Thee with my whole heart.*"

All Judah sought the Lord with their whole desire (or will), and He was found of them. God is longing to bless you, but is unable to do so as long as you are not willing to give yourself unreservedly and with all the strength of your will to let Him work out His will in you. Speak it out in God's presence: "*Father, I will seek Thee with all my heart and will.*"

December 21

Christ's Love to Us

A new commandment I give unto you, that ye love one another, even as I have loved you.—John 13:34

Even as the Father hath loved me, I also have loved you; abide ye in my love.—John 15:9

The Lord gave His disciples a perfectly new commandment, that *they should love one another as He had loved them.* To this end He wanted them to know what the love was wherewith He had loved them. Nothing less than *the love wherewith the Father had loved Him.* It is the everlasting, unchangeable, divine love wherewith the Father loved the Son, wherewith the Son loved us, and *wherewith we should love one another.*

The thought is so vast and so heavenly we need time to grasp it. Pray about it and let God's Spirit make it a blessed reality: the love of God to Christ, the love of Christ to me, my love to the brethren, is one and the same almighty, everlasting love.

God sent His Son to earth to manifest this love. The same love God had to His Son, He had in His heart for all mankind. This same love Jesus exercised toward His disciples. This love was given them when the Holy Ghost was poured out on the Day of Pentecost, that they might love one another, and more—even love those who were the enemies of Christ.

It is all one and the same love. Not merely a feeling or a blessed experience, but a living divine power, flowing from the Father to the Son, and working in the hearts of the disciples through the Son, and so streaming forth to the whole world.

We are ever ready to say: "We cannot love others as Christ has loved us." It is not impossible. The Holy Spirit, as the power of this holy love, *sheds it abroad in our hearts.* This is God's own word. He who meditates on it *until he believes it* will have courage to bring his petitions to the throne of grace, and to receive the love which passes all understanding.

December 22

Our Love to Christ

If ye love me, ye will keep my commandments.—John 14:15

In the Gospel of John, our Lord Jesus Christ speaks six times of our love to Him consisting in doing His will.

"If ye love me, *ye will keep my commandments*" (14:15). "He that hath my commandments *and keepeth them*, he it is that loveth me" (14:21). "If a man love me, *he will keep my word*" (14:23). "*If ye keep my commandments*, ye shall abide in my love" (15:10). "If ye abide in me, *and my words abide in you*" (15:7). "Ye are my friends *if ye do the things I command you*" (15:14).

It is not enough to read these words once. Take your Bible and go over them carefully. Notice how in each verse there is a wonderful promise. Then you will realize the blessedness of the life of the one who loves Christ, keeps His commandments, and abides in His love.

Notice the striking promise in verse 23 of this chapter. "If a man love me, he will keep my word: and my Father will love him, *and we will come unto him, and make our abode with him.*" The Father and the Son dwell in the hearts of those who love Jesus and keep His commandments. Such can say with Paul, "Christ lives in me," and will love the brethren and all around them with the love wherewith God loved His Son.

Paul says to all Christians: "Know ye not as to your own selves, *that Jesus Christ is in you*?" (2 Cor. 13:5). Many Christians do not realize this, or the love Christ has for them. If we are strengthened through the Holy Spirit, Christ will dwell in our hearts by faith, and *we shall be rooted and grounded in love.* Then it will be quite natural for the love of God to work within us in divine power, and we shall learn to love Him, even as He loved us, in the love of the Father.

Dear Christian, as Christ loved you, and you abide in His love, you will be enabled to keep His commandments. The measure of His sacrifice for you will be the measure of your willing surrender to Him in all things.

December 23

Our Love to the Brethren

This is my commandment, that ye love one another, even as I have loved you.—John 15:12

So many people deem it quite impossible to keep this command that they do not even attempt to keep it. But one who reads prayerfully and carefully the last two meditations in this series will see that the Lord has indeed made provision for the fulfillment of this command. The reader will learn that the great love wherewith the Father loved the Son is the love with which Christ loves us. Even as the love of the Father in the Son was His whole life, and worked with a divine power in Him, so the relationship between the Lord Jesus and ourselves is the same. As He loves us, His love comes to abide in us, because He himself dwells within us.

Even the world agrees that if a man says I love God, and hates his brother, he is a liar; for he that loveth not his brother whom he hath seen, how can he love God, whom he hath not seen? Hatred toward a brother is a sign a man does not love God. Love for a brother is an indication that he loves God.

Let us try to understand what the Lord really means by this command. He came to earth to make known God's love to us. He was returning to the Father. He had revealed the love of God the Father, and would leave this love on earth in charge of His disciples. He said to them: "Love one another, as I have loved you." Remember that through the Holy Spirit, whom I will send, I am dwelling within you and will enable you to love the brethren with My own love. I dwell in each one of My disciples. As you love others in the power of My love, they will also grow strong to love. And this will be a powerful sign that My love is in you, when the world is convinced, that as in Me, so in you, the Father had shed abroad His love.

Child of God, bow at the feet of your blessed Lord and worship and adore Him for His wonderful grace, and He will take up His abode in your heart, in the love of the Father, and give you the love wherewith to love your brethren, and so prove to the world that God is truly in our midst.

December 24

Love Demands All

Hereby know we love, because he laid down his life for us; and we ought to lay down our lives for the brethren.—1 John 3:16

It was not only on the cross that Christ gave His life for us: that was the consummation of a life that from the beginning was surrendered to the service and healing of man. The debt that rests upon each one of us as a consequence is not discharged if we are called upon suddenly to lay down our life. The example of Christ bids us give our whole life in service to our brethren.

Try to grasp this truth. The strength of God's love in Christ enabled Him to give up His life wholly for us. The same strength is available for us, and as we yield ourselves wholly to it we will be able to make the welfare of souls the central object of our lives. One who gives himself wholly into the keeping of God's love will feel its power and all-sufficiency. This is the blessedness of the Christian life—*giving our lives wholly for others even as Christ did.*

One sometimes finds, even among unlearned people, that where the fire of love to Christ burns there is an unquenchable desire to pray and work for others. I read recently a story of a young girl only ten years of age, whose heart had been so touched by the love of Christ that she began at once to lead others to Him. A few years later, when she went to a boarding school, it was her daily prayer and endeavor to bring others to know and love her Savior.

This continued until her nineteenth year, when she became a regular worker among soldiers, giving all her time and energy to the work. The Lord gave her such a spirit of prayer and such love to souls that for many years she continued that work, a living example to all of how God could enable one to spend her life in the service of others, and especially in winning them for Christ.

Dear reader, take this thought into your heart. Christ gave His life for you and you are a debtor who owes your life to the brethren. *The love of Christ constrains you and will supply all the power and strength needed.*

December 25

A New Commandment

A new commandment I give unto you, that ye love one another; even as I have loved you. —John 13:34

Let us once more consider the great wonder of the new command, that we should love our brethren with a Christlike love. One may think it foolish to imagine that in our wicked and perverse hearts, a love like that of the Son of God should grow up. Yes, but listen to what the Son of God says, for His command is not like the law given on Sinai, which was not accompanied with a gift of the power to keep it: "These things have I spoken unto you that my joy may remain in you, and that your joy may be fulfilled" (John 15:11). Power is given with the new command. A new spirit is promised which will enable us to love the brethren with Christ's love: "That Christ may dwell in your hearts by faith." He has promised to each one who loves Him and keeps His Word that He will come in unto him and take up His abode with him. It is in the power of this indwelling that He makes our hearts the dwelling-place of His love to His people.

Christ prayed to the Father: "That the love wherewith thou hast loved me may be in them, and I in them." He will indeed dwell in our hearts, bringing the love of God and manifesting His love to His children. As He dwells in our hearts with His divine love, He teaches us to love the brethren at all times and in all circumstances. He is the Vine, and we are the branches; he who dwells in Him as a branch in the vine bears much fruit, chiefly love to the brethren.

Let us say to ourselves: "My fellow Christians cannot see the Lord Jesus, but I have a charge to compensate them. I am commanded by my love to show forth His love as seen when He was upon the earth. Christ has given His love in my heart towards the brother who is so perverse and unloving in order that I may help him. Christ loved me while I was yet a sinner and He gives me His own love toward a wandering brother. That will bring blessing to the Lord Jesus, to my brother, and to myself."

O fellow Christians, let us believe in the love of Christ. Let us receive Christ into our hearts to abide there with His heavenly love, and let us have faith to reveal this love to our brethren. Christ will surely give the new Spirit, the Holy Spirit, to shed abroad His love in our hearts.

December 26

Lovest Thou Me?

Peter was grieved because he said unto him the third time, "Lovest thou me?"—John 21:17

After His resurrection from the grave, the Lord wanted to convince Peter of the lack of love which was shown by the denial of his Lord. To us, too, the Lord comes, time after time, with the question, "Lovest thou me?" until we are made to expostulate, "Thou knowest that I love thee, Lord," and to confess to the conviction of how little this love is shown in our hearts and lives.

Think of the tokens of a real true love. *A sincere longing for fellowship with the loved one.* We see in daily life how friends and relations like to be together. Our love to Christ can be tested by the joy we have in His presence when we meet with Him in the inner chamber.

Love seeks to please the loved one. Love strives to bring happiness to the object of its love. The extent of our love to the Lord is shown by the way we obey His will: "He that loveth me, keepeth my commandments. . . . If ye keep my commandments, ye shall abide in my love." Love does all it can to make the loved one happy.

Love seeks to become entirely at one with the loved one, and so attain to spiritual unity.

What a test this is for us when we try to answer the question, "Lovest thou me?" Let us apply this test to ourselves as in His presence. If we come short on any point, let us humbly confess it to our beloved Lord, and receive from Him on the throne of grace the power to love Him with our whole heart.

We read that when Peter was grieved and said, "Lord, thou knowest that I love thee," the Lord gave him power to feed His sheep and His lambs. Even as the Lord Jesus loved us when He sought and found us, so His own love will constrain us to win souls for Christ and His service.

December 27

The Love of Christ for the World

By this shall all men know that ye are my disciples, if ye have love one to another.—John 13:35

That they may all be one; even as thou, Father, art in me, and I in thee, that they may also be in us; that the world may believe that thou didst send me.... That the world may know that thou lovedst them, even as thou lovedst me.—John 17:21-23

In these two texts our Lord had the whole world in mind, and expressed His desire to save all men. The great power on which He built His hopes of winning the world was the wonderful love with which all people and nations would be welded into one, so that even the heathen could say: "Behold, how these Christians love one another."

The Lord has not saved us merely to make us happy. That is only the beginning. His great object is to use everyone who receives His love as a witness to win others to His service. It is not alone a witness in words that is needed, but the power of a heavenly love, by which selfish people, "hateful themselves and hating others," may be renewed into a life like that of Jesus Christ, a life of self-sacrificing love, which embraces all disciples in one Body.

Do you begin to realize why there is little power for conversion in some preaching? The world asks, what proof is there that Christians are any better than other people? The proof is that Christ can change really selfish people into *models of love and self-sacrifice.* It is a matter of deep concern for the church and for the world that Christians should demonstrate this heavenly love. For the Father loved them with the same love wherewith He loved the Son, and the Son gives this same love to us.

What does the world most need at the present time? *A revival of love in the hearts of men and women through the Holy Spirit.* This would bring untold blessing to every believer, to the whole church, and to all who realize what the love of God can do in hearts fully yielded to Him.

December 28

Love for Souls

He that is wise winneth souls.—Proverbs 11:30

Come ye after me, and I will make you fishers of men.—Matthew 4:19

Fear not; from henceforth thou shalt catch men.—Luke 5:10

When the Lord Jesus Christ taught Peter the great lesson about love (John 21:15-17), He gave him the right and the power to feed His sheep. This was in fulfillment of the promise made when the Lord first called Peter and said: "Follow me, and I will make you fishers of men."

Our Lord expects *that each one who receives into his heart His wonderful love will use that love in winning souls for Christ.* God's Word teaches us clearly that it is the duty of every Christian to be a soul-winner. When the heart is right with God the Christian has freedom in definite, believing prayer, and may expect God's blessing on personal work.

The principle is so simple that every Christian, old or young, rich or poor, may have a share in it. It is so important that a healthy spiritual life in the church and in the individual member can be preserved only when each one takes part.

The value of this principle will be seen when one realizes what the result would be if every Christian were to fulfill his obligation. Everywhere there are souls in need of help. Eminent ministers and evangelists agree it is not in the preaching of the Word alone, but in work for individual souls, that the largest results are to be found.

Personal work for souls means more love to our Lord and more joy in His service. This work consists not only in speaking to individuals about their souls, but also in speaking to God for souls. It is a great thing to be a soul-winner, a work angels might envy. God sent His only Son into the world to win souls for the kingdom. If you long to possess the love of God, surrender your lives to the Everlasting Love that you, through that love, may bring God's wandering children to their Father. A life consecrated to the winning of souls by the love of God in our hearts will bring joy to the heart of Christ, and glory to His name.

December 29

Not I, But the Grace of God

By the grace of God, I am what I am: and his grace which was bestowed upon me was not found vain; but I laboured more abundantly than they all; yet not I, but the grace of God which was with me.— 1 Corinthians 15:10

The word "grace" may be used in two senses. It points first of all to *the free and undeserved blessings bestowed by God,* upon which we can always reckon and for which we should thank Him daily, and then the word may be used of *the divine power* with which this compassionate love works within us. Grace is not merely an attribute of God, but a life-power which works in us every day and every hour, giving us the power to do God's will.

Paul speaks in this text of the goodness of God that made him, though all undeserving, what he was. God's grace in him was not found vain, for he had labored more abundantly than they all. He was by God's grace enabled to do his work. He felt it was all free grace, by means of which the divine power worked within him.

Let us hold fast these two thoughts as we approach the throne of grace. God will receive us and use us and bestow His grace upon us, not as we deserve, but according to the great love which He has for us. We will then be able to do what God requires each moment of the day. Hear what Paul says: "God is able to make all grace about unto you; that ye, always having all-sufficiency, *may abound unto every good work*" (2 Cor. 9:8). And again: "I was made a minister, according to that gift of the grace of God, which was given me, according to *the working of his power*" (Eph. 3:7). It is the constant stream of grace that gives us the power to be "abundant in every good work."

"Not I, but the grace of God that was with me." Let every thought of what the grace of God will work in you be linked with the words: *"Not I, but the grace of God."* Cultivate large thoughts of what God will do for you. Bow before the throne of grace fully assured of what His grace can and will do for you. "Be strong and of good courage, and he will strengthen your heart."

December 30

The God Who Doeth Wonders

I bow my knees unto the Father ... that Christ may dwell in your hearts through faith; to the end that ye, being rooted and grounded in love, may be strong to apprehend ... and to know the love of Christ, which passeth knowledge.—Ephesians 3:14-19

These meditations make us feel how sadly lacking in love we are toward God. More than one will be earnestly seeking to know how such a state may be overcome. God alone, the God who worketh wonders, can help us. He will help all who ask in faith. To gain that love we have to go to the throne of grace, from whence all love comes.

The gift of love is not bestowed separately. It comes to us when our hearts are filled with Christ. Our love for God will be sustained if we seek daily communion with Him. The apostle Paul, in our text above, refers to his bended knees: "I *bow my knees.*" When in all humility we bow before the throne of grace and humbly wait and worship there, then we will receive the indwelling Spirit, and the knowledge of the love of Christ will be bestowed.

It is not alone the forgiveness of sin we must seek; we must seek also for that abundant grace to help us be continually victorious over sin and enable us to be fitted for the continual indwelling of the Spirit. We must earnestly pray so to live that "the love of Christ which passeth all understanding" will be in the foremost place of our life. *At the throne of grace we will be rooted and grounded in that love.* And, having come to love God, that love will radiate from us to those around us and will even reach and enrich the hearts of those who do not themselves as yet love Him.

Such a state of blessedness will be obtained only in answer to much faith and prayer poured out at the throne of grace. Pray that "the Father, according to the riches of his glory, may strengthen us by faith." Only as we see the wonderful power of God and learn to know the love of Christ will we be able to love the brethren as we ought.

December 31

Grace and Love

Grace be with all them that love our Lord Jesus Christ in uncorrupt-ness.—Ephesians 6:24

In this series we have dwelt upon *grace* and love, and our text will serve to remind us how closely grace and love are linked together.

By faith the sinner first experiences the forgiveness of sins. When a sinner has partaken of the free grace of our Lord Jesus, then sincere, fervent love comes into his heart, and he, like the apostle Peter, may say: "Whom having not seen, we love, and rejoice with joy unspeakable." The great rule of the throne of grace, where God and the Lamb dispense eternal love, is this: "Grace be with all them that love our Lord Jesus Christ in *uncorruptness.*"

How that last word penetrates the secret of the terms under which the gift may be received! Does it indicate the reason why the wonderful power of grace is so often withheld? We should strive to live in the incorruptible, unbroken love of Jesus as the Father desires us. If we open our hearts to the Holy Spirit the pure love of God will enter and we will find "the grace of our Lord is exceedingly abundant with faith and love which is in Christ Jesus."

The wonder-working, almighty God, who "is able to do exceeding abundantly above all we ask or think, according to the power that worketh in us, unto him be the glory in the church and in Christ Jesus unto all generations for ever and ever" (Eph. 3:20).

"Unto him that sitteth on the throne and unto the Lamb be the blessing, and the honor, and the glory, and the dominion, for ever and ever" (Rev. 5:13).

"Unto him that loveth us and loosed us from our sins by his blood; and he made us to be a kingdom, to be priests unto his God and Father; to him be the glory and the dominion for ever and ever. Amen" (Rev. 1:6).